Achieving Excellence
in Preschool Literacy Instruction

SOLVING PROBLEMS IN THE TEACHING OF LITERACY
Cathy Collins Block, *Series Editor*

RECENT VOLUMES

Achieving Excellence in Preschool Literacy Instruction

★★★★★★★★★★★★★★

TOURO COLLEGE LIBRARY
Kings Hwy

edited by

**Laura M. Justice
Carol Vukelich**

Foreword by William H. Teale

THE GUILFORD PRESS
New York   London

KH

Printed in the United States of America

This book is printed on acid-free paper.

Last digit is print number: 9 8 7 6 5 4 3 2 1

Library of Congress Cataloging-in-Publication Data

Achieving excellence in preschool literacy instruction / edited by Laura M. Justice,
and Carol Vukelich.
     p. cm.–(Solving problems in the teaching of literacy)
  Includes bibliographical references and index.
  ISBN-13: 978-1-59385-610-6 (pbk. : alk. paper)
  ISBN-10: 1-59385-610-5 (pbk. : alk. paper)
  ISBN-13: 978-1-59385-611-3 (hardcover : alk. paper)
  ISBN-10: 1-59385-611-3 (hardcover : alk. paper)
  1. Language arts (Preschool) I. Justice, Laura M., 1968– II. Vukelich, Carol.
LB1140.5.L3A28 2008
372.6–dc22

                                                          2007027503

2/9/10

About the Editors

Laura M. Justice, PhD, is Professor in the School of Teaching and Learning at The Ohio State University. A certified speech–language pathologist, her research and teaching interests include language disabilities, early literacy acquisition, parent–child interactions, and preschool quality. Dr. Justice's research on these topics has been supported by grants from the U.S. Department of Education, the National Institutes of Health, the American Speech–Language–Hearing Association, and the International Reading Association, and has received recognition from the American Speech–Language–Hearing Association (Editor's Award, *American Journal of Speech–Language Pathology*), the Council for Exceptional Children (Early Career Publication Award from the Division for Research), and the U.S. President (2005 Presidential Early Career Award in Science and Engineering). Other books by Dr. Justice include *Language Development: From Theory to Practice* (with Khara L. Pence, 2007), *Scaffolding with Storybooks: A Guide for Enhancing Young Children's Language and Literacy Achievement* (with Khara L. Pence, 2005), and *Shared Storybook Reading: Building Young Children's Language and Emergent Literacy Skills* (with Helen K. Ezell, 2005).

Carol Vukelich, PhD, is the L. Sandra and Bruce L. Hammonds Professor in Teacher Education and Director of the Delaware Center for Teacher Education at the University of Delaware. Her research and teaching interests include children's early literacy development and teachers' professional development, specifically coaching and reflection strategies. Dr. Vukelich has served as President of the Association for Childhood Education International and the International Reading Association's Literacy Development in Young Children Special Interest Group. Other books by Dr. Vukelich include *Teaching Language and Literacy: Preschool through the Elementary Grades, Third Edition* (with James F. Christie and Billie Jean Enz, 2007); *Helping Young Children Learn Language and Literacy: Birth through Kindergarten, Second Edition* (with James F. Christie and Billie Jean Enz, 2008); and *Building a Foundation for Preschool Literacy: Effective Instruction for Children's Reading and Writing Development* (with James F. Christie, 2004). In addition, she is a contributing author (with James F. Christie and Kathleen A. Roskos) to an early literacy curriculum program, *Doors to Discovery* (2002).

Contributors

Mike A. Assel, PhD, is Assistant Professor of Pediatrics at the University of Texas Health Science Center at Houston, Associate Director of the Dan L. Duncan Children's Neurodevelopmental Clinic, and a licensed psychologist who assesses children with a variety of learning disabilities at the Children's Learning Institute (CLI). Dr. Assel's research interests include early childhood assessment, and he has worked with other CLI staff to develop classroom-based progress monitoring measures currently used in communities across the state of Texas and across the country. Dr. Assel is currently a coinvestigator on several grants sponsored by the National Institute of Child Health and Human Development and the Texas Education Agency, and is responsible for coordination of assessment data in several projects. Dr. Assel has published on the importance of early maternal interaction behaviors and their influence on children's later literacy skills and math achievement. His other research interests include the impact of curricula on early literacy, math, and social development.

April Bedford, PhD, is Associate Professor of Elementary and Literacy Education at the University of New Orleans, where she is also Chair of the Department of Curriculum and Instruction. She teaches a variety of graduate and undergraduate courses, including children's literature, early literacy, elementary reading methods, and qualitative research methods. Dr. Bedford is editor of the *Journal of Children's Literature* and has published book chapters and articles in a variety of journals, including *Language Arts*, *Social Studies and the Young Learner*, and *Book Links*. Currently, she is a Board member of the Children's Literature Assembly, an assembly of the National Council of Teachers of English; president-elect of the Children's Literature and Reading Special Interest Group of the International Reading Association; and chair of the Notable Books for a Global Society committee, a national children's literature award. Her research interests include representations of gender and diversity in children's literature, reader response, and teacher development. She has served as an evaluator for two Early Reading First grants and has worked extensively in urban elementary classrooms in New Orleans.

Tanis Bryan, PhD, is codirector of Southwest Institute for Families and Children, Adjunct Professor at Arizona State University, and Professor Emerita at the University of Illinois at Chicago. Her areas of specialization include children with learning disabilities, family–school linkages, and community-based participatory research. She has published more than 125 articles and two books in addition to manuals for teachers, parents, youth, and children. During the past 4 years, Dr. Bryan has worked on the development of curriculum-based assessment of early language strategies.

Martha Jane Buell, PhD, is Professor of Individual and Family Studies at the University of Delaware. Martha's research is dedicated to uncovering ways to improve the quality of early care and education for all children, especially children placed at risk due to economic circumstances and disabilities. She is a codirector of two Early Reading First grants.

Karen Burstein, PhD, is the director of the Southwest Institute for Families and Children, where she directs research and evaluation in the areas of early childhood education and health care. She consults with several Early Reading First and Reading First projects around assessment and curriculum alignment. Her current areas of interest include large-scale preschool assessment, new directions for evaluating community needs, and early language assessment.

Sonia Q. Cabell, MEd, is a doctoral candidate in Reading Education at the Curry School of Education, University of Virginia. Her current research projects investigate aspects of emergent literacy and language development among preschool children, including those exhibiting developmental language disorders. Prior to pursuing her doctorate, Ms. Cabell worked as a second-grade teacher and a literacy coach in both Oklahoma and Virginia.

Renée Casbergue, PhD, is Associate Professor in the Department of Education Theory, Policy, and Practice at Louisiana State University, where she teaches undergraduate courses in the Early Childhood Initial Certification Program and graduate courses in foundations of language and literacy, and early literacy development. Dr. Casbergue has also been a faculty member at Tulane University and the University of New Orleans, and has worked extensively with urban schools in New Orleans and Baton Rouge, Louisiana. She has coauthored two books: *Playful Learning and Teaching: Integrating Play into Preschool and Primary Programs* (with Judith Kieff) and *Writing in Preschool: Learning to Orchestrate Meaning and Marks* (with Judith Schickedanz). She has published book chapters about early literacy development and articles for a variety of journals, including the *Journal of Reading,* the *Journal of Reading Behavior, Childhood Education*, and *Book Links*. She is a past president of the Literacy Development of Young Children special interest group of the International Reading Association and has served as an external evaluator and researcher for two Early Reading First projects.

James F. Christie, PhD, is Professor of Curriculum and Instruction at Arizona State University, where he teaches courses in language, literacy, and early childhood education. His research interests include early literacy development and children's play. He is a member of the Early Literacy Development Commission of the International Reading Association, a member of the Board of Directors of Playing for Keeps, and past president of the Association for the Study of Play. He is project codirector for the Arizona Centers of Excellence in Early Education (ACE³) Early Reading First project.

David K. Dickinson, EdD, is Professor in the Department of Teaching and Learning at the Peabody School of Education, Vanderbilt University. He received his doctoral training at Harvard's Graduate School of Education after teaching elementary school in the Philadelphia area for 5 years. Since the early 1980s he has studied language and early literacy development among low-income populations. He also has created tools for describing the support for literacy and language learning in preschool classrooms, and developed and studied approaches to providing professional development to preschool teachers. He has served on numerous advisory boards and has published many articles and books, including two volumes of the *Handbook of Early Literacy Research*. He and Judith Schickedanz also coauthored a comprehensive preschool curriculum, *Opening the World of Learning (OWL)*. With support from the Institute for Educational Sciences, he and Ann Kaiser are currently studying approaches to supporting the language and literacy skills of children with deficient language skills. He also has led in creation of an innovative executive-style EdD program in early childhood leadership designed to provide doctoral training to leaders in the field while they continue in their current positions.

Virginia Dubasik, MAEd, MS, CCC-SLP, is a doctoral student at Arizona State University's Department of Speech and Hearing Science. She has many years of experience as a bilingual speech–language pathologist and working with preschool children.

Cevriye Ergul, MA, is a doctoral candidate at Arizona State University. Her areas of specialization include curriculum-based measurement (CBM), early literacy, children with disabilities, and second language learners. Over the past 3 years she has been involved in an Early Reading First project as the CBM coordinator. She has also coauthored several publications in peer-reviewed journals on subjects including use of CBM to monitor preschool children's early literacy development, family-centered intervention for young children at risk for language and behavior problems, and the social–emotional side of learning disabilities. She received her BS in psychology and a master's in special education.

Dale C. Farran, PhD, is Professor in the Departments of Teaching and Learning and Psychology and Human Development at Vanderbilt University. Dr. Farran has been involved in research and intervention for high-risk children and youth for all of her professional career, conducting research at the Frank Porter Graham Child Development Center in Chapel Hill, North Carolina, and the Kamehameha Schools Early Education Project in Hawaii. Dr. Farran is the editor of two books dealing with risk and poverty, and the author of more than 80 journal articles and book chapters. She is an Associate Editor of the *Early Childhood Research Quarterly* and is on the Editorial Board of *Infants and Young Children*. Her current research is on evaluating the effectiveness of alternative preschool curricula for preparing children from low-income families to transition successfully to school. She is currently directing several longitudinal studies to assess the effects of different preschool curricula.

Shelley Gray, PhD, CCC-SLP, is Associate Professor in the Department of Speech and Hearing Science at Arizona State University. Her research focuses on early literacy development, and assessment and treatment of language disorders in preschool- and school-age children. She is the principal investigator for the Tempe Early Reading First Partnership Grant and for research funded by the National Institutes of Health on lexical acquisition by young children with specific language impairment, and co-principal investigator for curriculum and treatment research funded by the U.S. Department of Education Institute of Education Sciences.

Bridget K. Hamre, PhD, is Research Scientist at the University of Virginia's Center for Advanced Study of Teaching and Learning. Dr. Hamre received a doctorate in clinical and school psychology from the University of Virginia. Her primary research interests lie in integrating psychological and educational theory and methodology. In particular, she is interested in identifying classroom-level processes that facilitate children's academic, social, and emotional development. Dr. Hamre also studies student–teacher relationships and coauthored the Student, Teachers, and Relationship Success System (STARS), an intervention aimed at helping teachers improve their relationships with students.

Myae Han, PhD, is Assistant Professor of Individual and Family Studies at the University of Delaware, where she teaches courses in early childhood education and early literacy. Her research interests are children's play and early literacy development. She is currently a codirector of the Delaware Early Reading First project and the Opening Doors to Literacy Early Reading First project.

Laura M. Justice, PhD (*see* "About the Editors").

Susan H. Landry, PhD, is a developmental psychologist and the Michael Matthew Knight Professor in the Department of Pediatrics at the University of Texas Health Science Center at Houston. She is also the Chief of the Division of Developmental Pediatrics and the Director of the Children's Learning Institute. Dr. Landry has been the recipient of multiple, large-scale grants funded by the National Institutes of Health, National Institute of Child Health and Human Development, Institute of Education Sciences, and the Texas Education Agency. Her research interests have focused on the impact of the caregiving environment on children's development and ways to promote quality environments in both home and school settings. More than 90 peer-reviewed publications and chapters describe the findings of these research studies.

Jennifer LoCasale-Crouch, PhD, currently works as an Institute of Education Sciences Research Fellow in Risk and Prevention at the University of Virginia in the Center for Advanced Study of Teaching and Learning (CASTL). Prior to this, Dr. LoCasale-Crouch worked as a clinician with children and families in schools and medical settings, developing and leading workshops for children, families, and professionals focused on enhancing quality of life and creating adaptive transitions. Her research focuses on teacher development and family–school–

community relations as avenues to support at-risk children during early childhood. She has also recently authored several articles on state-funded prekindergarten (pre-K) classroom quality, the transition to kindergarten, and the stability of children's experience from pre-K to kindergarten.

Andrew J. Mashburn, PhD, is a Senior Research Scientist at the Center for Advanced Study of Teaching and Learning at the University of Virginia and the author of numerous research articles, and policy and evaluation reports related to pre-K. Topics of his research include identification of the ecological features of pre-K programs that influence young children's development, measurement of young children's educational outcomes, and evaluation of the effects of education interventions, including state pre-K programs, curricula, and teacher professional development programs.

Lea M. McGee, PhD, is the Marie C. Clay Professor of Reading Recovery and Early Literacy at Ohio State University. She teaches graduate and undergraduate courses in beginning reading and language arts, and foundations of language and literacy development, and postgraduate classes in the theory and practice of Reading Recovery. She is coauthor of four books: *Teaching Literacy in Kindergarten* (with Lesley Mandel Morrow); *Literacy's Beginnings: Supporting Young Readers and Writers* (5th ed.) and *Designing Early Literacy Programs: Strategies for At-Risk Preschool and Kindergarten Children* (both coauthored with Donald J. Richgels); and *Teaching Reading with Literature* (with Gail Tompkins). She has published dozens of articles and book chapters in a variety of journals, including *The Reading Teacher, Language Arts,* and *Reading Research Quarterly.* She is past president of the National Reading Conference. Her research interests include alphabet learning, the role of fingerpoint reading in making the transition from emergent to conventional reading, and young children's responses to literature. She previously directed Project EXEL and Project CORE, and frequently works with teachers in their classrooms.

Carla K. Meyer, MS, is a doctoral student at the University of Delaware. She has school-based experiences as a classroom teacher, reading specialist, and literacy coach, including work for the *Middle School Reading Assistance Project* at The Johns Hopkins University. In addition, she has worked for the International Reading Association as a consultant to *Read Write Think.* She currently works on a survey project to understand better the needs of middle and high school literacy coaches. She is interested in schoolwide reform, professional development, and teacher quality.

Khara L. Pence, PhD, is a Research Assistant Professor at the University of Virginia in the Curry School of Education and the Center for Advanced Study of Teaching and Learning, with an appointment in the Preschool Language and Literacy Lab. Dr. Pence has participated in program evaluation activities as part of Early Reading First projects and serves as research faculty on two projects evaluating the effectiveness of language-focused preschool curricula. She coauthored *Scaffolding with Storybooks: A Guide for Enhancing Young Children's Language and Literacy Achievement* (2005) and *Language Development from Theory to Practice* (2007), and edited *Assessment in Emergent Literacy* (2007), as well as other book chapters and articles.

Robert C. Pianta, PhD, is the Novartis U.S. Foundation Professor in the Curry School of Education, and Professor of Psychology at the University of Virginia, where he also directs the University of Virginia Center for Advanced Study of Teaching and Learning. Dr. Pianta's research and policy interests are in research on classroom settings, their contributions to child outcomes in preschool and the early school years, and how to improve teaching and learning in classrooms Dr. Pianta is principal investigator and Director of the Institute of Education Sciences National Center for Research on Early Childhood Education and of MyTeachingPartner, a National Institute of Child Health and Human Development-funded clinical trial evaluation of web-based support for teachers in pre-K classrooms.

Yaacov Petscher, MS, is a doctoral student in developmental psychology at Florida State University and is the Director of Research at the Florida Center for Reading Research. He works as a methodologist on several center-related projects, applying advanced statistical models to examine the relationships among school, classroom, and student outcomes.

Terri Purcell, PhD, is Assistant Professor in the Department of Teacher Education at Cleveland State University (CSU). Dr. Purcell worked as a field faculty for the Reading First–Ohio Center, where she trained and supported literacy specialists in the Cleveland Municipal Schools. She is currently serving as the director of the Early Reading First program at CSU, working closely with three Head Start centers, 22 teachers, and more than 200 children and families. Dr. Purcell has been engaged in research on early intervention practices and professional development for preschool and elementary teachers, as well as a consulting author for Zaner Bloser's *Strategies for Writers–Kindergarten* curricular materials. She has served as a reviewer for Early Reading First and continues to work with teachers and schools throughout the country.

Craig T. Ramey, PhD, is Director of the Center for Health and Education at Georgetown University. He specializes in the study of factors affecting young children's development of intelligence, social competence, and academic achievement. Over the past 30 years, he and Sharon Landesman Ramey have conducted research involving more than 14,000 children and families in 40 states. Dr. Ramey is the author of more than 225 publications, including four books, and he frequently consults with federal and state governments as well as private agencies, foundations, and the new media. Dr. Ramey currently serves as Chairman of the National Board for Education Sciences, an advisory panel of the Institute of Education Sciences within the U.S. Department of Education.

Sharon Landesman Ramey, PhD, is the Director of the Center for Health and Education at Georgetown University's School of Nursing and Health Studies. She is a developmental psychologist whose professional interests include the study of the development of intelligence and children's competency, early experience and early intervention, the changing American family, and the transition to school. She has authored over 200 articles and six books. She and Craig Ramey received the 2007 Society for Research in Child Development Award for research contributions to children's policy.

M. Adelaida Restrepo, PhD, CCC-SLP, is Associate Professor at Arizona State University in the Department of Speech and Hearing Science. She specializes in language development, disorders, and intervention in Spanish-speaking children. She currently is the principal investigator of two federally funded grants that examine language and literacy intervention for English language learners.

Catherine A. Rosemary, PhD, is Associate Professor in the Department of Education and Allied Studies at John Carroll University. Dr. Rosemary worked for 16 years in public schools, serving in the positions of special education teacher, reading specialist, and director of curriculum and instruction. She currently directs the Literacy Specialist Project, a statewide professional development initiative for improving literacy teaching in preschools through grade 12, and codirects the Reading First–Ohio Center for Professional Development and Technical Assistance in Effective Reading Instruction. She conducts research on early literacy intervention and professional development in literacy. She is coauthor of *Designing Professional Development in Literacy: A Framework for Effective Instruction* (Guilford, 2007). Dr. Rosemary was instrumental in developing the Literacy Specialist Endorsement, available to Ohio's teachers as a new credential in literacy education.

Kathleen A. Roskos, PhD, is on the faculty of John Carroll University, where she teaches courses in reading instruction and reading diagnosis. Dr. Roskos has served in a variety of educational administration roles, including director of federal programs in the public schools and department chair in higher education. For 2 years she directed the Ohio Literacy Initiative at the Ohio Department of Education, providing leadership in primary through 12th-grade literacy policy and programs. Dr. Roskos studies early literacy development and learning, teacher cognition, and the design of professional education for teachers, and has published research articles on these topics in leading journals.

Christopher Schatschneider, PhD, is Associate Professor in the Department of Psychology at Florida State University and a faculty member of the Florida Center for Reading Research. Dr. Schatschneider has conducted research on early reading development and reading disabilities for over 15 years. He also serves as the primary methodologist on a number of federally funded grants and is the coeditor of the journal *Annals of Dyslexia*.

Judith A. Schickedanz, PhD, is Professor of Education in the Department of Literacy and Language, Counseling, and Development at Boston University, where she has taught courses in child development, early literacy, and curriculum and instruction, and has directed the laboratory preschool and coordinated the program in early childhood education. Dr. Schickedanz served as President of the International Reading Association's Literacy Development in Young Children Special Interest Group and was a member of its Commission on Early Reading and Early Literacy Committee. She studies early literacy development and learning, and instructional skills development in preschool teachers. She is senior author of *Understanding Children and Adolescents* (1998, 2001), author of *Much More Than the ABCs* (1999), and coauthor of *Writing in Preschool: Learning to Orchestrate Meaning and Marks* (2004), as well as numerous book chapters and articles.

Paul R. Swank, PhD, is a Professor in the Department of Pediatrics at the Children's Learning Institute. Dr. Swank supervises a staff of 12 statisticians and data management professionals in the Data Analysis Work Group. His expertise is in applied measurement, research design, and statistics, particularly linear models, mixed models for repeated measures, and structural equation modeling. He has applied his expertise in the areas of education, behavioral, and biomedical sciences for more than 25 years. He has published extensively in professional literature.

Carol Vukelich, PhD (*see* "About the Editors").

Sharon Walpole, PhD, is Associate Professor of Education at the University of Delaware. She has extensive school-based experience, including both high school teaching and elementary school administration. She has studied the design and effects of schoolwide reforms, particularly those involving literacy coaches. She works closely with the Reading First initiatives in Delaware and in Georgia. She is coauthor of *The Literacy Coach's Handbook: A Guide to Research-Based Reform* and *Differentiated Reading Instruction: Strategies for the Primary Grades,* as well as recent articles in *Reading Research Quarterly*; *Journal of Educational Psychology*; *Reading and Writing Quarterly*; *Language, Speech, and Hearing Services in the Schools*; *Early Education and Development*; and *The Reading Teacher.*

Betsy G. Watson, MEd, is a PhD candidate in reading education in the Department of Teaching and Learning at Peabody College, Vanderbilt University. Before returning to graduate school, she taught first, third, and fourth grades. She is involved in a research project that evaluates the implementation of a literacy curriculum in rural preschool classrooms funded by an Early Reading First grant. Her research focus is on the features of teacher–child verbal interactions that influence children's literacy outcomes.

Kellee M. Williams, MPH, is currently in the Master's in Public Health Program at Florida State University, and she is also a researcher for the Florida Center for Reading Research. Her interests lie in epidemiology and biostatistics, with emphasis on social and mental health and chronic disease prevention. She entered the Doctoral Program in Public Health in Epidemiology and Biostatistics in the Fall of 2007.

Foreword

The business of preschool today—the mission, the intent, the curriculum, the instructional activities—is not the business of preschool a generation ago. In fact, preschool has changed in a number of important ways even within the past decade. Discussion about the purpose of preschool education—should preschool provide helpful social and play experiences, or should it focus on fostering early academic skills?—has long been a topic of consideration. But now this issue has come to occupy center stage in a profound way, with increasing pressure to provide intentional instruction related to cognitive skills such as early literacy learning, especially to 3- and 4-year-olds.

During these early years of the 21st century, a high degree of consensus on this issue has developed, on one level at least. Part of this consensus stems from the greater attention paid by educators and even the general public to research suggesting that the preschool years are a critical time for learning vital skills in language, cognition, and foundational knowledge in a variety of domains. Another part of the consensus comes from teachers and assistants who work day-to-day in the early childhood classroom and witness what young children can do in reading and writing when they are given the chance. The informed approaches to preschool education that have emerged from this hands-on work and research presume that young children need and benefit from specific attention to literacy concepts and strategies during their preschool day.

In many respects, in the United States today, it is the best of times for preschool literacy. There is now near universal recognition of the importance of the fact that literacy development starts long before children enter first grade or even kindergarten. Current guidelines for federal and most state preschool programs explicitly incorporate standards or benchmarks for literacy. Professional organizations such as the International Reading Association (IRA) and the National Association for the Education of Young Children (NAEYC) have worked individually and collaboratively to get out the word and create professional materials related to preschool reading and writing instruction in the classroom. The organizations have issued a joint position statement "Learning to Read and Write: Developmentally Appropriate Practices for Young Children" (IRA, 1998; NAEYC, 1998), and more recently IRA put forth a "Literacy Development in the Preschool Years" (IRA, 2005) position statement. The *Handbook of Early Literacy Research* (Dickinson & Neuman, 2005) is now out in a second volume. And perhaps most indicative of all is the fact that the federal government is putting significant funding—approximately $100 million per year from 2003 through 2007—into the push for creating centers of excellence in early literacy with the Early Reading First initiative.

All of these developments sound great, but in some respects this era could also be ushering in a not-so-great period for the literacy education of America's preschool children. We are already witnessing growth in questionable assessment and instructional practices and policies in preschool classrooms. Research has amply shown that what has come to be known as the "Big Four"—vocabulary and other language abilities, phonological awareness, letter knowledge, and basic conventions of print—are crucial early building blocks for ensuring reading and writing success during the elementary school years and beyond. But it does not necessarily follow that, as has happened in many situations, the preschool literacy curriculum should be reduced to only these four areas. Research has also amply shown that ongoing child progress monitoring in the classroom helps teachers differentiate instruction and leads to enhanced achievement for children. But it is not necessarily true that an assessment program gives teachers appropriate data for making sound instruction decisions just because that program consists of a set of indicators determined to be reliable.

Two additional questions of crucial significance merit our deepest consideration if we are to avoid the pitfall of preschool literacy curriculum and instruction that misses the mark with children. First is a content question: *"What?"* In addition to the Big Four, what other aspects of early literacy development warrant explicit attention? I have some candidates that I believe research shows deserve a place at the instructional table: listening comprehension, familiarity with the rich body of children's literature (which will enhance knowledge in a number of important content area domains), literary understanding, and building positive attitudes toward literacy activities so that children will develop lifelong reading and writing habits.

Second is the question that applies to all areas related to children's preschool literacy development: oral language, vocabulary, text-based listening comprehension, phonological awareness, letter knowledge, print awareness, literature knowledge, literary understanding, and lifelong reading and writing habits. That question is *"How?"* It is how we go about fostering these concepts, strategies, and dispositions that counts. We must remember that we are teaching *preschool* children, 3- and 4-year-olds. We know they can do amazing things. But in our zeal to leave no child behind, to prevent reading difficulty, to create preschool centers of early literacy excellence, we must always remember the intimate bond between instruction and learning. An instructional plan, instructional strategy, or particular lesson may look appropriate on paper or logical to adult eyes. But what happens to a child when that plan or lesson is actualized in the classroom? What knowledge does the child learn—or not learn? What disposition toward literacy does it foster in the child? What insight about meaning-making or sounds or letters or language does it promote? It all depends on how the instruction is done.

The area of preschool literacy instruction is ready for a book like *Achieving Excellence in Preschool Literacy Instruction.* Early Reading First has the potential to bring enormous benefits to individual children, to agencies and schools that house programs, and to the field of early literacy itself. But we must closely examine our practices and policies, and we must use what we learn to improve what we do for and with our 3- and 4-year-olds. *Achieving Excellence in Preschool Literacy Instruction* offers information and insight from people who are "on the ground," doing the work in preschool classrooms. They help us see children and teachers and programs and policies in action. Nothing can be more helpful in moving forward the agenda for preschool literacy in an appropriate and productive way.

WILLIAM H. TEALE, EdD
University of Illinois at Chicago Reading Clinic

References

Dickinson, D., & Neuman, S. (Eds.). (2005). *Handbook of early literacy research* (Vol. 2). New York: Guilford Press.

International Reading Association. (1998). Learning to read and write: Developmentally appropriate practices for young children. *The Reading Teacher, 52,* 193–216.

International Reading Association. (2005). *Literacy development in the preschool years: A position statement.* Newark, DE: Author.

National Association for the Education of Young Children. (1998). Learning to read and write: Developmentally appropriate practices for young children. *Young Children, 53,* 30–46.

Preface

This book is about how every moment counts in the preschool classroom. More precisely, it is about how we must design programs and support teachers in fundamental ways that lead us to excellence in language and literacy instruction within the preschool classroom. Hundreds of research articles published every year give guidance in providing children with exemplary preschool language and literacy learning environments, so that they are poised to excel in the more academically oriented milieu of elementary schools. This volume, with contributions from 35 experts who are actively contributing to this research literature, helps to bridge research and practice, so that we can make every moment count for the young children in our preschool classrooms.

The 21st century is an incredibly exciting time for those of us who are invested in promoting and achieving high-quality learning environments for our country's preschoolers. The growing body of research indicating that early exposure to oral language and literacy skills (e.g., alphabetic knowledge and phonological awareness) places young children at an advantage for later reading achievement has pushed policymakers toward instituting new initiatives that change instructional practices in early childhood programs. States have developed language and early literacy standards (called voluntary guidelines by the federal government) detailing what young children should know and be able to do by the end of the preschool years (states called their standards by different names: "building blocks;" "learning foundations"). The George W. Bush administration has developed a plan (called Good Start, Grow Smart) to strengthen early learning to equip young children with the skills they need to begin school ready to learn. The administration put policies in place to hold Head Start programs accountable for every child's early literacy, language, and numeracy skills. Early Reading First (ERF), a competitive grant program that provides funding to organizations serving low-income preschool children, was created to address the growing concern that many of the nation's children begin kindergarten without the necessary skills to be successful. Funded ERF projects must use curricula, programs, and instructional methods that are supported by scientific research. The nation now realizes the importance of children's early years to their later academic success, particularly their reading achievement.

Achieving exemplary instruction is more important today than ever before. Current estimates indicate that the majority of American children from birth through age 6 (not yet in kindergarten) receive some form of childcare on a regular basis from persons other than their parents (Federal Interagency Forum on Child and Family Statistics, July 2005). At the same time, examinations of the quality of this care suggest that it is less than optimal. We now have a scientific base to guide our improvements in the coming years, much of which is detailed in this volume.

Scope and Audience

We organized this volume into four sections. Each section focuses on ideas central to achieving excellence in language and literacy instruction in our nation's preschools. Collectively, the sections provide a roadmap summarizing where the field is relative to the topic, and mapping a way forward. We describe each of these sections in detail below. Each chapter is prepared by one or more experts who are known nationally and internationally for research on their chosen topics. In addition, these professionals work "on the front lines," using their ideas to support preschool teachers' teaching and young children's learning. Several authors are consultants or evaluators, or project directors on ERF or similar projects, working directly with teachers and young children. They know what life is *really* like in preschool classrooms in America.

We envisioned, you, our readers, as we read the drafts of each chapter. We saw early childhood practitioners (teachers, center and project directors, ERF and other project coaches) reading and talking about the ideas presented and considering ways to use the ideas to inform their work with children and with each other. We also saw teachers-in-training to become teachers of young children, and their instructors and inservice teachers, seeking to become better preschool teachers and finding value in the ideas shared in this book. We'd love to hear from each of you. We include our e-mail addresses at the end of this preface.

Special Features

Before each section, we include a list of questions to guide your thinking as you read the chapters in that section. These questions relate to no single chapter in the section; rather, our intent is to help you think across the chapters in each section.

We also include three or four activities to help you extend and apply your knowledge. Typically these activities invite our readers who are not working in a preschool setting to connect with an early childhood program in their area to "test out" the ideas they read about, and those who are working in preschool settings to study their center's activities to reflect on their work with each other or with their children.

Acknowledgments

We acknowledge the outstanding contributors whose work and ideas are highlighted in this book. The chapter authors deserve a special thanks for working hard to meet deadlines, and to respond in a timely and graceful way to our revision requests. We are grateful to have worked with such an excellent group. We also want to thank Chris Jennison at The Guilford Press, who inspired us to pursue this work. And we must thank our families, husbands, and children. Addie got to play less with her mother, who was busy writing, reading, editing, and communicating with Carol. While we worked on this book, Addie acquired a brother, who sat in his mother's lap believing that she was attending to him when, in fact, she was reading a manuscript in her best storybook reading voice. Our spouses, Ian and Ron, gave us the time to work but periodically pulled us away from our computers and papers to make us have fun.

LAURA M. JUSTICE
(justice.57@osu.edu)

CAROL VUKELICH
(vukelich@udel.edu)

Contents

PART I

★★★★★★★★

BACKGROUND

The first three chapters of this book provide a framework for viewing preschool programs as essential contexts for improving educational outcomes for schoolchildren in the United States, particularly in the areas of early language and literacy. As you are undoubtedly aware, preschool programs are considered by society as holding great promise for addressing the "pernicious achievement gap between white and nonwhite students and between students from economically more advantaged vs. less advantaged families" (Meisels, 2006, p. 6). Andrew J. Mashburn, in Chapter 1, discusses the history of preschool programs in the United States and provides an interesting portrait of this segment of public policy through the 21st century, including a brief overview of research evidence that has helped to shape these policy decisions.

A topic of keen contemporary interest in the area of preschool programming scientifically based reading research (SBRR), is described in Chapter 2 by nationally recognized expert James F. Christie. Christie provides an excellent consideration of the "fit" between SBRR and preschool programming, and guidance to administrators and teachers on how explicit literacy instruction can be sensibly embedded into high-quality preschool programs.

In Chapter 3, Sharon Landesman Ramey and Craig T. Ramey provide a useful and well-articulated theory of professional development (PD) as applied to the field of early education and care. PD is currently seen as a critical mechanism for promoting the quality of early education, partic-

1

ularly in the areas of language and literacy, and decisions concerning the intensity, content, and pedagogy of PD should carefully articulate with theories of how adults learn best. The authors' important précis on this topic provides an important conceptual foundation for Part II of this book, which delves more deeply into current approaches to PD.

While reading these chapters, consider the following questions:

1. What are the major differences between using an emergent literacy approach and an SBRR approach in literacy instruction? What advantages are there in the blending of these two approaches?
2. How does the use of an SBRR approach to instruction relate to the creation of a high-quality preschool program?
3. Compare how public policy influenced both the movement toward the expansion of preschool programs and the movement for more scientifically based reading instruction.
4. Identify five principles of effective PD for early educators. Are these principles typically reflected in current PD approaches? Why or why not?

After you have completed your reading, consider one or more of the following activities to expand your knowledge further:

1. Observe in a preschool classroom for a morning. Note the opportunities for learning the key language and literacy skills that the teacher(s) provide the children. (If you are a teacher in a preschool classroom, reflect on the opportunities you provide your children for learning these skills.) Does this teacher, or do you, provide the children with explicit literacy instruction in each of the key language and literacy skills areas? Is this teacher's language and literacy instruction, or is your instruction, reflective of both the emergent literacy and SBRR perspectives on children's learning?
2. Explain how this program meets or does not meet the 10 structural benchmarks related to teachers' level of education and type of training; classroom characteristics, such as class size, child-to-teacher ratio, and curriculum, and additional services offered to children and families; and how this classroom exhibits or does not exhibit the specific classroom features that characterize high-quality processes set forth by Mashburn in Chapter 1.
3. Participate in a professional development opportunity—a study group, a workshop, or a conference. Explain how this opportunity

meets or does not meet the five principles of professional development articulated by Ramey and Ramey in Chapter 3. In what ways does it live up to these principles? In what ways does it not? What are the implications of this?

References

Meisels, S. J. (2006). *Accountability in early childhood: No easy answers.* Chicago: Erikson Institute, Herr Research Center for Children and Social Policy.

CHAPTER 1

★★★★★★★★

Evidence for Creating, Expanding, Designing, and Improving High-Quality Preschool Programs

Andrew J. Mashburn

"Preschool" refers to any formal program in which young children participate before they enter primary school that is designed to promote children's social–emotional, academic, language, and literacy skills, and health and well-being. Public preschool programs have been available throughout the history of the United States, the earliest of which were small-scale and targeted children from low-income families to prevent the negative impacts of living in poverty. This recognition that early interventions have the powerful potential to improve the well-being of children, families, communities, and societies has led to the widespread creation of public preschool programs by local, state, and the federal governments, and a majority of children currently attend some type of preschool program before they enroll in kindergarten.

Public policies determine whether preschool programs are created, who has access to them, and how they are designed and improved. For example, local, state, and federal legislators may propose policies to create public preschool programs, and citizens or their representatives may then vote on whether public funds should be spent to establish these programs. Once programs are created, policies determine a number of other features of the programs, such as who is eligible to attend, how many students and teachers are in each preschool class, what level of education and type of training teachers must have, and what services are available to teachers to improve teaching and learning in their classes. Each of these features may impact preschool program effectiveness in promoting the well-being of children who attend, and research that documents the effects of preschool may help inform policy decisions about whether programs are created, whom they should serve, how they should be designed, and ways to improve them. This chapter provides an overview of the history of preschool programs in the United States; describes policy questions related to creating, expanding, designing, and improving these programs; and reviews research evidence that has helped to shape these policy decisions.

History of Preschool Education in the United States

The system of public education in the United States was originally designed to begin at first grade, when children are 6 or 7 years of age. However, a variety of preschool programs have been created for children prior to their enrollment in primary school. The first preschool programs were established in the mid-19th century during the Industrial Revolution, when factory owners created "infant schools" where children could be cared for while their mothers worked in factories, and the primary goal was to spur economic and industrial growth (Pre-K Now, 2006). Public preschool programs were also established at this time with a different goal—to improve the well-being of young children and families from economically disadvantaged backgrounds. During the mid-19th century, urban poverty was rampant, and preschool programs were created in many cities to provide resources for young children that counter the negative effects of living in poverty (Pre-K Now, 2006).

The first public preschool programs were originally proposed in Boston in the 1830's to teach basic education skills for 3- and 4-year-olds; however, this initiative was rejected by the local school board (Pre-K Now, 2006). In 1853, New York City established 58 infant schools that served children from economically disadvantaged backgrounds. In 1848, Wisconsin amended its state Constitution to allow 4-year-olds to attend public school, and in 1873, created a kindergarten program specifically for 4-year-old children (4K) that in some school districts lasted for over 100 years (Pre-K Now, 2006).

In the 1870s, another widespread early education intervention—kindergarten—began to flourish in the United States. Kindergarten was originally created by Friedrich Froebel in Germany in the 1830s, with the goal of promoting children's socialization skills through play (Froebel Foundation, 2006). In 1873, St. Louis became the first city to offer kindergarten in every public school, and soon thereafter, public kindergarten programs gained widespread popularity nationwide. These programs were initially established in working-class neighborhoods to serve immigrant children and others who experienced the blight of urban poverty, but they were later expanded to include all children (Froebel Foundation, 2006). These were originally full-day programs; however, many kindergarten programs were scaled back to half-day programs in the 1930s due to the scarcity of resources brought on by the Great Depression (Education Commission of the States, 2005).

There has been a recent movement by states and districts to return kindergarten back to a full-day program. In 1977, 28% of children who attended kindergarten went to full-day programs, and by 2004, 65% of kindergartners attended full-day programs (Wirt et al., 2004). However, across states there is wide variability in state policies that determine whether school districts are required to have full-day kindergarten programs and whether children are required to attend them. For example, 41 states permit districts to offer full-day kindergarten and to require that children attend; seven states require districts to offer full-day kindergarten and permit them to require children to attend; and two states (Louisiana and West Virginia) require that districts offer full-day kindergarten and require children to attend (Education Commission of the States, 2005).

Despite the institutionalization of kindergarten programs in the U.S. system of public education at the end of the 19th century and its continuing reexpansion to a full-day program, children from socially and economically disadvantaged backgrounds who enter school have continued to lag behind their peers. As a result, the need for further early education experiences for children at risk for school failure has led to the creation of additional preschool programs. Small-scale, locally funded programs were established in a number of cities, such as the Perry preschool program, which began in Ypsilanti, Michigan, in 1962 (Schweinhart, Barnes, & Weikart, 1993), and the Chicago parent–child centers, which began in 1967 (Reynolds, Temple, Robertson, & Mann, 2001).

In 1965, Head Start was established nationwide as the first large-scale preschool program for 3- and 4-year-olds designed to help break the cycle of poverty among children of low-income families by providing comprehensive services to meet children's emotional, social, health, nutritional, and psychological needs (Administration for Children and Families, 2004). Although Head Start has served more than 23 million children over a 40-year period (1965–2005; Administration for Children and Families, 2006) many eligible children do not attend, because programs have either reached their capacity or are not available locally. As a result, most states have created their own programs to fill this gap in providing services to children with social and economic disadvantages. Currently 38 states offer one or more public preschool programs, most of which are targeted toward 4-year-old children who are poor, experience other family risks, or have developmental delays (Barnett, Hustedt, Robin, & Schulman, 2005). These preschool programs for 4-year-olds are typically referred to as "prekindergarten" (pre-K) programs because they serve children the year before they enroll in kindergarten. Twenty-seven of the 38 states that offer public pre-K programs also provide programs for 3-year-olds; however, these programs serve a relatively small percentage of 3-year-olds in each state (Barnett et al., 2005).

The current movements by states to expand kindergarten from half-days to full-days and to create preschool programs for 3- and 4-year-olds, combined with the continued expansion of Head Start enrollment, has resulted in a dramatic increase in the number of children who attend formal education programs prior to their enrollment in primary school. Since Head Start was created, there has been a 400% increase in the prevalence of 4-year-olds who attend preschool programs, with attendance rising from 17% in 1965 to 66% in 2002 (Barnett & Yarosz, 2004). Each year, approximately 800,000 children across the nation attend state-funded pre-K programs alone, which costs over $2.5 billion per year (Barnett et al., 2005). Table 1.1 provides an overview of the accessibility of preschool programs in each state, including the percentage of 3- and 4-year-olds who attend public preschool programs (state-funded and other public programs, including Head Start and the IDEA preschool grants program) during 2004–2005 (Barnett et al., 2005), and each state's policy regarding access to and attendance in kindergarten (Education Commission of the States, 2005).

The rapid growth and expansion of preschool programs described have been the result of local, state, and federal policies that create preschool programs, define who is eligible to attend, set program regulations, and offer services to improve preschool quality. Results from research studies have helped to inform policy decisions that contribute to the creation of effective preschool programs. The next section reviews research that documents the effects of attending preschool programs on children's development of social, academic, language, and literacy skills—the results of which have lead to the widespread creation of public preschool programs.

Evidence for Creating Preschool Programs

The primary purpose of preschool is to provide educational and social opportunities to help children enter school ready to learn; the next two subsections present findings from research studies providing evidence that preschool has positive benefits on developmental outcomes for children who attend and positive economic benefits for society.

TABLE 1.1. Percentage of 3- and 4-Year-Olds Attending State-Funded and Other Public Preschool Programs, and Policies Regarding Full-Day Kindergarten in Each State

	3-year-olds[a]		4-year-olds[a]		Kindergarten[b]
	% in state-funded programs	% in other public programs	% in state-funded programs	% in other public programs	State policy
Alabama	0	12	2	22	M
Alaska	0	15	0	24	P
Arizona	0	10	6	19	P
Arkansas	8	19	12	31	M
California	5	9	11	16	P
Colorado	1	8	11	14	P
Connecticut	2	11	15	14	P
Delaware	0	10	8	16	P
Florida	0	9	0	16	P
Georgia	0	11	55	13	M
Hawaii	1	10	5	16	P
Idaho	0	8	0	19	P
Illinois	12	12	26	18	P
Indiana	0	10	0	16	P
Iowa	1	11	4	17	P
Kansas	0	13	16	19	P
Kentucky	11	19	30	33	P
Louisiana	0	17	20	23	MR
Maine	0	19	14	27	P
Maryland	1	10	31	12	M
Massachusetts	7	10	8	15	P
Michigan	0	14	19	21	P
Minnesota	1	11	2	16	P
Mississippi	0	28	0	44	M
Missouri	2	13	4	19	P
Montana	0	18	0	29	P
Nebraska	1	12	3	18	P
Nevada	1	6	2	11	P
New Hampshire	0	8	0	13	P
New Jersey	15	9	26	12	P
New Mexico	1	14	1	28	P
New York	1	15	29	20	P
North Carolina	0	8	10	16	M
North Dakota	0	20	0	32	P
Ohio	2	13	5	18	P
Oklahoma	0	17	69	24	P
Oregon	3	10	5	17	P
Pennsylvania	1	12	5	18	P
Rhode Island	0	12	0	23	P
South Carolina	1	13	30	17	M
South Dakota	0	21	0	30	P
Tennessee	1	10	3	19	P
Texas	4	9	46	14	P
Utah	0	7	0	15	P
Vermont	13	14	45	19	P
Virginia	0	8	11	14	P
Washington	1	9	6	15	P
West Virginia	4	18	35	29	MR
Wisconsin	1	14	29	19	P
Wyoming	0	21	0	34	P

Note. P, state permits districts to offer full-day kindergarten and permits districts to require attendance; M, state mandates districts to offer full-day kindergarten and permits districts to require attendance; MR, state mandates districts to offer full-day kindergarten and mandates that attendance is required.
[a]Data from Barnett et al. (2005).
[b]Data from Education Commission of the States (2005).

Effects of Attending Preschool on Children's Development

Numerous research studies have investigated the effects of attending preschool programs on children's development of social, academic, cognitive, health, and language competencies, and findings from these studies
document very favorable benefits of high-quality preschool on children's
short-term and long-term outcomes (see Lamb & Ahnert, 2006). In the
earliest studies of the effects of attending preschool, children were randomly assigned to two groups: one group that attended preschool and the
other group that did not attend preschool. Children's skills and abilities
were compared at the end of preschool, into the later grades, and for
some studies, all the way to adulthood. These studies typically included
children from low-income families who attended a few very high-quality
preschool programs. Results of these studies provide powerful evidence
for short-term benefits of attending preschool (FPG [Frank Porter Gra-
ham] Child Development Institute, 2005; Lazar, Darlington, Murray,
Royce, & Snipper, 1982; Reynolds, 2000; Schweinhart et al., 1993). Some
of these studies also document benefits of attending preschool that last
into adulthood. For example, a longitudinal study of the effects of the
High/Scope Perry Preschool Study in Ypsilanti, Michigan (Schweinhart et
al., 1993, 2005) compared children who attended and did not attend preschool throughout elementary and secondary school and again at ages 27
and 40. Results indicated that children who attended a Perry Preschool
Program were more likely to graduate from high school on time and to
own a home and less likely to be referred for special education, to receive
Welfare as an adult, and to commit crimes.

Benefit–Cost Ratio of Preschool Attendance

Another method of documenting the effects of attending preschool is
benefit–cost ratios that compare the economic benefits to society that
result from children attending preschool and the costs of providing preschool. Economic benefits for society related to preschool attendance may
include fewer expenses in providing children with special education programs; less money spent on social programs, such as Welfare; and fewer
expenses for legal services resulting from crime. Results of benefit–cost
analyses show that the benefits of providing preschool for children who
experience social and economic risks strongly outweigh their costs. For
example, the High/Scope Perry Preschool Program yielded a benefit–
cost ratio of over 17 to 1, indicating that for each $1 invested in providing
preschool programs for children from economically disadvantaged families, society receives over $17 in return over the course of these children's
lives (Barnett & Massey, 2007). Two other studies of preschool programs—

the Abecedarian program, which randomly assigned infants from low-income families to receive preschool services through age 5 (Barnett & Massey, 2007; FPG Child Development Institute, 2005), and the Chicago child–parent centers, which compared children who attended and did not attend these programs available to 3-year-olds through third graders (Reynolds et al., 2001)—also had positive benefit–cost ratios. Specifically, for $1 invested in the Abecedarian program and the Chicago child–parent centers, there was a return to society of $3.80 and $7.10, respectively.

There are some criticisms of the results of these studies. For example, in the High/Scope Perry Preschool Study and the Abecedarian study, a relatively small number of children participated in the studies and rates of drop out (i.e., attrition) were high because the studies lasted for many years. In addition, because these studies included children from economically disadvantaged families who attended very high-quality preschool programs, the results may not be applicable to children who attend programs that provide lower quality services. In spite of these studies' limitations, their results provide powerful evidence of the potential of preschool programs to improve the short- and long-term well-being of individuals and society, and have fueled the creation and expansion of programs nationwide.

Evidence for Expanding Preschool Programs

With evidence showing that attending high-quality preschool has strong positive benefits on children's readiness for school and their well-being as adults, federal, state and local agencies have created preschool programs at a rapid rate. Once these programs have been established, another policy question is raised: Who is eligible to attend? The most common criterion determining access to preschool programs is age, and most state preschool programs are currently available for 4-year-old children. However, Head Start, as well as some state programs, offer services for 3-year-old children (see Table 1.1) (Education Commission of the States, 2006). Another common eligibility criterion for attending public preschool is the child's social and economic background. Most programs target children who experience risks, which may include family poverty, homelessness, low parental education, limited English proficiency, abuse or neglect, and health or developmental problems. The trend of expanding programs to serve more children who experience risks is occurring in many states: Alabama, Kansas, Louisiana, Nebraska, and Nevada each expanded enrollment in their state programs by 50% or more between 2001 and 2002, and 2002 and 2003 (Barnett, Hustedt, Robin, & Schulman, 2004).

Debates about Universal Preschool

Many state pre-K programs have removed economic and social risk as a requirement for enrollment altogether, which is moving public preschool toward a universal system that is available for any 4-year-old child. In 1995, the Georgia prekindergarten program became the first public program in the country that was available to any 4-year-old child who lives in the state (Georgia Department of Early Care and Learning, 2006). Universal programs have been created or will soon be created in other states, including Oklahoma, Maryland, West Virginia, New York and Florida (Barnett, Hustedt, et al., 2004). However, this movement toward universal preschool is not universally agreed upon, and in 2006, California voters rejected a state amendment creating a universal pre-K program in favor of the existing program that targets children who experience social or economic risks (Jacobson, 2006).

Whether it is a better use of resources to serve all children or to allocate resources to provide preschool services only for children who experience social or economic risks is hotly debated, and each side of this debate offers arguments about why programs should or should not be universally accessible (Barnett, Brown, & Shore, 2004). Advocates of programs targeting at-risk children cite evidence from research studies that indicates attendance in high-quality preschool programs has a stronger positive effect on children who experience risks of underachievement (e.g., Baydar & Brooks-Gunn, 1991; Bryant, Burchinal, Lau, & Sparling, 1994; Peisner-Feinberg & Burchinal, 1997). Thus, targeted programs may be a better investment of public resources, because they are likely to produce greater gains in development compared to programs that serve children who are not at risk for academic and social difficulties. In addition, providing resources to children from relatively privileged backgrounds, whose families may otherwise be able to afford to send their children to private programs, directs resources away from disadvantaged children who benefit the most, which may compromise the quality of provisions available to children with the greatest needs.

In contrast, some policy-related organizations and advocacy groups argue that public preschool programs should be available for any child who wishes to attend (Barnett, Brown, et al., 2004). They cite evidence that targeted programs may not reach the children they are intended to serve. In addition, many children who do not meet a targeted program's criteria for enrolling may still benefit from high-quality preschool experiences. There is also wide political appeal in providing universal preschool, which may be considered more equitable than targeted programs and more consistent with the notion that public education should include all children. Another argument about the potential benefits of universal compared to targeted programs is that universal programs result in a more diverse group of children enrolled in the same classroom. As a result, interactions with peers of different economic backgrounds and ability levels may have a positive effect on children's attitudes, behaviors, and educational outcomes (Henry & Rickman, 2007; Odom, 2000; Schecter, 2002).

Policies by local, state, and federal governments determine not only whether programs are created and who has access to preschool programs but also how programs are designed and regulated, which may influence the effectiveness of preschool programs in preparing children to enter school ready to learn, as well as the costs of providing preschool programs. On average, preschool programs for 4-year-olds cost over $3,500 per child per year for state pre-K programs and over $7,000 per child per year for Head Start (Barnett, Hustedt, Robin, & Schulman, 2004). To help inform policy decisions about how to design preschool programs that minimize costs and maximize benefits to children, professional organizations, advocacy groups, and researchers have identified a variety of preschool program features that lead to improved well-being for children.

Evidence for Designing High-Quality Preschool Programs

Almost every policy that pertains to designing preschool programs emphasizes the importance of providing high-quality services. In general, "high-quality preschool" refers to the characteristics of preschool programs that are believed to be beneficial to children, but parents, teachers, and policymakers may define the term differently. For example, parents may describe a preschool as high quality based on whether it is open for extended hours, has flexible scheduling, or has teachers who provide emotional support to their children. Teachers may describe quality in terms of the curriculum they use and the space, furnishings, and learning materials that support their implementation of this curriculum. Two broad definitions of quality of preschool programs have been described: structural quality and process quality (Lamb, 1998; Phillips & Howes, 1987; Vandell & Wolfe, 2000).

Quality of Structural Features

Policymakers tend to describe preschool quality in terms of "structural" features of programs that can be directly regulated through policies, such as the amount and type of training held by lead and assistant teachers, the maximum number of children that can enroll in a class, the maximum child-to-teacher ratio, the curriculum that is used, the amount of training and professional development in which teachers must participate, and the additional services that the programs provide, such as meals, health screenings, and family support. A number of professional organizations concerned with the well-being of young children (e.g., American Public Health Association and the American Academy of Pediatrics [1992], National Association for the Education of Young Children [2004], and National Institute for Early Education Research [NIEER; Barrett, Hustedt, Robin, & Schulman, 2005)] provide recommended standards of structural quality for preschool programs, which are often used to inform policymakers' and program administrators' decisions about how to design high-quality programs. For example, the NIEER defines high-quality preschool programs that serve 4-year-olds in terms of whether programs adhere to 10 structural benchmarks related to teachers' level of education and type of training; classroom characteristics, such as class size, child-to-teacher ratio, and curriculum; and additional services offered to children and families (see Table 1.2).

Despite the focus of professional organizations on promoting high-quality preschool based on these structural features, research provides mixed evidence that programs with these structural features lead to improved development for children. Some studies of preschool, child care, and informal early education programs that serve a wide range of children indicate that certain structural features—lower child-to-staff ratios, smaller class sizes, and higher levels of teacher education and training—lead to better outcomes for children (Burchinal, Roberts, Nabors, & Bryant, 1996; Dunn, 1993; Howes, 1997; National Institute of Child Health and Human Development [NICHD] Early Child Care Research Network, 2002a; Phillips, Howes, & Whitebook, 1992). For example, a large national study of children's early child care experiences conducted by the NICHD Early Child Care Research Network (1999) found that children at 6 months, 15 months, 24 months, and 36 months of age who were enrolled in child care centers that had higher structural quality regarding child-to-staff ratio, group size, caregiver training, and caregiver level of education, performed better on cognitive, language, and social competence measures compared to children enrolled in classes that met fewer of these standards. Similarly, Howes (1990) found that structural quality in pre-K—defined as whether classrooms met recommended standards for child-to-staff ratio, group size, caregiver training, and physical space—was associated positively with children's adjustment in kindergarten.

Thus, structural features of programs can be important components of a regulatory system aimed at providing classroom capacities that contribute to improvement in children's learning and social adjustment. However, other studies have found no evidence that structural characteristics

TABLE 1.2. Structural Quality and Process Quality in Preschool Programs

Structural quality

- Teachers have a bachelor's degree.
- Teachers' preservice training includes specialized training in early childhood education.
- Assistant teachers have a Child Development Associate (CDA) degree or equivalent.
- Teachers attend at least 15 hours of professional development per year.
- The state has comprehensive standards for curricula that are specific to pre-K.
- Classes have no more than 20 children.
- At least one teacher/staff member is present for every 10 children.
- Screening and referral services that cover vision, hearing, and health.
- Additional support services, including parent conferences or home visits, parenting support or training, referral to social services, or information relating to nutrition.
- At least one meal per day is served.

Process quality

Emotional support
- Positive climate
- Lack of negativity
- Regard for student perspectives
- Sensitivity to children's academic and emotional needs

Classroom organization
- Effective behavior management
- Productive use of class time
- Instructional formats that promote learning

Instructional support
- Feedback that extends learning and encourages participation
- Interactions that promote higher order thinking and problem solving
- Activities that facilitate and encourage language use

Data from Barrett, Hustedt, Robin, and Schulman (2005), and from Hamre and Pianta (2007).

benefit children's development. For example, in a recent compilation of seven large-scale studies of pre-K that involved over 7,500 children enrolled in nearly 3,000 public pre-K programs, two features of structural quality that are thought to benefit children's development—teachers' level of education and field of study—had little, if any, influence on the children's development of academic and language skills (Early et al., 2007). One explanation for these inconsistent findings across studies relates to when the studies were conducted. Early studies were conducted when there was wide variability in structural features such as class sizes, teachers' education, and fields of training; as a result, higher structural quality was found to be associated with children's development. Recently, preschool has become a more highly regulated system, which has reduced the variability in these features of programs; as a result, structural features are not as strongly related to children's development (Pianta, 2005).

Quality of Classroom Processes

Preschools that achieve high levels of structural quality do not necessarily deliver benefits to children who attend these programs. An alternative way to define preschool quality is in terms of processes that occur within a classroom that children experience directly (Lamb, 1998; Phillips & Howes, 1987; Vandell & Wolfe, 2000). Specifically, process quality concerns the nature of interactions between teachers and children, and Hamre and Pianta (2007) propose that classroom interactions are organized into three broad domains—emotional support, classroom organization, and instructional support. Specifically, high-quality preschool is characterized by interactions that are emotionally positive and sensitive to children's needs; an organizational climate in which learning materials, activities, and children's behaviors are effectively managed; and instructional interactions that effectively promote and extend children's academic, language, literacy, and social developments. Table 1.2 presents a list of specific classroom features that characterize high-quality processes within classrooms.

There is strong evidence across a number of studies that children enrolled in classrooms with higher process quality achieve greater academic and social benefits compared to children attending lower quality programs (Gormley & Phillips, 2003; NICHD Early Child Care Research Network, 2002b). There is also evidence that preschool programs with higher process quality have more positive effects for children who experience greater social or economic risks than for children with more privileged social or economic backgrounds. This suggests that attending preschools characterized by high process quality may have a compensatory effect on development for children who experience social or economic risks (e.g., Baydar & Brooks-Gunn, 1991; Peisner-Feinberg & Burchinal, 1997).

A recent large-scale study involving 11 states that offer public pre-K programs for 4-year-olds directly contrasted the influence of structural quality and process quality on children's development during pre-K (Mashburn et al., in press). There was little evidence that structural quality was associated positively with children's development of receptive language, expressive language, rhyming, problem solving, letter naming, or social skills during pre-K. In contrast, process quality was associated significantly with children's development. Specifically, higher quality instructional interactions were associated with faster rates of development of academic and language skills, and higher quality emotional interactions were associated with faster development of social skills. Thus, designing preschool programs so that they meet definitions of high quality based on structural standards may not be sufficient to ensure the programs deliver benefits to children who attend. Instead, high process quality is the mechanism through which preschool transmits benefits to children who attend (Hamre & Pianta, 2007; Pianta, 2003), and program resources that directly target improving classroom processes are likely to produce greater impacts on children's development than are resources aimed at improving structural features of programs.

Evidence for Improving Preschool Programs

For currently existing preschool programs, no matter who has access to them or how they have been designed, efforts to improve the quality of processes that occur within classrooms may be the most effective way to increase the benefits to children. Program policies may target two types of activities that focus directly on improving classroom processes—teacher professional development and program monitoring.

Professional Development

Traditional approaches for professional development practices have involved direct training of teachers through workshops (Birman, Desimone, Porter, & Garet, 2000) that tend to be ineffective, because the content is vague, irrelevant, or disconnected from classroom context; follow-up is limited; and methods involve passive learning techniques (Haymore-Sandholtz, 2002). A new vision for high-quality professional development for teachers has been promoted by No Child Left Behind, which describes good professional development activities as those that are intensive, sustained, and classroom-focused; as a result, there has been a recent movement to design professional development activities that are active, collaborative, embedded within a classroom context, and part of school culture (Abdal-Haqq, 1995; Darling-Hammond & McLaughlin, 1995; Lieberman, 1995; Putnam & Borko, 1997; Richardson, 2003). Two specific professional development techniques that have gained wider use are mentoring and consultee-centered consultation.

Through the process of mentoring, experienced teachers are agents of change through the support and guidance they provide to less experienced colleagues (Fideler & Haselkorn, 1999). In a review study of teacher mentoring, Ingersoll and Kralik (2004) found that mentoring programs for new teachers had a positive effect on teachers' job satisfaction and reduced teacher attrition. In another professional development technique, consultee-centered consultation, used in mental health fields (Caplan, 1970; Caplan & Caplan, 1993), and only more recently applied within schools (Rosenfield & Gravois, 1996), teachers and outside professionals, who bring a particular expertise and knowledge base, collaborate by using joint problem-solving techniques to address challenges that

teachers face in their classrooms (Knotek & Sandoval, 2003). These two
professional development techniques, in which teachers receive consistent, nonevaluative support from experts, and feedback on their practices
as observed in the classroom and in interactions with children, have
strong potential to improve the quality of teaching practices and, in turn,
children's developmental outcomes. This is particularly true when these
efforts are informed by a focus on dimensions of interactions and implementation shown to produce gains for children (Pianta, 2005).

Program Monitoring

Another approach to promote high-quality experiences for children within preschool programs, program monitoring typically involves observing
and rating the quality of provisions, instructional approaches, and interactions within classes that children directly experience, and results may be
used in a number of ways that promote high process quality. Results of
the observations may be used to provide feedback to preschool centers
about their areas of strengths and weaknesses, as well as resources to
implement changes. In addition, linking additional consequences to the
results of program monitoring may also be used to promote high-quality
experiences in pre-K. For example, the Los Angeles Universal Preschool
Program (Los Angeles Universal Preschool, n.d.) uses a five-star system
for rating the process quality in preschool programs. Only programs that
receive three or more stars are eligible to receive funding from the Los
Angeles Universal Preschool Program. In addition, programs that fall
below three stars may receive support from a "Quality Support Coach,"
who works directly with the preschool program, and offers support and
guidance for improving quality; also teachers are eligible to participate in
further education and training opportunities. Both of these approaches—
professional development and program monitoring—directly target the
quality of children's experiences within preschool classes, which in turn
has a direct influence on children's development of the skills needed to
enter school ready to learn.

Conclusions

Throughout the history of the United States, preschool programs have
been created for a variety of reasons—to provide an alternative form of
childcare, to promote industrial development, to counter the negative
effects of poverty on children, families and communities, and to provide
children with opportunities to learn skills they need to be successful in
school. Public policies determine whether preschool programs are cre-

ated and expanded, and how programs are designed and improved, and research about the effects of preschool programs on children's development offers some guidance that has informed these policy decisions that lead to effective preschool programs. However, it is important to note that these policy decisions are not influenced by research evidence alone. Policies are also shaped by the will of the people whose taxes fund these programs, by special interest groups who advocate for various policies, and by the perspectives of policymakers who seek to make decisions that are in the best interests of their constituents.

To the extent that research is used in making policy decisions, findings from a number of studies may help shape policies that lead to effective preschool programs. Research provides strong evidence that high-quality preschool programs benefit children and society, and as a result, public preschool programs have been created throughout the country. Research also offers guidance about whether programs should be universally accessible or target children with the greatest needs, and results of these studies are mixed. Some studies suggest that it is a better use of resources to provide public preschool for children who experience social and economic risks, because these children benefit the most from attending. Other studies suggest that universal programs result in classrooms with children who have more diverse abilities and backgrounds compared to classrooms in targeted programs, which may benefit children's development.

Findings from research studies may also inform decisions about where to invest program resources that result in effective programs. Evidence from current studies involving state-funded pre-K programs that serve 4-year-olds suggests that structural features of preschool programs, which are most often the target of policies and regulations, have few, if any, positive effects on the quality of children's experiences within classrooms and on the developmental outcomes of children who attend. Thus, state-funded pre-K program policies that require teachers to have bachelor's degrees and specialized training in early childhood education, and classes to have few students and many teachers drive up the costs of providing preschool programs without sufficiently ensuring that programs are effective. The features of preschool programs that do consistently relate to children's development are the quality of interactions that children experience directly—a positive emotional climate, a teacher who is sensitive to the emotional and instructional needs of children, productive use of class time, use of many different instructional materials and techniques, and language that extends children's understanding. Thus, providing teachers with professional development programs that comprise individualized, ongoing support that focuses on the specific needs they encounter within their classrooms, and providing systems of program monitoring that focus on the quality of children's experiences within classrooms, may be the most direct way to foster effective preschool programs that have powerful benefits to children.

Policies are the mechanisms through which public preschool programs are created, expanded, designed, and improved. As public school continues to expand downward to include more 3- and 4-year-olds, policies have the potential to be powerful tools in establishing effective early intervention programs, and research evidence may help guide these policy decisions. Specifically, future research that more precisely identifies the specific features of preschool programs with the greatest benefits for children, professional development techniques that support high-quality interactions within classrooms, and program monitoring strategies that ensure all children have high quality experiences may lead to preschool programs that more effectively promote the well-being of children, families, communities, and society.

References

Abdal-Haqq, I. (1995). *Making time for teacher professional development* (Digest 95-4). Washington, DC: Educational Resources Information Center (ERIC) Clearinghouse on Teaching and Teacher Education.

Administration for Children and Families. (2006). *Head Start Program fact sheet, fiscal year 2006*. Retrieved August 15, 2006, from *www.acf.hhs.gov/programs/ hsb/research/2006.htm*.

Administration for Children and Families, Department of Health and Human Services. (2004). *Head Start history*. Retrieved August 10, 2006, from *www.acf.hhs. gov/programs/hsb/about/history.htm*.

American Public Health Association & the American Academy of Pediatrics. (1992). *Caring for our children: National health and safety performance standards: Guidelines for out of home child care programs*. Washington, DC: American Public Health Association.

Barnett, S., Brown, K., & Shore, R. (2004). *The universal vs. targeted debate: Preschool Policy Matters, 6*. New Brunswick, NJ: National Institute for Early Education Research, Rutgers University. Retrieved July 30, 2006, from *nieer.org/docs/ index.php?dociD=101*.

Barnett, W. S., Hustedt, J. T., Robin, K. B., & Schulman, K. L. (2004). *The state of preschool: 2004 state preschool yearbook*. New Brunswick, NJ: National Institute for Early Education Research, Rutgers University.

Barnett, W. S., Hustedt, J. T., Robin, K. B., & Schulman, K. L. (2005). *The state of preschool: 2005 state preschool yearbook*. New Brunswick, NJ: National Institute for Early Education Research, Rutgers University.

Barnett, W. S., & Massey, L. N. (2007). Comparative benefit–cost analysis of the Abecedarian program and policy implications. *Economics of Education Review, 26*(1), 113–125.

Barnett, W. S., & Yarosz, D. J. (2004). Who goes to preschool and why does it matter? *Preschool Policy Matters, 8.* Retrieved August 11, 2006, from *www.nieer. org/resources/policybriefs/8.pdf.*

Baydar, N., & Brooks-Gunn, J. (1991). Effects of maternal employment and childcare arrangements on preschoolers' cognitive and behavioral outcomes: Evidence from the children of the national longitudinal survey of youth. *Developmental Psychology, 27*(6), 932–945.

Birman, B. F., Desimone, L., Porter, A. C., & Garet, M. S. (2000). Designing professional development that works. *Educational Leadership, 57*(8), 1–8.

Bryant, D., Burchinal, M., Lau, L., & Sparling, J. (1994). Family and classroom correlates of Head Start children's developmental outcomes. *Early Childhood Research Quarterly, 9,* 289–309.

Burchinal, M. R., Roberts, J. E., Nabors, L. A., & Bryant, D. M. (1996). Quality of center child care and infant cognitive and language development. *Child Development, 67,* 606–620.

Caplan, G. (1970). *Theory and practice of mental health consultation.* New York: Basic Books.

Caplan, G., & Caplan, R. B. (1993). *Mental health consultation and collaboration.* San Francisco: Jossey-Bass.

Darling-Hammond, L., & McLaughlin, M. W. (1995). Policies that support professional development in an era of reform. *Phi Delta Kappan, 76*(8), 597–604.

Dunn, L. (1993). Ratio and group size in day care programs. *Child Youth Care Forum, 22,* 193–226.

Early, D., Maxwell, K., Burchinal, M., Alva, S., Bender, R., Bryant, D., et al. (2007). Teacher education, classroom quality, and young children's academic skills: Results from seven studies of preschool programs. *Child Development, 78*(2), 558–580.

Education Commission of the States. (2005). *Full day kindergarten: A study of state policies in the United States.* Retrieved January 3, 2007, from *www.ffcd.org/ pdfs/ecs_fdk.pdf.*

Education Commission of the States. (2006). *State-funded pre-kindergarten programs student eligibility requirements.* Retrieved August 1, 2006, from *www.ecs.org/ dbsearches/Search_Info/EarlyLearningReports.asp?tbl=table.*

Fideler, E., & Haselkorn, D. (1999). *Learning the ropes: Urban teacher induction programs and practices in the United States.* Belmont, MA: Recruiting New Teachers.

FPG Child Development Institute. (2005). *The Carolina Abecedarian Project.* Retrieved August 15, 2006, from *www.fpg.unc.edu/~abc/.*

Froebel Foundation. (2006). *History.* Retrieved July 31, 2006, from *www. froebelfoundation. org/archive.html.*

Georgia Department of Early Care and Learning. (2006). *History.* Retrieved September 1, 2006, from *www.decal.state.ga.us/decalinfo/decalinfo.aspx?header=47 &Subheader=&position=8&headername=history.*

Gormley, W. T., & Phillips, D. (2003). *The effects of universal pre-K in Oklahoma: Research highlights and policy implications* (Crocus Working Paper No. 2). Washington, DC: Georgetown University.

Hamre, B. K., & Pianta, R. C. (2007). Learning opportunities in preschool and early elementary classrooms. In R. C. Pianta, M. J. Cox, & K. Snow (Eds.), *School readiness, early learning and the transition to kindergarten.* Baltimore: Brookes.

Haymore-Sandholtz, J. (2002). Inservice training or professional development: Contrasting opportunities in a school/university partnership. *Teaching and Teacher Education, 18*(7), 815–830.

Henry, G., & Rickman, D. (2007). Do peers influence children's skill development in preschool? *Economics of Education Review, 26*(1), 100–112.

Howes, C. (1990). Can the age of entry into child care and the quality of child care predict adjustment in kindergarten? *Developmental Psychology, 26,* 292–303.

Howes, C. (1997). Children's experiences in center-based child care as a function of caregiver background and adult:child ratio. *Merrill–Palmer Quarterly, 43,* 404–425.

Ingersoll, R., & Kralik, J. M. (2004). *The impact of mentoring on teacher retention: What the research says.* Denver, CO: Education Commission of the States.

Jacobson, L. (2006, June 14). California voters reject universal pre-k initiative. *Education Week,* pp. 15, 18.

Knotek, S. E., & Sandoval, J. (2003). Current research in consultee-centered consultation. *Journal of Educational and Psychological Consultation, 14,* 243–250.

Lamb, M. (1998). Nonparental child care: Context, quality, correlates, and consequences. In W. Damon (Series Ed.) & I. E. Spiegel & K. A. Renniger (Vol. Eds.), *Child psychology in practice: Handbook of child psychology* (5th ed., pp. 73–134). New York: Wiley.

Lamb, M., & Ahnert, L. (2006). Nonparental child care: Context, concepts, correlates and consequences. In W. Damon, R. M. Lerner, K. A. Renninger & I. E. Sigel (Eds.), *Handbook of child psychology: Child psychology in practice* (Vol. 4, pp. 950–1016). New York: Wiley.

Lazar, I., Darlington, R., Murray, H., Royce, J., & Snipper, A. (1982). Lasting effects of early education: A report from the Consortium for Longitudinal Studies. *Monograph of the Society for Research in Child Development, 47*(2–3, Serial No. 195), whole issue.

Lieberman, A. (1995). Practices that support teacher development. *Phi Delta Kappan, 76*(8), 591–596.

Los Angeles Universal Preschool, Quality Standards. (2005). *Abbreviated LAUP 5-Star Quality Rating Scale for Centers.* Retrieved August 11, 2006, from *www.laup.net/downloads/CenterStandards.star.pdf.*

Mashburn, A. J., Pianta, R. C., Hamre, B. K., Downer, J. T., Barbarin, O., Bryant, D., et al. (in press). Measures of pre-K quality and children's development of academic, language and social skills. *Child Development.*

Odom, S. L. (2000). Preschool inclusion: What we know and where we go from here. *Topics in Early Childhood Special Education, 20*(1), 20–27.

National Association for the Education of Young Children. (2004). *Position statements of NAEYC.* Retrieved August 11, 2006, from *www.naeyc.org/about/positions.asp.*

NICHD Early Child Care Research Network. (1999). Child outcomes when child care center classes meet recommended standards for quality. *American Journal of Public Health, 89,* 1072–1077.

NICHD Early Child Care Research Network. (2002a). Child-care structure–process–outcome: Direct and indirect effects of child-care quality on young children's development. *American Psychological Society, 13*(3), 199–206.

NICHD Early Child Care Research Network. (2002b). The relation of global first-grade classroom environment to structural classroom features and teacher and student behaviors. *Elementary School Journal, 102*(5), 367–387.

Peisner-Feinberg, E., & Burchinal, M. (1997). Relations between preschool children's child-care experiences and concurrent development: The cost, quality, and outcomes study. *Merrill–Palmer Quarterly, 43*(3), 451–477.

Phillips, D., & Howes, C. (1987). Indicators of quality in child care: Review of the research. In D. Phillips (Ed.), *Quality in child care: What does the research tell us?* (pp. 1–19). Washington, DC: National Association for the Education of Young Children.

Phillips, D., Howes, C., & Whitebook, M. (1992). The social policy context of child care: Effects on quality. *American Journal of Community Psychology, 20,* 25–51.

Pianta, R. C. (2003). *Standardized observations from pre-K to 3rd grade: A mechanism for improving access to high quality classroom experiences and practices during the P-3 years* (Foundation for Child Development Working Paper). New York: Foundation for Child Development.

Pianta, R. C. (2005). A new elementary school for American children. *SRCD Social Policy Report, 19*(3), 4–5.

Pre-K Now. (2006). *The history of pre-K.* Retrieved August 1, 2006, from *www.preknow.org/resource/abc/timeline.cfm.*

Putnam, R. T., & Borko, H. (1997). Teacher learning: Implications of new views of cognition. In B. J. Biddle, T. L. Good, & I. F. Goodson (Eds.), *The international handbook of teachers and teaching* (Vol. II, pp. 1223–1296). Dordrecht, The Netherlands: Kluwer.

Reynolds, A. J. (2000). *Success in early intervention: The Chicago Child–Parent Centers.* Lincoln: University of Nebraska Press.

Reynolds, A. J., Temple, J. A., Robertson, D. L., & Mann, E. A. (2001). Long-term effects of an early childhood intervention on educational achievement. *Journal of the American Medical Association, 285,* 2339–2346.

Richardson, V. (2003). The dilemmas of professional development. *Phi Delta Kappan, 84*(5), 401–406.

Rosenfield, S. A., & Gravois, T. A. (1996). *Instructional consultation teams.* New York: Guilford Press.

Schecter, C. (2002). *Language growth in low income children in economically integrated and segregated preschool programs.* West Hartford, CT: St. Joseph College.

Schweinhart, L. J., Barnes, H. V., & Weikart, D. P. (1993). *Significant benefits: The High/Scope Perry Preschool Study through age 27* (Monographs of the High/Scope Educational Research Foundation, 10). Ypsilanti: High/Scope Press.

Schweinhart, L. J., Montie, J., Xiang, Z., Barnett, W. S., Belfield, C. R., & Nores, M. (2005). *Lifetime effects: The High/Scope Perry Preschool Study through age 40*

(Monographs of the High/Scope Educational Research Foundation, 14). Ypsilanti, MI: High/Scope Educational Research Foundation.

Vandell, D. L., & Wolfe, B. (2000). *Child care quality: Does it matter and does it need to be improved?* Madison: Institute for Research on Child Poverty, University of Wisconsin–Madison.

Wirt, J., Choy, S., Rooney, P., Provasnik, S., Sen, A., & Tobin, R. (2004). *The condition of education 2004* (NCES 2004–077, U.S. Department of Education, National Center for Education Statistics). Washington, DC: U.S. Government Printing Office.

CHAPTER 2

★★★★★★★★

The Scientifically Based Reading Research Approach to Early Literacy Instruction

James F. Christie

The 1980s and early 1990s were relatively peaceful years in the field of early childhood literacy instruction. Unlike elementary grade reading instruction, which was locked in a seemingly endless series of "reading wars," there was a fairly widespread consensus as to how preschool-age children could best be prepared to learn to read. During this period, emergent literacy theory was the dominant perspective (Teale & Sulzby, 1986). According to this view, young children acquire written language in much the same way they acquire oral language—by observing written language in use, generating their own concepts and rules about how reading and writing work, then trying these out in social situations. Strategies emanating from emergent literacy were considered to constitute "best practice" in early childhood language arts instruction: print-rich classroom environments, frequent story reading, and opportunities for children to engage in meaningful emergent reading and writing activities such as literacy-enriched dramatic play (Christie, Enz, & Vukelich, 2007; Yaden, Rowe, & MacGillivary, 2000).

During this period of apparent calm, however, a storm was brewing. Two major shifts in early literacy policy were underway: (1) the standards movement, which has resulted in the rapid growth of state-level early childhood academic standards (Neuman & Roskos, 2005); and (2) the movement to prevent reading difficulties, which viewed failure to learn to read as a national public health crisis (Snow, Burns, & Griffin, 1998; Sweet, 2004). Roskos and Christie (2007, p. 89) point out that "underlying both initiatives is the premise that skill begets skill in a dynamic process—skills gained early in life help children gain additional skills in the next stage of development. . . . As a corollary, skills missed early in life are hard to compensate for later on."

By the late 1990s, many policymakers became disenchanted with the education establishment's rather relaxed emergent literacy approach to early reading instruction. There was an increased call for effective "science-based" methods of instruction to turn back the tide of rising reading disabilities. For example, Robert Sweet (2004, p. 18), a professional staff member of the Committee on Education and the Workforce for the U.S. House of Representatives, stated:

> Publishing companies have continued to sell textbooks that are based on the false premise that students learn to read naturally. Many teachers are still being trained in a method of instruction that is failing millions of students. . . . Illiterate prisoners, welfare recipients unable to read simple instructions on a medicine bottle, school dropouts that have given up school because they cannot read their assignments . . . and special education students who are placed on lifetime career paths simply because they have not been taught to read are all being shortchanged all because the education industry refuses to adopt the clear findings of scientific research supporting specific instructional practices that could reverse the terrible blight of illiteracy in America.

As Sweet's comment indicates, the paradigm shift that emerged in the field of education emphasized the importance of using science to inform practices and policies. The field of early childhood education has not been immune from such shifts, as discussed in the remainder of this chapter. A new perspective on early literacy known as scientifically based reading research (SBRR) has come into prominence and has had a tremendous influence on preschool language arts instruction. The chapter begins by defining SBRR and discussing the main tenets of this perspective. The controversy surrounding this perspective is also discussed. Then each of the "core" SBRR early literacy skills—vocabulary, phonological awareness, alphabet knowledge, and print awareness—is defined, and examples of how each skill can be directly taught to preschool children are provided.

SBRR Defined

The term "scientifically based research" was specifically defined in the No Child Left Behind Act. This legislation identified several features that must be present to meet the criteria of scientifically based research, as shown in Table 2.1. Because this definition of "scientifically based" research specified a preference for "experimental or quasi-experimental" methods, attention turned away from use of evidence derived from the qualitative studies favored by proponents of emergent literacy toward the types of quantitative studies that were popular in the fields of educational psychology and special education. The result was the rise of a new perspective on early literacy commonly referred to as Scientifically Based Reading Research (SBRR). Supporters of SBRR believe that rigorous experimental and correlational research can reveal (1) the skills and concepts young children need to master to become proficient readers and writers, and (2) the most effective strategies for teaching these skills and concepts to children.

The SBRR perspective was first introduced in Marilyn Adams's (1990) landmark book *Beginning to Read: Thinking and Learning about Print* and gained additional momentum with the publication of the

---

TABLE 2.1. No Child Left Behind's Definition of Scientifically Based Research

Scientifically based research includes research that:

(i) employs systematic, empirical methods that draw on observations or experiment;

(ii) involves rigorous data analyses that are adequate to test the stated hypotheses and justify the general conclusions drawn;

(iii) relies on measurements or observational methods that provide reliable and valid data across evaluators and observers, across multiple measurements and observations, and actual studies by the same or different investigators;

(iv) is evaluated using experimental or quasi-experimental designs in which individuals, entities, programs, or activities are assigned to different conditions with appropriate controls to evaluate the effects of the condition of interest, with a preference for random-assignment experiments, or other designs to the extent that those designs contain within-condition or across-condition;

(v) ensures that experimental studies are presented in sufficient detail and clarity to allow for replication, or, at a minimum, offer the opportunity to build systematically on their findings; and

(vi) has been accepted by a peer-reviewed journal or approved by a panel of independent experts through a comparably rigorous, objective, and scientific review.

Note. From No Child Left Behind Act of 2001 (pp. 126–127).

National Research Council's book, *Preventing Reading Difficulties in Young Children* (Snow et al., 1998). Adams (1990) introduced the concept of basing instruction on research about what young children need to know to be successful readers, and placed considerable stress on the importance of phonemic awareness and understanding of the alphabetic principle. *Preventing Reading Difficulties in Young Children*, edited by Snow and associates, specifically emphasized using empirical evidence or "science" to discover: (1) strong predictors of success and failure in reading, and (2) effective strategies for preventing reading difficulties. More recently, the scientifically based perspective has been used as the foundation for many initiatives by the U.S. Department of Education, including Good Start, Grow Smart, and the Early Reading First and Early Childhood Professional Development grant programs designed to increase the school readiness of low-income children by providing them with print-rich environments and science-based instruction on oral language, phonological awareness, alphabet knowledge, and print awareness.

In her booklet *Teaching Reading Is Rocket Science,* Louisa Moats (1999, p. 5) sums up the essence of the SBRR approach:

> Low reading achievement, more than any other factor, is the root cause of chronically underperforming schools, which harm students and contribute to a loss of public confidence in our school system. . . . Thanks to new scientific research—plus a long-awaited scientific and political consensus around this research—the knowledge exists to teach all but a handful of severely disabled children to read well. . . . In medicine, if research found new ways to save lives, health care professionals would adopt these methods as quickly as possible, and would change practices, procedures, and systems. Educational research has found new ways to save young minds by helping them to become proficient readers; it is up to us to promote these new methods throughout the education system.

Analogies between early literacy instruction, science, and the field of medicine have become a hallmark of the SBRR approach, and some of the major SBRR initiatives have been funded by the National Institute of Health (Lyon, 1998). This invocation of "hard science" and the medical model has caused some chagrin in the field of educational research in general and in literacy education in particular. In his critique of the National Research Council report that set SBRR into motion, David Berliner (2002, p. 18) pointed out, "It is not clear to me that *science* means the same thing to all who pay it homage, nor do I think that the distinctions between educational science and the other sciences have been well made." Noted language researcher Frank Smith (2003, p. vii) is even more blunt: "Reading instruction that is claimed to be 'scientific,' 'research-based,' and 'evidence-based'—imposed on many teachers and enforced through innumerable mandated tests—is founded on activities that are unspeakable and practices that are unnatural."

The harshest criticisms of SBRR are aimed at programs that provide children with a strict diet of direct instruction on core literacy skills and little else. However, SBRR instruction does not need to comprise only mindless drill and practice. In the remainder of this chapter, I demonstrate how SBRR instruction can be delivered in an engaging and age-appropriate manner to help preschoolers learn the skills they need to succeed in learning to read.

Core Science-Based Knowledge and Skills

Perhaps the most valuable contribution of the SBRR movement is that it has identified the "core" knowledge and skills that young children must have to become successful readers (see McCardle & Chhabra, 2004; Snow et al., 1998). Longitudinal studies have shown that preschool-age children's *oral language* (expressive and receptive language, including vocabulary development), *phonological awareness*, and *alphabet knowledge* are predictive of reading achievement in the elementary grades. *Print awareness*, which includes concepts (e.g., understanding how print can be used) and conventions (e.g., left-to-right, top-to-bottom sequence) of print, has also been found to be positively correlated with reading ability in the primary grades. These skills, sometimes referred to as the "Big Four," are the primary instructional objectives of SBRR programs within the field of education.

SBRR investigators have also focused on identifying effective strategies for teaching this core literacy content to young children. One of the most consistent research findings is that young children's phonological awareness and alphabet knowledge can be increased via *direct, systematic instruction* (National Reading Panel, 2000; Snow et al., 1998). This instruction may not only take the form of games and other engaging activities but it also involves preplanning and contains the elements of direct instruction: teacher modeling, guided practice, and independent practice. This emphasis on systematic instruction contrasts with the highly individualized instruction advocated by proponents of emergent literacy. For example, SBRR instruction usually involves systematic instruction on the letters of alphabet (all children are taught the same letters in the same order), whereas the emergent literacy approach advocates "personalizing" alphabetic instruction (e.g., teaching children the letters in their own names and in personally meaningful words). Of course, many teachers use a combined approach, teaching letters in a systematic way to the whole class and teaching highly salient letters to individual students.

To illustrate the nature of SBRR instruction, the remainder of this chapter presents descriptive vignettes of how children were taught the "core" early literacy skills with SBRR approaches in an Early Reading First project in southwest Arizona. All of the children were from low-income households, and more than 90% were English language learners. The sections that follow illustrate how each of the "Big Four" instructional objectives of Early Reading First—vocabulary, phonological awareness, alphabet knowledge, and print awareness—was taught in this project. The examples are intended to give readers the "feel" of developmentally appropriate, science-based early literacy instruction.

Vocabulary Instruction

"Vocabulary" refers to children's knowledge of word meanings. Although vocabulary acquisition is one of the key components of oral language development, it also plays an important role in early literacy. Research has shown that the size of children's vocabulary at age 3 is strongly associated with reading comprehension at the end of third grade (Hart & Risley, 2003). Research has also shown that vocabulary growth is promoted through direct instruction of targeted words and by arrangement of experiences so that children encounter these targeted words frequently in different contexts (McCardle & Chhabra, 2004). Because vocabulary size and rate of growth are central to the acquisition of early literacy skills, vocabulary development is one of the key instructional objectives in SBRR programs.

Early childhood teachers have traditionally used incidental approaches to provide vocabulary instruction, looking for "teachable moments" during storybook reading and classroom conversations to build children's knowledge of word meanings. What is new in SBRR programs is that vocabulary instruction is intentional and preplanned, as well as incidental. Specifically, teachers decide in advance to teach selected words to children, and both high-utility root words (Biemiller & Slonim, 2001) and rare words (Hirsch, 2003) are targeted for instruction. "High-utility root words" refer to uninflected words that occur with high frequency in oral language. These words are useful to know because they can be used to create many related words (*move* → *moved, moveable, remove,* etc.). "Rare words" refer to specialized vocabulary needed for development of domain knowledge in content areas (e.g., *excavate, backhoe, scoop, blueprint, plaster,* etc.). Often, these targeted words are connected to other parts of the academic curriculum—an ongoing thematic unit, books that are being read, field trips, and so forth. These vocabulary–curriculum connections provide opportunities for children to encounter the targeted words repeatedly in a short period of time—a crucial factor in word learning (Stahl, 2003).

Example: Integrated Vocabulary Instruction

San Luis Preschool teacher Mrs. Lopez uses a published curriculum to teach early literacy skills to the English language learners in her classroom. The curriculum is organized into thematic units centering on sets of children's books. This month, Mrs. Lopez's class is studying building and construction. The curriculum has identified approximately 20 target words that are to be directly taught to children, including the names of tools (*hammer, saw, safety goggles, tape measure, nails*) and construction equipment (*dump truck, backhoe, crane*). In addition, there are another 100+ "wonderful words" related to the construction theme that teachers are encouraged to use incidentally when the opportunity arises. On this particular day, Mrs. Lopez is teaching the target "tool" words. She begins circle time with the shared reading of a rhyme poster. Whereas the primary function of the poster is to teach rhyme identification, Mrs. Lopez also focuses the children's attention on the two "tool" words in the rhyme. She has children make a hand motion when *hammer* is mentioned and use their fingers to show how small the *tiny little nails* are. Next, Mrs. Lopez delivers a shared reading of a big book about building a doghouse. This informational book has very few text words but contains several photographs that contain pictures of tools. Even though the tools are not mentioned in the text, Mrs. Lopez pauses to discuss them. She first asks, "What kind of tools will they need to build the doghouse?" As she reads each page, she points to each of the tools in the illustrations and asks, "Does anyone know the name of this tool?" She chuckles when, after pointing to several nails in one picture, a child responds, "Tiny little nails," repeating the phrase used earlier in the rhyme poster. After the story is read, children go to center time. Mrs. Lopez has arranged the environment to provide additional opportunities to encounter and use tool words. Several regular-size copies of the doghouse book have been placed in the classroom library for independent or partner reading. There are blackline masters of tools for the children to color and label in the art center. Finally, the dramatic play center has a cardboard frame that resembles a doghouse, and it contains toy replicas of all of the tools mentioned in the doghouse book: plastic hammers, nails (actually wood golf tees), measuring tape, safety goggles, and a toy circular saw. Two girls and a boy spend a half hour playing together, pretending to build a doghouse. In this play, the names of tools are used numerous times, and the children help each other learn how to use each tool properly. For example, one of the girls reminds the boy to put on his safety goggles when using the saw!

Mrs. Lopez's instruction is consistent with the tenets of SBRR, because she directly teaches the meanings of preselected vocabulary words (in this case, the names of tools) and provides series of related activities that give children repeated opportunities to hear and use these words. This type of planned, intentional vocabulary instruction increases the likelihood that these words will become part of the children's receptive and expressive lexicon.

Phonological Awareness Instruction

Phonological awareness refers to an individual's awareness of the sound structure of speech. Phonemic awareness, an advanced stage of phonological awareness, involves awareness that spoken words are composed of individual sounds, or phonemes (e.g., *cat* is made up of the sounds /k/, /ă/, and /t/). Research has clearly established that these phonological processing skills, when measured in early childhood, are strong predictors of later reading achievement (Dickinson, McCabe, Anastaspoulos, Peisner-Feinberg, & Poe, 2003; National Reading Panel, 2000).

Research also has revealed a developmental trajectory in children's acquisition of phonological processing skills, as shown in Table 2.2. In general the movement of instruction is from larger to smaller units. Marilyn Adams (1990) suggests that before young children can become aware of phonemes—the individual sounds that make up spoken words—they first must become aware of larger units of oral language. Thus, children must first realize that spoken language is composed of words, syllables, and sounds. For example, they need to learn to recognize when words end with the same sound (i.e., rhyme) and begin with the same sound (i.e.,

---

TABLE 2.2. Phonological Processing Skills

Phonological awareness

1. Rhyme—words that end with same sound
2. Alliteration—words that start with same sound
3. Word and syllable segmentation—divide sentences into individual words and words into syllables

Phonemic awareness

4. Phoneme isolation (/fan/, /fork/, and /film/ begin with /f/ sound)
5. Phoneme blending (/d-o-g/ = /dog/)
6. Phoneme segmentation /dog/ = /d-o-g/
7. Phoneme manipulation
   - Deletion   /train/ – /t/ = /rain/
   - Addition   /f/ + /arm/ = /farm/
   - Manipulation   /rat/ – /a/ + /o/ = /rot/

---

alliteration). They also need to be able to segment sentences into words, and words into syllables. Once these skills are mastered, children can begin to focus on the individual sounds of language and develop phonemic awareness. When children have fully mastered phonemic awareness, they are able to take individual sounds and blend them into whole words, break words down into individual sounds, and even manipulate the sounds in words (e.g., replace the middle sound of a word with another sound, so that *cat* become *cut*, and *fan* becomes *fun*). This in turn lays the foundation for learning letter–sound relationships. In the next sections, I describe how teachers can adhere to principles of SBRR to help preschoolers develop an awareness of rhyme and alliteration.

Example: Rhyme Instruction

As mentioned earlier, San Luis Preschool teacher Mrs. Lopez uses song/rhyme posters from the project's curriculum to help her children learn to identify rhyming words and to learn word meanings. One day, she delivers a shared reading of the rhyme *Five Red Apples*:

> Five red apples in a grocery store,
> I bought one and then there were four.
> Four red apples in an apple tree,
> I ate one, and then there were three.

Mrs. Lopez reads the rhyme to her children several times on successive days. After the children have become familiar with the rhyme and its vocabulary, she begins to focus their attention on the rhyming words by pausing before the rhyming words and waiting for the children to supply the missing word. She tells the children, "We're going to read the *Five Red Apples* poster and I want you to tell me the word that I'm leaving out." She begins by reading, "Five red apples in a grocery store, I bought one and then there were. . . . " Several children shout out, "Four!" Mrs. Lopez responds, "That's right, *four*. OK, let's all say *four*," and all the children respond. Mrs. Lopez continues, "Four red apples in an apple tree, I ate one, and then there were . . . . " This time most of the children respond with "Three!" Mrs. Lopez says, "That's right, boys and girls, *three*. Listen to the words *tree* and *three*. They both end with the same sound. Words that end with the same sound are called rhyming words." She continues this pattern for the rest of the rhyme. On a subsequent day, Mrs. Lopez goes a step further and asks children to supply words that fit the rhyme pattern. For example, after reading the first rhyme segment in *Five Red Apples*, Mrs. Lopez says, "Yes, *store* and *four* both end with the same sound. Can you think of other words that rhyme with *store* and *four*?" The children come up with two: *more* and *poor*. Later, Mrs. Lopez will reinforce the concept of rhyme by having children play a rhyme categorization game in which they match objects (e.g., a miniature baseball bat, a real key) with pictures of objects that end with the same sound (e.g., hat and bee).

Example: Syllable Segmenting

Mrs. Vallejo, who teaches in a "reverse mainstream" preschool classroom in the Somerton School District in southwestern Arizona, is in the middle of a thematic unit on water and sea creatures. She focuses her instruction on syllable segmenting. First comes the "Name" part of the lesson. Mrs. Vallejo holds up a card with a child's first name written on it and asks the children to say whose name is on the card. The children then clap and count the number of syllables in the name. Mrs. Vallejo has been working with her children on this skill for several weeks, and they have become quite good at this. They quickly say the names (e.g., "Azael") and number of syllables ("three") for each card that Mrs. Vallejo holds up. The children enjoy the activity and are very engaged. Next up is the "Poster" part of the lesson. Mrs. Vallejo first asks children how many syllables are in the word *poster*, and the children shout out "Two!" Then she reads the rhyme poster, which is about a submarine. Although the main purpose of the poster is to teach rhyme recognition, Mrs. Vallejo focuses on both vocabulary and syllable segmenting. She reads the poster with the children, encouraging them to make motions that go with rhyme (e.g., putting their fingers together to make pretend glasses for the word *periscope*). Then she asks individual children to count the syllables in several words from the story (e.g., sub-mar-ine). The academic level of these activities is quite high for preschoolers who are learning English as a second language, especially because two-thirds of the children in this reverse mainstreamed classroom have been identified as having special needs. But all students seem able to participate successfully (two assistant teachers are there to help), and they appear to enjoy showing off their rapidly growing literacy skills.

These examples of phonological awareness instruction are consistent with the SBRR perspective. Mrs. Lopez and Mrs. Vallejo are both focusing their instruction on science-based skills: rhyme identification and production, and syllabic segmentation. This instruction is carefully planned rather than incidental. Mrs. Lopez does more than simply read the rhyme poster to the children. She provides children with opportunities to use their knowledge of rhyme to fill in missing words in the rhyme, and she explicitly explains the concept of rhyme. She then provides opportunities for children to produce rhymes that match the pattern in the poster. Mrs. Vallejo has taught her students to clap and count the number of syllables in words. In the earlier example, she provides children with repeated opportunities to practice these skills as she also teaches other skills, such as print recognition and vocabulary.

Alphabet Instruction

The ability to recognize and name the letters of the alphabet in kindergarten is a strong predictor of later reading achievement (Chall, 1996), and the National Early Literacy Panel has identified alphabet knowledge as a core component of early literacy instruction (Strickland & Shanahan, 2004). Alphabet knowledge can be divided into two subskills: identification and naming. Alphabetic identification involves being able to point out a letter that someone else names. For example, a teacher might ask a child to point to the letter *C* on an alphabet frieze (a chart that lists all of the letters in alphabetical order). Alphabetic naming requires naming a letter that someone else points to. For example, the teacher could point to the letter *C* on the alphabet chart and ask, "What's the name of this letter?" Of the two skills, naming is the more difficult.

In the next sections, I provide examples of how letter posters and the ABC Word Wall can be used to teach alphabet knowledge.

Example: Letter Posters

San Luis Preschool teacher, Mrs. Lopez, systematically introduces her children to a letter and its sound every two weeks, using letter posters in the *Sound, Rhyme, and Letter Time* (Wright Group/McGraw-Hill, 2002) program. These posters contain large upper- and lowercase letters and pictures of objects that begin with the "target" letter. For example, the letter *S* poster has pictures of a sun, a seal, a sailboat, a sandwich, sand, sunglasses, and a seashell. During the first week, Mrs. Lopez focuses on the sound of the letter, helping children to realize that all of the objects on the chart start with the same sound, /s/. During the second week, Mrs. Lopez teaches children about the letter *S*. She begins by reviewing the words represented on the poster, reminding the children that all these words begin with the /s/ sound. Next, she writes a label for each picture on a Post-it note, with the initial letter *S* in red and the rest of the letters in black. One by one, she places the Post-it labels on the pictures, having children say the names of the objects represented by the pictures. She points out that all of the words start with the same letter *S*. Next, Mrs. Lopez removes the Post-it labels from the poster and has children put the labels back on the chart next to the corresponding object. When they do this, Mrs. Lopez asks them to say the letter name, the letter sound, and the whole word. This is repeated over several days, so that all of the children get several turns. Mrs. Lopez also shows children how to write the letter *S* and gives them opportunities to write it on individual chalkboards and in their journals. By using this 2-week routine with each letter, Ms. Lopez is helping her children develop phonemic awareness and alphabetic recognition. Advanced children may also begin learning phonics by making connections between the letters and the sounds they represent.

Example: ABC Word Wall

Mrs. Lopez also uses an ABC Word Wall to teach alphabet knowledge. Large upper- and lowercase letters are arranged on the wall in alphabetical order. Printed words that begin with each letter are posted below, with visual support (a drawing or photograph) whenever possible. Each day, one or two special words are selected for placement on the word wall. These words can come from the stories, rhymes, songs, and poems that the class is reading. Words can also include children's names, familiar environmental print, and words from thematic units. These words are placed under the letters that they start with. Mrs. Lopez uses her word wall during transitions from large- to small-group instruction. She hands the pointer to a child and asks him or her to point to a letter that she says (letter identification), or Mrs. Lopez will point to a letter on the word wall and ask the child to name the letter. Each child gets a turn before leaving to go to the next activity, and Mrs. Lopez helps those who have difficulty. The children can usually point to or name the letters, because the pictures that go with the words and the familiar environmental print give helpful clues. This strategy promotes smooth transitions and gives children valuable practice with letters.

Mrs. Lopez' alphabetic instruction with the letter posters and her word wall are aligned with the principles of SBRR. She uses the posters systematically to teach children the letters of the alphabet in a preplanned order. She then uses the ABC Word Wall to provide opportunities for children to practice the alphabetic identification and naming skills they have been taught. Mrs. Lopez also provides individualized instruction, helping children learn the letters in their names and pointing out the names of letters that occur in salient environmental print. So her students are receiving a blend of SBRR instruction and the type of alphabetic instruction advocated by the emergent literacy perspective.

Print Awareness Instruction

"Print awareness" is a broad term that refers to children's ability to recognize print, ranging from contextualized environmental print (e.g., the word *Cheerios* on a cereal box) to decontextualized written words (e.g., the print in a children's book). Print awareness also encompasses concepts about print, including book concepts (author, illustrator, title, front, back) and conventions of print (directionality, capitalization, punctuation). Research has shown that young children's knowledge of concepts of print is moderately correlated with reading ability in the primary grades (Snow et al., 1998); thus, concepts of print are an instructional objective of SBRR instruction.

Concepts about print are strongly associated with the emergent literacy perspective, and these concepts are usually taught via shared reading of storybooks, shared writing (i.e., language experience dictation), and literacy-enriched play. Teachers who are firm believers in the SBRR philosophy may also use more direct forms of instruction to teach concepts about print.

Example: Environmental Print

Head Start teacher Mrs. Fernandez uses direct instruction to help her children in San Luis, Arizona, learn to recognize environmental print. She begins by pointing to words she has written at the top of a whiteboard—*I Can Read So Many Things*—and reads them to the class. She tells the children that this is the title of a book that they are going to write. Mrs. Fernandez then discusses how the children see many signs and symbols when they are riding around their community with their parents. She also tells the children about other places where they might encounter environmental print, such as cereal boxes and soda cans. She has a basket with pieces of paper that contain environmental print (drawing of a stop sign, a McDonald's logo, the logo of a local grocery store, a Pepsi logo, etc.), and she has written the phrase "I can read. . . . " repeatedly on the whiteboard. Individual children come up and take a piece of paper out of the basket, identify what the print says, then tape it onto the end of one of the unfinished sentences on the whiteboard. For example, Javier picks a Pizza Hut logo. He "reads" the logo, then tapes it on to the end of one of the sentences on the whiteboard. This produces the sentence, "I can read Pizza Hut." Javier then takes a pointer and tracks the print while the whole class reads this sentence. When the activity is finished, Mrs. Fernandez leaves the whiteboard up for several days for children to read with their friends during center time.

Example: Picture–Word–Letter Categorization

Mrs. Fernandez also uses direct instruction to help her children learn about the distinction between pictures, words, and alphabet letters. Mrs. Fernandez has prepared a large chart with three columns labeled "Picture," "Word," and "Letter." An example of each type of symbol is pasted next to the label: There is a photograph of an automobile next to the label "Picture"; the written word *cat* is next to the label "Word"; and the letter *A* is next to the label "Letter." Mrs. Fernandez has put a number of cards into a bag. Each card contains an example of a picture, a word, or a letter. She begins by explaining each of these concepts. The children are very interested, and several of them quickly recognize the examples that Ms. Fernandez has provided ("That's an *A*" and "It's *cat*"). Children take turns drawing a card out of the basket. When a child has drawn a card, he or she tells the class what is on the card, names the category to which it belongs, and tapes it to the correct column on the chart. If a child struggles, classmates help out. For example, Andrea picks a card with a classmate's name on it. She recognizes the name and says "Elias." Ms. Fernandez prompts her with the question, "Which type is it? A picture, word, or letter?" When Andrea does not respond, several classmates chime in: "It's a word." Andrea then places the card in the correct column and feels proud that she has done this correctly. The metalinguistic concepts of letter and word are quite abstract, but this direct instruction appears to be helping these 4-year-olds make the distinction between the two.

Mrs. Fernandez's instruction on environmental print recognition and the distinction between pictures, words, and alphabet letters are consistent with SBRR principles. She uses carefully planned, direct instruction to teach these print awareness skills. Mrs. Fernandez also takes advantage of "teachable moments" to teach these skills during shared reading, shared writing, and literacy-enriched play activity. However, she believes that direct instruction helps to ensure that all the children in her classroom have an opportunity to learn these important skills.

Conclusions

The examples from the Early Reading First project illustrate basic characteristic of the SBRR approach as applied to preschool literacy instruction, namely, that teachers are engaging in the direct instruction of core early literacy skills and content. The instruction is focused and relatively brief, with most of the lessons lasting between 5 and 10 minutes, often with several shifts in activity. The fact the children are highly engaged and able to participate successfully indicates that this instruction is also age-appropriate.

As mentioned earlier, direct instruction is not the only type of learning experience these children received. The program also included regular shared reading that focused on enjoyment of story, shared writing (language experience dictation), print-rich classrooms filled with functional and environmental print, and literacy-enriched play centers. This "blending" of SBRR and emergent literacy strategies provides children with the best of both approaches, creating a mix of learning opportunities that should meet the needs of most young learners (Christie et al., 2007).

Blending SBRR instruction with emergent literacy strategies is a value-added proposition (Christie et al., 2007). Young children still receive opportunities for meaningful engagements with reading and writing, and social support. However, they also are taught directly the important skills that they need to engage successfully in these activities. When SBRR instruction is blended with emergent literacy strategies, the bar is raised. Children have better opportunities to learn literacy skills and content than they did in programs that strictly adhered to the emergent literacy point of view.

References

Adams, M. (1990). *Beginning to read: Thinking and learning about print*. Cambridge, MA: MIT Press.

Berliner, D. (2002). Educational research: The hardest science of all. *Educational Researcher, 31*(8), 18–20.

Biemiller, A., & Slonim, N. (2001). Estimating root word vocabulary growth in normative and advantaged populations: Evidence for a common sequence of vocabulary acquisition. *Journal of Educational Psychology, 93*, 498–520.

Chall, J. (1996). *Learning to read: The great debate* (rev. ed.). New York: McGraw-Hill.

Christie, J., Enz, B. J., & Vukelich, C. (2007). *Teaching language and literacy: Preschool through the elementary grades* (3rd ed.). New York: Allyn & Bacon.

Dickinson, D. K., McCabe, A., Anastaspoulos, L., Peisner-Feinberg, E. S., & Poe, M. D. (2003). The comprehensive language approach to early literacy: The interrelationships among vocabulary, phonological sensitivity, and print knowledge among preschool-aged children. *Journal of Educational Psychology, 95*(3), 465–481.

Hart, B., & Risley, T. (2003). The early catastrophe. *American Educator, 27*(4), 6–9.

Hirsch, E. (2003, Spring). Reading comprehension requires knowledge of words and the world. *American Educator*, pp. 10–14.

Lyon, G. R. (1998). Why reading is not a natural process. *Educational Leadership, 55*, 14–18.

McCardle, P., & Chhabra, V. (Eds.). (2004). *The voice of evidence in reading research*. Baltimore: Brookes.

Moats, L. (1999). *Teaching reading is rocket science*. Washington, DC: American Federation of Teachers.

National Reading Panel. (2000). *Teaching children to read: An evidence-based assessment of the scientific research literature on reading and its implications for reading instruction*. Washington, DC: U.S. Government Printing Office.

Neuman, S., & Roskos, K. (2005). The state of the state prekindergarten standards. *Early Childhood Research Quarterly, 20*, 125–145.

No Child Left Behind Act of 2001. Available at *www.ed.gov/nclb/overview/intro/edpicks.jhtml?src=ln.*

Roskos, K., & Christie, J. (2007). Play in the context of the new preschool basics. In K. Roskos & J. Christie (Eds.), *Play and literacy in early childhood: Research from multiple perspectives* (2nd ed., pp. 83–100). Mahwah, NJ: Erlbaum.

Smith, F. (2003). *Unspeakable acts, unnatural practices: Flaws and fallacies in "scientific" reading instruction.* Portsmouth, NH: Heinemann.

Snow, C., Burns, M. S., & Griffin, P. (Eds.). (1998). *Preventing reading difficulties in young children.* Washington, DC: National Academy Press.

Stahl, S. (2003, Spring). How words are learned incrementally over multiple exposures. *American Educator,* pp. 18–19.

Strickland, D., & Shanahan, T. (2004). Laying the groundwork for literacy. *Educational Leadership, 61*(4), 74–77.

Sweet, R. (2004). The big picture: Where we are on the reading front and how we got here. In P. McCardle & V. Chhabra (Eds.), *The voice of evidence in reading research* (pp. 13–44). Baltimore: Brookes.

Teale, W., & Sulzby, E. (1986). Emergent literacy as a perspective for examining how young children become writers and readers. In W. Teale & E. Sulzby (Eds.), *Emergent literacy: Writing and reading* (pp. vii–xxv). Norwood, NJ: Ablex.

Wright Group/McGraw-Hill. (2002). *Sound, rhyme, and letter time.* Bothell, WA: Author.

Yaden, D., Rowe, D., & MacGillivary, L. (2000). Emergent literacy: A matter (polyphony) of perspectives. In M. Kamil, P. Mosenthal, P. D. Pearson, & R. Barr (Eds.), *Handbook of reading research* (Vol. III, pp. 425–454). Mahwah, NJ: Erlbaum.

CHAPTER 3

★★★★★★★★

Establishing a Science of Professional Development for Early Education Programs

The Knowledge Application Information Systems Theory of Professional Development

Sharon Landesman Ramey
Craig T. Ramey

The field of early childhood education has entered an era in which a solid foundation of knowledge supports large-scale implementation of educational and care practices and programs that effectively promote learning and well-being among children, particularly children at high risk for poor school achievement (cf. Donovan & Pelligrino, 2003; Neuman & Dickinson, 2006; NICHD Early Child Care Research Network, 2005; C. Ramey, Ramey, & Lanzi, 2006; Shonkoff & Phillips, 2000; Snow, Burns, & Griffin, 1998; Strickland, Snow, Griffin, Burns, & McNamara, 2002). The challenge in this era: How do we ensure success in implementing these proven practices and programs? Professional development (PD) of teachers has been widely endorsed as a highly promising strategy to support effective implementation. *At the heart of PD in the field of early childhood is the recognition that supporting active learning and healthy development in young children is a highly demanding endeavor–a professional endeavor that can benefit from systematic supports to improve teachers' and caregivers' everyday exchanges with young children and their families.*

In this chapter, we provide a selective overview of the history of PD in early childhood education and care, followed by a presentation of an integrative theory of PD. We have developed this theory of PD as a practical tool in conceptualizing, planning, providing, and evaluating the effectiveness of PD. The theory—named the knowledge application information systems theory, or KAIS theory, of PD—builds upon three distinct but interrelated strands. The first strand, Knowledge Application, represents a core commitment to putting into action the scientific knowledge about effective supports for positive learning, and the promotion of health and well-being in young children and their families. The second strand, Information, is included because PD itself needs to gather information about whether its intended outcome—namely, improved job performance that in turn supports children's positive development—is realized. Furthermore, information is hypothesized to be valuable in gauging PD participants' own attitudes, knowledge, skills, and performance. In the KAIS theory of PD, information gathering, analysis, and use are activities hypothesized to contribute directly to the quality of the early childhood education program. The third strand, based on formal Systems Theory (cf. Bertalanffy, 1975; Bronfenbrenner, 1979; Miller, 1978; Sameroff, 1983), requires thinking about children's learning opportunities from a systems framework that begins with the central axiom that the behavior and contributions of an individual (in this case, the professional receiving PD) depend on far more than just the person's own knowledge and skills. Thus, by taking into account a systems framework that assesses the natural supports and threats within a system, PD increases opportunities for timely and sustainable implementation of science-based practices. To close this chapter, we provide a case study from our ongoing research about PD effectiveness in diverse early education settings. This case study serves to illustrate the practical utility of the KAIS theory of PD and how effective PD can improve both teacher performance and children's school readiness in language and early literacy.

A History of PD in Early Childhood Education

Contemporary early childhood education, with an emphasis on empirical findings, in contrast to relying on philosophical writings and educational ideologies, can be traced directly to a landmark monograph in 1982 by Lazar, Darlington, Murray, Royce, and Snipper that summarized the findings from experimental studies designed to improve the academic and intellectual outcomes for children from disadvantaged families. The major conclusion reached in 1982 continued to receive extensive research support over the next 25 years—namely, that high-quality, intensive educational programs can lead to large and lasting improvements in children's outcomes. (We have noted [C. Ramey & Ramey, 1998; S. Ramey & Ramey, 2006] later programs that fail to show measurable benefits are weak, brief, and/or not driven by research findings about how young children learn.) The short-term benefits of these early educational programs can lay the foundation for long-term benefits, particularly when children attend schools that provide high-quality instruction and strong supports for learning. In 1982, the major long-term benefits identified were reductions in grade repetition and decreased placement in special education programs. Recently, S. Ramey and Ramey (2006) updated this synthesis of the research findings in terms of identifying principles of effective and sustained benefits from targeted early education programs. These principles of effective interventions form a solid foundation for providing PD to early childhood educators, although they need to be supplemented with particular content:

1. *The dosage principle.* In general, higher dosages (or greater intensity) of a high-quality program lead to larger benefits to children at risk for poor school performance than do lower dosages. In general, greater benefits are documented for at-risk children for whom educational interventions are provided for more hours per day and more total days, often over a multiyear period. We note, however, that several studies have demonstrated at-risk 4-year-olds can show educationally important gains in language and early literacy skills with 1-year programs that are full day. Furthermore, the dosage principle suggests that maximizing the amount of learning opportunities within a given program is likely to lead to greater developmental gains for at-risk children.

2. *The timing principle.* Overall, early educational programs that provide supports when children are younger tend to produce greater and longer lasting gains than do similar programs that start later and/or begin after children show delays. This principle is consistent with scientific findings about neuroplasticity being somewhat greater at earlier stages of development, although it is important for educators to realize that children learn many important things at different ages and stages of their development. The timing principle also suggests that there may be more (vs. less) ideal times and sequences for helping children to learn particular types of skills and knowledge.

3. *The academic instruction and language principle.* Research studies conclude that at-risk children exposed to systematic educational instruction and content, rather than mere custodial, non-educationally focused care, show more positive outcomes in the academic realm, with no reported negative consequences. Although young children learn through many modalities, including play and exploration, they also benefit signifi-

cantly from planned adult scaffolding, modeling, and interactions that introduce them to age-appropriate, stimulating types of language and literacy activities that promote early school success. This instructional principle supports the likely value of PD for teaching staff to increase their skills in specific, proven instructional strategies and adult–child transactions that promote children's language development and acquisition of early literacy skills.

4. *The differential benefits principle.* Some children show greater benefits from participation in early educational programs than do others (e.g., C. Ramey & Ramey, 1994). These individual differences relate to factors such as children's entry risk conditions and how well the educational program addresses the child's needs to prevent negative consequences of these risk factors. For instance, the same high-quality educational program may lead to even larger benefits for children who have extremely limited at-home supports in the areas of language and early literacy experiences (Vaughn, Linan-Thompson, Pollard-Durodola, Mathes, & Hagan, 2006) or for biologically at-risk children from lower resource homes (Hill, Brooks-Gunn, & Waldfogel, 2003).

5. *The educational continuity of supports principle.* Early educational programs are more likely to lead to lasting benefits when children continue to receive high-quality educational programs in subsequent years. Conversely, when at-risk children leave a high quality early educational program to attend inferior public schools, they are likely to suffer in terms of later educational attainment. Much of the so-called "fadeout effect" is attributable to poor-quality education given to at-risk children when they enter public schools (cf. Barnett, 2004; Currie & Thomas, 1995; Entwisle, 1995).

Another, often overlooked consideration in reviews about the scientific evidence of early educational interventions' impact is that all of the pioneering programs we know included *substantial levels of PD for staff, both prior to and throughout the period of educational treatment.* This was essential, because few professionals had been formally trained in providing instruction to children under the age of 5 when these educational interventions were launched (e.g., Gross, Spiker, & Haynes, 1997). Another feature of these pioneering studies is that the investigators actively monitored the performance of teachers and frequently assessed the children's developmental progress using well-standardized, objective assessment procedures.

To date, PD in the field of early childhood education has invested heavily in teachers earning a variety of degrees from institutions of higher education, ranging from a Child Development Associate (CDA) degree to an Associate of Arts (AA) degree, a Bachelor of Arts (BA), and a Master of Arts (MA) degree in early childhood education. These degrees alone have not been reliably associated with actual classroom instructional practices or direct benefits to young children (Early et al., 2006; Zaslow & Martinez-Beck, 2005). In addition, almost all early childhood education programs provide at least some annual PD to their teaching staff. The actual content, amount, and format of PD varies widely and, more importantly, has not been linked to specific classroom instructional practices that have proven effective in promoting children's positive developmental outcomes (S. Ramey & Ramey, 2005). Only now is a scientific body of knowledge beginning to emerge that can inform decisions about how to provide PD that yields demonstrated benefits to teachers, administrators, and children and their families.

As individuals who have developed and then tested early childhood educational programs over the past 35 years (cf. C. Ramey & Ramey, 2004a; S. Ramey & Ramey, 2006), we have firsthand experience in providing PD both for our own programs and for many school systems and community-based programs. Typically, the PD is provided in a workshop or traditional adult classroom setting, with no advance preparation or follow-up activities required of participants. This PD method appears to assume that by providing factual information to teaching staff, the teachers will change their classroom instruction and interactions with children. Most of the time, this form of PD is evaluated only by satisfaction ratings by the participants regarding individual presentations or sessions. Sometimes the PD evaluation includes administering pre- and post-tests of participants' knowledge about the topics covered in PD, although this is relatively rare. With the notable exception of PD provided in the research-driven educational programs, we know of few early educational programs that have explicitly evaluated the impact of PD on participants' performance in their classrooms.

We are aware through direct work in public schools and community-based pre-K and Head Start programs that many participants in PD are concerned that *what* they have learned through PD is not sufficiently practical or useful for their own everyday classroom situations. In other words, PD participants often state that they would prefer receiving PD that is more focused on actually *applying knowledge*, that is, translating the content of PD into specific classroom activities. In fairness, the resources of many school systems and community-based programs are limited and fluctuate, thus affecting the planning and delivery of a comprehensive program of high-quality PD. *We think that the widespread lack of a solid PD plan as an integral part of providing early educational programs is shortsighted.* Also, for reasons we do not understand well, PD in many large systems (e.g., public schools and Head Start programs) is not directly coordinated with the many external specialists who come into classrooms to advise teaching staff about a wide array of topics and types of children (e.g., literacy and math; children with speech and language problems, children in special education, English language learners, and children with behavioral and emotional difficulties); and to our knowledge, because the assistance these specialists provide usually focuses on particular children, it is not classified as PD. *In the absence of solid information to guide a continuous quality improvement effort, we predict that many early childhood education programs will fail to achieve their desired outcomes.* Accordingly, we present an integrative theory (below) designed to guide the planning, provision, and assessment of PD, building upon available scientific perspectives relative to those factors known to influence the performance of adults in educational settings, as well as to promote positive outcomes for young children.

Who Participates in PD?
Do Their Characteristics Matter?

In planning, providing, and evaluating PD in the field of early childhood education, we recognize that a wide range of individuals are participants in PD. The range of characteristics of individual participants in early childhood education PD is wide and far greater than many other practitioner professions with have a longer history and a process of formal examination, licensing, and mandated continuing education to maintain professional credentials (e.g., nursing, medicine, psychology, and therapeutic specialty areas). Accordingly, PD in early childhood education needs to take into account entry-level characteristics of PD participants and how these characteristics may influence decisions about the content, format, and intensity of PD provided. Furthermore, participants in PD may include individuals with distinctively different roles and responsibilities related to the implementation of an effective early childhood education program, including lead teachers, teaching assistants, supervisors and principals, and other specialty staff, such as reading instructors, English for speakers of other languages (ESOL) teachers, and special education professionals.

Figure 3.1 depicts one way of viewing PD participants in terms of four major dimensions: (1) their demographic and experiential characteristics, (2) their attitudinal and motivational characteristics, (3) their informational and knowledge base characteristics, and (4) their actual behavioral and job performance characteristics. We propose that each of these domains warrants consideration to achieve the positive impact of PD; that is, providing the same PD to all types of individuals, without considering who they are and the attitudes, knowledge, skills, and performance they bring to the PD setting, is unlikely to be an effective strategy. We consider these dimensions as a guideline to inventory PD participants in advance, and to inform us about the types of PD that are needed to increase its likelihood of having a measurable, positive benefit.

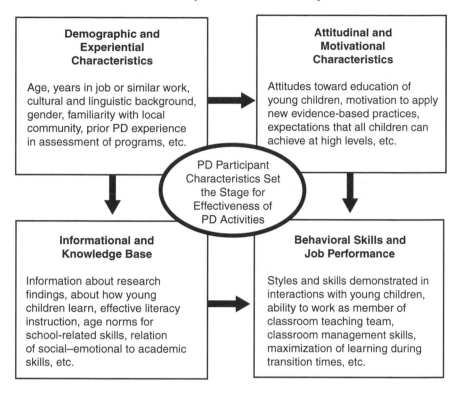

FIGURE 3.1. The relationship of characteristics of participants in professional development (PD) to behavioral skills and job performance. Based on an earlier ecological staff training model in Landesman-Dwyer and Knowles (1987).

We have used the framework in Figure 3.1 to guide the preparation of several programs of PD for different types of early educational programs and different types of PD participants. A common theme of these PD programs was promoting improved language and literacy instructional practices in classrooms or child care settings that served at-risk children from very low income or poverty-level families. For example, one program of PD we tested was provided to teachers who each had earned an MA degree with a specialty in early childhood education, and included both novice teachers and those with many years of teaching experience. In this same public school setting, we also developed the first systematic literacy-related PD for paraeducators (assistant teachers) in the classrooms, many of whom had only a high school degree or its equivalent, and about half of whom spoke a language other than English in their own homes. In a different geographical and cultural context, we evaluated PD that was provided only to child care providers and Head Start teachers with no more than a high school degree or its equivalent, but who each had at least several years experience serving at-risk children and spoke English as their native language.

In providing PD to these individuals with considerably different characteristics, we needed to think about approaches that could create positive receptivity to the knowledge being conveyed about effective instructional strategies for promoting language and early literacy. For instance, among those child care providers, Head Start staff, and paraeducators who had not previously considered their jobs in terms of being a major influence on young children's competence in early literacy and language, we needed to offer PD activities that would encourage shifts in attitudes and motivation that would in turn support changes in their interactions with young children. In contrast, for lead teachers with advanced degrees, we recognized that their attitudes and motivation to provide young children with formal instruction were already high, but we also learned that the education they had received differed tremendously in terms of specific skills that they were taught as being more (vs. less) effective. For some teachers, their own training had emphasized classroom practices that subsequently have been shown to be ineffective or, in some cases, counterproductive (e.g., the whole-language approach solely, or an anti-direct-instruction approach) to promoting early literacy skills in young children. Thus, we needed to consider how to engage these PD participants without alienating them. We also took into account information we had recently gathered about the quality of the classrooms and/or childcare environments in which the PD participants worked. This baseline information helped to inform PD in terms of positive instructional practices that were not being fully implemented, as well as the presence of nonoptimal classroom practices that needed to be eliminated. This information about the characteristics of the PD participants and classrooms also led us to design PD activities that we hypothesized would be more effective than just presenting information in a didactic and traditional format (e.g., primarily lectures and readings). This led us to include more demonstrations and various levels of job-embedded coaching, as well as use of video-based modules to convey key information through combined oral and visual formats. (Shortly, we provide an overview of PD outcomes associated with different dosages and formats intended to match the needs and learning styles of PD participants.)

The KAIS Theory of PD

We developed the KAIS theory of PD over the past three decades as we engaged in systematic research focused on improving the quality of care for a variety of young children with at-risk conditions and developmental delays or disabilities, and on providing PD training to staff (e.g., Gross, Spiker, & Haynes, 1997; Landesman-Dwyer & Knowles, 1987; C. Ramey & Ramey, 2004b; C. Ramey, Bryant, Wasik, Sparling, Fendt, & LaVange, 1992; S. Ramey et al., 2001). Our research experiences also included identifying highly academically capable young children whose demographic and family characteristics initially placed them in a broader, at-risk category, raising a key issue that "the bar" for academic achievement should not be set too low when providing PD for professionals who work with at-risk children (e.g., Robinson, Lanzi, Weinberg, Ramey, & Ramey, 2002). The KAIS theory, displayed in Figure 3.2, also builds strongly upon well established principles in basic Systems Theory and current ecological models about child development (cf. C. Ramey, Ramey, & Lanzi, 2006; Shonkoff & Phillips, 2000).

Figure 3.2 displays the key elements in our KAIS theory of PD. At the center of the figure, the PD activities are represented. The KAIS theory concentrates on the topic of "knowledge application," which is defined as

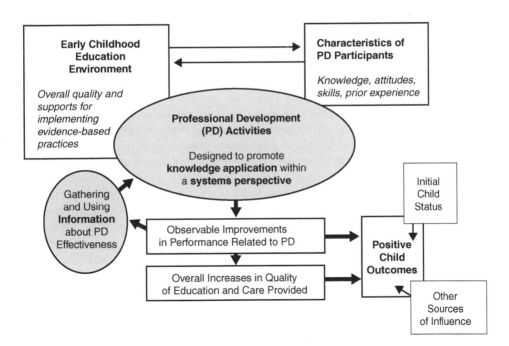

FIGURE 3.2. The knowledge application information systems (KAIS) theory of professional development for promoting positive child outcomes. The Ramey and Ramey KAIS theory of PD integrates research and conceptual frameworks that have informed our scientific investigations of early educational interventions (see C. Ramey & Ramey, 2004a; S. Ramey & Ramey, 2005, 2006; S. Ramey, 2005; S. Ramey, Ramey, & Lanzi, 2004).

implementing practices and behaviors that have been demonstrated to produce outcomes consistent with the goals for PD and for the early childhood education program. Synonyms for this include evidence-based practices, evidence-informed practices, scientifically supported practices, efficacious services and programs, and research-based practices. We realize that there are many forms of knowing and knowledge generation. Scientific methods that yield knowledge about young children's learning include many different approaches, including rigorous tests in randomized controlled trials (RCTs) that measure the efficacy of a practice or an intervention program, comparative longitudinal studies that observe children's development and measure their experiences over time, systematic case studies, ethnography, and individual subject designs. In the KAIS model, we emphasize that knowledge often relies on a synthesis of findings from multiple scientific investigations, and rarely can a single study generate definitive knowledge without being replicated in an independent study or conducted in multiple sites. *In conducting PD that has a central mission of translating research findings into widespread practice to benefit children, we think that the standards for judging evidence must be consistently high.* This is important to avoid providing PD that is trendy and quickly overturned, thus eroding confidence among PD participants that they can trust the validity of findings from research. This PD for practitioners should contain knowledge that has been vetted through peer review, replicated or supported in multiple studies, and ideally endorsed through consensus building and integrated sets of recommendations, such as research syntheses and practical guidelines provided by leading respected institutions, particularly those that do not have any proprietary interests or apparent conflict of interests (e.g., publishing their own materials, providing consultation or accreditation that yields profit to the organization). Groups that qualify for this respected role of providing systematic, balanced research reviews and recommendations include the National Academies (which establish working committees and task forces to review research evidence, particularly concerning unresolved or controversial topics), the National Institutes of Health (which sponsor select, special topic conferences and have a consensus conference mechanism available to achieve a professional resolution to highly controversial practices in a given field), and the Institute for Education Sciences (which has launched a "What Works" resource available for educators and policymakers).

In the KAIS theory of PD, plans for PD must include specification of the PD content (knowledge) that PD participants are to learn and then apply in their professional work. Just as importantly, PD participants need to understand the expected "observable improvements in performance related to PD" and the proposed "positive child outcomes" that are targeted to benefit from their knowledge application. Figure 3.2 illustrates these pathways. Furthermore, the KAIS theory of PD is designed to be shared openly with PD participants, so that they understand fully that their participation in PD is expected to result in specific changes that they and others can assess directly in terms of job performance. In other words, the KAIS theory can be specified and individualized by adding specific details to the major elements, so that both providers and participants in PD share a common perspective on the process of learning about effective practices and improving children's outcomes.

A distinctive feature of the KAIS theory of PD is the formal inclusion of information gathering, analysis, and reporting as integral components of PD itself. Just as students in any educational system are assessed through a variety of means to provide information about the degree to which their schooling and participation in the educational process has led to increased knowledge and skills, we think that PD itself must include this feature. At the time PD is planned, decisions should be made about what types of information to collect, how often, from whom, and for whom. Ideally, such information will be promptly shared in ways that can (1) refine subsequent PD provision, (2) determine the effectiveness of different forms and amounts of PD, and (3) provide supplemental assistance to PD participants who may be facing particular challenges. *This information component acknowledges that PD is a serious endeavor and a major investment of time and resources that are explicitly expected to support high levels of performance in staff and children.* In the past, PD participants have sometimes resisted being "evaluated" or "tested." Furthermore, the providers of PD rarely are assessed directly themselves. We think that a commitment to high-quality education for children cannot ignore the need to assess the PD thoroughly to see whether it is achieving its goals and objectives. This emphasis on information is consistent with a commitment to applying scientific findings in the classroom, where the implementation of effective practices is directly observable in the behavior of adults and young children. (*Note:* We do think that the wavering and often low levels of supports for PD reflect the fact that there has been little evidence to show PD makes a measurable difference. In some places, professionals are granted "PD days," with no formal activities planned, and professionals are just trusted to engage in some new learning of their own choice, with no documentation of the content of the PD or the expected benefits.)

Table 3.1 provides examples of some PD activities that are consistent with the KAIS theory of PD. These reflect a systematic process of planning, implementing, and evaluating PD that seeks to foster effective translation of scientific research findings into early educational programs and settings. We offer this theory as an alternative to typical PD in the field, which in the past has been characterized as largely unfocused, uncoordinated, and unproven.

TABLE 3.1. Features of Professional Development Activities Consistent with Key Elements (shown in CAPS) of the KAIS Theory of PD (see Figure 3.2)

PD is primarily and openly focused on KNOWLEDGE APPLICATION, as indicated by activities such as:

- Specifying with PD participants the exact knowledge to be acquired through PD and providing documentation of its support from scientific research
- Indicating to PD participants why the application of this knowledge is important for their job performance and positive outcomes for young children and their families
- Ensuring that those who plan and provide the PD have a solid understanding of the knowledge to be applied and indicators of its effective application
- Identifying behaviors and indicators that reflect incorrect application of knowledge or absence of knowledge application

PD explicitly identifies INFORMATION to be collected, analyzed, and reported regarding the effectiveness of the PD (i.e., PD that leads to increased knowledge application), such as:

- Instructing PD participants in how to gather and use information about their own performance in terms of knowledge application and about systematic assessment of children's progress related to the knowledge application
- Setting up procedures that include collecting, analyzing, and reporting on aspects of knowledge application focused on during PD
- Relating information about PD effectiveness to other systems goals

The PD provided directly addresses SYSTEMS factors that can be supportive and facilitate knowledge application, as well as systems factors that can threaten or lessen the effectiveness of the PD:

- Conducting a review of systems when planning the PD and including findings about this in the PD provided
- Problem-solving activities about how PD participants can actively engage others (administrators, parents, coworkers) in applying knowledge to benefit children's development
- Sharing case histories from other places where systems worked collaboratively to maximize knowledge application and to overcome potential obstacles
- Working directly with other individuals in the systems directly linked to the places where PD participants serve children, so that knowledge application is understood and supported

PD takes into account the ATTITUDES AND MOTIVATION of PD participants, such as engaging in the following:

- Considering existing information about recent performance of individuals for whom PD is planned in terms of attitudinal and motivational factors that may affect participation in PD and knowledge application
- Conducting surveys of potential PD participants about attitudes and motivation relevant to content of PD and knowledge application
- Contacting others who have provided PD on the same topic(s) and reviewing the scientific findings about PD efficacy for similar types of PD participants

(continued)

TABLE 3.1. *(continued)*

PD considers the characteristics and knowledge of the PD participants, as reflected in the following activities:

- Choosing an appropriate format(s) for presenting knowledge to be applied (e.g., taking into account the participants' reading and language skills, prior educational background, familiarity with terms and concepts relevant to PD)
- Ensuring that those who provide the PD are aware of the background characteristics of PD participants and their likely prior experiences related to the PD topic(s)
- Deciding about the dosage of PD (e.g., number of sessions, length of sessions), so that it is sufficient to allow participants to acquire the knowledge and skills needed for application in the work setting (*Note:* if ideal dosage is not possible, then the PD should include natural opportunities to continue to expand participants' competence over time)

Other issues for consideration in a KAIS theory-informed model of PD:

- PD provided should permit PD participants a voice in evaluating the PD they receive, especially in terms of its adequacy to support the stated "Observable Improvements in Performance" that are expected as a result of PD
- PD providers and participants should suggest how to improve future PD on the same topic(s), based on information collected, analyzed, and reported
- Those responsible for planning, providing, and evaluating PD should exchange information frequently and openly with those responsible for other aspects of the early childhood education program(s), including contributing to decisions about collecting, analyzing, and reporting about positive child outcomes

---

Case History

Here we provide a case history informed by the KAIS theory of PD. Over the past 5 years, we have conducted a series of RCTs designed to measure the impact of PD provided to teachers and caregivers in a variety of early childhood education settings in different states, including urban, suburban, and rural environments. In this chapter, we highlight results presented recently at national meetings to illustrate the practical usefulness of the KAIS theory of PD.

In all of these investigations, we have worked collaboratively with the local providers and school systems, as well as colleagues at other universities, in identifying PD priorities and formats for delivery. The many advantages of this partnership model of conducting research include increasing the probability that findings will be used to shape policy and be incorporated into ongoing systems of education and care for at-risk young children (see S. Ramey & Ramey, 1997). Our general conceptual framework about the quality of early education and care *transcends* any single type of program, such as Head Start, public pre-K, subsidized child care, Even Start, or Early Reading First, because scientific evidence about how young children learn best and the types of instructional practices or curricula that promote positive outcomes have not been limited to specific types of programs (i.e., administrative aegis). Figure 3.3 illustrates this conceptual framework known as the Four Diamond Model of quality for early education and care programs. (For a more extended discussion of the history and rationale for this, see S. Ramey & Ramey, 2005.) In the center is a diamond with four major components, each representing an area with extensive research support that children's actual types of experiences in these areas are reliably associated with more or less positive outcomes. The four diamonds include health and safety practices; adult–child interactions, primarily to support positive social and emotional development; language and learning activities, mostly focused on academic learning; and caregiver/teacher–family relationships, vital both to facilitate individualization of the care and education for a child and to encourage families to provide additional learning supports outside the school or child care setting.

The four-diamond model places these four central components (representing functional activities) within concentric circles that indicate proximal (near) and distal (far) supports hypothesized to influence the quality of education and care. This framework is quite different than those quality rating systems or accreditation criteria that include many structural, administrative, and staffing features, along with observed interactions, as actual indicators of a program's actual quality. In the Four Diamond Model, we consider features such as the educational and training background of teachers and other staff, recordkeeping systems, and physical plant dimensions to be valuable supports that facilitate positive interactions in the four diamond areas; but we do not credit programs solely for having these features. Instead, the emphasis is on the actual and observable transactions in the four diamonds. We think it reasonable to presume that more highly educated staff may on average have more knowledge and skills than less educated staff, but we also know of studies confirming that some teaching staff have excellent instructional skills but no formal higher education, and others have advanced degrees in the field of early childhood education, yet perform poorly. Undoubtedly, a physically spacious, beautiful, and well-stocked classroom can be an advantage to offering a high-quality program but, again, this cannot be equated with quality per se. Finally, the Four Diamond Model places PD in the circle of proximal influences—as a potentially powerful support to improve the quality of early education and care—but we would not rate a program highly simply because high amounts of PD are provided. Collectively, a large and consistently reviewed scientific body of knowledge supports the centrality of daily interactions in the four diamonds as vital for positive child outcomes in health and well-being; language, literacy, and other academic skills; and children's feelings about their social and learning supports—and this spans both the home and the educational or child care environ-

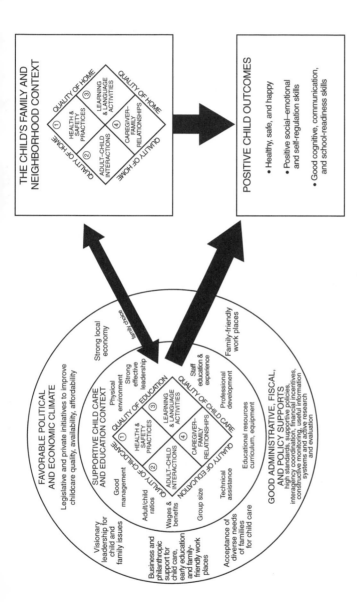

FIGURE 3.3. The Ramey and Ramey Four Diamond Model of the quality of early education and child care. The definition of a high-quality program is one that provides strong evidence-based practices and supports in each of the four diamonds, which represent the direct daily experiences children receive in the educational and care settings where they spend time. We developed this conceptual framework through partnerships and research collaborations with community and school providers over the past 15 years (see S. Ramey & Ramey, 2005). The Four Diamond Model provides an organizing framework for thinking about the role and the content of professional development, regardless of the administrative aegis of a program (e.g., public school pre-K, private childcare center, Head Start center, Even Start program, Early Reading First program). It also indicates that structural and administrative practices, as well as educational credentials should not be assumed to be adequate to identify a high-quality program; rather, the emphasis is on children's actual experiences and transactions with teachers and the environment.

55

ments (e.g., Borkowski, Ramey, & Bristol-Powers, 2002; Hart & Risley, 1995; C. Ramey & Ramey, 1999; C. Ramey et al., 2006; Shonkoff & Phillips, 2000).

In our program of research concerning the efficacy of PD to improve instructional activities and student achievement, we have concentrated primarily on the area of Language and Learning Activities based on national concern that children from very low resource families and communities lag considerably in their language development and early literacy skills when they enter kindergarten (cf. S. Ramey et al., 2001). In all our studies we have used an RCT design in which participating programs and staff understood and endorsed the research design and the purpose of the PD intervention. In this chapter, we present a case study from a very large public school system that operated both the county's educational program for Head Start and a public pre-K program for at-risk children from families considered to be at risk (low income but above the poverty level required for Head Start).

In this school system, the leadership (superintendent and other senior leaders) had made a strong public commitment to implementing evidence-based practices in pre-K/Head Start classrooms, with the explicit goal of increasing language, literacy, and math competencies. The school system had selected as a major curricular resource for all classrooms, the evidence-informed curriculum Building Language for Literacy (BLL) (Neuman & Snow, 2000) published by Scholastic, Inc. BLL is organized around major themes with named puppet characters who represent language and literacy skills areas (used in all themes). Systematic activities in each theme relate to promoting alphabetic knowledge, phonemic and phonological awareness, knowledge about print, and language development through storytelling, play activities, reading, songs, and poems. Teachers can readily add their own books and activities to supplement the formal ones provided in the BLL kit.

The school district did not provide specific training for teachers in the use of the BLL curriculum, although each teacher was given a full set of curriculum materials with the teacher's manual. (Note: other literacy curricular materials also had been given to all classrooms.) Prior to the study, however, many of the teachers had received PD from the school district regarding evidence-based practices in early literacy instruction. In this school district, the lead teachers in pre-K/Head Start classrooms had earned master's degrees with a specialty in early childhood education. Twenty-four classrooms were initially randomly assigned to one of two groups: (1) BLL coaching or (2) school district comparison. Then, the 12 BLL coaching classrooms were randomly assigned to receive different dosage levels of PD: (1) weekly BLL coaching or (2) monthly BLL coaching. BLL coaching involved the following PD activities:

1. A 3-day Summer Institute provided by Scholastic, Inc., and the lead developer of the BLL curriculum (Susan Neuman) for lead teachers, with the paraeducators (assistant teachers) joining for 2 of the 3 days.

2. Coaching in the classroom by specially trained BLL coaches with master's degrees in reading instruction, many years of experience as reading specialists in this school district, and project training related to BLL coaching and systematic classroom assessment to document the fidelity of BLL implementation. For both the monthly and weekly BLL conditions, the sessions lasted the entire day, 2.5 hours for the pre-K and 3.25 hours for the Head Start classrooms. Coaching involved individualized feedback to teachers based on the BLL Program Fidelity Checklist, as well as BLL coaches demonstrating evidence-based BLL curricular activities in the classroom.

3. Monthly, voluntary meetings in the early evening for BLL coaches and teachers in the weekly and monthly BLL conditions to exchange information about BLL in their classrooms and to receive additional PD on designated PD topics (usually selected by the BLL coaches to provide more in-depth materials about areas observed to need additional emphasis). Note: teachers were compensated for their participation at the school district rate paid for PD activities outside the regular school day. Attendance was consistently high, and PD participants rated sessions as highly useful.

The KAIS theory guided the PD at all stages, from planning through implementation, information gathering and reporting, and follow-up activities with participants, PD providers, and other stakeholders. All participating teachers, children and their families, school principals, and community superintendents were fully informed in advance and throughout the project about the purpose of the PD and the measures to be collected. The PD research was conducted in partnership with the school district and a steering committee met frequently to monitor the progress of the project. The major outcome measures (collected by trained research associates, who were not part of the PD intervention) were classroom observations of the literacy environment, using the Early Language and Literacy Classroom Observation (ELLCO; Smith & Dickinson, 2002), as a standardized tool, and the children's literacy skills, assessed primarily by the Test of Early Reading Ability, third edition (TERA; Reid, Hresko, & Hammill, 2002). Although we collected other measures as well, we focus on the two major outcomes in this chapter. Consistent with the KAIS theory of PD, we hypothesized that classrooms receiving focused PD to support knowledge application—in this case, implementation of the evidence-informed curriculum, BLL—would demonstrate significantly higher levels of language and literacy activities, as indexed in part by the ELLCO scores, and that students would in turn demonstrate benefits in terms of higher gains in their early literacy performance, reflected in their standardized TERA scores. We also had a second hypothesis about the dosage of PD: specifically, that teachers receiving weekly versus monthly BLL coaching would display significantly higher levels of competence in their knowledge application, and that the children in their classrooms (all of whom were considered to be at risk) would benefit the most of any of the conditions.

Figures 3.4 and 3.5 present the major findings about the ELLCO and the TERA performance of children for the three PD conditions. The two hypotheses about PD were supported; that is, the classrooms in which teachers received more PD—in a highly individualized format with ongoing support from other teachers during monthly meetings—showed observable benefits, and these extended to the children's development.

As KAIS theory specifies, the objective outcomes and the perspectives of those involved in PD are important to inform decisions about what types of PD to provide in the future and ways to improve the PD (even when proven to be efficacious). The steering committee designed

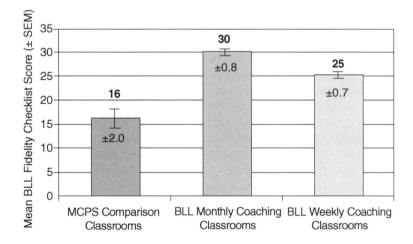

FIGURE 3.4. The effects of PD on classroom language and literacy environments as reflected in ELLCO scores. Classrooms were randomly assigned to receive additional professional development in the form of weekly versus monthly coaching in the implementation of Scholastic's Building Language for Literacy (BLL) curriculum for pre-K classrooms *or* to continue as part of the school district curriculum condition (Comparison group). See text for information about components of the BLL Coaching.

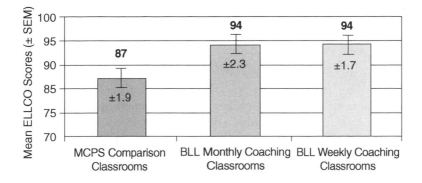

FIGURE 3.5. Children's reading achievement as indexed by percentile ranks for their TERA scores in classrooms receiving additional PD (weekly and monthly BLL coaching conditions) and in comparison classrooms. Children were assessed individually by trained research associates in the fall and the spring of the year in which their classrooms received the additional forms of PD or the comparison condition. All children were considered at risk by the school district. Children in the different PD conditions were comparable in demographic characteristics, and statistical analyses covaried for children's entry-level skills.

and conducted end-of-the-year feedback sessions in which teachers, para-educators, and principals shared their experiences, offered suggestions for future PD and research, and received public acknowledgment of their role in advancing the knowledge about PD itself. The steering committee reviewed the feedback, along with other information collected about the PD, then developed a set of interrelated recommendations for future activities to support the early literacy development of at-risk children. These recommendations include both expanding the PD, consistent with the types and amounts shown to be effective, and looking at the supportive system—most notably, the structural constraint of providing only a half-day program. The group responsible for the research study on this form of PD also actively monitored findings from other research and recognized the likely possibility that both the gains and the final achievement levels among the children were much lower than those reported by some other educational programs that provided full-day, year-round pre-K to similar, at-risk students. This case history illustrates that the KAIS theory can contribute to active inquiry among educators and key decision makers. In the process of utilizing the KAIS theory, the school district became increasingly aware of the many separate, and not always closely coordinated, endeavors occurring to "support" classrooms and the school district's goal of advancing achievement for at-risk children.

Conclusions

Our nation is launching its most vigorous, systematic, and costly efforts to improve what the public widely refers to as "the school readiness" of all young children. The investments are particularly strong and focused on at-risk students and the goal of "closing the achievement gap" between children from less and more advantaged families. Our experiences support the conclusion that PD is a highly promising means of increasing the quality of these educational interventions. As the knowledge base about effective early educational classroom practices continues to expand, there will be a growing need to share these new findings widely to ensure that teachers, experienced and novice, and key administrators and support staff are able to apply the knowledge to their educational settings. The cost of information gathering, analysis, and reporting is modest, particularly in comparison to benefits of documenting that the PD has resulted in anticipated benefits to children and society.

From a firsthand perspective, we think that the commitment to collecting trustworthy information and publicly reporting the findings may be a factor in promoting high-quality PD itself and high levels of active engagement by PD participants. This yet untested hypothesis—a system that highly values information about its own performance is more likely to achieve its goals—has received indirect support from decades of rigorous research on the impact of high-quality educational interventions for at-risk children and their families (S. Ramey & Ramey, 2005).

References

Barnett, W. S. (2004). Does Head Start have lasting cognitive effects?: The myth of fadeout. In E. Zigler & S. J. Styfco (Eds.), *The Head Start debates* (pp. 221–249). Baltimore: Brookes.

Bertanlanffy, L. V. (1975). *Perspectives on general system theory.* New York: Braziller.

Borkowski, J. G., Ramey, S. L., & Bristol-Powers, M. (Eds.). (2002). *Parenting and the child's world: Influences on academic, intellectual, and social–emotional development.* Hillsdale, NJ: Erlbaum.

Bronfenbrenner, U. (1979). *The ecology of human development.* Cambridge, MA: Harvard University Press.

Clinton, H. R. (1996). *It takes a village and other lessons children teach us.* New York: Simon & Schuster.

Coie, J., Watt, N., West, S., Haskins, D., Asarnow, J., Markman, H., et al. (1993). The science of prevention: A conceptual framework and some directions for a national research program. *American Psychologist, 48,* 1013–1022.

Currie, J., & Thomas, D. (1995). Does Head Start make a difference? *American Economic Review, 83,* 241–364.

Donovan, M. S., & Pelligrino, J. W. (Eds.). (2003). *Learning and instruction: A SERP research agenda.* Washington, DC: National Academy Press.

Early, D. M., Bryant, D. M., Pianta, R. C., Clifford, R. M., Burchinal, M. R., Ritchie, S., et al. (2006). Are teachers' education, major, and credentials related to classroom quality and children's academic gains in pre-kindergarten? *Early Childhood Research Quarterly, 21,* 174–195.

Entwisle, D. R. (1995). The role of schools in sustaining benefits of early childhood programs. *The Future of Children, 5,* 133–144.

Gross, R. T., Spiker, D., & Haynes, C. W. (Eds.). (1997). *Helping low birth weight, premature babies: The Infant Health and Development Program.* Stanford: Stanford University Press.

Hart, B., & Risley, T. R. (1995). *Meaningful differences in the everyday experience of young American children.* Baltimore: Brookes.

Hill, J. L., Brooks-Gunn, J., & Waldfogel, J. (2003). Sustained effects of high participation in an early intervention for low-birth-weight premature infants. *Developmental Psychology, 39,* 730–744.

Landesman-Dwyer, S., & Knowles, M. (1987). Ecological analysis of staff training in residential settings. In J. Hogg & P. Mittler (Eds.), *Staff training in mental handicap* (pp. 3–30). London: Croom Helm.

Lazar, I., Darlington, R. B., Murray, H., Royce, J., & Snipper, A. (1982). Lasting effects of early education: A report from the Consortium for Longitudinal Studies. *Monographs of the Society for Research in Child Development, 47*(2–3, Serial No. 195).

Miller, J. G. (1978). *Living systems.* New York: McGraw-Hill.

Neuman, S. B., & Snow, C. (2000). *Building language for literacy: Research-based early-literacy instruction.* New York: Scholastic.

NICHD Early Child Care Research Network. (2005). *Child care and child development: Results from the NICHD Study of Early Child Care and Youth Development.* New York: Plenum Press.

Ramey, C. T., Bryant, D. M., Wasik, B. H., Sparling, J. J., Fendt, K. H., & LaVange, L. M. (1992). Infant Health and Development Program for low birth weight, premature infants: Program elements, family participation, and child intelligence. *Pediatrics, 89,* 454–465.

Ramey, C. T., Campbell, F. A., Burchinal, M., Skinner, M. L., Gardner, D. M., & Ramey, S. L. (2000). Persistent effects of early childhood education on high-risk children and their mothers. *Applied Developmental Science, 4,* 2–14.

Ramey, C. T., & Ramey, S. L. (1994). Which children benefit the most from early intervention? *Pediatrics, 94,* 1064–1066.

Ramey, C. T., & Ramey, S. L. (1998). Early intervention and early experience. *American Psychologist, 53,* 109–120.

Ramey, C. T., & Ramey, S. L. (1999). Beginning school for children at risk. In R. C. Pianta & M. J. Cox (Eds.), *The transition to kindergarten* (pp. 217–251). Baltimore: Brookes.

Ramey, C. T., & Ramey, S. L. (2004a). Early educational interventions and intelligence: Implications for Head Start. In E. Zigler & S. Styfco (Eds.), *The Head Start debates* (pp. 3–17). Baltimore: Brookes.

Ramey, C. T., & Ramey, S. L. (2004b). Early learning and school readiness: Can early intervention make a difference? *Merrill–Palmer Quarterly, 50,* 471–491.

Ramey, C. T., Ramey, S. L., & Lanzi, R. G. (2006). Children's health and education. In I. Sigel & A. Renninger (Eds.), *The handbook of child psychology* (Vol. 4, pp. 864–892). Hoboken, NJ: Wiley.

Ramey, S. L. (2005). Human developmental science serving children and families: Contributions of the NICHD Study of Early Child Care. In NICHD Early Child Care Research Network (Ed.), *Child care and child development: Results from the NICHD Study of Early Child Care and Youth Development.* New York: Plenum Press.

Ramey, S. L., & Ramey, C. T. (2005). How to create and sustain a high quality work force in child care, early intervention, and school readiness programs. In M. Zaslow & I. Martinez-Beck (Eds.), *Critical issues in early childhood professional development* (pp. 325–368). Baltimore: Brookes.

Ramey, S. L., & Ramey, C. T. (2006). Early educational interventions: Principles of effective and sustained benefits from targeted early education programs. In S. B. Neuman & D. K. Dickinson (Eds.), *Handbook of early literacy research* (2nd ed., pp. 445–459). New York: Guilford Press.

Ramey, S. L., Ramey, C. T., & Lanzi, R. G. (2004). The transition to school: Building on preschool foundations and preparing for lifelong learning. In E. Zigler & S. J. Styfco (Eds.), *The Head Start debates* (pp. 397–413). Baltimore: Brookes.

Ramey, S. L., Ramey, C. T., Phillips, M. M., Lanzi, R. G., Brezausek, C., Katholi, C. R., et al. (2001). *Head Start children's entry into public schools: A report on the National Head Start/Public School Early Childhood Transition Demonstration Study* (Contract no. 105-95-1935). Washington, DC: U.S. Department of Health and Human Services, Administration on Children, Youth, and Families.

Ramey, S. L., & Sackett, G. P. (2000). The early caregiving environment: Expanding views on non-parental care and cumulative life experiences. In A. Sameroff, M. Lewis, & S. Miller (Eds.), *Handbook of developmental psychopathology* (2nd ed., pp. 365–380). New York: Plenum Press.

Reid, D. K., Hresko, W., & Hammill, D. (2002). *Test of Early Reading Ability, third edition.* Austin, TX: PRO-ED.

Robinson, N. M., Lanzi, R. G., Weinberg, R. A., Ramey, S. L., & Ramey, C. aT. (2002). Family factors associated with high academic competence in former Head Start children at third grade. *Gifted Child Quarterly, 46,* 281–294.

Sameroff, A. J. (1983). Developmental systems: Contexts and evolution. In P. H. Mussen (Ed.), *Handbook of child psychology.* New York: Wiley.

Shonkoff, J. P., & Phillips, D. A. (2000). *From neurons to neighborhoods: The science of early childhood development.* Washington, DC: National Academy Press.

Smith, M., & Dickinson, S. (2002). *Early language and literacy classroom observation toolkit.* Baltimore: Brookes.

Snow, C. E., Burns, M. S., & Griffin, P. (Eds.). (1998). *Preventing reading difficulties in young children.* Washington, DC: National Academy Press.

Strickland, D., Snow, C., Griffin, P., Burns, S. B., & McNamara, P. (Eds.). (2002).

Preparing our teachers: Opportunities for better reading instruction. Washington, DC: National Academy Press.

Vaughn, S., Linan-Thompson, S., Pollard-Durodola, S. D., Mathes, P. G., & Hagan, E. C. (2006). Effective interventions for English language learners (Spanish–English at risk for reading difficulties). In S. B. Neuman & D. K. Dickinson (Eds.), *Handbook of early literacy research* (2nd ed., pp. 185–197). New York: Guilford Press.

Zaslow, M., & Martinez-Beck, I. (Eds.). (2005). *Critical issues in early childhood professional development.* Baltimore: Brookes.

PART II
★★★★★★★★

PROFESSIONAL DEVELOPMENT AND TEACHER SUPPORT

Chapters 4 through 8 of this book consider how preschool programs can achieve excellence in language and literacy through the provision of high-quality professional development (PD), including classroom-based coaching and mentorship. Teachers who work in preschool programs are currently held to very high standards in the approaches, strategies, and curricula they use; interestingly, these standards seem to exceed those of many other disciplines (Meisels, 2006). Given that preschool teachers arrive at the classroom with great heterogeneity in their prior educational experiences and credentials, PD for the preschool teaching workforce has emerged as a critical mechanism for equalizing disparities in the instructional climate, classroom management, and emotional support observed across U.S.'s preschools (La Paro, Pianta, & Stuhlman, 2004). Importantly, not all PD activities are created equally, with recent evidence emphasizing the importance of providing teachers with sustained and intensive process-oriented training linked to their authentic experiences within the classroom (Garet, Porter, & Desimone, 2001).

Sharon Walpole and Carla K. Meyer, in Chapter 4, provide a framework for understanding various models of coaching, such as peer coaching, and describe how these models can be used effectively in preschool programs. Shelley Gray, in Chapter 5, extends this framework by providing a precise discussion of key principles for utilizing a mentorship approach to PD of preschool teachers.

Chapters 6, 7, and 8 each provide an in-depth description of specific approaches to PD that have been successfully used by the authors, all of which link teacher coaching and mentorship to classroom observational data. Bridget K. Hamre, Jennifer LoCasale-Crouch, and Robert C. Pianta (Chapter 6) focus their discussion on data-driven teacher coaching derived from observations of three general dimensions of instructional quality: emotional support, classroom organization, and instructional support. Extending this discussion, Mike A. Assel, Susan H. Landry, and Paul Swank (Chapter 7) describe an approach to coaching that is derived specifically from observations of instructional quality based on language and literacy instruction. In an excellent denouement to this section, David K. Dickinson, Betsy G. Watson, and Dale C. Farran (Chapter 8) describe use of an evaluation–feedback system that considers the moment-by-moment interactions between teachers and children and how a microanalytic perspective can guide effective professional development.

While reading these chapters, generate responses to these five questions. Join with others to share your responses in guided discussions:

1. In general, what characterizes effective coaching models?
2. What is the role of the supervisor, the mentor (or coach) and the mentee (the teacher) in a mentoring program? What is the relationship among these roles?
3. What coaching strategies might mentors use to achieve their goal of helping teachers improve their practices and their children's achievement?
4. How do data (e.g., from videotaped observations or behavior rating scales completed by mentors or transcripts) help focus and refine professional development for teachers?
5. How might mentors or coaches provide teachers with feedback about their teaching?

After you have completed your reading, complete one or more of the following three activities to expand your knowledge further:

1. Look on the U.S. Department of Education's website (*www.ed.gov/ programs/earlyreading*) to locate the nearest Early Reading First project. Contact the project administrators to see whether you might shadow one of its mentors or coaches for a day. (You may know of an early childhood program other than Early Reading First that uses coaches to support teachers' learning; this activity could be completed with that program.) How does what you

observe compare with what you have read about mentoring or coaching teachers of young children? How would you characterize the coaching you observed?

2. Interview the coach/mentor you shadowed. What coaching strategies does he or she use to mentor the teachers? How does this coach provide the teachers with feedback about their work with children? What data are used by this coach to help focus and refine professional development for the teachers?

3. Either independently or with a group of colleagues, develop a set of questions to interview a preschool center director. How does this center director view his or her role? Is the center director a supervisor, a coach/mentor, or does he or she assume aspects of both roles?

References

Garet, M. S., Porter, A. C., & Desimone, L. (2001). What makes professional development effective?: Results from a national sample of teachers. *American Educational Research Journal, 38*(4), 915–945.

La Paro, K. M., Pianta, R. C., & Stuhlman, M. (2004). The Classroom Assessment Scoring System: Findings from the prekindergarten year. *Elementary School Journal, 104*, 409–426.

Meisels, S. J. (2006). *Accountability in early childhood: No easy answers.* Chicago: Erikson Institute, Herr Research Center for Children and Social Policy.

CHAPTER 4

★★★★★★★★

Models for Coaching

Making Them Work for Preschools

Sharon Walpole
Carla K. Meyer

Coaching, in general, currently enjoys enormous popularity. Expectant mothers rely on labor coaches; individuals use nutritional coaches to establish healthy eating habits; families use coaches to help them rethink their finances; busy executives hire coaches to help them to improve their efficiency and management; athletes work with team coaches and individual coaches to build their competence. Think about why those coaches are sought and what they actually do. When people work toward a complex goal on their own, they may or may not have the tools to be successful; when they work with the support of a real coach, someone with specialized knowledge and experience who can provide direction, support, and continuous feedback, they are much more likely to succeed.

This sort of truly personalized support, coaching, is finally making its way into preschool programs. In particular, many preschools have begun to use coaches who provide support in the area of literacy instruction. In this chapter, we review models for coaching that have been developed outside of the preschool environment, and that provide some guidance for educators designing their own coaching models for use within preschool literacy programs. For a coaching model to really take hold, all stakeholders must feel comfortable with its design: administrators or directors, coaches, teachers, and parents. We invite preschool educators to consider coaching from any or all of these vantage points.

Why Consider Coaching?

One reason to consider the use of coaches within preschool literacy programs is that literacy experiences matter greatly for preschool children. Children who leave preschool with stronger emergent literacy skills are poised for more successful kindergarten experiences (Kaplan & Walpole, 2005; Whitehurst & Lonigan, 2002). Specific early literacy skills (phonological awareness, alphabet knowledge), along with oral language development, are targeted in some but not all preschools. In fact, preschool classrooms serving large numbers of children from poor families tend not to address these skills very effectively; observational studies of preschool classrooms indicate that they are often impoverished language and literacy environments (Dickinson, McCabe, & Clark-Chaiarelli, 2004).

This does not have to be the case. Preschool teachers are not always provided the tools—coherent, research-based curriculum materials—or the support high-quality preservice education and ongoing inservice education—they need. In fact, Whitebook (2003) collected data on the requirements for postsecondary education for kindergarten teachers, preschool teachers working in state-funded programs, and child care providers. Not surprisingly, kindergarten teachers are generally required to have more preservice training than educators who work in preschools; preschool teachers are generally required to have more training than childcare providers. Government statistics on the pre-service experiences of Head Start teachers indicate similar trends (U.S. Department of Health and Human Services, 2004). Despite external pressure to increase hiring standards for preschool staff members, very few come to their jobs with degrees in early childhood education. Given this fact, coaches might be especially necessary to bridge the gap between previous opportunities to learn and the demands on preschool educators to provide effective language and learning experiences for young children. Coaches do this by providing on-the-job, specific support.

The funding of Early Reading First is one strong indication that the tide is changing for preschool educators: in some settings, at least, preschool educators are getting the support they need continually to improve their knowledge and skills. Early Reading First, a federally funded program to increase the quality of preschool experiences for children, particularly children whose families are poor, targets increases in cognitive skills, language skills, and early reading skills. Early Reading First projects are charged with providing high-quality, intensive, on-the-job training. Coaching programs are one of the most common strategies for accomplishing these goals.

How Does Coaching Fit with Other Research on Teacher Support?

Establishment of excellent preschool centers that make a difference in the language skills, cognitive skills, and literacy development of young children demand improvements in preschool curriculum and practice. The targeted improvements go beyond the individual teacher or classroom to involve all teachers in a setting (school or center) or program. Often the improvements may demand wholesale changes that are extremely complex. Some changes may be initiated by the director of a preschool center: researchers call these top-down changes. Others may be initiated by teachers working together: Researchers call these bottom-up changes. Still other changes might involve both the administration and the teachers.

Coaches may be necessary to facilitate such comprehensive efforts. Research reviews of the literature on professional development for teachers (e.g., Richardson & Placier, 2001) have identified problems in unsuccessful reform efforts and also characterize successful ones. Table 4.1 lists lessons from that extensive professional development research that can guide a preschool coaching initiative.

One key to ensure that coaching works in a specific preschool setting is the extent to which the coaching meets the needs of the adults in that setting. Teachers' personal backgrounds, professional experiences, and educational beliefs must be considered when designing a coaching program. Given what is known about the diverse educational backgrounds of the current preschool teaching force, this concept is especially important. For us, this diversity suggests that a combination of top-down and bottom-up reforms may be the best, in which teachers have choice and voice, and are also held accountable to high expectations for both the quality of their teaching and evidence of child learning.

TABLE 4.1. Opportunities to Design Effective Teacher Change Projects

Research-based guidance for preschool coaching initiatives

- Make a long-term commitment to learning, across the entire year.
- Provide administrative support.
- Secure adequate funding to pay teachers and coaches for their time.
- Select goals from current research.
- Consider the strengths and needs of the staff.
- Collect teacher input before and during the initiative.
- Ensure the participation of the entire staff.
- Make the long-term goals clear and very specific to the setting.
- Plan for sufficient adult learning time outside the classroom.
- Plan for follow-up inside the classroom.
- Collect evidence about the quality of teaching and learning along the way.
- Use data to revisit goals.

Coaching is a framework, or a set of strategies, that a preschool community may find central to a well-designed staff support initiative. To integrate coaching, that community must set its goals, find a coach, and specify the role and responsibilities of the coach in addressing those goals. A coach is a site-based staff developer. In the most intensive efforts, the coach is a full-time staff member whose teaching duties are specific, but do not involve direct responsibility for children. A coach teaches teachers; teachers teach children.

Neufeld and Roper (2003a) proposed two general types of coaches. "Change coaches" include administrators as learners. They help administrators reorganize resources and build leadership and understanding related to site-based goals. "Content coaches" assume that resources are generally well allocated, and although they interact with administrators, their focus is more squarely on the teachers. They help teachers to learn and to implement new ideas during instruction, and they provide formative—not evaluative—feedback. Coaches serve as resources, providing feedback from the stance of a knowledgeable, critical friend to teachers who engage with young learners and in their own continuous learning. From our perspective, the best coaching model for a given site likely encompasses both "change" and "content," engaging administrators, teachers, and parents in a shared commitment to improving outcomes for young children. Below we present some possible guidance for the "how's" of coaching, again, with the hope that preschool educators will be able to fashion a model that fits the specific needs of their center. Remember, though, that before latching on to characteristics from a specific model, it is essential to consider whether the center has the resources (time, money, personnel) to implement the model, and whether the model is consistent with the teaching and learning goals of the center.

Training Models

Training models have a long and sometimes controversial history (for a review, see Hoffman & Pearson, 2000). In business, training is an ongoing cycle of opportunities designed to initiate new staff members into the inner workings of a particular company, and to introduce new ideas and procedures for experienced staff members. In education, training is part of nearly every educational innovation; to test the effectiveness of a new idea or to bring established innovations into new sites, teachers must engage in training to establish understanding and fidelity. Training is very specific and outcome-oriented; at the end of a training cycle, an individual is expected to know and to be able to do something. In teaching, training entails identification of a very specific teaching target and provision of a cycle of support that may include knowledge building, simulation and

TABLE 4.2. Characteristics of Training Models

Coach's roles
• Understanding and implementing an externally designed plan

School-level planning
• Commitment to external organization, including all of its requirements

Formal professional presentations
• Specified and required, usually delivered by external personnel

Role of student achievement data
• Lesson planning, grouping, reflection

Strategies for in-class support
• Observation
• Formal implementation walk-throughs

demonstration, and observation and feedback. This specificity invites criticism from those who favor a less rigid model (e.g., Duffy, 2004; Hoffman & Pearson, 2000), but we see many useful possibilities for training.

It is easy to envision training as an effective strategy for a particular aspect of the preschool curriculum. For example, coaches might use a training model to develop expertise in teaching rhyming or letter identification, or in interactive read-alouds or use of a new set of materials. It is more difficult to envision training applied to the entire preschool curriculum, because so many of the variables include the complicated interaction between the teacher and the children. However, in literacy education, training models have been applied to such very complex curricular objectives. The key is duration, intensity, and resources. Table 4.2 provides an overview of the shared characteristics of two training models for literacy curricula that are very different in their orientation; we describe each in turn to illustrate that training models employ similar strategies even as they target different underlying philosophies.

The Reading Recovery Training Model

One well-known training program in literacy, the Reading Recovery initiative, is an approach to tutoring first-grade struggling readers. We discuss this initiative here not because its instructional procedures are appropriate for preschoolers, but because its training program serves as a potential model for a preschool coaching program that includes training.

Reading Recovery relies on a "train the trainer" model. Reading Recovery teacher trainers must achieve a rigorous standard of professional development training, and they must attend refresher courses each year. Teacher trainers then train teachers—again, with specific require-ments for time and content. First, the teacher trainer builds teachers' understanding of the instructional procedures used in the program. Next the training includes extended observation with feedback: The teachers work with children while their trainers watch them. Debriefings are exten-sive and meant to develop very high levels of understanding and exper-tise. Extensive support and documentation of this training program are available in published materials (Reading Recovery Council of North America, 2004). This rigorous attention to organization results in high lev-els of consistency in the knowledge and practices of Reading Recovery teachers (Pinnell, 1985; Pinnell, Fried, & Estice, 1990).

Success for All

Success for All (SFA) is another example of a complex set of teaching objectives supported through training. SFA is a whole-school reform model with extensive effectiveness research in a variety of settings (Borman et al., 2005a, 2005b). Like Reading Recovery, SFA is an orga-nized, national movement. Again, we present this description to help pre-school educators understand the components of a training model rather than to endorse SFA.

SFA embeds training and site-based coaching within a specific new curriculum designed for the entire school. The model includes instruc-tional materials, a system for assessment and groupings, initial training of a site-based coach (called a "facilitator") and all teachers, and ongo-ing support from an SFA Foundation coach. SFA classrooms have spe-cific characteristics, including materials that must be displayed, and SFA facilitators use observation checklists to monitor fidelity to the program requirements. SFA coaches have ready-made tools to guide their work and can use a variety of strategies to support teachers who are strug-gling.

Both Reading Recovery and SFA are specific curricular models that rely on site-based coaching to support fidelity. Coaches are trained by the program designers. Coaches receive lesson planning templates speci-fying the type, amount, and time for instruction, and they are required to implement these lesson plans with teachers. Coaches also receive observation templates and must conduct specific observations. Both of these training programs are very expensive. However, many commercial preschool curricular packages offer some of these training services. Training may be adopted as part of any curricular initiative as long as the teaching outcome is very specific and there are specific supports (e.g., lesson-planning templates and observation templates) for the work of the coach.

Process Models

Other coaching models are much less directive about curricular goals. We identify two models—peer coaching and cognitive coaching—as process models because they were never meant to be connected to any specific curricular initiative. Rather, both are professional learning strategies that can be adapted to any curricular initiative. They differ in that they envision very distinct roles for coaches. Table 4.3 provides an overview of the characteristics of process models.

Peer Coaching

Developed in the early 1980s by Bruce Joyce and Beverly Showers, peer coaching has evolved into an effective model. Joyce and Showers originally envisioned the model as a bridge between researched-based teaching strategies presented in staff development and classroom implementation of these strategies. Peer coaching works within the context of school improvement in which the study of teaching and curriculum is imperative (Showers & Joyce, 1996).

The peer coaching model provides support for teachers attempting to implement strategies and models presented in traditional professional

TABLE 4.3. Characteristics of Process Models

	Cognitive Coaching (Costa & Garmston, 2002)	Peer Coaching (Showers & Joyce, 1996)
Coach's roles	• Encouraging teacher reflection of the teaching process through critical questioning	• Modeling and reflecting on a new instructional technique with a peer
School-level planning	• Fostering schoolwide commitment to learning	• Establishing a common goal throughout the school
Formal professional presentations	• Participating in inquiry-based course of study	• Participating in inquiry-based course of study
Role of student achievement data	• Informal data gathered and used to drive teacher's personal goals	• Used to select a focus for the course of study
Strategies for in-class support	• Planning conferences • Lesson observation • Postobservation reflection	• Collaborative planning • Modeling • Observations • Reflection

development. In this model, teachers act as coaches for one another. Teaching colleagues form groups of two or more to provide continuing support. After participating in staff development, collaborating teachers meet to discuss instructional goals to develop lesson plans and corresponding materials. Using goals developed during planning as a guide, one teacher observes another teacher's lesson. The observation is in no sense evaluative. In fact, Showers and Joyce assert that the "coach" should be the teacher teaching the lesson, and no feedback should be provided from the observer. They maintain that the learning occurs through the observation of the teaching process (Showers & Joyce, 1996).

Peer coaching has been modified and used in preschools. In a Head Start center participating in a peer coaching program, one teacher reported that receiving and providing feedback helped her become more aware of her interactions with the children (Vail, Tschantz, & Bevill, 1997). Although valuable to many educators, observational feedback should not be the central component of peer coaching; rather, the central focus should be the collaboration and support provided by peers as each educator focuses on improving his or her own teaching.

Peer coaching models are appropriate for schools or centers committed to a specific instructional change but not a complete curricular overhaul. Nonetheless, individuals in the school or center must agree to work together, and the schedule must include time for planning and collaboration. Eliminating teacher isolation is an important component of peer coaching. Encouraging teachers to pool resources and become experts through collaboration improves the implementation of strategies presented through staff development. Preschools that elect to implement a peer coaching model must have teachers and administrators who are committed to self-regulated learning and professional collaboration.

Cognitive Coaching

Using a blend of cognitive psychology and collaboration, Cognitive Coaching promotes the self-directed learning of teachers. Like peer coaching, cognitive coaching strives to reenvision the dynamics of professional development. The Cognitive Coaching model encourages teachers to identify their concerns and promotes reflective dialogue with their coach. Unlike other models of supervision, Cognitive Coaching emphasizes the intellectual processes involved in teaching (Costa & Garmston, 2002). Figure 4.1 summarizes essential strategies in Cognitive Coaching.

The Cognitive Coaching model utilizes a three-step cycle during which the coach and teacher plan, engage in a lesson observation, and reflect (Ray, 1998). The planning conference allows the coach and teacher to meet, identifies the teacher's goals, and establishes the coach's role for

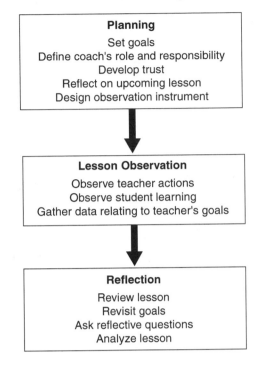

FIGURE 4.1. Procedures from Cognitive Coaching.

observation. However, the planning conference must also be an opportunity for the coach to establish trust and encourage the teacher to engage in mental analysis and reflection prior to the implementation of the lesson. Part of this process includes coach and teacher working together to develop data-gathering instruments based on the teacher's specific goals for the lesson (Costa & Garmston, 2002). The observation provides the coach with the opportunity to gather data. During the observation, the coach simply monitors the teacher's actions and student learning, and collects data as determined in the planning conference. Finally, during the postlesson conference, the coach helps the teacher recall the events of the lesson and reflect on how well the actual lesson compares with the teacher's own goals. The coach uses reflective questioning and data from the observation to help the teacher analyze the lesson's effectiveness.

To promote the reflective planning, instruction, and study of the teaching, Cognitive Coaching coaches must have an excellent understanding of the teaching process. However, the central focus of Cognitive Coaching is that the teacher, not the coach, is in charge of his or her learning, with the strength of the model based on the coach's questioning techniques (Brooks, 2000); hence, the model may be ideal for expert teachers who are transitioning into a coaching role. The model encourages the coach to recognize the importance of listening to the concerns of the teachers. Furthermore, because the Cognitive Coaching model does not present the coach as the "expert" who will "fix" the problem, the coach avoids the potentially awkward shift of authority from teacher to coach. However, Cognitive Coaching may not be appropriate for schools or centers initiating broad-based changes, and the teachers participating in the Cognitive Coaching model must accept continuous learning and reflection as a centerwide initiative.

Hybrid Models

Some coaching models focus on multiple coaching strategies applied within a specific curricular context. The three models we have located, which we have termed "whole-school reform," "team-based reform," and "demonstration-based reform," each rely upon a specific research and theory base, and a specific set of strategies for the coach. Table 4.4 provides an overview of the characteristics of these models.

Whole-School Reform

Walpole and McKenna's *The Literacy Coach's Handbook: A Guide to Research-Based Practice* (2004) provides a coaching model designed for whole-school reform efforts in struggling elementary schools. The underlying curricular changes in this model are reflective of the cognitively-oriented experimental research in early reading that was reviewed by the National Institute of Child Health and Human Development (2000). The model may apply in settings where data indicate that large numbers of children are not mastering basic early literacy benchmarks, and teachers and administrators are committed to school- or centerwide restructuring.

We think that such center-based reform strategies will apply to preschools "starting from scratch"—preschools in which the reform is comprehensive and includes an intensive focus on new curriculum and new assessments. In this model, coaches help the staff to reconsider the schedule, creating longer blocks of instructional time, shared time for planning and collaboration during the day, and efficient use of the entire instructional team. Coaches also provide guidance in the design of an assessment system that serves two broad goals. First, it informs instructional decisions through a sequence of screenings, diagnostic tests, and progress-monitoring assessments. Second, data also provide feedback to direct continuous changes in the program. The model assumes that the program must be defined from within and refined based on child achievement data.

TABLE 4.4. Coaching Strategies in Hybrid Models

	Reform model (Walpole & McKenna, 2004)	Team-based model (Neufeld & Roper, 2003a)	Demonstration classroom model (Poglinco et al., 2003)
Coach's role	• Design, implement, and evaluate a new curriculum	• Facilitate study groups and demonstration lessons	• Model an external curricular model at each grade level
School-level planning	• Scheduling • Designing assessment systems • Selecting curricular resources	• None	• Formal commitment to the external curricular plan
Formal professional presentations	• Research presentations • Data presentations • Book studies	• Participating in inquiry-based course of study	• Teacher meetings • Study groups
Role of student achievement data	• Periodic feedback on effectiveness of whole-school project • Ongoing feedback on effectiveness of instruction: screening, diagnosis, progress monitoring	• Used to select a focus for the course of study	• Reflection on student work products with standards-based rubrics
Strategies for in-class support	• Formative observation of all teachers • Modeling for struggling teachers	• Lab site for demonstration and observation	• Model classrooms • Demonstration classrooms • Observations

This reform model directs coaches to work with teachers in two important ways. Coaches conduct formal outside-the-classroom professional development by presenting research findings to inform teachers' work, sharing summarized child achievement data, and choosing and leading professional book studies. Coaches also conduct ongoing inside-the-classroom professional development by observing teachers and providing formative, supportive, specific, confidential feedback, and by modeling for them, if they need additional support. Again, this model assumes that the exact balance struck in these activities is a function of the characteristics of the specific center.

Team-Based Reform

The Boston Plan for Excellence in the Public Schools has developed an ambitious coaching model called Collaborative Coaching and Learning (CCL), a district-sponsored professional development approach whose most salient feature is a specific team-based cycle of work. CCL is used as a strategy for enacting district curricula in Boston, but it includes teacher choice. It also stands out as an organized strategy for coaches who work in multiple sites. We think that this type of team-based reform has much to offer to preschool settings as teachers are fine-tuning their instructional practices.

This team-based approach relies on 8–week cycles for teams of five to eight teachers to work together twice each week. From an individual coach's point of view, two teams may work simultaneously for 8 weeks, either at the same site or at two different ones. The coach spends 2 days each week with each team, and then the fifth day is reserved for the coach's own preparation. Teachers start by using student achievement data to guide them toward a very specific focus. In this part of the model, the inquiry, teachers work with the coach to design a course of study: They agree on a focus and on a schedule for a set of professional readings related to that focus. They meet once each week to discuss these readings and their application to instruction.

The second part of the model, the lab site, is the classroom of one member of the cohort where team members experiment with the new instructional practices. They begin with a preconference, determining the focus of the lesson and the observation. Then one member of the team teaches while the others watch. Finally, the team debriefs, focusing on ways that the observation/demonstration provided insight into effective instruction. Follow-up procedures include coaches visiting individual team members in their own classrooms to observe or model lessons.

Demonstration-Focused Reform

America's Choice is a comprehensive, standards-based school reform system in which coaching features specifically and prominently. We describe coaching in this model based on information from an external description of the program (Poglinco et al., 2003); this strategy for coaching has much to offer to preschools, and we refer to it as demonstration-based coaching, in that it may be applied outside the America's Choice model. In this model, the school is already committed to a specific curricular plan that specifies allocated time for specific activities in reading, writing, and math instruction.

The most salient feature of this coaching model is the use of the demonstration classroom. The coach spends 6–8 weeks teaching in a colleagues' classroom (called the "model classroom"), so that he or she can build personal knowledge and expertise with the curriculum. Then the coach moves to a demonstration classroom, where the goal is to show teachers what he or she learned in the model classroom. All teachers visit the demonstration classroom and watch the coach teaching there over the course of 3 or 4 weeks. Finally, the coach observes the teachers in their own classrooms, providing feedback and support as needed. After supplying all teachers on a particular team with the support they need, the coach begins another demonstration classroom, working with a different team.

In this demonstration-focused model, the coach does provide outside-the-classroom professional support in the form of teacher meetings and study groups. The America's Choice team provides materials to direct these meetings. Teacher meetings include discussions and presentations on specific aspects of the curriculum. Study groups include procedures for reviewing student work samples and for understanding the standards that inform the program's design.

Resounding Themes

Preschool instruction is important to children, and preschool teachers do not always receive the support they need. We are excited about the possibilities of literacy coaching in preschools, particularly their potential to bridge the "knowledge" gaps that often exist for preschool teachers who may have had little preservice training, and to do so in a way that builds collaboration and collegiality in the preschool center. Coaching models have several broad characteristics. First, they provide a specific structure to enable teachers to learn both inside and outside the classroom. Second, they specify roles for coaches that allow them to provide support for teacher learning rather than evaluation of teacher competence. And third, they are informed by data—in the form of child achievement data, observational data, or both. We encourage preschool educators to consider these themes as they build a coaching model for their center.

Rather than start from scratch, we urge preschool educators to draw from the coaching models we have identified in developing their own: training models, process models, and hybrid models. Remember our caution, though, as we introduced the models: It is essential that two questions guide selection of individual, site-based preschool coaching models:

1. Is the model consistent with the available resources in terms of money, time, and personnel?
2. Is the model consistent with the site's goals for teaching and learning, such that full implementation leads to the outcomes the preschool is seeking?

Our work with coaches in a variety of settings convinces us that there is no single, "right" way to implement coaching. Rather, there is a right way and also many wrong ways for each site. Remember that coaching influences all of the stakeholders in a preschool center of excellence—children, parents, teachers, coaches, and administrators. Readers who coach may wish to read *Coaching Families and Colleagues in Early Childhood* (Hanft, Rush, & Shelden, 2004), which provides some reflective tools to help them to consider all of their stakeholders. We urge preschool educators to take care at the beginning of their initiative to learn from existing models, and to think through the goals and logistics of the coaching plan.

References

Borman, G. D., Slavin, R. E., Cheung, A., Chamberlain, A. M., Madden, N. A., & Chambers, B. (2005a). Success for All: First-year results from the national randomized field trial. *Educational Evaluation and Policy Analysis, 27,* 1–22.

Borman, G. D., Slavin, R. E., Cheung, A., Chamberlain, A. M., Madden, N. A., & Chambers, B. (2005b). The national randomized field trial of Success for All: Second-year outcomes. *American Educational Research Journal, 42,* 673–696.

Brooks, G. R. (2000). Cognitive coaching for master teachers and its effect on student teachers' ability to reflect on practice. *Delta Kappa Gamma Bulletin, 67,* 46–50.

Costa, A. L., & Garmston, R. J. (2002). *Cognitive coaching: A foundation for renaissance schools,* Norwood, MA: Christopher-Gordon.

Dickinson, D. K., McCabe, A., & Clark-Chaiarelli, N. (2004). Preschool-based prevention of reading disability. In C. A. Stone, E. R. Silliman, B. J. Ehren, & K. Apel (Eds.), *Handbook of language and literacy: Development and disorders* (pp. 209–227). New York: Guilford Press.

Duffy, G. G. (2004). Teachers who improve reading achievement: What research says about what they do and how to develop them. In D. S. Strickland & M. L. Kamil (Eds.), *Improving reading achievement through professional development* (pp. 3–22). Norwood, MA: Christopher-Gordon.

Hanft, B. E., Rush, D. D., & Shelden, M. L. (2004). *Coaching families and colleagues in early childhood.* Baltimore: Brookes.

Hoffman, J., & Pearson, P. D. (2000). Reading teachers education in the next millennium: What your grandmother's teacher didn't know that your granddaughter's teacher should. *Reading Research Quarterly, 35,* 28–44.

Kaplan, D., & Walpole, S. (2005). A stage-sequential model of literacy transitions: Evidence from the Early Childhood Longitudinal Study. *Journal of Educational Psychology, 97,* 551–563.

National Institute of Child Health and Human Development. (2000). *Report of the National Reading Panel. Teaching children to read: An evidence-based assessment of the scientific research literature on reading and its implications for reading instruction* (NIH Pub. No. 00-4769). Washington, DC: U.S. Government Printing Office.

Neufeld, B., & Roper, D. (2003a). *Coaching: A strategy for developing instructional capacity.* Providence, RI: The Annenberg Institute for School Reform.

Neufeld, B., & Roper, D. (2003b, July). *Year II of collaborative coaching and learning in the effective practice schools: Expanding the work.* Cambridge, MA: Education Matters.

Pinnell, G. S. (1985). Helping teachers help children at risk: Insights from the Reading Recovery program. *Peabody Journal of Education, 62,* 70–85.

Pinnell. G. S., Fried, M. D., & Estice, R. M. (1990). Reading Recovery: Learning how to make a difference. *Reading Teacher, 43,* 282–295.

Poglinco, S. M., Bach, A. J., Hovde, K., Rosenblum, S., Saunders, M., & Supovitz, J. A. (2003, May). *The heart of the matter: The coaching model in America's choice schools.* Philadelphia: Consortium for Policy Research in Education.

Ray, T. M. (1998). Implementing the NCTM's standards through cognitive coaching. *Teaching Children Mathematics, 4,* 480–483.

Reading Recovery Council of North America. (2004). *Standards and guidelines of Reading Recovery© in the United States.* Columbus, OH: Author.

Richardson, V., & Placier, P. (2001). Teacher change. In V. Richardson (Ed.), *Handbook of research on teaching* (4th ed., pp. 905–947). Washington, DC: American Educational Research Association.

Showers, B., & Joyce, B. (1996). The evolution of peer coaching. *Educational Leadership, 53,* 12–16.

U.S. Department of Health and Human Services. (2004, January). *Status of efforts to increase the qualifications of Head Start teachers.* Retrieved July 29, 2006, from *oig.hhs.gov/oei/reports/oei-07-01-00560b.pdf.*

Vail, C. O., Tschantz, J. M., & Bevill, A. (1997). Dyads and data in peer coaching. *Teaching Exceptional Children, 30,* 11–15.

Walpole, S., & McKenna, M. C. (2004). *The literacy coach's handbook: A guide to research-based practice.* New York: Guilford Press.

Whitebook, M. (2003). *Early education quality: Higher teacher qualifications for better learning environments–a review of the literature.* Retrieved July 29, 2006, from *www.iir.berkeley.edu/cscce/pdf/teacher.pdf.*

Whitehurst, G. J., & Lonigan, C. J. (2002). Emergent literacy: Development from prereaders to readers. In S. B. Neuman & D. K. Dickinson (Eds.), *Handbook of early literacy research* (pp. 11–29). New York: Guilford Press.

CHAPTER 5

★★★★★★★★

Mentoring Preschool Teachers

Shelley Gray

Did you have a mentor in your life who gave unselfishly, with your best interests at heart? Maybe an aunt who showed you the secrets of her sugar cookie recipe or a coach who helped build your character and stamina? Do you have a mentor at school or work who watches patiently and encourages you when you make mistakes, stands by, ready to help when you need it, and is devoted to learning in ways that inspire you?

Mentors have been around for a long time. The original Mentor was a character in *The Odyssey*, written by Homer. Mentor's job was to coach Odysseus's son while he was away at war, a position that required knowledge and wisdom. "Mentor" has come to mean an experienced and trusted friend, counselor or teacher. A "mentee" is a person who has a mentor. When all goes well, the mentor–mentee relationship is powerful and rewarding for both people. When it doesn't, it can be a waste of time, or worse, can create negative feelings. The information in this chapter is designed to help readers develop a successful preschool mentoring program that can be both powerful and rewarding for the mentee (typically a teacher) and the mentor.

Successful mentoring depends on many factors. At the top of the list is careful consideration of why a mentoring program is needed and whether all colleagues want one. After all, it is one thing to be a mentee when it is the mentee's idea, or when a mentor–mentee relationship emerges as a pleasant surprise from an existing relationship. It is quite another when someone is told that he or she is going to have a mentor. The natural reaction of many people to this news is concern that they must be doing something wrong, or that their supervisor doesn't think they are performing up to par. This type of mentor–mentee relationship might not begin successfully. Luckily, there is a growing research base about how to build successful mentoring programs.

What the Research Says

Authors of earlier chapters in this volume build a compelling case for the importance of improving young children's early language and literacy skills. Preschool centers of excellence that promote children's language and literacy development cannot be developed without competent, knowledgeable, and creative teachers. Such teachers are developed and nurtured—not born. Professional development should support teachers' acquisition and implementation of important skills, yet research suggests that it often does not. Professional development training frequently focuses on skills that do not help teachers prepare preschoolers for kindergarten success (Freeman & King, 2003). The content of the training is often haphazard (Birman, Desimone, Porter, & Garet, 2000; Little, 2001) and may not actually improve teachers' performance (Crow & Snyder, 1998). One reason may be that trainers do not understand that adult learners differ from their younger counterparts and that training must be of sufficient intensity to have an impact (Birman et al., 2000). Here is where mentors play a critical role. Research on adult learning suggests that adults like to take responsibility for their own learning. They want to learn relevant skills that fulfill a need, and they want to practice real-world application of what they are learning in a safe environment over time (Knowles, 1970). For teachers, that safe environment is their own classrooms. By providing modeling, feedback, support and accountability, mentors help teachers improve their teaching where it counts, with the children in their classroom.

Although studies investigating the effectiveness of early childhood mentors are limited, research in teacher education suggests that mentors can have a positive impact on teachers' behavior. The results of several studies that illustrate the positive impact that mentoring can have on teaching and teacher retention are provided in Table 5.1.

Another study illustrates what can go wrong in a mentoring program. Pavia, Nissen, Hawkins, Monroe, and Filimon-Demyen (2003) evaluated the relationships of six mentor–mentee pairs over a 9-month period. All of the participants were women who worked full time in classrooms serving children between the ages of 3 and 5 years. The classrooms included private nonprofit, Head Start, and public school programs. Experienced

TABLE 5.1. Studies Illustrating the Positive Impact of Mentoring on Teaching and Teacher Retention

Authors	Study description	Results
Odell & Ferraro (1992)	• Surveyed two groups of beginning teachers 4 years after they had participated in a first-year teacher mentoring program or no mentoring program.	• Ninety-six percent of mentored teachers were still teaching compared to a national retention rate of approximately 91%. • A higher percentage of the teachers who received mentoring also reported that they intended to keep teaching as compared to the national average. • Teachers who had been mentored reported valuing the emotional support, the support using instructional strategies, and the help obtaining resources for their classroom they received from their mentors.
Birman, Desimone, Porter, & Garet (2000)	• Surveyed a national sample of more than 1,000 teachers who were participants in the Eisenhower Professional Development Program aimed at developing classroom teachers' math and science knowledge and skills.	• Traditional workshops and more innovative educational practices were effective training models. • Successful professional development programs included training of sufficient duration, a focus on content knowledge, inclusion of active learning, and a concentration on activities consistent with teacher goals. • Mentors extended the duration of training by modeling skills after the workshop's end, shared knowledge with their mentees, and promoted active learning of skills that teachers valued.
Schepis, Ownbey, Parsons, & Reid (2000)	• Evaluated the effectiveness of a professional development training program for teaching assistants and substitute teachers in a community-based preschool that served children with developmental disabilities. • Training included the modeling of basic teaching skills, role playing, and on-the-job monitoring and feedback by the supervising teacher or professional development trainer in the classroom	• All staff members reached criterion in the training program. • The staff continued to use the teaching procedures after the training was concluded.
Vaughn & Coleman (2004)	• Studied the extent to which mentor teachers effectively taught fellow teachers the instructional practice of Collaborative Strategic Reading and the extent to which mentees effectively implemented what they had learned.	• Mentors and mentees liked working with a partner and preferred it to more traditional inservice training. • Mentees used the strategy with varying degrees of success. • Mentors implemented the strategy but most modified it from the model they had been taught.

teachers served as mentors. Mentors and mentees met formally at an orientation meeting, then at six additional meetings during the year. Mentors and mentees both reported some positive benefits from the program, but a number of difficulties also became apparent. Mentors reported that they were not clear on what their role should be with their mentee and how they should act. Some mentors felt that they were not wanted or needed. Mentees felt that it was difficult to find mutually acceptable times to meet or even talk on the phone with their mentors. They felt that they had to come up with problems to discuss with their mentor, and that when real problems occurred in their classroom there was such a delay between the problem and the meeting with their mentors that the problem was already resolved. Furthermore, the cultures of these different programs made it difficult for mentors and mentees to relate to one another. Mentees also felt that they had contributions to make to the mentor–mentee relationship, but that these were not acknowledged. By the end of the project many mentors and mentees were discouraged that they had not "connected" with each other. They viewed their participation in the program as another "job." These results illustrate that good intentions are not sufficient to build an effective mentoring program. It takes careful thought, planning, ongoing evaluation, and flexibility to change what doesn't work. The remainder of this chapter is devoted to describing how organizations can create a successful mentoring program for preschool teachers.

How to Build a Successful Mentoring Program

Develop a Clear, Well-Defined Purpose

The first step in developing a mentor program requires consensus by all key participants on the purpose of having mentors, how mentors will support the mission of the organization, and how they will help achieve the project's goals. This assumes that a written mission statement and clearly written project goals are already in place. If not, writing these becomes the first step. This leads to the second step, preparing a written job description for the mentors, whether they are paid participants or volunteers. This step must include input from potential mentors, mentees, administrators, and advisory groups. A review of published research is in order to incorporate evidence-based practice into discussions and decision making. Without this job description, mentees may misunderstand the mentor's purpose and be reluctant to participate. The third step is a written "job description" for the mentees. This should specify who in the organization is expected to participate in mentoring and why. The fourth step is to clearly define the mentor–mentee relationship by creating a document that both will sign.

When preschool programs want to transform themselves purposefully into centers of excellence that promote language and literacy development, mentors are likely to focus on the following program goals: (1) effective implementation of a scientifically based language and early literacy curriculum to include class schedules and lesson planning; (2) effective teaching strategies for children from a variety of developmental levels, cultures, and home languages; (3) effective modeling and scaffolding of oral language in the classroom to include high-level vocabulary, syntax, and language used for a variety of purposes; (4) creation of language- and print-rich classroom environments; and (5) nurturing of mentees to help them become confident, self-directed learners. The knowledge base for these components comes from professional development training designed with research in mind. Training supports teachers' acquisition of content knowledge in language and early literacy development, includes hands-on activities in the mentees' classrooms, and provides opportunities for the mentees to assess and reflect on their own performance and growth. Mentors are central to the mentees' learning. They attend training with their mentees, model skills in their mentees' classrooms, and help their mentees reflect on their growth and what is needed next.

Specify What Mentoring Is and Is Not

It is critically important to define clearly a mentor's role within the organization and the project. The mentor's job description should delineate what mentoring is *and* what it is not, what mentors are expected to do and what they are *not* expected to do. A list of possible mentor roles is provided in Figure 5.1. This work lays the groundwork for recruiting mentors and retaining those who support the organization's mission and goals.

It is important to distinguish between the roles of supervisors and mentors. One hopes that the organization's supervisors are mentors. However, given the responsibility overload experienced by educational administrators, it is rare to find them modeling in classrooms or watching teaching performance over time. Thus, supervisors may mentor, but mentors should not be supervisors. Mentees cannot easily admit their failures to their supervisor or ask for help from the person who evaluates their job performance. Where supervisors cannot tread, mentors can. Mentors help teachers be risk takers by providing support when they try out new skills. Mentors revel in their mentees' successes and brainstorm solutions when things do not work.

Another word of caution: Mentors should not share information with supervisors except in clearly defined ways that have been agreed upon by supervisors, mentors, and mentees. This should be spelled out carefully in

Mentoring is . . .	Mentoring is not . . .
• Helping • Providing support • Modeling • Sharing • Giving • A partnership • Leading by example	• Teaching another person everything you know • Showing off • Power seeking • Ladder climbing
Mentors are . . .	Mentors are not . . .
• Trusted • Available • Coaches • Encouragers • Knowledgeable • Experienced • Facilitators • Catalysts • Lifelong learners • Adaptable • Respectful • Teachers • Patient • Truthful • Fans of their mentees • Committed • Good communicators	• Psychotherapists • Go betweens • Teaching assistants • Servants • Supervisors • Superhuman • Judges • Perfect • Rescuers

FIGURE 5.1. Mentor roles.

written "rules of engagement" for supervisors, mentors, and mentees. In general, sharing should be limited to issues of safety and legality. Lest this sound overly dramatic, envision the wrath of a teacher who confides a worry to her mentor, then later receives a call from her supervisor, who wants to discuss the problem. Nothing torpedoes a mentoring program faster than a lack of trust between mentors and mentees. This does not mean that mentors should not be responsive to training needs identified by supervisors. Rules of engagement should include ways that supervisors can request help from mentors for their teachers, and that mentees can share confidential information, such as personnel reviews, with their mentors.

Select Mentors Carefully

All mentors should be good teachers, but all good teachers should not be mentors. As suggested in Figure 5.1, teaching is an important part of mentoring, but it is only one part. Likewise, good supervisors do not necessarily make good mentors. Teaching, supervising, and mentoring are different behaviors. Mentors must be comfortable speaking uncomfortable truths and sharing confidences. They must be patient and have their mentees' best interests at heart. They must be willing to hold others accountable and to show their own weaknesses. They should enjoy cheerleading and celebrating others' successes. They must be knowledgeable, experienced, and credible.

Good mentors within an organization often can be easily identified: They are already mentoring others because they enjoy it and people seek them out. They are (or were) strong, knowledgeable teachers. They are not people one is trying to get out of the classroom or out of a supervisory position. Mentor candidates are likely to be gifted teachers or administrators at a stage in their careers when they are seeking new challenges. These are not people who have lost their passion for teaching, or who are tired. They are people who want to stretch and to help others stretch.

When selecting mentors, an important first consideration is whether their knowledge base matches the one needed for the program. Several years of experience teaching children the same age and developmental level as those of the mentee is an important criterion. Mentees expect to be mentored by teachers who have "been there and done that." As the old saying goes, there is no substitute for experience. Second, mentors must possess a keen grasp of oral language and early literacy development, and how to teach it in a preschool classroom. Third, mentors should have previous successful mentoring experience. Fourth, mentors should understand the organization's educational culture. Teachers in Head Start programs have different requirements than those in faith-based or public school programs. Mentors who understand the ins and outs of working in the organization also understand the challenges the organization's teachers face.

Train Mentors

The people selected to become mentors benefit tremendously from training designed specifically for mentors. It is tempting to ask mentors to begin working with their mentees immediately, but the early investment in mentor development pays dividends later. Most mentors come to the job directly from teaching or supervising; therefore, they need to understand the differences between their previous job and mentoring, and they need guidance during the transition.

Paid mentoring positions in early childhood education are a relatively recent development in this field. Consequently, there is not a body of research to help determine the effectiveness of particular mentor training models, and the number of training resources is limited. In the absence of research, readers may find two resources helpful. One is *The Early Child-*

hood Mentoring Curriculum: A Handbook for Mentors (Bellm, Whitebook, & Hnatiuk, 1997), which provides a course outline for prospective mentors. The other is *Mentoring Matters: A Practical Guide to Learning-Focused Relationships* (Lipton & Wellman, 2003), which is geared toward mentoring for new teachers and provides a comprehensive overview of the mentoring process.

At a minimum, mentors should demonstrate understanding of the mission, objectives, policies, and procedures of the organization, especially as these relate to the role of mentors and mentees, before they begin their mentoring. They should receive training on adult learning; how to establish successful mentor–mentee relationships; how to model, coach, observe, and provide feedback to teachers; what to do when conflicts arise; and how to assess their own performance. Just as teachers need to practice new skills in the classroom, mentors need to practice mentoring skills and to receive feedback about their performance. Mentors might receive support from a consultant or from each other to develop and refine their skills through use of videotaped and live observations. An organization with only one mentor might develop a relationship with other organizations that use mentors to create a network of support.

Match Mentors and Mentees Carefully

The more mentors and mentees have in common, the more likely their relationship will flourish. This does not mean that a mentee should be a clone of his or her mentor, but it suggests that project leadership should thoughtfully assign mentor–mentee pairs. By the same token, if a mentor and mentee do not develop a trusting relationship, the leadership should reconsider the arrangement. The goal of mentoring is to strengthen teaching skills and to increase children's learning. This will not be accomplished if a mentor and mentee devote more time to resolving conflicts than to achieving program goals.

Protect Mentor–Mentee Time

Relationships require time. Teachers and their mentors need time to get to know one another and to develop trust. Mentors should be in their mentees' classrooms on a regular basis for sufficient lengths of time to become familiar with the children, the curriculum, the classroom environment, and the schedule, and to watch it all unfold. Once they have this foundational background, mentors are much better equipped to be proactive in their mentoring. This also provides mentees the opportunity to watch the mentors interact with children. This is a crucial time for mentors to be centrally involved in the classroom, not to sit and watch. First impressions are important, and mentors should show their capability and their vulnerability. This is also an important time for mentors to set the expectation that they will be coaching or modeling in the classroom, not acting as another teacher or teaching assistant.

Very soon the mentors and mentees tackle the work of new skills development and practice. This also requires protected time. Dedicated time should be set aside for mentors and mentees to carry out the important steps in the mentoring process—to learn, model, practice, observe, receive feedback, and begin again. In addition to classroom time, meeting time must be set aside when the teacher does not have responsibility for children. Less that 1 hour per week is insufficient; 2 hours is more realistic, and 3 hours would be best.

Develop a Reward and Accountability System

A system of accountability should be developed for mentors and mentees based on project goals and the mentor job description. Project goals specify the knowledge and skills that teachers are to demonstrate, and the mentor job description details how to support mentees in achieving those goals. For example, a mentor and mentee might attend a professional development class together. The mentor models the skill for the mentee in the classroom; and then the mentee demonstrates the skill, receives feedback, and practices again. Once the skill is implemented consistently in the classroom, the project should acknowledge this increased competence through some type of reward system. This might be professional development credit, certificates, or recognition at meetings. It is important to recognize the achievements of both mentors and mentees, because they work as a team.

Set guidelines for teachers and mentors so that they know how often they are expected to meet, how many and which skills they should work on, and how they should document progress. Develop a form that documents mentor–mentee interactions. This form may specify the objective on which the mentee is working, the dates and type of modeling and support provided by the mentor, the dates on which the mentee demonstrated the skill for the mentor, the feedback and discussion between the mentor and mentee as a result of this observation, and the plan for future development. An example of such a form may be found in Appendix 5.1.

To achieve consistency across classrooms there must be clear expectations regarding what constitutes best practice in areas of language and literacy teaching. One important step in this regard is to use objective-based lesson plans that specify what children will learn as a result of each teaching activity. Mentors can play a key role in helping teachers develop these lesson plans. When everyone in the classroom knows what the children are supposed to be learning, it is easier to identify strengths and weaknesses in the curriculum, the environment, and the teaching that can then be addressed by mentors. To take this one step further, agencies may wish to develop checklists for the most important teaching skills. The checklist becomes a tool to plan the training and to evaluate the teachers' skills. An example of a dialogic reading checklist may be found in Appendix 5.2.

Evaluate Your Mentoring Program

Mentors and mentees should have the opportunity to evaluate the success of the mentoring program on a regular basis and to share perceived strengths and weaknesses with their supervisors. Because many aspects of the mentor–mentee relationship are confidential in nature, participants may feel more comfortable providing anonymous evaluations. One way to encourage feedback from all participants is to have mentees and mentors meet separately in a focus group. The focus group leader should be from outside the organization. The focus group leader comes to an evaluation session with questions designed to elicit feedback about how well the mentoring program is meeting its specific goals, suggestions for improvement, and ideas for new goals. This process promotes constructive criticism and brainstorming, and provides valuable information for mentors, mentees, and project supervisors. Findings from these sessions should be summarized by the focus group leader and incorporated into a document available to all participants. The document summarizes progress in meeting project goals and provides a starting place for an action plan for improvement.

Guard against Codependence

It is natural for people who work closely together to depend on one another, and in good mentor–mentee relationships teachers come to rely on the advice and support of their mentors, but there should be a planned obsolescence of the formalized mentor–mentee relationship. More new teachers need mentoring, and project goals change as old ones are achieved. For this reason it is important for mentors and mentees to know the expected duration of their relationship from the beginning. This should be spelled out in the project description. One year seems like the shortest length of time required for a mentor and mentee to develop an efficient working relationship and to achieve a small set of goals. Two years is better.

It is also wise for mentors to do some "cross-mentoring" in other classrooms so that mentees receive guidance from more than one experienced mentor and mentors have an opportunity to see how other teachers are progressing. One way to do this is to specify certain skills that the "home-based" mentor will address and others that might be covered by a mentor who has special expertise in that area. For example, the home-based mentor may work with his or her mentee on lesson planning, classroom environment, and dialogic reading, because these are critical to the everyday success of a quality program. Another mentor may work with several mentees on integrating technology into early literacy activities, because it is a specialized area of expertise. This kind of arrangement provides mentors with opportunities to mentor skills they especially like and also encourages them to continue their own professional growth.

Give careful consideration to where mentors' offices should be. If they "live" where their mentees live, it may be difficult to keep an appropriate distance. If they live where supervisors live, it may be difficult to keep confidentiality. Ideally, mentors have a space where they can meet and plan together, convenient to mentees' classrooms but in a different building. They should have resources such as laptop computers they can use at different sites and sufficient storage to organize their teaching materials.

Grow New Mentors

Good mentors are difficult to find. One solution to this dilemma is for projects to grow their own mentors. Identify within the organization skilled teachers who develop good relationships with others. If they are interested in becoming mentors, offer incentives for attending mentor training while they are still teaching, and give them the opportunity to apprentice under one of the best mentors. In this way the project supports the professional growth of the staff, and new mentors are ready when they are needed.

Use Mentors as a Valuable Resource

Mentors are valuable not only for their role with teachers but also as experts within the organization. Mentors may be the project's best "point people" for trying out new teaching approaches or materials, because they know the children, classrooms, and curricula, and have lots of teaching experience themselves. They also have an uncanny knack for knowing what will and what won't work, because they interact with people at all levels of the organization. Include mentors in project planning and evaluation meetings. Recognize and reward their efforts.

Conclusions

Preschools are being challenged to improve their language and early literacy programs to achieve instructional excellence. Mentors are one of a preschool's best assets when the goal is to implement new teaching strategies and curricula relatively quickly, while also achieving a high level of quality. Like teachers, expert mentors are made, not born. A mentoring program should be thoughtfully designed based on the information in this chapter and other research-based resources. Program evaluation should determine the strengths and needs of the mentoring program each year so that it improves with age.

References

Bellm, D., Whitebook, M., & Hnatiuk, P. (1997). *The early childhood mentoring curriculum: A handbook for mentors.* Washington, DC: Center for the Childcare Workforce.

Birman, B., Desimone, L., Porter, A. C., & Garet, M. (2000). Designing professional development that works. *Educational Leadership, 57,* 28–33.

Crow, R., & Snyder, P. (1998). Organizational behavior management in early intervention: Status and implications for research and development. *Journal of Organizational Behavior Management, 18,* 131–156.

Freeman, G. D., & King, J. L. (2003). A partnership for school readiness. *Educational Leadership, 60,* 76–79.

Knowles, M. S. (1970). *The modern practice of adult education: Andragogy versus pedagogy.* New York: Association Press.

Lipton, L., Wellman, B., & Humbard, C. (2001). *Mentoring matters: A practical guide to learning-focused relationships.* Sherman, CT: Miravia, LLC.

Odell, S. J., & Ferraro, D. P. (1992). Teacher mentoring and teacher retention. *Journal of Teacher Education, 43,* 200–204.

Pavia, L., Nissen, H., Hawkins, C., Monroe, M. E., & Filimon-Demyen, D. (2003). Mentoring early childhood professionals. *Journal of Research in Childhood Education, 17,* 250–260.

Schepis, M. M., Ownbey, J. B., Parsons, M. B., & Reid, D. H. (2000). Training support staff for teaching young children with disabilities in an inclusive preschool setting. *Journal of Positive Behavior Interventions, 2,* 170–178.

Vaughn, S., & Coleman, M. (2004). The role of mentoring in promoting use of research-based practices in reading. *Remedial and Special Education, 25,* 25–38.

MENTOR LOG FOR LEVEL I SKILLS
(COMPLETE WITH THE TEACHER)

Teacher: _____   Mentor: _____

Example is not the main thing in influencing others. It is the only thing.—
Albert Schweitzer

With the teacher, select one of the skills checklists:

☐ Trophies Curriculum   ☐ Curriculum-Based Measures

☐ Big Math Curriculum   ☐ Kindergarten Transition

☐ Dramatic Play   ☐ School–Home Connection

☐ Vocabulary   ☐ Technology

☐ Scaffolded Conversation   ☐ Post Office Pals

☐ Outdoor Literacy   ☐ Dialogic Reading (see

☐ Lesson Planning I   Appendix 5.2)

☐ Other: ☐ Classroom Environment I

FOCUSED MODELING PLAN

Which skills from the checklist would you particularly like to see modeled?

What setting? (e.g., small-group book reading, block area, dramatic play area)

What date and time?

Will this be videotaped?   Yes   No   If yes, who will set up?

(continued)

FOCUSED TEACHER OBSERVATION PLAN

☐ Date–time for teacher observation

_____

☐ Setting for teacher observation

_____

☐ Will the session be videotaped?   ☐ Yes   ☐ No   If yes, who will set up?

☐ Mentor completes the entire skills checklist focusing especially on skills that were modeled

☐ Teacher completes self rating of the entire skills checklist focusing especially on targeted skills

☐ Date, time, location for feedback conference

_____

☐ Script the teacher and children during the observation if applicable

Teacher–Child Sample	Mentor Notes

(continued)

FEEDBACK CONFERENCE NOTES

1. Ask teacher to summarize her impressions and assessment of the skills demonstrated by referring to her skills checklist.
   "Looking at your skills checklist, how would you assess your teaching?"

2. Ask teacher to reflect on positive aspects of her assessment.
   "Which skills were you most pleased with?"

3. Build on the positive aspects of the teacher's reflections.
   "Yes, and I saw you X" (referring to your notes on the skills checklist or sample).

4. Ask teacher to reflect on what they might do to improve their teaching.
   "What would you like to change or improve?"

5. Build on that goal by reviewing comments and examples from the Mentor's Skills Checklist.
   "OK, I noted that you did X . . . perhaps X would have a better result."

6. Review remainder of skills checklist for additional goals.
   "What other skills from the checklist should we work on?"

7. Develop action plan for the following 5 days.
   "OK let's prioritize our goals for the next 5 days. What specifically do you want to work on and how can I help you?"

(continued)

ACTION PLAN

Goal 1:

Teacher will prepare by:

Mentor will support by:

Goal 2:

Teacher will prepare by:

Mentor will support by:

Goal 3:

Teacher will prepare by:

Mentor will support by:

Teacher Signature	Mentor Signature	Date

DIALOGIC READING CHECKLIST

Score _____ out of 50 _____%

Evaluator Name: _____

Date–Time of Observation: _____

☐ Observation 1   ☐ Observation 2   ☐ Observation 3

Description: Dialogic reading is to be observed in action. Review lesson plans for the skill objectives to be taught. Dialogic reading should be developmentally appropriate and engaging for children. Evaluators should check the strategies observed (not all strategies will be used at one time). Evaluators should write brief, objective comments supporting their rating under each item.

Dialogic reading	5 Exemplary	4 Consistent	3 Some	2 Minimal	1 None
1. Teaching objectives for dialogic reading are specified on the weekly lesson plan.					
2. Teaching team has pre-read book, developing questions corresponding to the story/theme.					
3. Teaching team uses the interaction strategies of **PEER**:					
☐ **P**rompts the child to say something about the book					
☐ **E**valuates the response					
☐ **E**xpands the child's response by rephrasing and adding information					
☐ **R**epeats the prompt to make sure the child has learned from expansion?					
4. Teaching team uses the question strategies of **CROWD**:					
☐ **C**ompletion prompts					
☐ **R**ecall prompts					

(continued)

Dialogic reading	5 Exemplary	4 Consistent	3 Some	2 Minimal	1 None
☐ **O**pen-ended prompts ☐ **Wh**- prompts (what, where, when, why, how) ☐ **D**istancing prompts					
5. Teaching team ensures that children are involved in dialogic, small-group reading, storytelling, book choice activities, and/or narrative computer instruction a minimum of 50 minutes per day for 5-hour programs or 110 minutes per day for 8- to 11-hour programs.					
6. Teaching team ensures that children are read a variety of developmentally appropriate text types that directly support teaching objectives and themes each week, including: ☐ Narratives ☐ Pattern books ☐ Expository books					
7. Teaching team uses expression and voice to make the story come alive for the children.					
8. Children are active learners, involved and engaged in the story being presented.					
9. The children are given sufficient time (pause) to respond to questions/prompts.					
10. Teaching team enhances children's print and word awareness (verbally and nonverbally).					
Total Points					**/50**

CHAPTER 6

★★★★★★★★

Formative Assessment of Classrooms

Using Classroom Observations
to Improve Implementation Quality

Bridget K. Hamre
Jennifer LoCasale-Crouch
Robert C. Pianta

It would be ideal if all one had to do to ensure young children's exposure to the highest quality learning environments was to provide classrooms and teachers with sufficient materials and an evidence-based curriculum. Anyone who has worked in school settings, however, knows that ensuring high-quality learning environments is not that easy. Although teacher qualifications, curricula, and adult–child ratios are important to consider in the development of high-quality early childhood settings, none of these is sufficient to guarantee that children will receive high-quality instruction and social supports (Early et al., 2006; LoCasale-Crouch et al., 2007; Pianta et al., 2005). In other words, if we give the same curriculum to 20 teachers, children in each of their classrooms will experience something quite different, even if all of these teachers are well-educated and experienced, and the curriculum has been shown to be effective.

We saw a vivid illustration of this phenomenon as a part of a recent project in which 160 teachers across one state were provided with explicit daily lesson plans from research-based curricula in literacy, language, and social development. Each teacher sent in videotapes of themselves teaching lessons from the curricula every other week. These tapes were viewed by both consultants, who worked with the teachers, and trained observers, who coded the tapes using a standardized measure of classroom quality. Both the consultants and the neutral observers noticed significant variation in the quality of teachers' lesson implementation. Some teachers were well prepared, had positive relationships with students, used effective behavior management, and were able to engage students in the lessons. Other teachers clearly hadn't looked at the lessons before implementing them, were quite negative in their interactions with students, read directly from lesson scripts without intonation or interest, and had such significant management problems that none of the children benefited from the lessons. Even among teachers following the same lesson plan who were well-prepared and effective at engaging the children, one teacher might focus on vocabulary, whereas another might focus on the structure and layout of print materials—same lesson, effective teachers, but different outcomes for children.

It has long been understood that teachers show considerable variability in their instructional interactions with children, and the observations we have described converge with this understanding such situations occur frequently in the early childhood field, particularly as centers and preschools move to using formal curricula but fail to provide adequate supports for high-quality implementation of them. In this chapter, we describe ways to make data-driven decisions based on systematic classroom observations to help address the problem of variable implementation among teachers. We discuss the use of observational formative assessments of classrooms to provide teachers with individualized, ongoing, and collaborative feedback targeted explicitly on practices that we know make a difference to children's development. Because this process is based on standardized classroom observations, it has the benefit of providing early childhood program administrators with direct evidence of the effectiveness of their programs and efforts to improve them.

A Model for Using Formative Assessment with Teachers

"Formative" assessment is any assessment process in which evidence is gathered to provide ongoing feedback to the person being assessed, so that person can change or adapt his or her performance in response to the feedback. This term has typically been used in relation to student learning, with consistent evidence that students of teachers who use formative assessment effectively make greater academic progress than do students of teachers who fail to use these practices (Black & William, 1998). This type of assessment is also very common in the business world, where quality control and adherence to performance standards are strong foci. However, the concept of formative assessment is also applicable to teachers' performance, although it has rarely been used in that regard, particularly when standardized performance metrics are the source of data and feedback. Many professional development efforts with teachers are aimed at improving the quality of their social and instructional interactions with students, but few of these efforts are guided by any evidence as to how to make the professional development experiences most relevant and helpful to individual teachers. Rather, in the typical model for professional development, all teachers within a school attend inservice trainings, with the content based on the interests of principals or other administrators, or assumptions about the needs of faculty. We assert that just as student learning can be significantly enhanced when teachers use a formative assessment model, the quality of teaching can be improved through the systematic use of observation as a formative assessment tool.

One of the tenets of formative assessment is that there is an ongoing feedback loop between information gained in assessments and the types of interventions offered (Boston, 2002). Figure 6.1 depicts a model in which the systematic use of observations with teachers can function as an assessment tool to create a feedback loop between the practice of teaching and professional development opportunities, including workshops and more targeted mentoring and support programs (Pianta, 2005). In this way, professional development opportunities are targeted to the individual needs of a teacher or group of teachers.

A critical feature of this model lies in the definition of what constitutes high-quality early childhood instruction. Despite a long history of debate over this issue, there is growing consensus around a set of practices linked to children's social and academic development (Hamre & Pianta, 2007). Consistent with recent converging evidence from large studies of early childhood environments (Howes et al., in press; Mashburn et al., in press), in this chapter we take the view that teachers' daily interactions with students are the most important part of teaching practice and the components of the classroom environment most closely associated with students' positive development. Thus, when we talk about quality teaching practices, or implementation quality, we are referring to the ways in which teachers and children interact with one another. In the next section we describe in more detail a framework for understanding and measuring these high-quality interactions.

There are three steps that early childhood centers and preschools can take to implement formative assessment consistent with the model presented in Figure 6.1; each is explained in greater detail below. The first step involves the systematic use of a validated observational tool to help assess the needs of teachers, at both center and individual levels. It is not sufficient to use any available observational tool for this process. Rather,

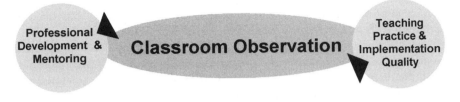

FIGURE 6.1. Formative assessment for teachers using standardized observation.

to ensure that professional development efforts target classroom components that actually make a difference for young children, it is critical that the tool used for observation provides evidence of links to children's social and academic development. The second step is to develop targeted professional development experiences based directly on information from the classroom observations. We discuss one model of supervision and mentoring that can be used to provide individualized feedback and support to teachers to improve their implementation of any curriculum. The final step involves use of observation to document changes in practice, thus providing direct evidence of the success of interventions or information about ways interventions may need to be modified to provide teachers with the support they need.

Selecting and Using Standardized Observational Tools

Systematic observation in teaching has long been identified as a powerful way to describe educational practices, investigate inequities, and improve both teachers' classroom practice based on feedback and teacher education programs (Millman & Darling-Hammond, 1990). However, until recently, few programs used *standardized* observational measures, which is a key part of targeting professional development resources systematically to improve implementation quality.

Two important features of standardized observation tools make them more useful than other observation systems for classroom formative assessment: reliability and validity. A reliable tool is one that provides a process for training observers to make reliable judgments about what they see; a valid tool is one that provides evidence that what is observed is linked to important child outcomes.

Reliability is an essential characteristic of a good observation tool, because if the tool does not measure things consistently, or reliably, then one cannot assume that the scores are an accurate reflection of the actual classroom processes. For example, if two persons observe in a classroom for 20 minutes, then provide that classroom a quality score from 1 to 10, without any common agreement on what quality is, they are very unlikely to give similar scores. Each person may end up looking at, and making judgments about, different parts of the classroom. One person may think the teacher is very nice and give the classroom a 10, whereas the other might dislike the way she is teaching and give the classroom a 2. Although individual thoughts and reflections about classrooms are important, it is essential that programs adopt a more standardized view of quality implementation to make systematic progress toward improved practice. To do this, standardized observational tools provide training and also typically require observers to pass a reliability test prior to use of the measure.

Validity, also an essential characteristic of a good observation tool, refers to whether what is being observed actually captures what is important; in other words, validity considers whether we are measuring something about classrooms that actually matters. We could easily have a measure that provides reliable scores on things that we do not care about, but this measure would not be a valid indicator of processes related to children's social and academic development. For example, we could measure the number of desks in a classroom. It would be easy to learn how to use this measure reliably, but it would not be very important in terms of child outcomes.

In the choice of a standardized observational tool for observing what happens in classrooms, program administrators should look for tools that have a formal and well-documented training protocol, and empirical evidence linking observations to child outcomes. In terms of the latter, research supports the view that components of classrooms most closely associated to children's social and academic development are their daily interactions with teachers and peers (Hamre & Pianta, 2005; Mashburn et al., in press; National Institute of Child Health and Human Development [NICHD] Early Child Care Research Network [ECCRN], 2000). Thus, we recommend using observational tools that focus explicitly on these interactions. An additional reason to focus on interactions rather than on other aspects of classrooms (e.g., furnishings and curricula) is that teachers have much more control over these aspects of the classroom; thus, they are more amenable to change through professional support and development.

The Classroom Assessment Scoring System

One observational tool designed explicitly to characterize the quality of the interactions between teachers and children is the Classroom Assessment Scoring System (CLASS; Pianta, La Paro, & Hamre, in press), which provides reliable and valid measures of classroom interactions and has been used widely in research, including the National Center for Early Development and Learning's (NCEDL) two large-scale studies of state pre-K programs in 11 states (Early et al., 2005; Pianta et al., 2005). Other standardized observational systems, such as the Early Childhood Environ-ment Rating Scale (ECERS; Harms, Clifford, & Cryer, 1998) and the Early Literacy and Language Classroom Observation toolkit (ELLCO; Smith, Dickinson, Sangeorge, & Anastasopoulos, 2002), may also be used in a formative assessment process, although both measures focus on a mixture of interactions and other, more structural features of classrooms.

Derived from developmental theory and validated by decades of research in educational settings that directly connect teacher interactions with children's classroom experience, the CLASS focuses exclusively on teachers' instructional, language, and social interactions with children (La Paro, Pianta, & Stuhlman, 2004). CLASS describes three broad domains of teacher quality: emotional support, classroom organization, and in-structional support. Each domain comprises individual dimensions pro-viding unique information about implementation quality. Table 6.1 pro-vides a complete description of these dimensions. Below, we briefly review studies that have used the CLASS to provide an overall description of classroom quality and links between this quality and student outcomes.

Research using the CLASS, including the over 700 preschool class-rooms in 11 states in the NCEDL Multistate and statewide early education program (SWEEP) studies (Early et al., 2005), shows that, in general, emo-tional support and classroom organization are typically only at moderate levels of quality within preschool programs; instructional support is typi-cally at a low level of quality. Interestingly, one of the most dramatic find-ings from these studies was the high degree of variability among pro-grams (LoCasale-Crouch et al., 2007; Pianta et al., 2005). As displayed in Figure 6.2, out of 700 pre-K classrooms studied using the CLASS, 15% were rated as showing high levels of support to children, whereas 19% provided moderate to low levels, across the CLASS domains; the rest fell somewhere in between (LoCasale-Crouch et al., 2007). This variability was not equally distributed across the population: Classrooms with the lowest quality were also those with the heaviest concentration of disadvan-taged children.

There is strong evidence that this variability in classroom quality is important to children's development. Within the NCEDL studies, even though only a small percentage of pre-K children actually experience high-quality classrooms as measured by CLASS, children in the highest quality classrooms finished the pre-K year with higher academic achieve-ment than their peers in other classrooms (Howes et al., 2006; Mashburn et al., in press). These findings are consistent with results from other stud-ies showing that children in higher quality preschool classrooms enter school with better language development, math skills, and reading skills (Burchinal, Peisner-Feinberg, Bryant, & Clifford, 2000; Howes et al., in press; Pianta, LaParo, Payne, Cox, & Bradley, 2002). Clearly, pre-K pro-grams that provide sufficient emotional, organizational, and instructional

TABLE 6.1. CLASS Framework for Early Childhood Classroom Quality

Area	Dimension	Description
Emotional support	Classroom climate	Reflects the overall emotional tone of the classroom and the connection between teachers and students. Considers the warmth and respect displayed in teachers' and students' interactions with one another as well as the degree to which they display enjoyment and enthusiasm during learning activities.
	Teacher sensitivity	Encompasses teachers' responsivity to students' needs and awareness of students' level of academic and emotional functioning. Highly sensitive teachers help students see adults as a resource and create an environment in which students feel safe and free to explore and learn.
	Regard for student perspectives	Considers the degree to which teachers' interactions with students and classroom activities place an emphasis on students' interests, motivations, and points of view, rather than being very teacher-driven. This may be demonstrated by teachers' flexibility within activities and respect for students' autonomy to participate in and initiate activities.
Classroom organization	Behavior management	Encompasses teachers' ability to use effective methods to prevent and redirect misbehavior, by presenting clear behavioral expectations and minimizing time spent on behavioral issues.
	Productivity	Considers how well teachers manage instructional time and routines, so that students have the maximum opportunity to learn.
	Instructional learning formats	Considers the degree to which teachers maximize students' engagement and ability to learn by providing interesting activities, instruction, centers, and materials. Considers the manner in which teachers facilitate activities, so that students have opportunities to experience, perceive, explore, and utilize materials.
Instructional support	Concept development	Examines the degree to which instructional discussions and activities promote students' higher order thinking skills versus focus on rote and fact-based learning.
	Quality of feedback	Considers teachers' provision of feedback focused on expanding learning and understanding (formative evaluation), not correctness or the end product (summative evaluation).
	Language modeling	Examines the quality and amount of teachers' use of language-stimulation and language-facilitation techniques, including self and parallel talk, open-ended questions, repetition, expansion/extension, and use of advanced language.
	Literacy focus	Examines the degree to which teachers explicitly, purposefully, and systematically make connections for students about precursory concepts of written and oral language related to literacy development, including print units, alphabet letters, book organization and print concepts, and phonological units (syllables, onset–rime, phonemes).

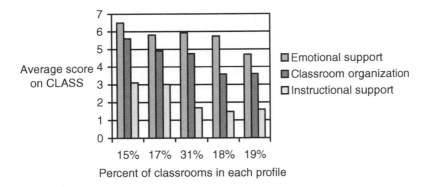

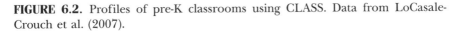

FIGURE 6.2. Profiles of pre-K classrooms using CLASS. Data from LoCasale-Crouch et al. (2007).

supports offer a potentially powerful intervention in addressing school readiness for children at risk for school failure. Thus, the promise of early childhood education depends in large part on the professional development and training of teachers in the high-quality instructional and interaction skills that matter most for children's development (Zaslow & Martinez-Beck, 2006).

Conducting Observations to Assess Program and Classroom Needs

Once program administrators have chosen an observation tool for use, they need to develop a plan to assess classrooms. This typically begins with the necessary training on the observation tool. In the case of CLASS, this includes a 2-day training in which observers watch and practice scoring multiple videos, discuss these scores with a CLASS expert, and take a reliability test. Trained observers can then return to their programs and conduct observations. We typically recommend that observers arrange to visit a classroom at an unannounced time within a specific week, rather than scheduling a specific day and time to go to the classroom. By knowing roughly when a visit will occur, teachers typically feel prepared for the visit but do not develop specific plans or lessons that are atypical of their normal practice.

These classroom observations form the basis for decisions about staff professional development opportunities. For example, one common CLASS finding is that preschool classrooms tend to provide particularly low-quality instructional supports. Teachers rarely make use of strategies known to promote cognitive development, such as encouraging children to make predictions, engaging in conversations that follow the child's lead, or providing feedback that scaffolds the children's learning. Thus, program administrators may choose to bring in an expert on promoting cognitive development to provide a workshop to the whole staff. The observations also help identify teachers in need of support and provide specific information about the types of supports they need. In the next section, we discuss ways in which these initial assessments can be used to provide individualized feedback and support to teachers.

Providing Individualized Feedback and Support to Enhance Implementation Quality

Once program staff have conducted observations and identified specific goals for particular teachers, they must decide on the best way to intervene. Here, we draw upon our experiences providing individualized feedback and support to teachers within MyTeachingPartner (MTP), a University of Virginia professional development program for preschool teachers (Pianta et al., 2007). Although MTP shares many components with other models for supervision and mentoring, it is unique in its reliance on standardized observations as the central target for intervention. MTP uses the CLASS to define high-quality teaching and set targets for teachers. There are four basic steps to the MTP process: building supportive, collaborative relationships; developing a system for regular feedback based on observation; working with teachers to target discussions of practice on specific CLASS dimensions; and systematically working to enhance teachers' observational skills, reflection, feelings of effectiveness, and implementation quality.

Building Consistent, Positive, Collaborative Mentor–Teacher Relationships

In the MTP model, relationships form the foundation of a successful mentoring experience. Just as students perform best when they develop warm and supportive relationships with teachers, teachers need to form positive connections with mentors.[1] Teachers who feel that their mentors are interested in their professional development and lives outside of the classroom feel more comfortable talking openly about their struggles in the classroom. Yet time limitations and a push to meet external evaluation criteria often lead mentors to forget that their work with teachers is most effective if it occurs within the context of a warm, supportive rela-

---

[1]Throughout the sections below, which describe each of these steps in more detail, we refer to the person working with the teacher as a mentor, but this could be an outside consultant, supervisor, expert teacher, or other individual specifically identified to work with teachers.

tionship. Some specific steps mentors can take to support the development of these relationships include the following:

Be consistent. Establishing consistency in relationships is essential to relationship development. It is difficult for teachers to reach a level of comfort with any single mentor if they have to change every few months. To be most effective, mentoring relationship may continue over several years, with periods of more and less intensive work. However, it is possible to work for shorter periods of time. In either case, it is imperative that the mentor emphasize consistency in the work by establishing and keeping regular meeting times.

Be positive. Most people need to hear positive feedback even to begin to listen to more critical feedback. Teachers are no different. In fact, teachers are often exceptionally critical of their own work, and they need help seeing the things they are doing well. Focusing on the positive is important throughout the MTP process, but is most critical in the initial stages of relationship development and during stressful times, such as when a new, difficult child is enrolled in the class. This focus on the positive does not preclude the provision of more critical feedback but simply points to the importance of providing this more critical feedback within the context of a supportive relationship. Ultimately, feedback should provide a balance between noticing things teachers are doing well and supporting their focus on areas that are more challenging.

Support autonomy. A major goal of the MTP approach is to develop collaborative relationships in which teachers feel equally responsible for making mentoring sessions productive and useful. Although there are often inherent power imbalances in mentor–teacher relationships, particularly when a supervisor or center director is acting as mentor, teachers make the most progress when their mentors make an active effort to empower them in the process. This process of empowerment often occurs over time, with mentors providing more guidance in work early on and slowly working with teachers to take more responsibility.

Developing Systems for Regular Feedback

Systems need to be put in place to provide regular communication and feedback. Although the exact format may be adapted to fit the individual needs of preschools, and the technology used to support this process may vary, several key features that should be kept in mind when developing these systems:

• *Engaging teachers in the process of self-observation is critical.* The MTP model relies heavily on the use of videotapes, a feature central to the success of the model. It is not sufficient for mentors to go into classrooms to observe and to take notes, then meet with teachers to discuss these observations. Teachers consistently tell us that they are so busy during lesson implementation that they often barely remember what happened after it is over. In addition, the CLASS focus of attention on minute-to-minute interactions is impossible to do if teachers are not able to watch themselves teach. Often during our conversations following their viewing of videotapes, teachers tell us they noticed important behaviors of certain children that they had missed, or realized that they sounded harsh and critical. These types of revelations are much more powerful when made by teachers themselves rather than when a mentor simply tells them they are negative in interactions with students.

• *Change in practice is most likely if feedback occurs on a regular basis over an extended period of time.* As discussed earlier, consistency is critical to relationship development, but it is also important as a mechanism for maintaining momentum and moving teachers toward change in practice. In our initial MTP project, we worked with teachers on a 2-week cycle. During each 2-week period, the teachers videotaped themselves, received an edited version of the videotape to watch and reflect upon (with guided prompts), and engaged in a feedback session with a mentor. These 2-week cycles continued over the course of 2 years. Modifications to these time periods are possible. However, it is important not to let too much time elapse between meetings if progress is to be made.

• *The process requires engaging teachers in self-reflection, as well as targeted discussions with a mentor, to help move this reflection toward change in practice.* As described below, there is a structure for allowing teachers to watch and reflect on the videotapes independently and a time in which they can engage in these processes with a mentor. Although shared viewing of the videotape without an opportunity for independent observation and reflection is possible within the MTP model of mentoring, we find that their combination provides much more powerful intervention. Teachers are able to watch videotapes of themselves as many times as they want and to think about them, without the pressure of someone else commenting or looking on. In this way, teachers come to the mentoring session much more prepared and ready to discuss their teaching practice in an open way.

MTP uses a four-step cycle of feedback, as depicted in Figure 6.3. The first step of the mentoring cycle begins when the teacher videotapes herself teaching once every 2 weeks. The content of what she is teaching may vary depending on the focus of the mentoring work (e.g., literacy and language activities).

In the second step, the mentor then edits the classroom observation videotape and writes prompts designed to promote the teacher's reflec-

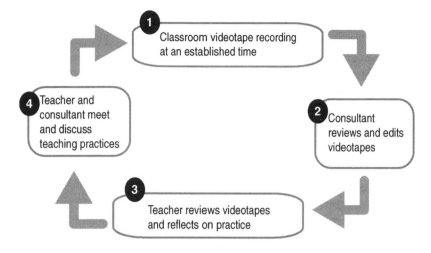

FIGURE 6.3. MTP mentoring cycle.

tive thought about specific classroom interactions as defined by CLASS. The edited videotape is a powerful tool, because it helps focus mentors' and teachers' attention on specific aspects of teaching practice. Most new computers come with videotape editing software that makes this process fairly simple from a technical standpoint, particularly when using digital video cameras. However, if editing in this way is beyond the technological capacities of staff, it is possible simply to choose a start and end time and have the teacher watch and reflect on that segment of the videotape. In our initial MTP work, which relied heavily on the Internet for providing professional development support to teachers across the state, these edited videotapes and prompts were posted on a secured website that only the teacher could view. However, this process can be completed in more low-tech ways by mailing or hand-delivering videotapes directly to teachers.

In the third step, the teacher views edited videotape and responds to prompts. The final step involves a mentoring session between the teacher and the consultant. These sessions can occur in person, over the phone, or via videoconference software on the Internet. During these sessions the teacher and the mentor discuss the edited classroom videotape and issues related to classroom performance, and determine goals for future cycles. The use of videotapes allows the consultant to provide support to the teacher without having to travel to the classroom. As a follow-up to the session, teachers can explore a website that includes several hundred videotaped examples of real teachers engaged in high-quality interactions with students, aligned with each CLASS dimension (e.g., teacher sensitivity, quality of feedback). These videotapes, each with accompanying text highlighting the high-quality teaching practices of relevance, are an incredible resource for teachers, because they provide explicit, real-world examples of how to actually implement evidence-based practices across a variety of teaching dimensions (e.g., relationship building, providing feedback, developing higher order thinking skills, etc.).

Deciding on a Focus for Mentoring Sessions

The MTP model is based on the premise that feedback and support are most helpful if they target specific areas of practice known to relate to children's social and academic development. Thus, each mentoring cycle focuses on a particular dimension of the CLASS. Due to the importance of relationships in the MTP model, we typically start work with teachers by focusing on a positive climate. Every teacher has examples of times in their classroom that illustrate a positive climate, and it is an aspect of the classroom to which teachers find it easy to relate. With some teachers we may keep working on the positive climate for a while, whereas with others we move quickly to other dimensions.

From that point on, decisions about the area of focus are made collaboratively with the teacher, based on the observational assessments described earlier, as well as on conversations about teachers' interests. Collaborating in this way allows teachers to take an active role in the process and increases their motivation for the work. Because we see this work as ongoing, we are able to be flexible in the focus of mentoring cycles, such that over time we cover both areas that may be most interesting to teachers and those indicated by the assessment as needing particular support.

In cases in which a school or center has led a CLASS inservice training, teachers may already be familiar with the CLASS dimensions. If not, we recommend having teachers spend time watching videotaped examples of the CLASS dimensions in order to help them decide which area seems most interesting (see the CLASS Video Library at *www.classobservation.com*).

Working toward Systematic Improvements in Implementation Quality

The ultimate goal of mentors' work is to help teachers improve their teaching practices. To do this, mentors help teachers to do the following:

- Become better *observers* of their own practice.
- *Reflect* on ways in which their knowledge about themselves, their students, and the practice of teaching are associated with their actual classroom practice.

- Feel more *effective* in their interactions with students.
- Increase the quality of their *implementation* of curricula and lessons.

In the MTP model, mentors help teachers meet these goals through an ongoing process of observation, discussion, and feedback. The goals are listed in order, from those we tend to focus on most heavily during initial work to those that come into focus during later sessions. However, we are usually working across these goals throughout our work with teachers. Even the most experienced teachers benefit from practice in self-observation, and even the most inexperienced novice teachers should start to think about ways they might change their interactions with students. Some examples of prompts that focus on these different goals are provided in Table 6.2.

Documenting Effectiveness and Modifying Interventions

Documenting the effectiveness of this type of professional development work with teachers is increasingly a requirement of federal grant packages, as well a necessary step for informing and modifying future work with teachers. In this final step of the process, program administrators return to the standardized observational protocols used in the initial step and examine changes in classroom processes that may have resulted from the professional development supports offered to teachers. There are a few factors to keep in mind when conducting these final assessments.

First, we recommend planning a formal system for evaluation from the beginning of the project that includes a timeline for collecting data in line with the planned mentoring and professional development work. This data collection includes, at the very minimum, a system for conducting observations at regular intervals throughout the intervention. To avoid bias, these observations should be conducted by someone other than the mentor. It is also a good idea to find ways to document teachers' and mentors' perceptions of the effectiveness of their work together, because this may be a critical factor in the ultimate success of the intervention.

Second, it is essential to recognize that behavioral change takes time, so looking for changes too soon can result in a lack of significant findings. The time required to effect change depends on several factors, including the intensity of the intervention, and the investment of the mentor and teacher in the process. In general, we recommend completing at least 8–10 mentoring cycles before expecting to document changes in behavior. Decisions about when to end mentoring supports need to be made on an individual basis and depend on a variety of factors, including available resources, teacher motivation, and the results of observations.

TABLE 6.2. Strategies and Sample Prompts for Improving Self-Observation, Reflection, Feelings of Self-Efficacy, and Implementation Quality

Teacher goals— improvements in . . .	Mentor strategy	Example strategy or prompt
Self-observation	Move teacher from making global to more specific observations.	*Global*: "I was really struggling with behavior during this lesson." *Specific*: "I notice that I spent a lot of time telling the students to sit still with their hands in their laps. Each time I remind them it works for about a minute and then I have to remind them again. It is taking a lot of time out of the lesson."
	Model observational statements while watching video with teachers.	"I see you are asking a lot of close-ended questions in this segment of the lesson, and students are responding with 'yes' and 'no.' "
Reflection	Ask questions focused on links between knowledge and observed practice.	"I know you are taking a course right now in child development and that you just covered attachment theory. How do you see your students' relational history impacting the way they interact with you in the classroom? During this video clip, tell me about one student who you see may be struggling with relationships and what you are doing to support him or her."
Feelings of self-efficacy	Draw attention to things teachers are doing well.	"In this video I notice that you are really working to promote your students' abilities to think deeply about the world around them. What specific strategies and questions are you using to promote their thinking? How can you tell when they seem to get it?"
	Focus attention on situations when teachers' behaviors have a direct effect on a child.	"In this clip I notice that you are struggling to get Kayla's attention. What specific strategy finally worked? How might you think about doing this differently next time so that she is able to attend more quickly?"
	Engage in discussions of challenging children, with a focus on disconfirming stereotypes.	"We've often talked about how hard it is for Elena to get along with her peers. What do you notice about her in this clip? What factors do you think may be helping her get along with others during this activity?"
Implementation quality	Generate ideas about alternative approaches.	"We've been talking a lot about finding ways to promote children's language during whole-group lessons. In this clip the children are sitting listening to you talk for about 5 minutes before they get to join in. How might you introduce this lesson differently next time to get them talking and participating a bit earlier?"

Finally, program administrators should remember that implementation quality is not simply a function of the teacher, but a complex interaction between the teacher and students, and other classroom factors. Although the feedback process we described focuses heavily on the teacher's role in making changes, it is sometimes the case that, through this process, program staff recognize that systematic changes are needed to promote real change in classroom practices. For example, because some teachers work much better with specific populations of students, such as English language learners or children with emotional difficulties, changes in classroom assignment of students may be helpful. Or mentors may find that, across many teachers, they are having a hard time increasing their teachers use of language modeling and concept development strategies, in large part because of the way their current curricula structure activities. In these cases, program administrators may consider alternative curricular packages. Mentors and program administrators can come together on a regular basis to discuss the mentoring and assessment process to facilitate discussion of some of these outside influences on implementation quality that may warrant attention.

Conclusions

This chapter describes a process through which preschool programs engage in a process of self-assessment and improvement. Critical to the success of this work is the use of standardized measures for observation to make data-driven decisions about the needs of individual teachers. Observation tools used in this way should have documented information on reliability and validity. The development of supportive mentoring relationships is also critical, because these relationships provide teachers with ongoing opportunities to reflect upon and change their interactions with students. Although this type of intensive assessment and professional development support requires a significant investment of time and resources, it is also much more likely than the more typical inservice workshop to lead to real changes in practice. Given what we know about the current quality of preschool programs, it is clear that as preschool programs expand, adapt new curricula, and hire new teachers, provision of this type of ongoing, personalized support for teachers will be a key to their success.

Acknowledgments

This work was conducted as a part of the MyTeachingPartner Research Group, supported by the National Institute of Child Health and Human Development and the Interagency Consortium on School Readiness. It was also supported by a grant from the Foundation for Child Development.

References

Black, P., & William, D. (1998). Inside the black box: Raising standards through classroom assessment. *Phi Delta Kappan, 80*(2), 139–148. Available at *www.pdkintl.org/kappan/kbla9810.htm*.

Boston, C. (2002). The concept of formative assessment. *Practical Assessment, Research and Evaluation, 8*(9). Retrieved August 25, 2006, from *pareonline.net/getvn.asp?v=8&n=9*.

Burchinal, M. R., Peisner-Feinberg, E., Bryant, D. M., & Clifford, R. (2000). Children's social and cognitive development and child care quality: Testing for different associations related to poverty, gender, or ethnicity. *Journal of Applied Developmental Sciences, 4*, 149–165.

Early, D., Barbarin, O., Bryant, O., Burchinal, M., Chang, F., Clifford, R., et al. (2005). *Prekindergarten in eleven states: NCEDL's Multistate Study of Pre-Kindergarten and Study of State-wide Early Education Programs.* Retrieved December 1, 2005, from *www.fpg.unc.edu/NCEDL/pdfs/SWEEP_MS summary_final.pdf*.

Early, D., Bryant, D., Pianta, R. C., Clifford, R., Burchinal, M., Ritchie, S., et al. (2006). Are teachers' education, major, and credentials related to classroom quality and children's academic gains in pre-kindergarten? *Early Childhood Research Quarterly, 21*, 174–195.

Hamre, B. K., & Pianta, R. C. (2005). Can instructional and emotional support in the first grade classroom make a difference for children at risk of school failure? *Child Development, 76*(5), 949–967.

Hamre, B. K., & Pianta, R. C. (2007). Learning opportunities in preschool and early elementary classrooms. In R. C. Pianta, M. J. Cox, & K. Snow (Eds.), *The new American elementary school.* Baltimore: Brookes.

Harms, T., Clifford, R. M., & Cryer, D. (1998). *Early Childhood Environment Rating Scale: Revised Edition.* New York: Teachers College Press.

Howes, C., Burchinal, M., Pianta, R., Bryant, D., Early, D., Clifford, R., et al. (in press). Ready to learn?: Children's pre-academic achievement in pre-kindergarten programs. *Early Childhood Research Quarterly*.

La Paro, K., Pianta, R., & Stuhlman, M. (2004). Classroom Assessment Scoring System (CLASS): Findings from the pre-K year. *Elementary School Journal, 104*(5), 409–426.

LoCasale-Crouch, J., Konold, T., Pianta, R., Howes, C., Burchinal, M., Bryant, D., et al. (2007). Profiles of observed classroom quality in state-funded pre-kindergaten programs and associations with teacher, program, and classroom characteristics. *Early Childhood Research Quarterly, 22*(1), 3–17.

Mashburn, A. J., Pianta, R. C., Hamre, B. K., Downer, J. T., Barbarin, O., Bryant, D., et al. (in press). Pre-k program standards and children's development of academic and language skills. *Child Development*.

Millman, J., & Darling-Hammond, L. (Eds.). (1990). *The new handbook of teacher evaluation: Assessing elementary and secondary school teachers.* Newbury Park, CA: Corwin Press.

National Institute of Child Health and Human Development, Early Child Care Research Network. (2000). The relation of child care to cognitive and language development. *Child Development, 71*(4), 960–980.

Pianta, R. (2005). Standardized observation and professional development: A focus on individualized implementation and practices. In M. Zaslow & I. Martinez-Beck (Eds.), *Critical issues in early childhood professional development* (pp. 231–254). Baltimore: Brookes.

Pianta, R. C., Howes, C., Burchinal, M., Bryant, D., Clifford, R., Early, C., et al. (2005). Features of pre-kindergarten programs, classrooms, and teachers: Do they predict observed classroom quality and child–teacher interactions? *Applied Developmental Science, 9*(3), 144–159.

Pianta, R. C., La Paro, K. M., & Hamre, B. K. (in press). *Classroom Assessment Scoring System [CLASS].* Baltimore: Brookes.

Pianta, R. C., La Paro, K., Payne, C., Cox, M., & Bradley, R. (2002). The relation of kindergarten classroom environment to teacher, family, and school characteristics and child outcomes. *Elementary School Journal, 102*(3), 225–238.

Pianta, R. C., Mashburn, A. J., Downer, J. D., Hamre, B. K., & Justice, L. (2007). *Effects of web-mediated professional development resources on teacher–child interactions in pre-kindergarten classrooms.* Manuscript submitted for publication.

Smith, M., Dickinson, D., Sangeorge, A., & Anastasopoulos, L. (2002). *Early Literacy and Language Classroom Observation Scale (ELLCO).* Baltimore: Brookes.

Zaslow, M., & Martinez-Beck, I. (2006). *Critical issues in early childhood professional development.* Baltimore: Brookes.

CHAPTER 7

★★★★★★★★

Are Early Childhood Classrooms Preparing Children to Be School Ready?

The CIRCLE Teacher Behavior Rating Scale

Mike A. Assel
Susan H. Landry
Paul R. Swank

The pre-K classroom is alive with activity. Without being able to see inside the mind of a child, the adults in the classroom observe imagination and creativity in the dramatic play area, multiple writing stations, science corner, and building areas. The lead teacher in the classroom is sitting in the middle of a group of children taking down dictation and asking questions like "What kind of things are you thankful for?" Another adult, Sarah Granbery, is sitting unobtrusively in the classroom with a clipboard, intently listening to how the lead teacher responds to children, as well as occasionally smiling at children who approach her during this classroom observation session. Part of Ms. Granbery's job as a mentor to 20 pre-K teachers in her school district is to complete the Center for Improving the Readiness of Children for Learning and Education (CIRCLE) Teacher Behavior Rating Scale (TBRS). She plans to be in the classroom for 2½ to 3 hours. Ms. Granbery is actively scanning the TBRS and rating the classroom teacher on a variety of activities, such as writing down children's responses so that they can see what they said in print. When one of the children tells the classroom teacher that she is thankful for her grandmother's cooking, the teacher listens intently and then responds to the bright-eyed 4-year-old by prompting, "Tell me about some of your favorite foods that your grandmother cooks." The child immediately responds that she "loves Granny's cookies because they have chocolate chips." Ms. Granbery casually flips to the Oral Language subscale of the TBRS and makes a few marks to indicate the quality of the teacher's verbal responses to children.

Following this dictation activity, the teacher announces in an excited voice, "It's time for circle time," and leads children into "The Name Game" song during this transition. The children become giddy if their teacher uses their name in this silly rhyming song. Many of the children join the singing.

Jack, Jack, bo-back,

Banana-fana fo-fack

Mee-mi-mo-mack

Jack

Ms. Granbery, who is still observing the classroom activities, moves to the section of the TBRS labeled Phonological Awareness and makes a few notations in the Rhyming section. Although Ms. Granbery recognizes that singing one song will not be likely to make children successful academically, she also knows that children's exposure to rhyming is one of the steps along the phonological continuum. Turning back to her classroom observation, in which she sees that the teacher is preparing the children for a book-reading session about the approaching Thanksgiving holiday, Ms. Granbery notices that the classroom is decorated with Thanksgiving artwork and that centers across the classroom contain themed materials. Ms. Granbery makes a notation of this observation in the Centers subscale of the TBRS.

While the children nap a little later in the day, Ms. Granbery meets with the classroom teacher and details all of the strong early literacy and math activities she observed. She also highlights goals for upcoming weeks and reminds the teacher that she will be back next month. This meeting between mentor and teacher can best be described as a conversation between colleagues. Although she commends the teacher for providing opportunities for child dictation, Ms. Granbery suggests that this small-group activity could be somewhat stronger if children were allowed access to writing materials while the teacher was taking dictation. She also suggests that children's writing samples be placed into portfolios to track their written expression skills progress across the course of the year. Upon leaving the school, Ms. Granbery recalls that this classroom looks very different now compared to when she first visited in August.

The importance of the classroom environment and the impact that this environment has on children's learning have been of interest to educators and researchers for years. Determining the most efficient ways to evaluate the quality of the teaching environment in pre-K settings is critically important as programs strive to achieve excellence. Reports on the portrait of American children entering kindergarten suggest that many children leaving pre-K lack the language, literacy, and social skills needed to succeed in the kindergarten classroom (Zill & West, 2001). This occurs to a large degree because too many of the nation's children are attending early child care programs of such low quality and do not achieve school readiness skills (Helburn, 1995); this problem is magnified for children from low-income households, who are more likely than advantaged children to attend low-quality programs (Smith, Blank, & Collins, 1992). A large body of research documents the critical importance of early experiences for learning (Bradley, Caldwell, & Rock, 1988; Landry, Smith, Swank, Assel, & Vellet, 2001; Molfese, 1989; Neville et al., 1998). Because of this research, we are beginning to understand that improving the quality of early childhood education must be a key goal for the 21st century.

In this chapter, we discuss a tool that may be used to determine the extent to which an early childhood classroom exhibits features consistent with high-quality language and literacy instruction. We describe the research behind the tool, based on the premise that educators and administrators must select tools that are developed in a rigorous empirical process. This tool is used to help classrooms become high-quality learning environments. For our purposes in this chapter, "high quality" refers to early childhood classroom environments that provide children who enter kindergarten with the full range of skills they need to succeed in elementary school, including the foundational skills necessary to learn to read (i.e., early literacy skills) and the ability to use language as a tool of expression. Skills across the language and literacy domains are established as important ingredients for school readiness. The mounting research evidence on reading precursors (e.g., print knowledge, phonological awareness) also confirms the importance of foundational reading skills, and readers are referred to James F. Christie (Chapter 2, this volume) for a review of this literature.

As they strive to improve children's skills in these areas, program staff often use tools to provide formative and summative guidance on how staff members are doing. However, some of the most widely used early childhood classroom observation measures, such as the Early Childhood Environment Rating Scale—Revised Edition (ECERS-R; Harms, Clifford, & Cryer, 1998) and the Early Language and Literacy Classroom Observation toolkit (ELLCO; Smith & Dickinson, 2002), do not include measurement of classroom practices that are most likely to promote skills in fundamental areas associated with school readiness. Rather, these measures attempt to identify whether programs exhibit relatively general aspects that are consistent with positive and supportive caregiving environments. Although these types of measures are frequently used to assess the quality of early childhood classrooms, and are certainly beneficial in many regards, there is limited evidence that high scores on these measures predict better child outcomes (Dickinson, 2006).

In this chapter, we focus most intensively on use of a tool that is well-aligned with instructional practices geared toward improving children's early literacy and language skills. Ensuring that early childhood classroom environments support skills within the domains of reading and language is critical, because both are necessary for early decoding and later reading comprehension (Juel, Griffith, & Gough, 1986). When children are exposed to instructional activities that promote print knowledge and phonological awareness, for instance, they are more likely to have success in learning to read (e.g., Box & Aldridge, 1993; Lonigan, 2003; Lonigan, Burgess, Anthony, & Barker, 1998). Building language skills through activities (e.g., read-alouds and word walls) support later skills, such as literacy, problem solving, and social competence.

Researchers at University of Texas Health Science Center at Houston developed the CIRCLE Teacher Behavior Rating Scale (TBRS; Landry, Crawford, Gunnewig, & Swank, 2001) because of the lack of an available classroom observation measure to target enriched learning activities in these important skill areas. The first goal in the development of this classroom observation measure was that it would be sensitive to classroom environments and instructional practices that promote the skills important for school readiness. A second goal was to ensure that the instructional areas measured were predictive of change in children's literacy and language skills, thus providing documentation that improvement in teaching practices would promote improvements in children's academic readiness. (A more recent version of the tool includes a focus on mathematics as well; however, given the focus of this book, in this chapter we focus our discussion on an earlier version of the tool that focused primarily on language and literacy skills.)

The opportunity to evaluate whether the TBRS met these goals was initiated in 1999, with the development of an extensive professional development (PD) program whose aim was to improve the quality of Head Start programs in Texas (Landry, Swank, Smith, Assel, & Gunnewig, 2006) and to evaluate whether the programs were effective (i.e., whether they improved participating children's literacy, math, and social skills). The PD program delivered to the Head Start teachers focused on the following content areas: (1) general professional practices (including room organization, daily routines, and use of supportive and responsive interactive teaching styles); (2) language enrichment and "scaffolding" of children's language throughout the day; (3) book reading in ways that promote language/literacy skills; (4) effective teaching strategies to build language comprehension and expression; (5) strategies that promote print and book awareness; (6) age-appropriate literature to enhance children's motivation to read; (7) instructional approaches focusing on phonological awareness; (8) developmentally appropriate activities that foster alphabet knowledge and early word recognition skills; and (9) approaches that develop early written expression skills. Training in this PD program emphasized research-based means of enhancing early literacy skills, which included developing lesson plans and integrating literacy materials and activities into all parts of the day (e.g., centers, transition activities). In particular, the practice of conducting effective book readings to target specific vocabulary and to build learning activities, such as "story extenders," was an integral focus of PD activities. Because the TBRS targeted these same behaviors, observations of classroom teachers prior to and following training was combined with pre- and posttesting of children's gains in early literacy skills. The TBRS was used in this PD program as both a process measure (i.e., a means to guide the practices of mentors working directly with the Head Start teachers enrolled in the project) and an outcome measure (i.e., a means to determine whether quality improved in the classrooms of the Head Start teachers who received the PD program).

Overview of the TBRS

The TBRS contains 63 items across 13 separate content areas. Most items utilize both a 3-point scale to evaluate the *quantity* of the observed behavior and 4-point scale to evaluate the *quality* of the observed behavior. The use of separate quantity and quality ratings for most items allows observers to account for discrepancies in these dimensions (e.g., a teacher engages in multiple read-alouds, but they are of poor quality). Appendix 7.1 provides information to familiarize readers with the specific TBRS subscales and to provide details of the number of items within each subscale. Furthermore, it describes the types of ratings that are completed with sample questions. Appendix 7.2 includes the Oral Language subscale of the TBRS that was completed by the mentor in the vignette.

The TBRS was designed to be completed by a trained observer in approximately 2½ to 3 hours of classroom observation. Users of the instrument must schedule their classroom observations during that portion of the day when teachers are implementing the majority of their literacy and language activities. Users are required to observe at least one large-group activity, one small-group activity, and transitions between activities. In addition, they must examine teachers' weekly lesson plans and samples of student work (i.e., portfolios).

Training for the TBRS

Users of the TBRS undergo significant training before they are able to use the instrument reliably. This training on how to administer the TBRS follows a prescribed scope and sequence of specific activities. First, those being trained—the trainees—are presented with a didactic overview of the measure, including the purpose, procedures, and constructs that underlie the development of the measure. Then they are exposed to components of the checklist and taught how to complete the form accurately. Specific attention is paid to the type of scale used in each item (e.g., frequency counts versus 4-point rating scales) and the anchors associated with the instrument's quality rating scales.

The trainees then practice their skills via observation of videotapes of teachers in action in their classrooms. During this phase of training, trainees are asked to code specific activities (i.e., a book reading demonstration by a classroom teacher). The intention here is to prevent trainees from becoming overwhelmed by the amount of information that they are required to process—that is, multiple scales at the same time. One helpful technique during the videotaped portion of the training is to provide for trainees both raw and choreographed footage of pre-K settings that can be used to view, discuss, and critique positive and negative aspects of the teaching environment, classroom organization, book readings, and other important aspects of early literacy and language.

Once a trainee has demonstrated the ability to code reliably from a videotape, he or she begins a process of field certification. During this portion of the training, expert coders work side by side with trainees learning the system within a classroom. Following the first few live practice coding sessions, trainers compare a trainee's coding and that of a veteran coder by using percentage agreement calculations, which are an efficient means to determine whether the training is progressing as expected. Following training, a substantial proportion (i.e., 20%) of all observations are "double-coded" for calculation of interrater reliability. This approach allows a comparison of individual raters' scores to a "gold standard" by calculation of generalizability coefficients. This method is recommended for studies using continuous behavioral observational data, and has the advantage of evaluating both the consistency across a variable for each rater and the variance across participants for those variables used in the analyses (Frick & Semmel, 1978). Coefficients above .50 indicate adequate reliability (Mitchell, 1979, for research purposes). Generalizability coefficients of at least .65–.70 are required prior to certification of a trainee as eligible to conduct independent observations. Once a trainee demonstrates proficiency coding "live" data (i.e., observations in a classroom), he or she is ready for field work, with oversight and continued interrater reliability checks. The trainee is now a reliable rater.

Piloting Phase

As described earlier, the TBRS was used in a large Head Start PD study in 1999 and 2000. The TBRS developers trained classroom mentors from across the state of Texas on both the use of the instrument and how to use it to guide their feedback to the Head Start teachers to facilitate the fidelity of the implementation of the PD content. (See the nine PD features identified earlier in this chapter.)

Two approaches were employed to document teachers' fidelity of implementation of the PD content. First, TBRS data were collected at least five times per year in classrooms receiving the PD program; that is, mentors delivered PD training during the summer months, then assessed whether or not the teachers' instructional practices reflected the PD content across the school year. These data revealed that 60% of the Head Start teachers demonstrated strong growth and 30% exhibited moderate growth on most of the TBRS rating scale areas based on analysis of effect sizes. Thus, 90% of the teachers incorporated the knowledge presented in the professional development sessions into their classroom teaching. The second approach used to documenting fidelity of implementation of PD content was through multiple site visits by TBRS expert coders. The expert coders and the mentors sat side by side in the same classroom, observing each teacher as he or she implemented the language and literacy activities. Agreement between mentor and the expert coder ratings was .78, demonstrating the ability of the mentors to track changes in teachers' behaviors.

Developing Adequate Psychometric Data on the TBRS

Continued examination of the psychometric properties of the TBRS was conducted as part of several state and federally funded pre-K classroom intervention projects. These examinations resulted in changes to the TBRS to improve its sensitivity in capturing what may be measured effectively in a 3-hour classroom period. (Full details on the psychometric properties of the TBRS are available from Mike A. Assel.)

After determining that the TBRS could be coded reliably by well-trained persons, the research team evaluated the validity of the instrument. They conducted multiple examinations of validity using their own data and that of outside research groups that used the TBRS. As an

TABLE 7.1. Generalizability Coefficients for CIRCLE TBRS Subscales

Subscale	Year 1	Year 2
Best Practices	.84	na
General Sensitivity	na	.72
Classroom Structure	na	.50
Book Reading	.87	.70
Centers	.95	.77
Lesson Plans	.96	.75
Math	.98	na
Oral Language	.92	.88
Team Teaching	.96	.93
Print Concepts	.91	.70
Written Expression	.94	na
Phonological Awareness	.80	.83
Total Scale	.96	.87

Note. Due to differences in the items and subscale names, all subscales were not administered in both years.

example of our findings, generalizability coefficients are presented in Table 7.1.

Evaluating the Validity of the TBRS

The research team initially sought evidence for validity based on positive changes in teachers' behavior being predictive of positive changes in child outcomes. Findings from a Houston-based Preschool Curriculum Evaluation Research (PCER) study revealed that the instructional practices of the teachers, as measured by the TBRS, predicted child outcomes. Specifically, higher scores on the TBRS were significantly and positively correlated with child language and literacy outcomes (see Table 7.2) These analyses also provided evidence of discriminant validity; that is, the Houston PCER study evaluated children's outcomes within two language and literacy curricula, Let's Begin with the Letter People (Abrams & Co., 2000) and Doors to Discovery (Wright Group/McGraw-Hill, 2001). Based upon the type of curriculum that was utilized in the classrooms, both of which reportedly were literacy- and language-focused, higher scores on the TBRS were expected to correlate with higher scores on the child outcomes measures. There were multiple instances of convergent validity in which target teachers who scored higher on checklist subscales had students who scored higher on measures of early literacy.

TABLE 7.2. Correlations between the CIRCLE TBRS and Child Outcomes

	TBRS subscales			
Child outcomes	General Teaching Behaviors	Oral Language Use	Phonological Awareness	Print and Letter Knowledge
PLS-IV Auditory Comprehension subscale	.54*** (.0001)	.61*** (.001)	.34*** (.0004)	.46*** (.0001)
Expressive Vocabulary Test	.57*** (.0001)	.63*** (.0001)	.37*** (.0002)	.53*** (.0001)
WJ-III Letter–Word ID subscale	.36*** (.0002)	.51*** (.001)	.25* (.011)	.37*** (.0001)
WJ-III Sound Awareness (rhyming) subscale	.35*** (.0003)	.62*** (.001)	.39*** (.0001)	.55*** (.0001)
DSC Auditory subscale	.40*** (.0001)	.47*** (.001)	.31** (.0017)	.44*** (.0001)

Note. Associated p values in parentheses.
*Significant at the .05 level; **significant at the .01 level; ***significant at the .001 level.

In terms of the instructional practices stressed in the target curricula, a teacher's oral language use (verbal scaffolding, rich vocabulary, descriptions, etc.) was highly correlated with child outcomes on language measures. For instance, correlations were .60 and .63 between the Oral Language subscale of the TBRS and child scores on the Preschool Language Scale–IV Auditory Comprehension subscale (PLS-IV AC; Zimmerman, Steiner, & Pond, 2002) and Expressive Vocabulary Test (EVT; Williams, 1997), respectively ($p < .0001$). Also, a teacher's use of rich language (as rated by the TBRS) was positively correlated ($r = .51$) with child scores on the Woodcock–Johnson III Test of Academic Achievement Letter–Word identification subscale (WJ-III Letter–Word ID; Woodcock, McGrew, & Mather, 2001) and the Auditory subscale of the Developing Skills Checklist (DSC; $r = .47$; CTB/McGraw-Hill, 1990).

Additionally, the teacher's ability to incorporate phonological awareness activities into the classroom, as measured by the TBRS, was correlated with the WJ-III Sound Awareness subscale ($r = .39$), the DSC Auditory subscale ($r = .31$), PLS-IV AC ($r = .34$), EVT ($r = .37$), and WJ-III Letter–Word ID subscale ($r = .25$). These higher correlations indicate that the teachers' use of phonological awareness activities in the classroom predicted child scores on phonological awareness outcome measures.

A teacher's score in the Print and Letter Knowledge subscale of the TBRS, which evaluates instructional practices such as the teacher's ability to discuss concepts of print and letters (e.g., discussing words that begin with a certain letter, words that begin with the same sound), skill at incorporating print into centers, and the effective use of a letter wall, were related to all child outcomes. Correlations between scores on this subscale and child outcome measures ranged from .36 to .55 ($p < .01$ for all correlations).

Overall, teachers' scores on the Best Practices/General Teaching Behaviors subscale of the TBRS were correlated with child outcomes at high levels (.36–.57, $p =.001$), which indicates that what the checklist considers to be high-quality teaching skills correlates with higher outcome scores for children. Significant correlations between center structure and child outcomes were expected. These significant correlations were likely related to the fact that our center items tend to be weighted more toward the ability of the classroom teacher to incorporate thematic content of the curriculum and literacy activities into centers. In other checklists (e.g., ECERS-R), Environment/Materials is weighted heavily. In the TBRS Center subscale, high scores were obtained by teachers who were able to infuse centers with related language and early literacy activities.

Comparison of Validity Characteristics of the TBRS and the ECERS-R

Our preliminary evaluations suggested that the TBRS was sensitive to changes in teachers' behavior and demonstrated adequate generalizability properties. Furthermore, it was clear that observers could be reliably trained to use the instrument. We then turned our attention to determining the extent to which the TBRS was able to predict children's growth within preschool classrooms compared to other, widely used observational tools, such as the ECERS-R (Harms et al., 1998). We were able to address this question when the Institute of Education Sciences (IES) chose to use the TBRS in the national cross-site evaluation project (known as the PCER study). The data reported here were collected by a national evaluation team trained in early 2003 to use the instrument. This data-collection team also was trained to use the ECERS-R to evaluate classroom characteristics.

This validity study involved 39 classrooms in the greater Houston area. Classrooms were evenly dispersed between Title 1 classrooms in public schools and Head Start. There were differences in the educational background of teachers across the program types. For instance, all of the teachers in the Title 1 classrooms had 4-year degrees, whereas the majority of the teachers in the Head Start setting had 2-year child development certificates or associate's degrees (for additional details, see Assel, Landry, Swank, & Gunnewig, 2007).

All children were individually assessed in the fall and spring of the pre-kindergarten year using the following measures: Peabody Picture Vocabulary Test–3 (Dunn, & Dunn, 1997), Test of Early Reading Ability–3 (Alphabet and Conventions subscales; Reid, Hresko, & Hammill, 2001), and subtests from the W–J III (e.g., Letter–Word ID subscale; Woodcock et al., 2001).

All classrooms were evaluated with both the ECERS-R and the TBRS in the spring of 2003. Observations lasted approximately 4 hours. Data collectors were part of a national team of classroom observers working on the PCER study. Findings showed that the TBRS, in a mixed-model analysis controlling for time (t) between pre- and posttesting and child age, significantly and positively predicted children's gains across the year in knowledge of print (t =2.39, degree of freedom [df] = 129, p = .02) and print conventions (t = 2.08, df = 129, p = .04), as well as identification of letters and sounds (t = 2.33, df = 129, p = .02). It also showed a positive but nonsignificant relation with receptive vocabulary (t = 1.5, df = 129, p = .14). In contrast, higher scores on the ECERS-R showed a significant but negative prediction with vocabulary gains (t = –2.22, df = 191, p = .03) and negative trends with knowledge of print (t = –1.88, df = 193, p = .06) and identification of letters and associated sounds (t = –1.85, df = 193, p = .06). These findings demonstrate that a classroom observation instrument that specifically targets pre-K instructional practices reported to enhance early literacy skills (i.e., TBRS) is more effective in identifying whether a classroom and/or teacher is preparing children to be school-ready than a measure of the general quality of the classroom environment (i.e., ECERS-R).

Conclusions

The CIRCLE TBRS appears to be sensitive to teacher and classroom changes in response to training in the use of practices that promote language and early literacy skills, and is predictive of school readiness abilities. In terms of the validity of the scale, multiple approaches were used to evaluate whether the TBRS would be predictive of child outcomes and to compare the predicative utility of the TBRS against a widely used observational rating system that attempts to capture positive and nurturing caregiving environments (i.e., the ECERS-R). Findings show that teachers who score higher on TBRS subscales have children who perform better on standardized measures of child outcomes. This has been compared to the pattern of findings between the ECERS-R and child outcomes that show negative or no correlation with language and literacy outcomes across a relatively large dataset collected by outside raters.

Thus, the TBRS appears to be a reliable and valid measure that fills a void in early childhood education. The subscales were developed to evaluate those teacher behaviors that many early childhood programs target (e.g., a teacher's use of rich language, providing students with activities to encourage letter knowledge and print acquisition) in their efforts to prepare children for school. Its ability to measure change in characteristics of the classroom environment and teachers' instructional practices is due in part to the inclusion of items that target aspects of an early childhood environment demonstrated to predict school readiness. Additionally, the TBRS provides those working with teachers (e.g., mentors, administrators, and researchers) with specific information about what is actually occurring at the level of an adult–child interaction. With this knowledge, teachers can be encouraged via mentoring or ongoing PD activities to increase the frequency of those behaviors that have been shown by research to be critical for success in school.

> It has been 5 weeks since Ms. Granbery visited one of her favorite classrooms. In the car, Ms. Granbery spends a few minutes poring over all of her printed notes on the TBRS that was administered prior to Thanksgiving. Although her notes occasionally aggravate the university's data-collection staff, who preach about avoiding making marks close to any of the "choice fields," these notes form the basis of what she will observe in the classroom. She is particularly interested in whether suggestions from the previous month's visit have been incorporated. After entering the classroom and exchanging pleasantries with the teacher, Ms. Granbery takes a seat and begins to complete the TBRS. The classroom teacher looks up and smiles as she is taking dictation, and all of the children can be seen with pencils, markers, stamps, and different types of paper. Ms. Granbery observes that most children are able to make some recognizable letters (usually letters contained in their names) and have no trouble making "letter-like" forms that progress from left to right. As Ms. Granbery continues to score the TBRS, the teacher encourages language development by sensitively responding to children's comments during dictation. Ms. Granbery notices that compared to her visit prior to the Thanksgiving holiday, the teacher's questions appear more fluent and less scripted, and there is less emphasis on ensuring that every child gets asked the same questions about Thanksgiving foods. In short, the teacher is sensitively responding to each child's utterances during dictation. Ms. Granbery smiles, because she is sure that this teacher, who initially needed help with basics (classroom schedules, room arrangement, etc.), now seems to understand the joy of working with pre-K children.

Acknowledgments

The findings reported here are based on research conducted by us as part of the Preschool Curriculum Evaluation Research (PCER) program funded by the Institute of Education Sciences (IES), U.S. Department of Education; through Grant No. R305J020014 and multiple grant awards from the Texas Education Agency (TEA). The PCER Consortium consists of representatives from IES, the national evaluation contractors, Research Triangle Institute (RTI) and Mathematica Policy

Research, Inc. (MPR), and each grant site participating in the evaluation. The content of this publication does not necessarily reflect the views or policies of the PCER Consortium members, including IES, RTI, and MPR, nor does mention of trade names, commercial products, or organizations imply endorsement by the U.S. Government.

References

Abrams & Co. (2000). *Let's begin with the letter people.* Waterbury, CT: Author.

Assel, M., Landry, S. H., Swank, P. R., & Gunnewig, S. (2007). An evaluation of curriculum, setting, and mentoring on the performance of children enrolled in pre-kindergarten. *Reading and Writing: An Interdisciplinary Journal, 20,* 463–494.

Box, J. A., & Aldridge, J. (1993). Shared reading experiences and Head Start children's concept about print and story structure. *Perceptual and Motor Skills, 77,* 929–930.

Bradley, R., Caldwell, B., & Rock, S. (1988). Home environment and school performance: A ten year follow-up and examination of three models of environmental action. *Child Development, 59,* 852–867.

CTB/McGraw-Hill. (1990). *Developing Skills Checklist.* Monterey, CA: CTB/McGraw-Hill.

Dickinson, D. K. (2006). Toward a toolkit approach to describing classroom quality. *Early Education and Development, 17,* 177–202.

Dunn, L. M., & Dunn, L. M. (1997). *Peabody Picture Vocabulary Test* (3rd ed.). Circle Pines, MN: American Guidance Service.

Fleiss, J. L. (1986). *The design and analysis of clinical experiments.* New York: Wiley.

Frick, T., & Semmel, M. (1978). Observer agreement and reliabilities of classroom observational methods. *Review of Educational Research, 48,* 157–184.

Harms, T., Clifford, R. M., & Cryer, D. (1998). *Early Childhood Environment Rating Scale–Revised Edition.* New York: Teachers College Press.

Helburn, S. W. (Ed.). (1995). *Cost, quality, and child outcomes in child care centers* (Technical Report). Denver, CO: University of Colorado at Denver, Department of Economics, Center for Research in Economic and Social Policy.

Juel, C., Griffith, P. L., & Gough, P. B. (1986). Acquisition of literacy: A longitudinal study of children in first and second grade. *Journal of Educational Psychology, 78,* 243–255.

Landry, S. H., Crawford, A., Gunnewig, S., & Swank, P. R. (2001). *Teacher Behavior Rating Scale.* Unpublished research instrument, Center for Improving the Readiness of Children for Learning and Education, University of Texas Health Science Center at Houston, TX.

Landry, S. H., Smith, K. E., Swank, P. R., Assel, M. A., & Vellet, S. (2001). Does early responsive parenting have a special importance for children's development or is consistency across early childhood necessary? *Developmental Psychology, 37,* 387–403.

Landry, S. H., Swank, P. R., Smith, K. E., Assel, M. A., & Gunnewig, S. (2006). Enhancing early literacy skills for pre-school children: Bringing a professional development model to scale. *Journal of Learning Disabilities, 39*, 306–324.

Lonigan, C. J. (2003). Development and promotion of emergent literacy skills in preschool children at-risk of reading difficulties. In B. Foorman (Ed.), *Preventing and remediating reading difficulties: Bringing science to scale* (pp. 23–50). Timonium, MD: York Press.

Lonigan, C. J., Burgess, S. R., Anthony, J. L., & Barker, T. A. (1998). Development of phonological sensitivity in two- to five-year-old children. *Journal of Educational Psychology, 90*, 294–311.

Mitchell, F. (1979). Interobserver agreement, reliability, and generalizability of data collected in observational studies. *Psychological Bulletin, 86*, 366–370.

Molfese, D. L. (1989). Electrophysiological correlates of word meanings in 4 month old human infants. *Developmental Neuropsychology, 5*, 79–103.

Neville, H. J., Bavelier, D., Corina, D., Rauschecker, J., Karni, A., Lalwani, A., et al. (1998). Cerebral organization for language in deaf and hearing subjects: Biological constraints and effects of experience. *Proceedings of the National Academy of Sciences USA, 95*, 922–929.

Reid, D. K., Hresko, W. P., & Hammill, D. D. (2001). *Test of Early Reading Ability: Third eEdition*. Austin, TX: PRO-ED.

Smith, M. W., & Dickinson, D. K. (2002). *Early Language and Literacy Classroom Observation (ELLCO) toolkit*. Baltimore: Brookes.

Smith, S., Blank, S., & Collins, R. (1992). *Pathways to self-sufficiency for two generations: Designing welfare-to-work programs that benefit children and strengthen families*. New York: New York Foundation for Child Development.

Williams, K. T. (1997). *Expressive Vocabulary Test*. Circle Pines, MN: American Guidance Service.

Woodcock, R. W., McGrew, K. S., & Mather, N. (2001). *Woodcock–Johnson III Tests of Achievement*. Itasca, IL: Riverside.

Wright Group/McGraw-Hill. (2001). *Doors to Discovery: A new pre-kindergarten program*. Bothell, WA: Author.

Zill, N., & West, J. (2001). *Entering kindergarten: A portrait of American children when they begin school* (U.S. Department of Education, OERI, NCES 2001-035). Washington, DC: U.S. Government Printing Office.

Zimmerman, I. L., Steiner, V. G., & Pond, R. E. (2002). *Preschool Language Scale–Fourth Edition*. San Antonio, TX: Psychological Corporation.

DESCRIPTION OF TBRS CONTENT AREAS
AND SAMPLE QUESTIONS.

Subscale	No. of items	Type of rating	Sample question
General Teaching Behaviors	9	Quantity (3 point) and quality (4 point)	Uses encouragement and positive feedback that provides children specific information regarding what they are doing well.
Lesson Plan Portfolios	3	Quantity (3 point) and quality (4 point)	Lesson plan shows strong thematic connection in written lesson plans (detailed information that ties theme-related material to learning objectives).
Progress Monitoring	3	Dichotomous (i.e., yes or no)	Recent dated documentation of children's developmental progress across all emergent literacy areas through the use of cognitive checklists/assessments.
Portfolios	2	5-point scale with anchors to capture frequency of occurrence	Dated documentation in portfolios of child developmental progress with children's art work, samples of written expressions, journals, children's notes, or children's dictations.
Centers	7	4-point quality rating. Frequency count of number of centers.	Materials, activities, and objectives follow the current theme and are linked to learning goals (exciting and obvious theme = high; look for appropriate rotation of seasonal items and refreshing materials).
Book Reading Behaviors	9	Quantity (3 point) and quality (4 point)	Vocabulary words are combined with pictures or objects when preparing to and/or reading books aloud.
Print and Letter Knowledge	6	Quantity (3 point) and quality (4 point)	Discusses concepts about print (text contains letters, words, sentences, reading progresses left to right, top to bottom, etc.)
Math Concepts	2	Quantity (3 point) and quality (4 point)	Involves children in organized, hands-on activities that support one or more of the math strand concepts (i.e., counting, 1:1 correspondence, sorting, patterning, graphing).
Phonological Awareness	7	4-point quality rating and indication of what PA activities were observed.	Did the observer see a specific PA activity (e.g., alliteration) and what was the quality (i.e., *low, medium-low, medium-high, high*).
Written Expression	3	Quantity (3 point) and quality (4 point)	Provides children with a variety of opportunities and materials to engage in writing (e.g., journals, response to literature).
Oral Language Use	7	Quantity (3 point) and quality (4 point)	Uses "thinking" questions (open-ended, "why," "how") or comments to support children's thinking or activity of interest.
Team Teaching (if applicable)	5	Quantity (3 point) and quality (4 point)	Teacher and assistant work together so that small groups of children receive ongoing instruction in center activities, small-group activities, and read-alouds.

ORAL LANGUAGE SUBSCALE OF THE TBRS COMPLETED ON THE TEACHER MENTIONED IN THE VIGNETTE

Oral Language Use with Students

Ratings should be based on a 2-hour visit. However, a second visit may be needed to observe a specific situation, such as book behavior or center time, if not observed in the first visit.

Rating	Quantity Frequency of Speech			Quality			
	Rarely	Sometimes	Often	Low	Medium Low	Medium High	High
1. Speaks clearly and uses grammatically correct sentences.	□	□	■	□	□	■	□
2. Models for children how to express their ideas in complete sentences.	□	□	■	□	□	□	■
3. Uses "scaffolding" language (nouns, descriptors, action words, linking concepts).	■	□	□	□	(■)	✗	□
4. Uses "thinking" (open-ended, "wh," "how") questions or comments to support children's thinking or activity of interest.	□	□	■	□	■	□	□
5. Relates previously learned words/concepts to activity.	□	■	□	□	□	■	□
6. Encourages children's use of language throughout the observation period irrespective of type of activities.	□	■	□	□	■	□	□
7. Engages children in conversations that involve child and teacher taking multiple turns (e.g., 3–5 turns).	■	□	□	□	■	□	□

Notes from actual TBRS form:

#3. The teacher infrequently used scaffolding language. She briefly discussed the function/use of calendars during "morning circle"—low quality. *Note:* Mentor changed rating from "medium high" to "medium low."

#4. Lots of "wh" questions but most felt scripted and repetitive (e.g., "What do you eat for Thanksgiving?"). She never followed up with deeper level questions.

#5. Related vocabulary from book-read back to center activities. Specifically, she discussed Pilgrims and turkeys from the book-read while children were making art projects—fairly high quality.

CHAPTER 8

★★★★★★★★

It's in the Details

Approaches to Describing and Improving Preschool Classrooms

David K. Dickinson
Betsy G. Watson
Dale C. Farran

The first decades of the 21st century appear likely to be an era in which public schooling is extended to an increasingly larger numbers of four-year-old children, especially children from low-income families (National Institute for Early Education Research, 2005). This expansion of services reflects the well-established fact that children who enter kindergarten from homes where parents have limited education and income are at greater risk of short- and long-term educational failure (National Assessment of Educational Progress, 1999; Snow, Burns, & Griffin, 1998). Furthermore, mounting evidence pointing to the beneficial effects of preschool attendance is sufficient to merit committing substantial public funds to provide these children a preschool education (Barnett, 2001; Dickinson, McCabe, & Essex, 2006; Reynolds, 1994; Schweinhardt, Barnes, Weikart, Barnett, & Epstein, 1993). Attention has focused on the early years because the language and literacy skills of children from the preschool years through grade 1 are predictive of later academic success (Dickinson & Sprague, 2001; Farran, 2001; Gormley, Gayer, Phillips, & Dawson, 2005; Snow, Burns, & Griffin, 1998; Snow & Dickinson, 1991).

The need to target young children from economically disadvantaged homes is heightened by the fact that children from low-income families fall far behind their peers on measures of cognitive ability at entry to kindergarten (Hamre & Pianta, 2005).

With increasing awareness of the importance of the preschool years, the desire to extend services to more children and to garner support for the funding required to deliver these services increases the need to demonstrate that programs are of high quality (Farran, 2000). In this chapter we first briefly discuss how the quality of classrooms typically has been described, then present two alternative approaches that examine classrooms in far greater detail than has been typical. Also, we report how we are striving to share the information generated by our observations with teachers to help them improve their classroom practices.

Accountability for Children's Learning

As early education programs are expanded to serve more children, those funding the programs (e.g., federal and state governments) increasingly are holding the programs accountable for demonstrating measurable improvement in children's academic abilities. In many cases this pressure has necessitated a change in program focus. Prior educational philosophies and accreditation standards have tended to emphasize children's social and emotional adjustment, and to downplay academic goals (Dickinson, 2002). For example, a study of Head Start classrooms in the mid-1990s found substantially stronger practices related to the provision of an organized and nurturing environment than to language and early literacy development (Smith, Dickinson, Sangeorge, & Anastasopoulos, 2002). The focus on providing children with an organized and nurturing environment may help to explain the results of a national study of Head Start; the researchers found that children were making scant progress in letter knowledge and vocabulary (West, Xtria, & CDM Group, 2003). Other observational research revealed that minimal time was spent in interactions in which the teachers appeared to have a clear pedagogical agenda, and only the exceptional teacher frequently engaged children in extended, cognitively rich conversations (Dickinson, McCabe, & Clark-Chiarelli, 2004; Dickinson & Tabors, 2001).

The combination of changes in the field's understanding of the importance of early literacy and increased demands that programs demonstrate their contribution to children's learning already has had an effect. Recent data indicate that Head Start contributes to improvement in children's print-related knowledge (Administration for Children and Families, 2005). Observations in classrooms funded to be models of excellent practice reveal that instruction includes substantial attention to teaching alphabet knowledge and basic aspects of phonological awareness (e.g., rhyming, initial sounds in words) (Farran, Kang, Aydogan, & Lipsey, 2005). These improvements in child outcomes, along with the changes seen in teacher instruction, demonstrate that early childhood programs are responsive to shifts in accountability requirements. However, despite the incremental gains, many 4-year-old children from low-income homes continue to perform well below national norms on early assessments of language and literacy, with the deficiencies being most pronounced in the area of oral language skills (Administration for Children and Families, 2005; Administration on Children, Youth and Families, 2004; Bryant, Burchinal, Lau, & Sparling, 1994; Dickinson, St. Pierre, & Pettengill, 2004).

We are at a historical moment for early childhood education. Public policy, bolstered by academic research, is expanding services to increasing numbers of needy children and their families. At the same time, these policymakers expect the programs receiving the funds to measure teachers' and children's performance on academic achievement outcomes that traditionally have not been embraced by many early childhood educators. One product of this convergence of forces could be a radical change in the character of preschool education. Assessment pressures could lead programs to narrow the focus on skills for which they are held accountable, with these being heavily weighted toward the basic literacy and numeracy skills that are most easily and reliably measured (e.g., letter knowledge, phonological awareness, print concepts, counting and number recognition). Some federally funded systems, such as the Head Start National Reporting System, include a measure of receptive language, but many local initiatives likely will continue to limit their focus to the more easily assessed "basic" skills. Evidence is mounting that strong long-term literacy success is rooted in a cluster of related print and language skills (Dickinson, McCabe, Anastasopoulos, Peisner-Feinberg, & Poe, 2003; Early Child Care Research Network (ECCRN), 2005; Storch & Whitehurst, 2002). A narrow focus on discrete preacademic skills does a disservice to children from low-income homes, those served by Head Start, and most public pre-K programs. These children's greatest need is in the area of oral language.

Publicly funded preschools are having little effect on these complex language skills. For example, the newly released Head Start Impact Study (Administration for Children and Families, 2005) indicates that Head Start fostered growth in children's letter knowledge skills, but that Head Start children made no more progress than the comparison children in the areas of complex language skills and math, or in fostering acquisition of self-regulatory and social skills. Vocabulary—a competence that goes far beyond identifying letters—has been one of the most difficult child competencies to improve through current preschool practices, yet as children get older, its importance increases to the point that it may become the most important predictors of reading skills (Dickinson & Porche, 2007; Snow et al., 1998; Spira, Bracken, & Fischel, 2005). If we are to hold early childhood programs accountable for children's learning, it is vital that the methods we adopt encourage instruction that fosters basic skills *and* language abilities, while also building world knowledge and social skills.

An Alternative Approach: Detailed Descriptions of Classroom Life

Accountability demands have taken varied forms with children of different ages. School districts and states have long assessed children and child-based accountability has been bolstered by the federal government, with the National Reporting System for Head Start being the prime example in the early childhood world. Another approach is to examine the quality of instruction in individual classrooms. Assessments that focus on practices in individual classrooms are used by the National Board for Professional Standards (National Board for Professional Teaching Standards, 2006), and by the National Association of Education of Young Children (NAEYC; 2005) in its accreditation system. A classroom-based rather than a child-based approach has a number of attractive elements: There is no intrusion on instructional time; the link between the assessment and practices that merit improvement is relatively clear; and support for a broader spectrum of outcomes can be captured. The potential for using such assessments as part of program improvement efforts is particularly intriguing, because teachers have few opportunities to receive objective feedback about their teaching.

We might be able both to describe and to bolster quality if we can create tools that describe classrooms in a way that is meaningful to teachers, and devise ways to share feedback in a manner that enables teachers to understand and use it as part of their instruction. This is the challenge we are grappling with in the research we discuss in this chapter. We outline two approaches to describing early childhood classrooms and giving teachers information from our observations. Both describe classrooms in a "fine-grained" manner and include a focus on interactions between teachers and children; both have been used to provide feedback to help teachers improve their practice.

By describing the details of interaction, we follow a path that is different than the dominant approach used to assess classroom quality. Typically, efforts to describe the quality of early childhood classrooms have employed tools such as the Early Environment Rating Scale (Harms, Clifford, & Crye, 1998), the Early Language and Literacy Classroom Observation Toolkit (ELLCO; Smith et al., 2002), and the Classroom

Assessment Scoring System (CLASS; La Paro, Pianta, & Stuhlman, 2004), all of which assign single ratings to broad dimensions of classroom practice. This method has utility for researchers and for policy-makers seeking to identify strong classrooms because it yields a small number of readily interpreted scores. However, such tools tend to account for only modest amounts of variance in children's development and provide rather global guidance for improving practice (Dickinson, 2003, 2006). For example, the FACES study, a large study of Head Start children's home and classroom experiences, and their academic and social development, has not been able to find associations between its measures of quality, collected primarily using tools that describe broad features of classrooms, and children's fall-to-spring growth (Zill & Resnick, 2006).

Detailed descriptions of what teachers are doing might enhance our ability to describe the ways in which classrooms affect children's growth. Support for this proposition comes from findings of studies that examined in detail the language teachers use with preschool-age children and found significant associations between aspects of teacher input and children's syntactic development (Huttenlocher, Vasilyeva, Cymerman, & Levine, 2002; Vasilyeva, Huttenlocher, & Waterfall, 2006) and mathematical knowledge (Klibanoff, Levine, Huttenlocher, Vasilyeva, & Hedges, 2006). Studies have also shown that the language used by preschool children's teachers correlates positively with children's language and literacy performance at the end of kindergarten (Dickinson & Smith, 1994) and fourth grade (Dickinson & Porche, 2006), after controlling for home factors and age 3 language skill (i.e., mean length of utterance).

Use of detailed observations to assess classroom quality raises some thorny challenges. One major problem is that to gain detailed information, one must focus on a narrow range of aspects of classrooms, and have methods for collecting and analyzing these data in a reliable and reasonably timely manner. Selection of specific dimensions requires a strong theoretical rationale and, ideally, empirical validation of the importance of the features being observed. Valid collection of detailed information and analyses of these data in a timely manner are two vexing challenges because, by their very nature, such data can be time consuming to process. If collecting fine-grained samples of teacher language in the classroom, one would need to collect and analyze language samples. However, language samples need to be transcribed, and the transcripts must be verified, then analyzed either by coding them or using an automated analytic system. Researchers have used such methods (e.g., Dickinson & Tabors, 2001; Hart & Risley, 1995; Huttenlocher et al., 2002), but the effort required to process the data is considerable and the time lag between data collection and ready-to-report findings can be lengthy, so that the information is of little value for professional development or quality monitoring. Nonetheless, although there are hurdles to overcome related to the use of fine-grained descriptions of classrooms, we believe it is possible to create mechanisms for collecting and using such data for fostering professional development of teachers (feedback to teachers) and for research purposes.

Feedback to Teachers

As we have increased our ability to identify and describe specific features of classrooms that foster student learning, we have improved our capacity to create descriptions of classroom life that can help teachers become cognizant of critical aspects of their practice and make needed changes. Traditionally, early childhood programs have been evaluated by external entities (e.g., NAEYC, Head Start Bureau, state accreditation systems) and have received feedback on the extent to which they meet standards required for accreditation. The processes set in motion by reviews can require changes in programs; thus, feedback may lead to improvements (e.g., better financial systems, enhanced safety, improved learning). In such evaluation systems, feedback is given at the end of a high-stakes review process and is tied to the program's ability to demonstrate practices consistent with standards, some of which may be specific (e.g., handwashing routines) and others of which may very general (e.g., providing an emotionally supportive environment).

The approaches to providing feedback that we describe are different than traditional evaluation–feedback systems in several respects. First, feedback is given during the course of an evaluation or intervention; thus, is not linked to a high-stakes assessment of the classroom or program. Second, feedback is about very specific features of classroom life that are under the control of the teacher. Third, teachers are the recipients of the information and are the agents responsible for making—or not making—changes in practices. This teacher-focused approach contrasts with typical program evaluation systems in which teachers are not the primary audience and rarely are central to the decision-making processes after evaluation results are received. We hypothesize that providing teachers feedback tightly linked to practice has the potential to put teachers in the position to make informed decisions about changes they need to make in their classrooms.

Two Approaches to Describing Classrooms and Giving Teachers Feedback

In this section we first describe an approach to professional development that employs methods that were initially developed to study ways that teacher–child interactions support children's learning (Dickinson & Tabors, 2001). We then introduce an approach devised as part of an evaluation of an Early Reading First program (Farran & Lipsey, 2004).

Objectifying by Transcribing

Given the research we reviewed earlier indicating that particular teacher behaviors are related to enhanced language and early literacy learning, Dickinson devised a professional development approach intended to help teachers adopt strategies for interacting with children (e.g., use and encourage children's use of varied vocabulary, engage in sustained conversations). In creating this approach Dickinson made several key assumptions:

1. It is the moment-to-moment interactions between teachers and children that are most likely to affect children's learning. Because the teacher must be the central agent in efforts to bring about changes, he or she must be motivated to make changes and be directly involved in establishing goals.
2. People tend not to be aware of the details of how they use language; language is a tool used to achieve ends, but it is transparent to the user; that is, people tend not to notice the language they use to achieve their goals.
3. To change how they use language, teachers need to become aware of how they use language. Transcripts can objectify language in a way that may give teachers the ability to begin making changes in how they use language.
4. Making changes in how one uses language is difficult, because patterns of language use reflect a lifetime of practice using language, and patterns of language use reflect adaptive responses to the complexities of classroom life.
5. Teachers need to understand why specific kinds of changes can benefit children, because this knowledge provides the motivation needed to make difficult and possibly uncomfortable changes in language use.
6. Changing how one converses with children requires time, specific feedback on multiple occasions, and external support.

Building on these assumptions, Dickinson devised and pilot-tested a means to help teachers study the strategies they use when interacting with children. The approach included aspects of means employed in the Literacy Environment Enrichment Project (LEEP), which he previously had developed and helped to implement (Dickinson & Brady, 2005), and elements of the mentoring approach used by Wasik and Bond (2006). The context for this pilot test was a state-funded preschool in a rural Tennessee school district using the curriculum Opening the World of Learning (OWL; Schickedanz & Dickinson, 2005). District leadership nominated three teachers for participation in the field test of the procedure; all agreed to participate. Dickinson made clear that his intention was to help teachers become aware of and, he hoped, improve the way they supported children's language development, not to "enforce" appropriate use of the curriculum.

Delivery of the Intervention

The project began with a workshop on research and theory about the nature of early literacy, with a focus on the importance of oral language skills. Research findings related to specific strategies known to foster language were discussed and illustrated with videotaped vignettes. Dickinson asked the three teachers to select one of two strategies that had been highlighted: (1) providing children increased opportunities to hear and use new vocabulary, or (2) engaging children in conversations that spanned multiple turns, with a goal of achieving at least five or more back-and-forth exchanges. Each was given a tape recorder and asked to tape-record herself and to complete a self-reflection form that required consideration of the extent to which she had achieved specific goals. The vocabulary reflection form asked whether or not she had used new words being taught as part of the curriculum, whether she had used them in ways that communicated their meanings, whether the children had used them, and whether she had heard children use the words at other times of the day. The conversation reflection form for focusing on the quality of their conversations asked whether the teacher had stayed on a topic for five or more exchanges, responded to a child's questions or comments effectively, and engaged in extended conversations with children during other times of they day (see Appendix 8.1 and 8.2). After each teacher recorded herself and completed the self-evaluation, Dickinson sent them to the research team at Vanderbilt University, where the tapes were immediately transcribed. The transcripts were sent to the teacher and were the basis for a telephone conversation about what the teacher and Dickinson noted about the transcribed interaction. Following two such rounds, Dickinson provided a second half-day of professional development. On this occasion the focus was on strategies for improving conversations with children, and on a videotape showing one of the teachers during block play. After this session there were two more rounds of audiotaping, reflection, and discussion.

Evidence of Effectiveness

Did this procedure result in changes in how the teachers interacted with the children? To answer this question, Dickinson videotaped each teacher, who wore a wireless microphone, before the project began, at the midpoint of the project after about 6 weeks, and after the final professional development experience. These videotapes, in which the teacher interacted with the children during small-group times (20-minute instructional times in which the teacher worked with about eight children) and centers time (the period of the day when children engage in self-selected activity and the teacher moves from one center), were transcribed either in full (small-group times) or selectively (approximately 6 minutes from the beginning, middle, and end of the centers time). The transcripts were analyzed by the software Systematic Analysis of Language (SALT; Language Analysis Lab, 2006), a set of computer programs that analyzes transcripts along a number of dimensions. Teachers also were interviewed before and after the project. Transcripts and notes were made of the phone conversations, and the transcribed teacher–child interactions were retained.

The procedure played out differently with each of the three teachers. Mrs. Day, a veteran who had taught first grade for 27 years and was interested in teaching preschool-age children, wanted to focus on improving her ability to sustain conversations with children. She quickly became aware of her tendency to overwhelm children with talk and sought to increase her wait time and engage children in more extended interactions. Several SALT measures provide indices of the role of children in interactions and of teacher engagement in sustained conversations: mean length of the teacher's and the children's turns, number of words used per minute by the teacher and children, and percentage of one-word utterances by children. Mrs. Day's rate of speech was quite high during the first and third small-group instructional times (129 and 135 words per minute [wpm]), respectively, but was lower during the second session (114 wpm). Her average rate of speaking was somewhat slower during centers time but did not show a significant decrease (95, 102, and 114 wpm, respectively) across the sessions. Other measures do suggest changes in children's participation in conversations. During small-group times, the children increased the number of words they used nearly fivefold (4.4, 16.1, and 20.2 wpm, respectively) and between the first videotaping and the middle and end of videotaping, the average length of their turns increased (1.9 vs. 3.0 and 2.5). During both small-group and centers times the percentage of one-word utterances by children declined dramatically in small groups (72.4, 45.6, and 44.1%, respectively) and centers (51.1, 32.3, and 25.7%, respectively).

An examination of how Mrs. Day spent centers time also suggested changes in her approach. During the first videotaping, she visited the centers 24 times, for an average of 1 minute, 5 seconds per center. Midway through the project, she stopped in different centers 17 times, for an average of 3 minutes, 34 seconds per center and at the end of the project she was in 19 centers, for an average stay of 2 minutes, 52 seconds. Thus, her average stay in a center was more than twice as long later in the project, suggesting an effort to sustain interactions.

The second teacher, Mrs. Johnson, previously had taught fourth grade prior to moving to preschool for the past 2 years. She chose to focus on increasing the children's opportunities to hear and use new vocabulary. In her interviews, Mrs. Johnson indicated that she was more aware of her own vocabulary use, as well as the children's, and felt she was able to make changes in how she supported children's word learning. Dickinson's study of her talk revealed the changes during centers time. There was a modest increase in the number of different words she used per minute, from 18.6 wpm during the first videotaping to 23.7 and 20.9, respectively, in the middle and last videotapings. An increase in the number of different words used can occur if a teacher simply talks more, but this was not what happened, because the ratio of different words relative to the total number of words per minute increased from 0.28 different words relative to total words in the first videotaping to 0.34 at the middle and end videotaping. Changes were not apparent in measures of children's talk or during small-group instructional time.

The third teacher, Ms. Thomas, had taught preschool for over 20 years, was enrolled in a master's degree program, and had minimal energy for the intervention due to her studies and responsibilities at home. She indicated that the project asked her to initiate interactions during centers time in a manner that she found inconsistent with her preferred habit of standing back and observing children, and interacting only when problems arose. Her interview responses indicated minimal engagement in an effort to change her interaction style, and the quantitative data showed no evidence of changes.

An encouraging finding of the field test of this procedure is that with the use of digital technologies, it was possible to provide support for teachers that included the careful consideration of the details of interaction. On one day a teacher could record herself, and complete and send the reflection form and the audio file to Dickinson, who resided some 100 miles away. The very next day, the audio file could be transcribed and returned in the form of a transcript. Dickinson and the teacher could have a conversation about an interaction that had taken place 1 or 2 days earlier. The results also indicated that it is possible to help teachers reflect on how they converse with children, and that awareness, *coupled with efforts to change*, can translate into new ways of conversing with children.

In the coming months, Dickinson and a team of colleagues intend to refine this approach by asking teachers to set more specific goals and giving them both the transcripts and some quantitative data about their progress in effecting changes in how they converse with children. The team will collect data on teacher–child interactions and examine relationships between specific features of each teacher's language use and children's language and literacy growth, thereby providing additional assurance that the behaviors the team is asking teachers to adopt are associated with improved learning.

Observing Fidelity of Implementation

The second project we describe also is based in a rural southeastern U.S. preschool system that is part of a federal Early Reading First (ERF) grant; the program has been evaluated by Farran and Lipsey since its inception (for details see Farran, Lipsey, Hurley, et al., 2006). The program adopted OWL, a comprehensive preschool curriculum that emphasizes language and literacy (Schickedanz & Dickinson, 2005). Although the OWL curriculum includes a Curriculum Implementation Form as a means of determining fidelity, the instrument is a rating form with a 1- to 3-point scale; Farran and Lipsey did not feel that this would provide the degree of specificity the ERF administrators and teachers needed. For the purpose of providing more specific feedback to teachers, they developed procedures to examine in detail the teachers' implementation of the curriculum.

Many "full-day" curricula, such as OWL, provide a schedule of activities (or components) for teachers to enact during the day. The OWL curriculum indicates a suggested length of time each of these activities is to occur, as well as descriptions of the curricular content to be addressed in each component. The first attempts by Farran and Lipsey to assess fidelity of implementation involved assessing whether the components were being enacted for the amount of time the developers suggested. Also they examined whether the type of content outlined in the manual was observed during each component. Watson made substantial contributions to the development and refinement of both instruments. The attempt to speak to both of those issues is the focus of this part of the chapter.

The tools the project devised were created specifically to capture those two essential features of the OWL curriculum; however, the same general approach could be used with other curricula as long as it is possible to articulate the activities and behaviors expected throughout the day. The data we discuss were collected during three 6-hour observations to evaluate the fidelity of implementation of the curriculum across the academic year and illustrate the instruments; Watson has been a classroom observer throughout the project.

The Tools

The first instrument is the Narrative Record. This form can be used in any curriculum to document how time is spent in the classroom. Observers record the start and stop time for each instructional episode. An instructional episode is defined as "changing" when either the mode (e.g., whole group to small group) or the focus of the instruction changes (e.g., language arts activity to math activity, but children remain in a whole group). Each instructional episode is coded by the observer on the spot when it changes. The observer's narration serves as a documentation of the decisions made about the activity. Reprinted in Figure 8.1 are the top several lines of a Narrative Record recording sheet, and the notes and ratings of a classroom observation. The final column documents specific components of the OWL curriculum and allows determination of how much time is spent in each classroom on each component.

The Instructional Content Observation Form was developed to track how much teachers are able to address the content the OWL curriculum

Time	Narrative Description of Activities	Mode WGT WG SGT SG IAT IAC Seat Out Test	Type Rdg LngA Math Sci SS Art/M Cntr Oth Tms	Tchr Instr 0 none 1 low 2 skills 3 inf 4 hi inf	Class Inv 1 2 3 4 5	OWL SCHD Cntrs MM SL SWPL SG FT OD
8:35	Teacher and five students writing recipe for ice cream. Teacher models writing. Students ask questions and discuss ice-cream flavor. Students point out differences between capital *A* and *V.*	SGT	Rdg	3	4	Cntrs

FIGURE 8.1. Partial Narrative Record recording sheet (Farran & Lipsey, 2004).

recommended. Created for OWL, it uses the language, math, and science domains from the OWL program guide and evaluation materials. For example, the OWL curriculum includes Story Time (ST), Centers (C), and Small Groups (SG), and one of the academic domains is vocabulary. If the teacher provided vocabulary instruction during ST, C, and SG, then the observer would check each of those components for the vocabulary domain on the Instructional Content Observation Form. Figure 8.2 is a partial Instructional Content Form for oral language only, to show how the system works.

To illustrate use of these forms in action, Watson has provided a vignette of an actual observed classroom segment. Following the vignette, she provides the codes obtained from the Narrative Record and the Instructional Content Observation Form. Note that these are not the details that would be written in an actual observation session. Watson has reconstructed a classroom segment to provide an illustration of coding.

Language and Literacy	Where Observed	*Score 0–10
Oral Language		
1. Vocabulary	MM__ SL__ ST__ SWPL__ SG__ FT__ T__ C ✓OD__ NO__	__
2. Conversation	MM__ SL__ ST__ SWPL__ SG__ FT__ T__ C ✓OD__ NO__	__
3. Using Language to Resolve Conflicts	MM__ SL__ ST__ SWPL__ SG__ FT__ T__ C__ OD__ NO__	__
4. Using Language to Tell Personal Narrative and Engage in Pretend Play	MM__ SL__ ST__ SWPL__ SG__ FT__ T__ C ✓OD__ NO__	__
5. Using Language to Learn Information and How To Do Things	MM__ SL__ ST__ SWPL__ SG__ FT__ T__ C__ OD__ NO__	__
6. Learning information	MM__ SL__ ST__ SWPL__ SG__ FT__ T__ C__ OD__ NO__	__
7. Inferential questions	MM__ SL__ ST__ SWPL__ SG__ FT__ T__ C__ OD__ NO__	__
8. Literacy connections	MM__ SL__ ST__ SWPL__ SG__ FT__ T__ C__ OD__ NO__	__
		*Score = # of places observed

FIGURE 8.2. Partial Instructional Content Observation Form recording sheet (Farran & Lipsey, 2004).

Center Time: Recipe Writing

During morning center time, the lead teacher brought a large pad of chart paper to one of the open student tables to write the recipe for homemade ice cream. One of the centers for that morning was an ice-cream-making station. The teacher had gathered all the materials and ingredients; she just needed to write the recipe before she began the center activity. One student noticed that the teacher was about to write, and asked to "watch." The teacher picked up on this cue and invited the student to help her write the recipe. In the course of 5 minutes, four other students became interested and involved in the recipe writing. What started as a spontaneous teacher–child interaction became a 40-minute, small-group literacy lesson that captivated five children. During the "lesson," students initiated talk about beginning sounds, production and repetition of letters and words, links to personal experiences, number comparisons, ingredients in ice cream, and inferential thinking about relationships. This excerpt from the "lesson" shows some of the teacher–child interactions.

> TEACHER: OK, we need to write the recipe. Mary, do you want to come sit over here by me? (*Mary sits across the table from the teacher.*)
>
> MARY: Is that the ingredients for it (*points to bag with sugar, vanilla, plastic bags, and measuring cups*)?
>
> TEACHER: (*Nods.*) OK, we're going to write it [recipe] on here [chart paper] and you're going to help me with the words. OK? OK, we need to write the title up here. What are we making today?
>
> MARY: We are making ice cream (*talking "chorally" like the students do when they read the morning message*).
>
> TEACHER: OK. Now did I tell you what flavor we're making?
>
> MARY: Yes. Strawberry.
>
> TEACHER: No, that's one of the sauces that we're going to put on top. What flavor is the ice cream?
>
> MARY: Chocolate?
>
> TEACHER: Now remember, Mary. I'll have chocolate syrup for you and strawberry syrup. But I said everyone's ice cream is going to be . . .
>
> MARY: Va . . . vanilla.
>
> TEACHER: Vanilla. OK. Are you ready to write "vanilla ice cream" at the top? (*Writes "vanilla" on the top line of the chart paper. Then, she writes a capital* I.)
>
> GINA: That's like a *t*.
>
> TEACHER: Well, it looked like a *t* at first, and then I put this line on the bottom of it. Now what did I make it?

GINA: *I.*

SEAN: (*sitting to the side of the writing*) You know what? If it was like that, with that (*pointing to the* V–*which is almost upside down to him, and making a cross with his hand, to indicate capital* A), that be my big brother's name.

TEACHER: You know what? Your big brother's name starts with an A. That looks a lot like an *A,* doesn't it? But you know what it needs to be if it's an *A?* We'd have to turn it upside down. This is a *V.* (*Writes on scrap sheet.*) That's what letter I used. But, if you turn it upside down and then put another line across it, that's the *A* that you're talking about. (*Writes an A on scrap sheet.*) That's what Austin's name begins with. You are exactly right.

[later]

CARRIE: What's that *t*-word there (*pointing to "tsp." on recipe*)?

TEACHER: You know what? That's an abbreviation. I didn't write the whole word. Sometimes in recipes you can shorten words. That means teaspoon. But it doesn't have all the letters in it. This whole word is *teaspoon.* (*Writes the word on a scrap of paper.*)

Instructional Content Form Codes

For the example of the recipe writing, the academic domain rows marked in the Instructional Content Observation Form, in the column for center time (C), would include *vocabulary, conversation, using language to tell personal narrative* (on the section of the form that is presented in Figure 8.2). If the entire form were presented, you would see that the following content was also checked: *beginning sounds, meaning and uses of print, early writing, early reading,* and *alphabetic letter knowledge.*

Vocabulary would be marked because the teacher used vocabulary words (*ingredients, recipe*) from the unit. The multiple-turn conversation (approximately 11 turns) between the teacher and Mary is evidence for *conversation. Using language to tell personal narrative* would be the appropriate domain to categorize when Sean talked with the teacher about his brother's name. The teacher's talk about the letters *I* and *V* as the beginning sounds of *ice cream* and *vanilla* would fall under the academic domain of *beginning sounds.* The students were learning about the format of recipe writing, including abbreviations for measurements (tsp. = teaspoon), which would be considered *meaning and uses of print. Early writing* would be marked, because the teacher modeled writing for the students, and compared and contrasted the formation of letters (*A* and *V*).

The students' dictation of the title for the teacher ("We are making ice cream") and the student's question ("What is that *t*-word there?")

would be considered *early reading*. Last, the discussion of the characteristics of *I*, *A*, and *V* is the evidence for *alphabet knowledge*.

Illustrative Results from Both Instruments

Over the 2-years of evaluation, the project staff tried various methods for providing feedback to the teachers and the school administrators from the observations. None of the methods has been unequivocally successful. Teachers are not accustomed to there being observers in their classrooms and are even less accustomed to using data to reflect on their own classroom practices. In this section, Farran and Watson provide two examples of overall results obtained and how they could be used by systems.

TIME ALLOCATION FROM THE NARRATIVE RECORD

As the project has proceeded and teachers have become more experienced with the curriculum, the allocation of their instructional time has moved closer to the times recommended by the curriculum. In Table 8.1, the average time spent by individual teachers is presented as they enacted each of the OWL components across the second year of the ERF project. Individual times are given, along with the average for the group and a comparison to the times recommended by the curriculum. As indicated by the columns on the right, teachers continued to spend more time on caretaking activities (naps, snacks/lunch, toileting) and transitions than the curriculum recommends. During the first year, Farran and Watson discovered that transitions were extended by the inclusion of curricular content (e.g., dismissal from whole group by recognizing certain letters). The first-year time spent in transitions totaled over 60 minutes; by the second year, perhaps as a result of the feedback, that time had been reduced to 43 minutes.

The biggest difference between the OWL recommended time and the time spent by the classrooms was on center-based activities, with the ERF classrooms spending about half the time recommended by the curriculum developers. One reason for this discrepancy may be the number of whole-group activities prescribed by the curriculum—four—and the time taken by the teachers to get children into and out of these various groups. The other intrusion into time was a category the staff had to invent, called "Non-OWL." Many teachers had their own favorite activities, as well as songs and books that they preferred. A portion of the observational day in all classrooms was coded Non-OWL as teachers incorporated these additional activities. Table 8.1 shows clearly that teachers differed greatly on this aspect, from a low of a little less than 2 minutes to a high of more than 30 minutes, averaged across the three

TABLE 8.1. Time Allocation Averaged across Three Observations Compared to Recommended Times

Teacher	Centers	Morning Meeting	Story Time	Small Groups	Songs, Wordplay and Letters	Find Out about It	Outdoors	Snack/ Lunch	Transition	Nap	Non-OWL
A	65.3	15.0	22.3	23.7	22.7	20.3	28.0	46.3	53.3	58.7	4.3
B	49.3	8.7	17.3	12.7	18.0	12.3	19.7	47.7	60.7	81.3	32.3
C	63.7	17.3	19.7	22.3	22.0	16.3	33.0	45.3	32.3	71.3	16.7
D	56.0	11.0	18.0	23.3	26.7	14.7	41.7	53.0	41.7	68.0	6.0
E	61.3	20.7	20.3	16.3	22.7	15.7	27.0	52.0	46.3	66.3	11.3
F	76.0	14.7	21.3	17.0	18.3	14.7	28.7	69.3	36.3	56.0	7.7
G	54.0	19.3	24.0	18.7	24.3	13.7	24.7	47.0	31.3	80.7	22.3
H	68.3	6.0	21.3	18.7	22.3	12.0	27.7	73.7	33.7	74.7	1.7
I	69.3	14.3	19.7	15.0	20.7	14.3	29.0	40.0	57.0	68.3	12.3
J	51.7	16.3	21.0	18.0	29.3	15.3	26.3	47.3	42.0	66.7	26.0
Average	61.5	14.3	20.5	18.6	22.7	14.9	28.6	52.2	43.5	69.2	14.1
OWL Recommends	110.0	15.0	25.0	20.0	20.0	20.0	35.0	45.0	10.0	60.0	

observations. The time spent in transitioning students among activities, in caretaking, and in covering non-OWL materials had to come from somewhere; the two most flexible times were centers and outdoors, both of which were shorter than either the curriculum or most early childhood educators would advocate.

Data from an instrument such as the Narrative Record are useful because they describe the way in which time is allocated in the classroom, therefore providing a measure of teachers' and a program's priorities. The data demonstrate individual differences among teachers that could form the basis for peer discussions in professional development. There is also information here for the curriculum developers. Two whole-group activities (Story Time and Find Out About It) were uniformly lower than the amount of time the curriculum manual prescribed. Evidence from these 10 classrooms suggests that the developers might want to revisit either the time prescribed or the suggestions to teachers for how best to use that time.

CONTENT AREAS EMPHASIZED

In Table 8.2, the results on instructional content covered during a full year of curriculum implementation are reported. These data show the degree of emphasis each content area received across the day.[1] The areas receiving the most attention throughout the day were vocabulary, generating interest in books, and the meaning and uses of print, and early reading. Content related to phonological awareness appeared to be the most difficult to incorporate into various parts of the day. Of concern to the evaluation staff was the fact that many content areas decreased in emphasis over the year, with a notable drop off at Time 3, the late spring (see, e.g., the scores for conversation, inferential questions, literacy connections, and responses to books). It is hard to sustain rich interactions throughout the academic year, and prekindergarten programs in the public school are susceptible to the wind down that comes before the summer holidays. But these are areas that should be naturally self-sustaining. More investigation is clearly needed.

Although not demonstrated in Table 8.1, this process of data collection also leads to analyses of where during the day teachers are incorporating the most content. For example, in the first year, the evaluation staff discovered that two of the shortest components of the curriculum were being loaded with a great deal of content. The OWL component called "Songs, Word Play and Letters" received the majority of attention to

---

[1]The procedure for determining content emphasis has been changed to allow us to determine the actual number of times teachers address the content within each component. Those data will be available in 2007.

TABLE 8.2. Instructional Content for OWL, 2005–2006.

Language and Literacy	Number of areas observed		
	Time 1	Time 2	Time 3
Oral Language			
Vocabulary	4.9	4.4	5.3
Conversation	3.8	3.2	3.0
Using Language to Resolve Conflicts	1.2	1.1	0.7
Using Language to Tell Personal Narrative & Engage in Pretend Play	2.0	3.5	3.2
Using Language to Learn Information and How to Do Things	3.3	2.2	2.8
Learning Information	3.3	3.0	3.4
Inferential Questions	3.6	3.0	2.4
Literacy Connections	3.9	3.7	2.6
Phonological Awareness			
Syllable Awareness	0.0	0.2	0.2
Beginning Sounds	1.8	2.1	2.7
Rhyme Awareness	1.2	1.3	1.0
Phonemic Awareness	0.3	0.4	0.6
Book Interest and Understanding			
Interest in Books	4.4	3.9	3.7
Understanding of and Responses to Books	3.8	3.4	2.5
Print Understanding and Use			
Meaning and Uses of Print	4.0	4.3	3.9
Early Writing	1.7	1.7	2.3
Early Reading	4.0	5.0	4.6
Alphabet Letter Knowledge	2.7	3.0	3.0
Mathematics			
Numbers and Operations	2.9	2.0	2.8
Patterns, Relationships, and Functions	0.9	0.9	1.3
Geometric and Spatial Relationships	1.0	1.3	1.0
Measurements	0.2	0.2	0.6
Science			
Inquiry Skills	1.8	2.0	1.9
Physical Sciences	2.5	2.7	2.3
Earth and Space Sciences	0.1	0.0	0.0
Life Sciences	0.7	0.0	1.5

Note. OWL contains 10 components in a day. Scores could range from 0–10.

letter–sound correspondence, rhyming and beginning sounds. Feedback on these aspects allowed teachers to make changes in their instructional routines, changes that we saw reflected in the data collected the following year.

Conclusions

These two forms illustrate the process of creating a fidelity system that derives directly from the curriculum itself. Each allows administrators to compare classrooms to each other and to the dictates of the curriculum. Each of these instruments may be thought of as a template. Although Farran and Lipsey have structured them to reflect the emphases in OWL, each could be adapted for any curriculum, as long as the expected activities and curricular content are specified by the curriculum developers.

The unresolved issue continues to be how to allow teachers to have ownership of their curriculum and at the same time to determine how closely their practices match those recommended by the curriculum. Once a system (or researcher) adopts instruments such as the two described here, resulting actions must still be determined. For example, how close to the time recommendations do teachers need to be? Will child outcomes improve if the teachers work harder to do what the curriculum says they should? Another example is how to weight attention to different types of content? Should teachers attempt to work harder on learning how to include conversations and vocabulary during the day or to include more phonemic awareness activities? These instruments can provide the description of what *is*, but they do not say what *should be*. The latter has to be left to the preschool program or school system.

Concluding Thoughts

Early childhood educators and researchers are far ahead of educators who teach older children in efforts to devise tools that describe the quality of classrooms and identify specific kinds of classroom experiences that foster learning (Lambert, 2003). As a result, we are in the enviable position of having a track record of different kinds of efforts to describe classrooms and creating a toolkit of approaches to evaluate program quality that can be employed in a flexible manner according to the needs of a project (Dickinson, 2006). We are convinced that a new wave of development of tools for describing classrooms is needed, one that strives to capture the fine-grained details of classroom life. We speculate that such descriptions will benefit researchers and those interested in measuring and improving quality, because they will yield enhanced insight into the classroom dynamics that give rise to improved learning and increase our capacity to track the extent to which new curricula are being implemented. Here we have described promising approaches in two different projects that might be employed by others in a fashion tailored to their particular situation.

An added benefit of attending to the details of classroom life is that such descriptions hold the promise of being able to give teachers feedback that they can understand and use to enhance their teaching. We caution that careful thought needs to go into how teachers are given this information: Issues of importance include spoken or unspoken messages about ways the data might be used as part of supervision and evaluation of teachers' performance. As we discovered, it is also important that those providing feedback present it in a manner that highlights key information and makes clear the links to classroom practices.

Acknowledgments

We thank the teachers in both programs for their collaboration on these projects. We also thank Brittany Aronson, Molly Handler, Catherine Darrow, Ann Morse, Shani Shalev, and Titilayo Tinubu for assistance with data collection and analysis with the Dickinson project. We thank Sean Hurley, Aimee Servais, Karen Hyden, and Nancy Richardson for assistance with data collection and analyses on the Farran and Lipsey project. Funding for one project was supplied by a grant from Peabody College of Education, Vanderbilt University, and for the other, by an award from the Early Reading First program of the U.S. Department of Education.

References

Administration for Children and Families. (2005). *Head Start impact study: First year findings.* Washington, DC: U.S. Department of Health and Human Services.

Barnett, W. S. (2001). Preschool education for economically disadvantaged children: Effects on reading achievement and related outcomes. In S. B. Neuman & D. K. Dickinson (Eds.), *Handbook of early literacy research* (pp. 421–443). New York: Guilford Press.

Bryant, D. M., Burchinal, M., Lau, L. B., & Sparling, J. J. (1994). Family and classroom correlates of Head Start children's development outcomes. *Early Childhood Research Quarterly, 9,* 289–309.

Dickinson, D. K. (2002). Shifting images of developmentally appropriate practice as seen through different lenses. *Educational Researcher, 31*(1), 26–32.

Dickinson, D. K. (2003). Are measures of "global quality" sufficient? *Educational Researcher, 32,* 27–28.

Dickinson, D. K. (2006). Toward a toolkit approach to describing classroom quality. *Early Education and Development, 17*(1), 177–202.

Dickinson, D. K., & Brady, J. (2005). Toward effective support for language and literacy through professional development. In M. Zaslow & I. Martinez-Beck (Eds.), *Critical issues in early childhood professional development* (pp. 141–170). Baltimore: Brookes.

Dickinson, D. K., McCabe, A., Anastasopoulos, L., Peisner-Feinberg, E., & Poe, M. D. (2003). The comprehensive language approach to early literacy: The interrelationships among vocabulary, phonological sensitivity, and print knowledge among preschool-aged children. *Journal of Educational Psychology, 95*(3), 465–481.

Dickinson, D. K., McCabe, A., & Clark-Chiarelli, N. (2004). Preschool-based prevention of reading disability: Realities vs. possibilities. In C. A. Stone, E. R. Silliman, B. J. Ehren, & K. Apel (Eds.), *Handbook of language and literacy: Development and disorders* (pp. 209–227). New York: Guilford Press.

Dickinson, D. K., McCabe, A., & Essex, M. A. (2006). A window of opportunity we must open to all: The case for high-quality support for language and literacy. In D. K. Dickinson & S. B. Neuman (Eds.), *Handbook of early literacy research* (Vol. II, pp. 11–28). New York: Guilford Press.

Dickinson, D. K., & Porche, M. (2007). *The relationship between teacher–child conversations with low-income four-year olds and grade four language and literacy development.* Manuscript submitted for publication.

Dickinson, D. K., & Smith, M. W. (1994). Long-term effects of preschool teachers' book readings on low-income children's vocabulary and story comprehension. *Reading Research Quarterly, 29*(2), 104–122.

Dickinson, D. K., & Sprague, K. (2001). The nature and impact of early childhood care environments on the language and early literacy development of children from low-income families. In S. B. Neuman & D. K. Dickinson (Eds.), *Handbook of early literacy research* (pp. 263–280). New York: Guilford Press.

Dickinson, D. K., St. Pierre, R., & Pettengill, J. (2004). High quality classrooms: A key ingredient to family literacy programs. In B. Wasik (Ed.), *Handbook of family literacy* (pp. 137–154). Mahwah, NJ: Erlbaum.

Dickinson, D. K., & Tabors, P. O. (Eds.). (2001). *Beginning literacy with language: Young children learning at home and school.* Baltimore: Brookes.

Early Child Care Research Network. (2005). Pathways to reading: The role of oral language in the transition to reading. *Developmental Psychology, 41*, 428–442.

Farran, D. C. (2000). Another decade of intervention for disadvantaged and disabled children: What do we know now? In J. P. Shonkoff & S. J. Meisels (Eds.), *Handbook of early childhood intervention* (2nd ed., pp. 510–548). New York: Cambridge University Press.

Farran, D. C. (2001). Experience-dependent modifications of the brain and early intervention: Assumptions and evidence for critical periods. In D. B. Bailey, F. Symons, J. Bruer, & J. Lichtman (Eds.), *Critical thinking about critical periods* (pp. 233–266). Baltimore: Brookes.

Farran, D. C., Kang, S. J., Aydogan, C., & Lipsey, M. (2005). Preschool classroom environments and the quantity and quality of children's literacy and language behaviors. In D. Dickinson & S. Neuman (Eds.), *Handbook of early literacy research* (Vol. 2, pp. 257–268). New York: Guilford Press.

Farran, D. C., & Lipsey, M. (2004). *Evaluation Subcontract. Wayne County Literacy Acceleration Project: Early Reading First, Elementary and Secondary Education.* Washington, DC: U.S. Department of Education.

Farran, D. C., Lipsey, M., Bilbrey, C., & Hurley, S. (2006, April). *Comparing the effects of a literacy focused to a developmental curriculum in rural prekindergarten classrooms.* Poster presented at the annual meeting of the American Educational Research Association, San Francisco, CA.

Farran, D. C., Lipsey, M., Hurley, S., Watson, B., Richardson, N., & Curry, S. (2006, June). *Multifaceted evaluation of a literacy curriculum during the first year of an Early Reading First project.* Poster presented at the 8th annual Head Start Research Conference, Washington, DC.

Gormley, W. T. J., Gayer, T., Phillips, D., & Dawson, B. (2005). The effects of universal pre-K on cognitive development. *Developmental Psychology, 41*(6), 872–884.

Hamre, B. K., & Pianta, R. C. (2005). Can instructional and emotional support in the first-grade classroom make a difference for children at risk of school failure? *Child Development, 76*(5), 949–967.

Harms, T., Clifford, R., & Crye, D. (1998). *Early Childhood Environment Rating Scale (ECERS-R) Revised Edition.* New York: Teacher's College Press.

Hart, B., & Risley, T. (1995). *Meaningful differences in the everyday lives of American children.* Baltimore: Brookes.

Huttenlocher, J., Vasilyeva, M., Cymerman, E., & Levine, S. (2002). Language input and child syntax. *Cognitive Psychology, 45*, 337–375.

Klibanoff, R. S., Levine, S. C., Huttenlocher, J., Vasilyeva, M., & Hedges, L. V. (2006). Preschool children's mathematical knowledge: The effect of teacher "math talk." *Developmental Psychology, 42*(1), 59–69.

Lambert, R. (2003). Considering purpose and intended use when making evaluations of assessments: A response to Dickinson. *Educational Researcher, 32*(4), 37–52.

Language Analysis Lab. (2006). *Systematic Analysis of Language Transcripts (Version Windows Research V9).* Madison: Waisman Research Center, University of Wisconsin.

La Paro, K. M., Pianta, R., & Stuhlman, M. (2004). The Classroom Assessment Scoring System: Findings from the prekindergarten year. *Elementary School Journal, 104*(5), 409–426.

National Assessment of Educational Progress. (1999). *Trends in academic progress: Three decades of student performance.* Washington, DC: U.S. Department of Education, Office of Educational Research and Improvement.

National Association of the Education of Young Children. (2005). *New NAEYC early childhood program standards and accreditation criteria.* Washington, DC: Author.

National Board for Professional Teaching Standards. (2006). *Assessment process.* Retrieved November 21, 2006, from www.nbpts.org/become-a-candidate/assessment-process.

National Institute for Early Education Research. (2005). *The state of preschool: 2005 State preschool yearbook.* New Brunswick, NJ: Rutgers University.

Reynolds, A. J. (1994). Effects of a preschool plus follow-on intervention for children at risk. *Developmental Psychology, 30*, 787–804.

Schickedanz, J., & Dickinson, D. K. (2005). *Opening the World of Learning: A comprehensive literacy program.* Parsippany, NJ: Pearson Early Learning.

Schweinhardt, L. J., Barnes, H. V., Weikart, D. P., Barnett, W. S., & Epstein, A. S.

(1993). *Significant benefits: The High/Scope Preschool Study through age 27* (Monographs of the High/Scope Educational Research Foundation, No. 10). Ypsilanti, MI: High/Scope Educational Research Foundation.

Smith, M. W., Dickinson, D. K., Sangeorge, A., & Anastasopoulos, L. (2002). *The Early Language and Literacy Classroom Observation Toolkit (ELLCO)*. Baltimore: Brookes.

Snow, C. E., Burns, M. S., & Griffin, P. (Eds.). (1998). *Preventing reading difficulties in young children*. Washington, DC: National Research Council, National Academy Press.

Snow, C. E., & Dickinson, D. K. (1991). Skills that aren't basic in a new conception of literacy. In A. C. Purves & E. Jennings (Eds.), *Literate systems and individual lives: Perspectives on literacy and school*. Albany: State University of New York Press.

Spira, E. G., Bracken, S. S., & Fischel, J. E. (2005). Predicting improvement after first-grade reading difficulties: The effects of oral language, emergent literacy, and behavior skills. *Developmental Psychology, 41*(1), 225–234.

Storch, S. A., & Whitehurst, G. J. (2002). Oral language and code-related precursors to reading: Evidence from a longitudinal structural model. *Developmental Psychology, 38*, 934–947.

Vasilyeva, M., Huttenlocher, J., & Waterfall, H. (2006). Effects of language intervention on syntactic skill levels in preschoolers. *Developmental Psychology, 42*(1), 164–174.

Wasik, B., & Bond, M. A. (2006). The effects of a language and literacy intervention on Head Start children and teachers. *Journal of Educational Psychology, 98*(1), 63–74.

Westat, Xtria, & CDM Group. (2003). *Head Start FACES 2000: A Whole-Child Perspective on Program Performance* (Pub. No. *www.acf.hhs.gov/programs/opre/hs/faces/reports/faces00_4thprogress/faces00_4thprogress.pdf*). Retrieved July 7, 2007, from U.S. Department of Health and Human Service Administration for Children and Families, Washington, DC.

Zill, N., & Resnick, G. (2006). Emergent literacy of low-income children in Head Start: Relationships with child and family characteristics, program factors, and classroom quality. In D. K. Dickinson & S. B. Neuman (Eds.), *Handbook of early literacy research* (Vol. 2, pp. 347–371). New York: Guilford Press.

VOCABULARY REFLECTION FORM FOR CENTERS
OR SMALL-GROUP TIMES (DICKINSON)

(circle the activity you focused on)

Teacher: _____

Date: _____

Reflection on the Activity		Comments
Before the activity **I planned** to focus on particular words.	Yes No 0–1 2–3 4–5 6–8 9+ (# of occasions)	Words
During this activity **I used** words in a way that I thought would help children learn their meaning.	Yes No 0–1 2–3 4–5 6–8 9+ (# of occasions)	Words
During this activity I made a special effort to get a **child(ren) to use** a word that was hard for that child (or children).	Yes No 0–1 2–3 4–5 6–8 9+ (# of occasions)	Event:
During this activity I heard a child **spontaneously use** a word that I had taught this year.	Yes No 0–1 2–3 4–5 6–8 9+ (# of occasions)	Event:
Full-Day Reflection		
During this day I heard children **spontaneously use** a word that I had taught during the year.	Yes No 0–1 2–3 4–5 6–8 9+ (# of occasions)	
During this day **I praised** a child (or children) for using a good word.	Yes No 0–1 2–3 4–5 6–8 9+ (# of occasions)	Words

Other comments:

CONVERSATION REFLECTION FORM FOR CENTERS
OR SMALL-GROUP TIMES (DICKINSON)

(circle the activity you focused on)

Teacher: _____

Date: _____

Reflection on the Activity		Comments
Before the activity **I planned** to help children learn or think about new concepts.	Yes No 0 1 2 3+	Ideas/concepts
During this activity I had conversations that explored one topic for **5 or more exchanges**.	Yes No 0 1–2 3–4 5+ (# of occasions)	(May include efforts to solve a problem)
During this activity I had conversations during which a child(ren) **thought hard** about a problem or a new idea.	Yes No 0 1–2 3–4 5+ (# of occasions)	Event:
During this activity **I responded to a child's comment or question** that reflected curiosity, puzzlement or grasp of an idea.	Yes No 0 1–2 3–4 5+ (# of occasions)	Event:
Full-Day Reflection		
During this day I had conversations with a child or small group that explored one topic for 5 or more exchanges.	Yes No 0–1 2–4 5–6 7+ (# of occasions)	
During this day **I praised** a child (or children) for good thinking or for asking an interesting question.	Yes No 0 1–2 3–4 5+ (# of occasions)	
During this day I had conversations with children about something that **had happened to them** or about their home or family.	Yes No 0 1–2 3–4 5+ (# of occasions)	

Other comments:

PART III

★★★★★★★★★★

OPTIMIZING EARLY
LEARNING ENVIRONMENTS

Chapters 9 through 13 of this book consider how preschool teachers and other educators who work with preschool children (e.g., speech–language pathologists, reading specialists) can accelerate children's language and literacy accomplishments within the preschool classrooms. A rapidly accumulating literature shows that preschool teachers need to give careful thought to the targets they address within the their classrooms (e.g., vocabulary, phonological awareness), the techniques they use to address these targets (e.g., direct systematic instruction, scaffolding during authentic events), and the contexts in which instruction takes place (e.g., shared storybook reading, dramatic play). This section provides explicit guidance to preschool educators on such issues.

We organized these chapters to move from broad to more focal considerations of the classroom milieu. Renée Casbergue, Lea M. McGee, and April Bedford (Chapter 9) give specific guidance on how preschool educators can best organize their classrooms and interact with pupils to help them learn language and literacy across a range of different activity contexts. Sonia Q. Cabell, Laura M. Justice, Carol Vukelich, Martha Buell, and Myae Han (Chapter 11) focus specifically on the storybook reading context and consider how interactions around storybooks can be organized explicitly to promote specific language and literacy objectives. Judith A. Schickedanz (Chapter 10) carefully considers teacher responsiveness, an important element of high-quality preschool instruction, and describes how teachers can be responsive to children in ways that maximize their language and cognitive development within various learning activities.

Chapters 12 and 13 focus on a very important topic in any consideration of how to achieve excellence in the preschool classroom: the diversity of our pupils. On the first day of school, preschool educators look across their classrooms and see children who differ in so many ways, from the languages they hear at home to the educational accomplishments of their parents. Despite such differences, the children in our preschool classrooms have much in common, including a love of playing and pretending, learning new words, building their background knowledge through exploring topics important to understanding themselves and the world, and showing others what they know and can do. To guide preschool educators as they work with heterogeneous learners, Terri Purcell and Catherine A. Rosemary (Chapter 12) discuss the concept of differentiated instruction, and show how it can help educators provide developmentally appropriate instruction to classrooms in which children arrive with diverse understandings, skills, and experiences. M. Adelaida Restrepo and Virginia Dubasik (Chapter 13) provide additional guidance on this topic by summarizing the literature on how to provide quality instruction to children who are not native English speakers and are learning a second language within the preschool classroom.

While reading these chapters, generate responses to these five questions, and be prepared to share your responses in guided discussions with others:

1. Beyond providing children with a print-rich environment, what key aspects of interactions among children and their teachers positively affect children's achievement?
2. What language and early literacy skills can adults teach through storybook reading?
3. Why is it important for teachers to exhibit cognitive sensitivity toward children in their classrooms? How does this affect children's learning?
4. How can supporting English language learners' development of their native language and literacy be beneficial to the development of their English language and early literacy skills learning? Which language and early literacy skills areas most easily transfer from the native language to English?
5. What is differentiated instruction, and how does it compare with developmentally appropriate practice?

After reading the chapter, complete one or more of the following four activities to expand your knowledge further:

1. Observe a teacher-directed activity (large or small group) in a classroom. Did the teacher extend the lesson to the children's free play or centers time? If so, how? If not, how might you have done so?

2. Eavesdrop on a teacher's talk with children during center time or audiotape your interactions with children during center time. Is this teacher's language helpful to children's language and literacy development? Did this teacher attend to a child's misunderstandings, and use evaluative and elaborate feedback to guide a child toward greater understanding? If not, were there any missed opportunities to do this? How might you have handled such an opportunity?

3. Audiotape yourself reading a storybook to a preschooler. Use Appendix 11.1 in Chapter 11, this volume, to understand the language and literacy skills you taught or reinforced during this storybook reading.

4. Observe a preschool classroom. What kinds of groupings for instruction were evidenced? In what ways did these groupings seem to improve children's learning opportunities and experiences? In what ways might they have detracted?

CHAPTER 9

★★★★★★★★

Characteristics of Classroom Environments Associated with Accelerated Literacy Development

Renée Casbergue
Lea M. McGee
April Bedford

Two 4-year-olds, Kendara and Li'Tisha, playing in the housekeeping area in their preschool classroom decided to pretend that they were getting ready for a party. As they selected party clothes and prepared party foods in the kitchen, their teacher said from the block area beside them where she was interacting with other children, "Have you already sent your invitations?" The girls immediately chose paper and pencils, and Kendara began to write. Seeing this, their teacher moved into their center and knelt beside the table, encouraging the children to consider what information they would need to include, and supplying conventional spelling when the children requested it. When they finished, Kendara and Li'Tisha took their invitation to the children sharing books in the library center and invited them to the party. At that point, Li'Tisha decided that she also needed to make an invitation. Returning to the housekeeping center, she too began to write, using Kendara's invitation as a model, with Kendara pointing at various symbols written on her invitation for Li'Tisha to copy.

This rich and meaningful literacy interaction among these children and their teacher was observed during one of our many trips to visit this preschool site. We found that occurrences such as these were common in the language- and print-rich environments created as a result of two federally funded Early Reading First (ERF) projects. This chapter describes our discoveries about how to help teachers transform ordinary preschool classrooms into extraordinary environments that accelerate children's language and literacy development.

Going Beyond the Mandates

In 2002 (but not in later funded projects), ERF grantees were required to demonstrate that project classrooms provided high levels of language and literacy support using the Literacy Environment Checklist of the Early Language and Literacy Classroom Observation Toolkit (ELLCO; Smith & Dickinson, 2002) on yearly reports to the U.S. Department of Education. We provided two ERF project teachers with considerable professional development and in-classroom coaching relative to the classroom environment; in particular, we taught these teachers how to rearrange their classrooms to match the elements on the Literacy Environment Checklist. It is not surprising that as a result of this professional development and coaching, the classrooms in these two projects exhibited the elements on the Literacy Environment Checklist.

We noticed that despite maintaining perfect scores on the Literacy Environment Checklist during the entire first year, not all classroom environments were *really* language- and literacy-rich. Despite having the same scores, some teachers tremendously accelerated their students' language and literacy growth in comparison to other teachers. This led us to explore two questions:

1. According to current research, what are the characteristics of language- and literacy-rich classroom environments? Does the ELLCO capture these elements?
2. What characteristics were evident in the classrooms where teachers were more successful in accelerating children's language and literacy development that were missing in other classrooms?

Examining Research on the Characteristics of Language- and Literacy-Rich Environments

We examined three strands of research that we believed would inform us about the elements defining high-quality language and literacy environments. These included research on (1) children who are successful beginning readers or who arrive in kindergarten already reading (Clark, 1976; Clay, 1975; Durkin, 1966; Heath, 1983; Taylor, 1983; Taylor & Dorsey-Gaines, 1988; Teale, 1978); (2) successful preschool and kindergarten classrooms (Cochran-Smith, 1984; Dickinson & Smith, 1994; Dickinson & Sprague, 2001; Dickinson & Tabors, 2001; Neuman, 1999; Rowe, 1998); and (3) interventions designed to change classroom environments to be more supportive of language and literacy (Justice, Chow, Capellini, Flanigan, & Colton, 2003; Taylor, Blum, & Logsdon, 1986; Morrow & Rand, 1991; Vukelich, 1990, 1994; Neuman & Roskos, 1992, 1993, 1997). In each of these research studies we sought to identify characteristics of the environment that seemed related to children's successes. We also examined research on the nature of "ideal" book and writing centers (e.g., Fractor, Woodruff, Martinez, & Teale, 1993).

From this research we developed over 50 research-based components of a language- and literacy-rich environment. These components may be categorized as teachers' practices and language; reading, and writing routines; literacy materials and classroom space; and classroom displays. Table 9.1 summarizes and condenses these components. The better known characteristics of well-designed book or writing centers are not reiterated here.

Then, we compared the Literacy Environment Checklist to our list of research-based components of language- and print-rich environments. This comparison revealed that the majority of the components were reflected in the checklist. What was missing was the assessment of the purposes of the written displays, the language used in these displays, or their usefulness to children. The checklist also does not include an assessment of the types of language the teacher uses or the evidence of daily encouragements, acknowledgments, and scaffolding of the children's reading and writing.

Using the data we collected from classroom observations as part of our external evaluation of the two projects' classrooms, we attempted to uncover the differences between classroom environments where children's learning was accelerated at a higher rate than that of children in other classrooms.

Observational Data Collection

The external evaluators visited each classroom twice, once early in the fall semester and again at the end of the school year. Classroom environments were evaluated with the ELLCO Literacy Environment Checklist. Additional data were collected during observations of three key routines across all classrooms. First, whole-group literacy activities were observed

TABLE 9.1. Research-Based Components of High-Quality Language- and Literacy-Rich Classrooms

Teacher practices and language	Reading and writing routines	Literacy materials and classroom space	Classroom displays
Teacher provides opportunities for extended talk.	Teacher provides daily modeling of several reading and writing routines (read aloud, shared and interactive reading and writing).	Materials are age-appropriate, authentic, and functional.	Print displays represent a variety of purposes for writing, including furthering pretense, experimenting with print, recording ideas, etc.
Teacher frequently uses "rare words."	Teacher provides access to abundant reading and writing materials, including those that the teacher has read or written.	Materials are varied, clustered thematically, located in proximity to props, and easily accessible.	Print displays include materials that are produced by the teacher with input from the children.
Teacher regularly employs language extension strategies.	Teacher encourages children's daily participation in reading and writing activities.	Room is divided into clearly defined and labeled play spaces that include reading and writing materials.	Print displays include pieces produced by children.
Teacher provides opportunities for children to use analytic and predictive talk.	Teacher acknowledges children's attempts to read and write.	Ample space is provided for more than one dramatic play center.	Print displays include connected text and themed words.
Teacher plans for conversations with children throughout the day.	Teacher scaffolds children's reading and writing efforts.	Dramatic play centers include themes and "scripts" that are familiar to children.	Print displays are usable and accessible to children.
Teacher plays with and talks to children in centers.		Purpose of centers is evident.	Print displays change frequently in content, format, and sophistication.
Teacher extends children's dramatic play by modeling new "scripts."		Centers are organized for children's independent use.	

for 20 minutes during each classroom site visit. These activities included a variety of approaches to morning message and shared writing routines, interactive read-alouds of picture books, and oral language routines. Next, the evaluators observed 20-minute small-group literacy activities. These sessions designed for 8–10 children were intended to call children's attention to specific aspects of print. For these two sources of data, evaluators took extensive field notes that described each activity and captured language interactions among teachers and children. Finally, children's free play in centers was observed for an additional 20 minutes. During this period, the evaluators used time sampling procedures to note the number of children engaged in any form of literacy activity at specific intervals, and whether that literacy activity included interaction with a teacher or teaching assistant. Teachers' and assistants' activities were also recorded at set intervals within the 20 minute period. The form used by the external evaluators to gather these data is included in Appendix 9.1.

From these data, it appeared that three aspects of interactions among children and their teachers within the language- and print-rich environments were closely related to differences in children's achievement: (1) extensions of teacher-directed activities from whole- and small-group lessons to children's free play or centers time; (2) the quantity and quality of teachers' interactions with children during free play; and (3) the amount of children's spontaneous interactions with print during their free play. In the following sections, we discuss each of these aspects of interactions.

Extensions of Teacher-Directed Activity

In classrooms with some of the most impressive gains in children's literacy knowledge, children frequently extended activities from whole- or small-group routines into their own play during centers time. These extensions were often encouraged by teachers and took many different forms.

Almost all teachers regularly placed books shared during whole-group activities in a prominent place in the book center or on an easel in the whole-group area for the children's use during centers time. Children reread the books independently when the teacher made a point of saying, "I'm going to put this book here so you can read it yourself later, if you like." Children appeared to be especially eager to interact with the book on their own when their teacher suggested a specific aspect of the book they might enjoy exploring. For example, while sharing *The Three Billy Goats Gruff* (Stevens, 1995), one teacher pointed out the troll's captive frog in each illustration, commenting on how it was gradually freed. As she placed the book on the easel for children to read later, she said, "You might want to find that frog on every page and see how much happier he gets each time!" Of course, this enticed a number of children to look at the book together and retell the story to each other.

Books were not the only materials that teachers made available to children after teacher-directed activities. One especially effective routine in these classrooms was "step up," an extension of more typical shared writing activities. After reading a book, sharing some experience, or engaging in a discussion of objects that teachers or children brought to share with the class, the teachers engaged children in the creation of a language experience or shared writing display. Children were then invited to "step up" to the chart and circle, underline, or write some feature of print on which instruction was focused that day. After talking about hurricanes, for example, one teacher elicited a list entitled "What We Remember about Hurricane Katrina." Children shared their recollections, resulting in a list that read as follows: rain, water, trees, rumbling, dark, and hot. Upon completion of the list, the teacher invited the children to step up to the chart and find specific letters on which they had been focusing during small-group time. As she held up magnetic letters, the children found corresponding letters in the dictated list and circled them. At the conclusion of the group activity, the teacher told the children that they could continue to find letters on the chart during centers time. Magnetic letters corresponding to many of those on the dictated list were placed on the whiteboard below the chart, and a number of children eagerly engaged in that activity during their free play time, taking turns either being the teacher holding up letters or circling letters and writing on the chart. Photo 9.1 provides an illustration of this activity.

PHOTO 9.1. Children pay careful attention to particular aspects of print as they are invited to "step up" individually to find, circle, or write letters following a shared writing activity.

Other teachers also made a point of making materials from activities they directed accessible for children's independent use. These included, for example, puzzle cards into which children placed foam letters representing beginning or ending sounds, mats and small objects to be sorted according to beginning sounds, and blocks for building words and blending sounds. The key to extending all of these activities into children's free play was the teachers' reminders, both at the conclusion of the teacher-directed activity and again just before children moved into centers, that the materials were available for children's independent use.

At other times, children extended whole- and small-group activities into their own play without any direct encouragement from their teachers. In one classroom, the children had been pursuing an "ocean" theme. They read books about ocean life, shared stories about their own visit to a Gulf Coast aquarium, and pretended to be divers in an "under the sea" dramatic play center. During one small-group activity, the teacher made individual, simple brochures from folded paper with the title "Come to the Aquarium" on the outside. He printed, "Come see the . . . inside," leaving space to write in the name of an animal dictated by a child. Children drew pictures to represent their favorite fish or aquatic mammal beneath this dictation, and many of them copied the teacher's print to label their pictures themselves. This activity was focused as much on vocabulary and oral language development as on writing as children discussed their choices of animals with each other and the teacher. Later that day, two children were observed attempting to create their own brochures independently in the writing center. Each boy had drawn a line down the center of the page to represent the fold in the paper, and both had drawn pictures and labeled them with the animal's name. One boy had even spelled *jelly* conventionally—obviously copied from the jellyfish label on a finished brochure hanging near the center. Photo 9.2 provides an illustration of this work.

In all of these examples, children's interaction with print was directly extended from teacher-directed activities into the free play time by the children's choice. As a result, not all children engaged in these extensions. Those that did, however, significantly increased the time they were engaged with meaningful print, often doubling their exposure to target sounds, letters, and words.

Teacher Interactions during Free Play

A second feature of classrooms with the largest gains in children's literacy achievement was the quantity and quality of the teachers' interactions with children during their free play time. As noted earlier, data were collected to document how teachers spent their time during children's free play in centers. Even among this dedicated group, there was a surprising

PHOTO 9.2. Children extend whole-group activity into their own independent play here as they draw or print near the writing center for their own creations.

degree of variance in both how much teachers interacted with children during their play and the manner in which they did so. In many cases, this variance could be explained by outside influences and school policies that prohibited teachers from interacting more effectively.

The most glaring example of a policy that inhibited teachers' interactions with children was the requirement in one school that teachers record a narrative account of which center each child selected, and the specific activities in which he or she was engaged every day. The result of this policy was that both the teacher and the teaching assistant spent the entire free play period every day moving from center, to center furiously taking notes. When asked how those notes were used one of the teachers shrugged and said, "We just have to put them in the children's folders each day."

In another school, the free play time in centers seemed to be viewed by administrators as nonteaching time, during which teachers could be called away from the children to deal with administrative issues. Teachers in that school fairly regularly found themselves standing in the doorway to their classrooms, discussing calls from parents, changes in carpool arrangements, or administrative responsibilities, while monitoring the various classroom centers for behavior issues. Their interactions with children during that time included offering guidance for behavior management from their spot by the door.

This use of teachers' time is in sharp contrast to that in other classrooms, where teachers were able to spend all of their center activity time supporting and extending children's play. In the most effective classrooms, teachers frequently joined children in their play, extending their conversations and inviting them to use props that encouraged engagement with print, as in the example that opened this chapter. There were as many instances of teachers suggesting writing activities to children as there was variety in the dramatic play centers they established. Beyond the expected invitations for children to create grocery lists and write telephone messages in the housekeeping center, or to create menus and take orders in restaurant centers, these teachers found many more creative possibilities for children's engagement with print. One teacher set up his own "Oceanarium" and provided actual brochures from a local marine center, blank checks and receipts, schedule cards indicating when boat tours would leave the dock, a reservation book for group and individual tours, a telephone and message pad, and books and photographs of marine life. As the children pretended to be workers and visitors at the oceanarium, the teachers periodically stopped in to buy tickets, to book tours, or to ask about the feeding habits or habitat of specific animals pictured in the center display, pretending that the children were expert marine biologists. These interactions resulted in conversations that incorporated rich vocabulary related to the ongoing theme and opportunities for teachers to observe and to scaffold children's use of print.

Another wonderful interaction occurred when one teacher spotted a little boy sitting on a chair in a library center, quietly reading aloud from an open book on his lap, and very accurately retelling the story of the little red hen as he turned each page. She approached him and asked if he would read the book to her. He started to get up to give the chair to her, but she stopped him and sat on the floor in front of him saying, "No, you're reading to me, so you're the teacher." He was delighted, and immediately assumed the "teacher" role, holding the book facing outward toward his "pupil" so that she could see the pictures as he reread the book.

Whereas these teachers encouraged language and literacy by circulating around the room and playing with the children, others occasionally chose to remain in one center for the majority of free play time. This usually resulted in children gravitating toward those centers and enjoying extensive interactions with their teachers. In some classrooms, children spent much more time in the library center when the teacher was there sharing books the children requested than when the children were in the center without an adult.

Two teachers skillfully meshed extended time in the library center with the theme of their dramatic play centers. Toward the end of the school year, these teachers each set up a beach dramatic play center in their respective classrooms, with items including beach toys, towels, sunscreen bottles, goggles, inflatable rings, and print materials for beach equipment rental. One teacher asked her students to dictate a list of all the items they might find at the beach, and created a mural displaying all

PHOTO 9.3. Children enjoy reading with their teacher "at the beach" in their library center, here sharing a book related to their ongoing investigation of oceans.

of their suggestions as a backdrop for the book center. During free play time, one teacher donned a sun visor and the other put on sunglasses as they both brought plastic beach bags full of books to their library centers. Children soon put on their own sun visors or sunglasses and settled in with their teachers for summer beach reading. Photo 9.3 provides an illustration.

Children's Spontaneous Interactions with Print

A final characteristic of classrooms in which children demonstrated impressive language and literacy gains was the degree to which the children spontaneously engaged with print. The external evaluators, using a time point sampling procedure, documented the number of children engaged in any form of interaction with print. Examples of literacy interactions included looking at books or listening to them being read anywhere in the classroom; writing of any kind; using alphabetic materials such as puzzles, matching word games, and letter–sound sorting activities; and engaging in print-related computer activities. Classrooms that consistently had the greatest number of children using print on their own tended to be those in which children made the strongest gains in their language and literacy skills.

The most obvious print engagement occurred in the library, listening, and writing centers. In some classrooms, children spent significant portions of their free play time in the library center, reading books either alone or to each other. Frequently, they could also be observed reading to dolls or to stuffed animals. In many classrooms, the listening center was also a popular attraction, particularly when it was accessible and set up so that children could select books and tapes, and start listening with little or no assistance from adults. Well-stocked writing centers that contained a variety of shapes, sizes, colors, and textures of paper, as well as a broad variety of writing implements, were also favored by many children.

Interactions with print also abounded in dramatic play centers. Whether taking orders in restaurants, scheduling appointments in barber shops or doctors' offices, making shopping lists and writing receipts for items in a store, or listing types of plants for sale in a nursery, children wrote prodigiously in classrooms with creative dramatic play centers equipped with props that induced engagement with print. The more a dramatic play center reflected children's experiences beyond their homes, the more engaged children seemed to be. This was certainly the case with the "Oceanarium" established by the teacher after children had visited a marine center. It was also true for a dramatic play center set up as a book fair. The introduction of this center was timed to coincide with a schoolwide book fair conducted as a fund-raiser in the school auditorium. All of the children visited the book fair with their classes during school time, and many returned with their parents to buy books at the end of the day. Children reenacted this experience time and again in the dramatic play center with books drawn from the library center and an ample supply

PHOTO 9.4. This dramatic play center, set up to mimic the school's book fair, enticed many children into both reading and writing as they bought and sold books to each other.

of book order forms, blank checks, credit cards, and receipts. Photo 9.4 provides an illustration.

Implications for Early Literacy Interventions

Experience with the two ERF projects highlighted here provide some insight into characteristics of early literacy interventions that are likely to lead to increases in children's language abilities and literacy. Clearly, establishing environments within which children are able to interact with print in a variety of ways, and for many different purposes, is a necessary first step. However, a literacy-enhanced physical environment alone is not sufficient to ensure optimum language and literacy gains. Instead, it is the interactions that occur within that environment that appear to accelerate children's development.

Three characteristics of effective classrooms appeared to relate to the differences documented in children's language and literacy achievement: (1) extensions of teacher-directed activities to children's free play; (2) interactions between teachers and children during free play time that invite children to engage with print; and (3) children's spontaneous inter-action with print in centers and during dramatic play. In classrooms in which the children appeared to receive the most encouragement to read and write for their own purposes, children made the strongest language and literacy gains.

Although some aspects of teachers' interactions with preschool children may be related to personal style, other aspects may be relatively easy to teach as part of ongoing professional development. Simply having teachers place materials used in teacher-directed activities where they are accessible for children's independent use might be a routine that significantly increases children's engagement with print, especially if teachers habitually remind children that those activities are available. Encouraging teachers to alternate between movement among centers and extended periods of time in library and writing centers may also be an easily learned strategy that increases the time children opt to spend reading and writing.

Observation in these classrooms also suggests that effective early literacy interventions may require advocating for changes in policies and practices that interfere with teachers' ability to engage their children in meaningful literacy activities. Teachers need to understand both the importance of allowing children to choose their own centers and moving freely among centers, and the importance of their own language and literacy interactions with children during center time. Teachers may need assistance to help administrators understand the importance of these teacher–child interactions during play and to recognize those interactions as teaching.

The examples of rich language and literacy interactions described in this chapter, however, illustrate the power of play in literacy-infused preschool classrooms. Early literacy interventions that structure physical environments, provide appropriate materials, and enhance language and literacy interactions among children and teachers paid substantial dividends in the literacy development of the children we observed. We urge other educators to implement these same types of interventions to enhance the development of young learners in their classrooms.

References

Clark, M. (1976). *Young fluent readers*. London: Heinemann Educational Books.

Clay, M. (1975). *What did I write?* Portsmouth, NH: Heinemann.

Cochran-Smith, M. (1984). *The making of a reader*. Norwood, NJ: Ablex.

Dickinson, D. K., & Smith, M. W. (1994). Long-term effects of preschool teachers' book readings on low-income children's vocabulary and story comprehension. *Reading Research Quarterly, 29*, 104–122.

Dickinson, D. K., & Sprague, K. E. (2001). The nature and impact of early childhood care environments on the language and early literacy development of children from low-income families. In S. B. Neuman & D. K. Dickinson (Eds.). *Handbook of early literacy research* (pp. 263–280). New York: Guilford Press.

Dickinson, D. K., & Tabors, P. O. (2001). *Beginning literacy with language*. Baltimore: Brookes.

Durkin, D. (1966). *Children who read early*. New York: Teachers College Press.

Fractor, J., Woodruff, M., Martinez, M., & Teale, W. (1993). Let's not miss opportunities to promote voluntary reading: Classroom libraries in elementary school. *Reading Teacher, 46*, 476–484.

Heath, S. B. (1983). *Ways with words: Language, life, and work in communities and classrooms*. Cambridge, UK: Cambridge University Press.

Justice, L. M., Chow, S., Capellini, C., Flanigan, K., & Colton, S. (2003). Emergent literacy intervention for vulnerable preschoolers: Relative effects of two approaches. *American Journal of Speech–Language Pathology, 12*, 320–332.

Morrow, L. M., & Rand, M. (1991). Preparing the classroom environment to promote literacy during play. In J. F. Christie (Ed.), *Play and early literacy development* (pp. 141–165). Albany: State University of New York Press.

Neuman, S. B. (1999). Books make a difference: A study of access to literacy. *Reading Research Quarterly, 34*, 286–311.

Neuman, S. B., & Roskos, K. (1992). Literacy objects as cultural tools: Effects on children's literacy behaviors in play. *Reading Research Quarterly, 27*, 202–225.

Neuman, S. B., & Roskos, K. (1993). Access to print for children of poverty: Differential effects of adult mediation and literacy-enriched play settings on envi-

ronmental and functional print tasks. *American Educational Research Journal,*
30, 95–122.

Neuman, S. B., & Roskos, K. (1997). Literacy knowledge in practice: Context of
participation for young writers and readers. *Reading Research Quarterly, 32,*
10–32.

Rowe, D. (1998). The literate potentials of book-related dramatic play. *Reading
Research Quarterly, 33,* 10–35.

Smith, M. W., & Dickinson, D. K. (2002). *User's guide to the early language and literacy classroom observation (ELLCO) toolkit.* Baltimore: Brookes.

Stevens, J. (1995). *The Three Billy Goats Gruff.* New York: Harcourt.

Taylor, D. (1983). *Family literacy: Young children learning to read and write.* Portsmouth, NH: Heinemann.

Taylor, D., & Dorsey-Gains, C. (1988). *Growing up literate: Learning from inner-city
families.* Portsmouth, NH: Heinemann.

Taylor, N., Blum, I., & Logsdon, D. (1986). The development of written language
awareness: Environmental aspects and program characteristics. *Reading
Research Quarterly, 21,* 132–149.

Teale, W. H. (1978). Positive environments for learning to read: What studies of
early readers tell us. *Language Arts, 55,* 922–932.

Vukelich, C. (1990). Where's the paper?: Literacy during dramatic play. *Childhood
Education, 66,* 203–209.

Vukelich, C. (1994). Effects of play interventions on young children's reading of
environmental print. *Early Childhood Research Quarterly, 9,* 153–170.

CLASSROOM OBSERVATION CODING FORM

Classroom: <u>Ms. Walker/Ms. Washington</u>   Date: <u>5/10/06</u>

Center observation protocol

Sampling time	# Children engaged in literacy activities	Teacher supporting? (Indicate which if yes)	Aide supporting? (Indicate which if yes)
3 minutes 9:50	3 listening center 1 rhyme word game 1 computer reading game 2 writing center 2 Play Doh™—making letters	✓ Helping child read "boat" on picture card—child saying "ship" and couldn't find rhyme.	✓ Providing letter cookie cutters for children to make letters.
8 minutes 9:55	3 listening center 1 rhyme word game 1 computer reading game 2 writing center 2 Play Doh™—making letters	✓ Helping children sound out words in writing center.	✓ Helping children roll out Play Doh.
13 minutes 10:00	2 reading center 1 writing center 1 computer reading game 1 grocery list/drama 2 Play Doh™—making letters	✓ Reading completed grocery list with child.	✓
18 minutes 10:05	2 writing home drama 1 writing center 2 reading center 1 writing center 2 reading center 1 computer reading game	✓ Reading *The Three Billy Goats Gruff* with two children.	No

	Teacher activity	Aide activity
6 minutes 9:53	Helping one child complete math pattern chain.	Supervising blocks while suggesting letters to children with Play Doh.
11 minutes 9:58	Suggesting items for shopping list in dramatic play center.	Block area.
16 minutes 10:03	Reading to two children in book area.	Helping two children with word puzzles.

CHAPTER 10

★★★★★★★★★

Increasing Children's Learning by Getting to the Bottom of Their Confusion

Judith A. Schickedanz

A number of years ago, a teacher shared her puzzlement with me about a child's unusual reaction one day at the end of story time. Immediately after the teacher had finished reading the story, the child asked, "Is that the end of the story?" She looked worried. The teacher opened the book again to show the last page, and then she turned to the book's end papers. "There are no more words," she explained. The child's eyes began to fill with tears.

The child had never before become upset at the end of story time. Why, then, on this day? The teacher knew of the new baby at home, and wondered whether mother had stopped reading stories at bedtime. After talking with the child's mother, however, she learned that the nightly story reading routine had not changed.

Given the child's love of stories, the teacher wondered whether the child had liked this story so much that she had not wanted it to end. Out of curiosity, the teacher and I looked at the book to determine why it might have appealed so much to this child. All of a sudden, we had an idea about the child's upset feeling. We thought the ending was somewhat unusual and that the child might not have considered it adequate.

In the story *The Little Polar Bear and the Brave Little Hare* (de Beer, 1998), two young animals find themselves far away from their home in the Arctic. While exploring, the bear cub falls through the rooftop of a polar research station operated by humans, then the little hare devises a plan to help the bear cub escape. When she thumps her foot on the rooftop to prompt the researcher to open the door, her trapped friend runs out. As they run home, they discuss how frightened they had been. The text indicates that they found their home.

On the last pages of the book, the two young animals are pictured atop a mound of snow, talking with one another. On the last page, they are pictured sleeping side by side, under the nighttime sky. In this book, "home" means habitat or the region where one lives, not a specific shelter. If a child's understanding of the word "home" is confined to shelter, then he or she might be concerned that the animals do not make it home; thus, they are not yet safe when the story ends.

The next day, the teacher talked with the child and asked why she had become upset the day before. The child's explanation revealed that she indeed thought the young animals did not arrive at their home. As a consequence of this misunderstanding, she thought the humans might find the animals and hurt them. The teacher and child looked at the book again, and the teacher read the part of the text that stated explicitly that the young animals were far from the polar station when they stopped once, while running home, to catch their breath. The teacher further explained that they ran more after this pause, as she referred to the picture depicting this event. Then, she explained that in this story, the word "home" means habitat or a region, not a house or a cave or a nest. She also explained that humans are scared of polar bears, especially adult bears that probably live near the little bear and hare; thus, they are unlikely to go very far from their research station. For all of these reasons, she explained, the little animals were safe at the end of the story.

Teacher Sensitivity and Children's Learning

This teacher in this situation was warm and supportive of a child who was emotionally upset. Often the concept of teacher sensitivity is restricted to these attributes. In this specific case, however, the child's reaction was the consequence of her limited understanding of the word *home*. To deal with the child's emotional upset, the teacher provided information to help the child draw a likely inference about the situation at the end of the story. As the anecdote illustrates, emotional and cognitive states are sometimes intertwined in young children. This should not be a surprise given the young child's limited store of information and limited reasoning ability.

A considerable body of research suggests that responsiveness to both emotional and cognitive needs supports learning. For example, a positive emotional climate in a classroom promotes emotional understanding and self-regulation (e.g., control of behavior; Birch & Ladd, 1998). These, in turn, lead to more positive social interactions with both peers and teachers (Howes, 2000). Children with higher levels of self-regulation also tend to pay attention and to follow directions better (Arnold et al., 1999; McClelland, Morrison, & Holmes, 2000). They also receive more positive feedback and instruction from teachers (Arnold et al., 1999; McEvoy & Welker, 2000). Thus, a teacher's warmth and nurturance can have major effects on children's learning.

The cognitive dimension of teacher sensitivity involves noticing and caring about children's misunderstandings, and using evaluative and elaborate feedback to guide a child toward greater understanding. Cognitive sensitivity is likely to have an effect on a child's learning, because explanations involve information, which constitutes a form of instruction. Not surprisingly, one study of parent–child interactions in the home (Weizman & Snow, 2001) labeled the highest level of support provided to children "instructive" to capture its highly informative nature. In the storybook example, the teacher explained the meaning of the word *home* in the book's specific context and also reread some text to provide critical information about the story characters' physical position in relationship to humans in the research station. Then, she provided information about the typical human perspective on bears (i.e., dangerous animals) and drew the inference that the researchers were not likely to venture out to look for the young cub and the hare. Then, considering together the distance of the young animals' home from the research station and the human inclination to avoid contact with bears, the teacher drew the inference that the young animals were safe when the story ended. In doing this, the teacher modeled the kind of thinking required to comprehend this story. It was the instruction the teacher provided, not solely her emotional support, that helped to allay the child's concerns. The importance of both of these dimensions, instruction and teacher sensitivity, and their interaction, has prompted a number of researchers to study emotional and instructional dimensions together as they seek to determine how classroom processes affect learning (Hamre & Pianta, 2005; Peisner-Feinberg et al., 2001).

As another example, consider this very common situation in any preschool—the accidental knocking over of a block building. Typically, the child whose building is toppled is upset. To calm the child, a teacher usually explains that the other child did not mean to bump into the building. A teacher sometimes provides additional information that helps the upset child learn to consider factors that reveal another person's intentions. For example, the teacher might explain that the other child would not have wanted to knock down the building: "She was helping you build. She wouldn't have wanted the building to fall." A teacher might also explain how the accident happened, if indeed the teacher knew: "She stepped back a little to get a good view of the back of the block shelf, when she was trying to find another long block. She wasn't looking at the building, and she forgot the building was so close to the shelf. That's why she accidentally bumped into it when she backed up." The teacher in this situation provides not only emotional support but also full and rich information.

This chapter explores the cognitive dimension of teacher sensitivity through consideration of a variety of examples of young children's misunderstandings. The examples are from my observations of many preschool classrooms and my own experience in teaching preschool children. The examples provided do not involve overt displays of intense emotion of the kind described in the chapter's opening vignette. Often, however, a child's tone of voice and facial expression did convey puzzlement or a tinge of frustration. I do not provide emotional details for the examples, because most preschool teachers are exceptionally warm and caring toward children. They comfort children when they are upset, and they offer words of encouragement (e.g., "We'll read stories again tomorrow"; "I'll help you rebuild your building. We can fix it"). They also label and accept children's emotions (e.g., "I know how disappointed you are. You had worked so hard on that building").

Often less adequate, however, is cognitive sensitivity—caring about and especially responding fully to children's misunderstandings. Although teachers typically do respond to children's misunderstandings, they very often do so in a limited way, without really getting to the bottom of children's confusion. In part, this occurs because adults take too much for granted. Adults assume that a child notices what they notice, knows what they know, and can reason in ways that adults are able to reason. Of course, this isn't true. Yet, in a busy classroom, it is truly difficult for teachers to set aside all that they know to see things from a young child's perspective. It is also sometimes difficult to figure out exactly what is causing a child's confusion in a current situation.

My goal in this chapter is to increase preschool teachers' interest in looking more closely at this aspect of their teaching, and to interest teachers in studying preschool children's confusions. In addition to providing many examples to think about, the chapter provides a tool and some strategies for undertaking this kind of study, and linking it to instruction.

Preschool Children's Cognitive Confusion: Some Examples

A wide variety of examples of children's confusion is considered, along with information about their likely sources. Examples that illustrate the same or a very similar kind of confusion are grouped together.

Confusion about Things with Closely Related Functions or Features

This kind of confusion is very common among preschoolers. This is not surprising given their limited knowledge about the world. Young children often ignore facts provided in a current situation, or dispute them, relying instead on their own relatively limited experiences and background knowledge (Neuman, 1990).

Goose, Not Duck, and Tortoise, Not Turtle

The two examples provided here are drawn from read-aloud times. They involve the child's thinking that an animal pictured in a book is one kind of animal when, in fact, it is another, closely related kind of animal.

In the first example, the teacher was introducing a new storybook to the children (*Farfallina & Marcel* [Keller, 2002]). Immediately after holding up the book for the children to see, she started reading the title. But before she had pronounced even half of the first word, a child shouted out, "That's a duck!" The child was referring to the picture of a young bird on the book's cover. The teacher said, in a kind and informative tone, "Well, actually, it's not a duck. It's a gosling. " Then, she resumed reading the title.

The second example also occurred as a teacher began to introduce the storybook for the day. This time, the story was *Hi, Harry* (Waddell, 2003). As in the previous example, a child immediately focused on the cover's illustration, which shows a large turtle. The child shouted, "That's a turtle!" The teacher said, "Yes, he's a tortoise, a turtle." Then she read the title of the book to the children.

A Little Turkey Baster

This example of a child's confusion occurred while a teacher was introducing activities available in the classroom's activity centers. On this day, the teacher started to show the children some small, plastic eyedroppers that they would use to transfer colored water to paper toweling. As the teacher held up an eyedropper, which she intended to name and then demonstrate, a child called out, "Hey, a little turkey baster!" The teacher said, "Well, it looks kind of like the turkey basters you played with at the water table a few weeks ago. But it's really an eyedropper, not a turkey baster."

Thinking about the Sources of Children's Confusion

First consider the confusion about ducks versus geese. A duck's appearance is very similar to that of a goose, and a child's more common experience, both in books and in real life, is probably with ducks, not geese. Given that a specific animal of any kind can differ somewhat from another animal *of the same kind* (e.g., some cats have long fur, whereas others have short fur, yet both are called cats), it is perfectly sensible for a child to think that baby geese can be labeled ducks. A baby duck and a baby goose differ no more than baby ducks differ from one another.

This situation is similar to those often seen in toddlers who have learned to recognize and name a specific kind of animal, such as cows. When a child with knowledge of cows first sees a horse, the child likely will say, "Cow!" Because the horse's features are very similar to a cow's, the young child thinks this is just another kind of cow and overextends the meaning of the word *cow*. As adults provide information about the features that differ between these two animals and provide a name for the new animal, children gradually learn to make the correct distinctions and attach names correctly.

The tortoise/turtle confusion differs just a bit from the duck and goose confusion. Calling a tortoise a turtle is not incorrect, although it is not the most precise label. This confusion is somewhat on the order of the situation in which a child calls a cocker spaniel a dog, and an adult says, "Yes, it's a dog. It's a cocker spaniel." Though not incorrect, the label "dog" is not the most precise label of the animal. On the first page of the book *Hi, Harry,* the text introduces Harry as a tortoise. Had the story's text said simply that Harry was a turtle, the teacher probably would not have introduced the more precise label for the animal pictured on the book's cover, when a child used the word *turtle* to label the animal pictured.

Eyedroppers and turkey basters share a very similar physical design, although they differ in size and function. Part of a child's confusion in labeling these items probably stems from experiences wherein the same name applies to objects having the same features, despite obvious differences in their size (big tree, little tree; big glass, little glass; big dog, little dog; etc.). In all of these examples, the function or behavior of the items does not differ. Thus, it is not incorrect to call any size of one of these objects by the same name—tree, glass, dog—and to distinguish among them by adding a modifier (e.g., that's a *big* dog; that's a *tall* glass; that's a *big* tree). To use an example relevant to adult labeling, adults often specify the kind of table to which they are referring as coffee table, kitchen table, dining room table, or end table. In these cases, however, the word *table* remains in the label. Adults just add a modifying word to indicate which table is being talked about.

In the case of an eyedropper and a turkey baster, the situation is somewhat different. Here, two objects with the same basic design are given completely different names, based on each object's specific function. One object is used to moisten a turkey as it cooks in the oven; the other is used to place drops of medication in our eyes. Given that young children are unlikely to have experienced either of these situations first-hand, they simply use the name of the item they encounter *first* to name the item they encounter second, then add the appropriate modifier to distinguish between the different sizes of the two items. In other words, had the children experienced the eyedropper and colored water first, the child who labeled the eyedropper a "little turkey baster" would likely have called the turkey baster a "big eyedropper." It makes sense given how naming works for many other objects in the child's world.

Adequate Responsiveness to a Child's Misunderstanding

Knowing the likely sources of the children's confusion in the examples presented, was the teacher's response in each case adequate? An adequate response is one that provides information of the appropriate kind and amount to truly help a child move past his or her confusion.

Although, in each case, the teacher responded to the child, the information provided was probably not adequate to help a young child achieve true cognitive clarity. At best, the child was alerted to the fact that he or she used an incorrect or inadequate term to name something, was made aware that something about the two animals or objects differ and must be noticed or known, and that a new and different word exists for his or her use. On the Adult Involvement Scale (AIS) (Howes & Stewart, 1987), a tool for measuring teacher responsiveness, the responses would receive a rating of *simple* ("responds but does not elaborate"). Unless a response qualifies as *Elaborative* or *Intense* on the AIS, it is rather unlikely that the child would truly have understood *why* the new term offered by the teacher was more adequate than the one the child had used.

Without such an increase in understanding, a child is likely to misname the animals or objects again. Mistakes are likely even when adequate information has been provided on the first occasion of confusion. Children typically need several encounters to learn the necessary distinctions and to attach the correct word to the correct animal or item on a consistent basis. The confusion can persist for much longer than necessary, however, and may even worsen, when adults deal too superficially with the confusion on each occasion it arises.

These examples of confusion require information that helps a child learn to distinguish one animal or item from another. For example, rather than saying, "Well, actually, it's not a duck. It is a gosling," the teacher must acknowledge that the bird pictured does resemble a duck, then provide information about how the two birds differ. For example, a teacher might say, "Yes, this bird does look a lot like a duck, like a baby duckling with soft feathers. It is a large bird with webbed feet and a long neck like a duck. It's not small like a robin or a sparrow. But this bird is a baby goose, which we call a gosling. Geese have even longer necks than ducks, and their bodies are bigger, too. A duckling would not be quite as big as this gosling."

Of course, the teacher would point to the picture of the gosling, as appropriate, while providing this explanation. Then, outside of the current story reading context, a wise teacher also provides some information books about large birds, such as ducks and geese, for children to look at. The teacher could help children use the books' pictures of the two birds in both their immature and adult forms. In this way, the children would learn to distinguish between the birds based on physical features, and would then have more opportunities to associate the correct name with each one.

The turtle/tortoise situation is similar, in that the teacher provided the correct term but did not provide any information about how to distinguish between a tortoise and other kinds of turtles. A tortoise is a large kind of turtle that lives on dry land in areas where it is fairly warm all the time. Turtles that are not tortoises live in or near bodies of water, where it is sometimes cold, and they range in size from quite small to very large. A teacher can provide information somewhat briefly in a book reading context, then follow up with books about various kinds of turtles, and with more discussion of their differences in that context.

The turkey baster and eyedropper situation is also similar, in that the correct term for the eyedropper was provided, whereas additional information about why each item is called by a unique name was not. A teacher should acknowledge that the two items certainly resemble one another and also work similarly (i.e., both are used to draw a liquid inside, then squirt it out). The teacher could then add that the bigger of the two items—the turkey baster—is used to gather the liquid from the cooking pan and to squirt it onto the turkey that is baking. This is done to keep it moist—to keep it from drying out in the heat of the oven. We use an eyedropper, on the other hand, to put medicine in our eyes. The teacher would surely want to comment that a turkey baster is much too big to serve as an eyedropper, and that an eyedropper is much too small to baste a big turkey.

As with the duck/goose and tortoise/turtle situations, the children would be helped the most if a verbal explanation provided in the initial context were followed up with suitable pictures and demonstrations (e.g., a doll's eye used with an eyedropper demo) (Weizman & Show, 2001). Knowing each tool's intended use, and seeing this use demonstrated, would help children to remember the specific name for each item.

Confusion Due to a Child's Limited Understanding of a Word

In the examples considered previously, children's limited understanding of words has been involved in their misunderstandings. In these examples, children extended the use of a word they knew to a new item or animal that resembled something they had experienced previously. Children demonstrated two problems: (1) They had not learned to distinguish between things that closely resemble one another in physical appearance, and (2) they had not yet learned the name, or the precise label, for the newly encountered item or animal.

In the next three examples, children's difficulties stem from a failure to extend the use of a known word to quite dissimilar physical situations, when its use is in fact appropriate. Because the new situation appears to children to differ remarkably from the situation of previous use, they are reluctant to use it in the new situation, even though the teacher or another adult has used it. These are instances in which children experience variations in a word's meanings. Some words are used across a variety of settings, and the meaning of the word varies somewhat depending on the context.

"That's Not a Foot"

A child made this comment as he was observing snails. The large muscle at the bottom of the snail's body, which it uses to move itself from one place to another, is called a "foot." Before the children had seen live snails, the teacher read a book about snails to them. One large picture of a snail in the book provided labels for the snail's body parts. One label was "foot." No one said anything when the teacher reviewed the picture and read this label.

The next day, the children observed live snails as they climbed up the sides of their clear plastic containers. As one pair of children observed, the teacher reached over to point to the snail and said, "There's its foot." One child said, "Its foot? That's not a foot!" The teacher replied, "Yes, it is. That's what a snail's foot looks like."

"Rainbows Aren't Real"

The behavior in this example occurred at the writing table, where several children had gathered to draw pictures in blank books. A teacher talked with children about their drawings and frequently offered to write, or help the children write, labels. One child explained to the teacher that she had drawn a rainbow, and a picture of herself standing beside it. The teacher commented that the rainbow was very colorful, and also asked the child whether she had ever seen a real rainbow in the sky. The girl said that she had, and began to tell about it.

A child sitting nearby listened attentively to the conversation between this child and the teacher. After hearing about his classmate's experience in seeing a rainbow, he said that he had seen one, too. Then he added, "but rainbows aren't real." The teacher, unsure at this point about whether she understood correctly what the child had said about his own rainbow experience, asked, "So, have you ever seen a rainbow?" The child said, "Yes, I've seen one. When I was riding in the car with my mom, I saw one out the window. But rainbows aren't real," he added.

"But you saw one," the teacher replied. "So, they are real."

"No, they aren't," said the child once again.

At this point, the teacher wondered whether the child's understanding of the word "real" was more restricted than hers. Next, she asked, "Have you ever sneezed?" The child said that he had. "Are sneezes real?" she asked. The child said, "No, they aren't real." The teacher then said, "They exist. People do sneeze. Even though we can't hold a sneeze in our hand, they happen. Once a sneeze is over, it's gone." The child nodded his head in agreement. "Sneezes are like rainbows in that way," the teacher continued. "They exist, even though they don't last and we can't hold onto them." The child again agreed.

The teacher then explained that when we say that something is "real," we mean that something really exists, or that something really happens. If something is real, it is not something that we only pretend or imagine to happen. To summarize, the teacher said, "So, we can say that a rainbow is real, and that a sneeze is real, even though they disappear right away, and we can't hold them." The child said, "Oh." His facial expression and tone of voice suggested that he meant "Thanks for the information. I didn't know that, and I understand what you are saying."

"They Not Be Crying"

A child made this statement to the teacher who was reading to him individually. The book they were reading was *Mouse Paint* (Walsh, 1989). In this story, three white mice find jars of paint: one red, another yellow, and still another blue. Each mouse climbs into a jar. They emerge, covered with paint; the excess paint drips from their bodies to the floor, making a puddle. Then, the red mouse does a little dance in the yellow puddle of paint, turning it orange. The other two mice are watching as this happens, and one comments in surprise to the other. The text says, " 'Look,' he cried." Then the mouse describes what he has observed—that red paint mixed with the yellow paint puddle turns it orange.

After the teacher had read the page to him, the child placed his hands on the book to prevent her from turning the page. He looked very closely at the pictures, then, in a very authoritative tone, said, "They not be crying." The teacher knew why he was interpreting the word cry in terms of its usual meaning—to shed tears. In the days prior to this incident, a teacher had read *Oonga Boonga* (Wishinsky, 1998) to the children a number of times. In this story, a baby cries all the time. The word *crying* is used numerous times to refer to the baby's behavior, and great big tears are pictured coming from her eyes. No wonder, then, the child had this understanding of the word *cried*.

The teacher said, "Oh, you are right. The mice are not crying like Baby Louise in *Oonga Boonga*. The book is telling us what one of the mice said, and how he said it." The teacher read that part of the text again, and then continued to explain the word's meaning in this context: "Here, *cried* means that the mouse said 'Look' very loudly to the other mouse. He cried out, shouted probably, when he said it. He didn't say it in a soft voice."

The child looked at the pages again, and said, "That's right. They not be crying tears like Baby Louise." The teacher agreed, then continued reading the story.

Thinking about the Sources of Children's Confusion

In two of these examples, the teachers quickly figured out the source of the child's confusion. With the source in mind as a guide, the teachers provided explanations that helped one child understand a broader meaning for the word *real* and another to understand a second meaning for the word *cried*.

In the third example, involving the word *foot*, the teacher did not get to the bottom of the child's confusion, perhaps because the real animal was there and she assumed that pointing to the snail's foot, and repeating that this part of the snail's body is indeed called a "foot," was sufficient. The child might have benefited, however, had the teacher gone further in explaining why this part of the snail is called a "foot," and what the word *foot* means, more generally.

For example, it might have been useful to explain to the children that the foot of something is its bottom part, and that we even talk about the foot of a hill or the foot of a table leg or bed. With respect to animals, a foot is their lower part, too, and they use this part to move their body from one place to another. A teacher might explain further that the feet of different animals differ in appearance, that horses and cows, for example, don't have toes like people, but they have hooves instead; and that bears, cats, and dogs have paws, not feet like ours. Finally, a teacher might add that some animals have four feet, others have two, and that still others, such as snails, have just one. *What Do You Do with a Tail Like This?* (Jenkins & Page, 2003) is very useful for such a discussion. (This book discusses animals' tails, and also their feet, eyes, mouths, and noses.)

As this example illustrates, it is sometimes helpful to convey to children the most basic meaning of a word, such as *foot*, and to explain the very basic properties of items qualifying for use of this label. *Foot* is a term used to refer to the bottom of quite a number of things, not just to the bottom part of animals' bodies. Of course, depending on the children's prior experience and current knowledge, a teacher might find that he or she needs to explain that fish and snakes don't have any feet at all!

Confusions Due to a Child's Limited Ability to Combine Information and to Reason

In the examples considered so far, there is a sense in which the children have lacked both information and the ability to reason with it. For example, a child needs to know the features of both ducks and geese, to contrast and compare these features in his or her mind when seeing a bird, to decide which kind of bird it is on this occasion, and then select the accurate name. Yet except for the opening vignette in this chapter, the examples considered have involved fairly simple situations in which a lack of information and direct experience with the two things in question are the basic problems. Piecing together a lot of information, reasoning about it, then drawing an inference has not been very much at stake in the previous examples. In the final two examples considered, the child's confusion stems as much from a failure to integrate information through reasoning to draw an inference as from a lack of information itself. Two more examples of situations that resemble the opening vignette follow.

"The Peddler Shouldn't Have Let the Monkeys Take His Caps"

A child made this statement at the end of story time, after the teacher had read *Caps for Sale* (Slobodkina, 1968) and discussed various aspects of the story with the children. Just as the teacher closed the book and started to say that story time was over for the day, a boy said, "The peddler shouldn't have let the monkeys take his caps!"

In response to the question, the teacher opened the book again and turned to the pages where the peddler sitting under the tree with empty branches was pictured. The teacher pointed to the tree and asked the children whether there were monkeys there. They answered "no." Then, she asked whether the peddler's eyes were closed. They said "yes." Then the teacher commented that apparently the peddler had fallen asleep before the monkeys had come to the tree. The teacher then asked whether people usually know what goes on around them when they are asleep. The general consensus among the children was that they do not. Then, the teacher explained that the peddler didn't know that monkeys would come while he was asleep, and not knowing they were going to come, he really couldn't have prevented them from taking his caps. It appeared that most children in the group followed the reasoning the teacher modeled.

"Why He's Got That Flashlight?"

A second example of confusion stemming from a young child's failure to consider all of the facts at hand, and to reason with them, is also drawn from the story reading context. On this occasion, the teacher was reading the story *Corduroy* (Freeman, 1976). She had reached the page where the night watchman is riding down the escalator to find out what had crashed on the floor below. As the teacher turned to this page, a child asked, "Why he's got that flashlight?"

The teacher responded by explaining that it was nighttime, and she reviewed the previous page of text, where it stated that it was late in the evening. She also pointed out the darkness in the background of the illustrations on the nighttime pages, then flipped back a page or two to show the white background in previous illustrations that depicted daytime scenes in the store. She then returned to the page where the night watchman was pictured and pointed out that the store was dark in a lot of places. She said that the night watchman needed a flashlight to explore everywhere to find out what had caused the crash.

Thinking about the Sources of a Child's Confusion

In the *Caps for Sale* situation, one problem, of course, is that preschool children don't necessarily know all of the relevant circumstances to consider at the time they are presented in the book. Preschool children might not notice that the branches of the tree are bare when the peddler its down, and they might not be able to reason logically about this information, even if they have noticed it. A child who notices the bare branches when the peddler sits down under the tree might not notice that the peddler's eyes are closed, which indicates the peddler is sleeping. Perhaps the child missed this detail, then thought the peddler was still awake when the monkeys arrived.

Even with relevant information in hand, however, quite a long sequence of reasoning is required to draw the inference that the peddler couldn't have prevented the monkeys from taking his caps. This kind of reasoning is not easy for preschool children. Preschoolers often understand the inference an adult has drawn when the adult models his or her reasoning by talking out loud to the children. On their own, however, this kind of thinking is difficult for preschoolers. With preschool children, especially, a teacher must provide a model of the kind of thinking that is necessary for comprehending stories (Cochran-Smith, 1984).

In the situation with the misunderstanding about the flashlight in the story, Corduroy (a stuffed bear) had stated earlier in the story that he would go and see if he could find his button that night. Then, on the next page, the first sentence of the text starts with, "Late that evening . . . ";

moreover, starting on this page, the background in the illustrations is black, whereas on the previous pages it is white. When reading the page where Corduroy climbs down from his toy department shelf, the teacher had explained the meaning of "Late that evening" after reading the whole sentence. She had said that "late evening" is after dinner, and maybe about bedtime.

The illustrations themselves are a bit confusing given that they are light enough to allow one to see clearly what is in the foreground—the night watchman, the sides of the escalator on which he is riding, and the casing of the flashlight. On the opposite page, where we see the night watchman after he has arrived in the furniture department, we can see clearly the head of a bed, even though the flashlight's beam is not aimed directly at it. In other words, the illustrations do not convey the total darkness that a child might associate with the use of a flashlight, such as during a storm, when the electricity fails.

Although the previous text, the teacher's previous comments, and the contrast we see in the book's illustrations, before and after Corduroy left his shelf, provide a lot of clues about the time of day when the night watchman rode down the escalator, there are also some contradictory clues, such as the lack of total darkness on the nighttime pages. Thus, a young child might not be able to piece things together well enough to understand why the night watchman was carrying a flashlight.

Providing Instruction
That Decreases Children's Confusion

My insights about children's confusion, whether encountered in my own teaching or observed while others are teaching, have often come to mind a day or two after I have mulled some situation over and over in my mind. Insights increase when I discuss various situations with teachers in study groups, for example. By keeping track of children's confusion, and by thinking about and analyzing it, either by ourselves or in discussion with others, teachers can gain more insight into young children's minds and can increase their own ability to respond adequately when such situations arise in the classroom.

Teachers can use a simple tool to keep track of incidences of confusion in children, in order to study them over time, and to compare and contrast them. Keeping track of children's confusion not only provides teachers with information about the general kinds of things that cause problems for most preschoolers but also helps to pinpoint children who might have more problems than others. In conjunction with the list of incidences of confusion, teachers can study carefully the storybooks, and other materials and contexts involved in the various times of confusion, and can often find clues as to how to proceed in explaining something to children to prevent misunderstanding as a story is read (McGee & Schickedanz, 2007).

Discussions of these lists provide not only a wonderful activity for teacher study groups but also an important focus for discussions between a teacher and a coach or mentor. It is, after all, improving children's understanding that should be the ultimate goal of teaching. Finding a way to focus squarely on what children understand in situations such as those described in this chapter helps teachers with instructional planning and implementation in ways that truly keep the children very much on their minds.

References

Arnold, D. H., Ortiz, C., Curry, J. C., Stowe, R. M., Goldstein, N. E., Fisher, P. H., et al. (1999). Promoting academic success and preventing disruptive behavior disorders through community partnership. *Journal of Community Psychology, 5*, 589–598.

Birch, S. H., & Ladd, G. W. (1998). Children's interpersonal behaviors and the teacher–child relationship. *Developmental Psychology, 34*, 934–946.

Cochran-Smith, M. (1984). *The making of a reader.* Norwood, NJ: Ablex.

de Beer, H. (1998). *The little polar bear and the brave little hare.* New York: North–South Publishers.

Freeman, D. (1976). *Corduroy.* New York: Puffin Books.

Hamre, B. K., & Pianta, R. C. (2005). Can instructional and emotional support in the first-grade classroom make a difference for children at risk of school failure? *Child Development, 76*, 949–967.

Howes, C. (2000). Social–emotional classroom climate in child care, child–teacher relationships and children's second grade peer relations. *Social Development, 9*, 191–204.

Howes, C., & Stewart, P. (1987). Child's play with adults, toys, and peers: An examination of family and child care influences. *Developmental Psychology, 23*, 423–430.

Jenkins, S., & Page, R. (2003). *What do you do with a tail like this?* Boston: Houghton Mifflin.

Keller, H. (2002). *Farfallina & Marcel.* New York: HarperCollins.

McEvoy, A., & Welker, R. (2000). Antisocial behavior, academic failure and school climate: A critical review. *Journal of Emotional and Behavioral Disorders, 8*, 130–140.

McGee, L. M., & Schickedanz, J. A. (2007). Repeated interactive read-alouds in preschool and kindergarten. *Reading Teacher, 60*, 742–751.

McLelland, M. M., Morrison, F. J., & Holmes, D. L. (2000). Children at risk for early academic problems: The role of learning-related social skills. *Early Childhood Research Quarterly, 15*, 307–329.

Neuman, S. B. (1990). Assessing inferencing strategies. In J. Zutell & S.

McCormick (Eds.), *Literacy theory and research* (pp. 267–274). Chicago: National Reading Conference.

Peisner-Feinberg, E. S., Burchinal, M. R., Clifford, R. M., Culkin, M. L., Howes, C., Kagan, S. L., et al. (2001). The relation of preschool child-care quality to children's cognitive and social developmental trajectories through second grade. *Child Development, 72*(5), 1534–1553.

Slobodkina, E. (1968). *Caps for sale.* New York: HarperCollins.

Waddell, M. (2003). *Hi, Harry.* Cambridge, MA: Candlewick Press.

Walsh, E. S. (1989). *Mouse paint.* New York: Harcourt.

Weizman, Z. O., & Snow, C. E. (2001). Lexical input as related to children's vocabulary acquisition: Effects of sophisticated exposure and support for meaning. *Developmental Psychology, 37*(2), 265–279.

Wishinsky, F. (1998). *Oonga Boonga.* New York: Puffin Books.

CHAPTER 11

★★★★★★★★★

Strategic and Intentional
Shared Storybook Reading

Sonia Q. Cabell
Laura M. Justice
Carol Vukelich
Martha Jane Buell
Myae Han

Experts conceptualize children's emergent literacy development as encompassing two separate domains: inside-out skills and outside-in skills (Whitehurst & Lonigan, 1998). "Inside-out skills" are children's code-related insights, such as print knowledge and phonological awareness. These are akin to the code-based skills that children draw upon to "crack" the alphabetic code, and evidence points to such skills as being critically linked to later achievements in reading (e.g., Storch & Whitehurst, 2002). "Outside-in skills" are no less important to longitudinal success in reading, and comprise comprehension-related or meaning-based abilities, such as vocabulary and inferential language skills. These two domains of emergent literacy development are differentially related to later reading outcomes. The code-related inside-out skills play a role early in the reading acquisition process, as children learn to decode words and develop understanding of the alphabetic principle. As they move beyond the early years of reading development, comprehension becomes the more important focus as children read to learn, and they increasingly draw upon their outside-in skills to successfully read for meaning. Because both decoding and comprehension are essential components of reading (Gough & Tunmer, 1986), it is important for preschool educators to strategically and intentionally develop children's inside-out and outside-in skills within the classroom.

In this chapter, we discuss how educators can capitalize upon shared storybook reading interactions as a vehicle for strategic and intentional teaching of important inside-out and outside-in skills. Specifically, we describe how educators can organize "extratextual conversations" during reading interactions to promote children's print knowledge, phonological awareness, vocabulary, and inferential language skills. Extratextual conversation refers to the dialogues between teachers and children that extend or expand upon the content of the storybook. Educators can readily capitalize on extratextual opportunities for developing children's inside-out and outside-in skills, and many studies have shown this to afford great benefit to the developing child (e.g., Justice & Ezell, 2002; Penno, Wilkinson, & Moore, 2002; van Kleeck, Vander Woude, & Hammett, 2006; Whitehurst et al., 1988). This chapter is therefore designed to provide explicit guidance to preschool educators on how they might capitalize on extratextual opportunities and go beyond the "limited input" style of reading that often is characteristic of many adults, in which too few opportunities for in-depth discussion are made available to children (e.g., Hammett, van Kleeck, & Huberty, 2003).

Interactive Reading at Tier One and Tier Two

Interactive reading involves an extended, meaningful exchange between adults and children, during which both parties are actively engaged in the learning process. There are two benefits to interactive reading. First, interactive storybook reading can serve as an ideal context for *scaffolding* children's emerging literacy and language skills (e.g., van Kleeck, 2006). As adults read with children, they provide the support children need to work at a level that surpasses their independent capabilities. Teachers can utilize their book-related discussions to gauge where children are in their understanding of a particular concept, such as the role of print in telling a story, then extend that understanding through explicit discussions. When educators create this type of interactive environment, they help children to develop the metalinguistic and explicit insights that are necessary precursors to skilled reading. Second, interactive storybook reading also encourages children's active, rather than passive, involvement as they create dialogues with their adult reading partners. Whether children are pointing, turning pages, opening flaps, asking or answering questions, or making comments, evidence suggests that active participation is better than passive participation for children's development (Sénéchal, Thomas,

& Monker, 1995); in fact, active engagement is seen as an important mechanism for explaining children's accelerated gains in language and literacy skills that occur in interactive reading compared to more passive experiences (e.g., Sénéchal et al., 1995; Wasik & Bond, 2001; Whitehurst et al., 1988).

High-quality book reading may be especially beneficial for young children who experience risk factors for later reading difficulty. Indeed, young children from lower socioeconomic backgrounds are often behind their more advantaged peers in terms of both inside-out and outside-in skills (e.g., Chaney, 1994; Hart & Risley, 1995; Justice & Ezell, 2001). Young children reared in poverty often have reduced opportunities to engage in valuable literacy routines, including book-sharing interactions, consequently resulting in fewer opportunities to develop important inside-out and outside-in skills, such as vocabulary (Hart & Risley, 1995). In contrast, their middle- and upper-class peers tend to engage in more literacy interactions and continually gain increasingly sophisticated vocabulary, concepts, and print knowledge as adults read regularly to them (Neuman, 2006). The knowledge gap between these groups of children widens over time, a principle described as the "Matthew effect" (Stanovich, 1986). It is clear that once children fall behind in reading, it is very difficult for them to catch up with their peers, and they often stay behind their peers year after year (Juel, 1988).

In many preschool programs today, educators are paying attention to the response-to-intervention (RTI) literature that advocates the need to "layer support" to meet children's diverse needs and proactively reduce individual children's risk for academic difficulties (see Fuchs, 2003; Justice, 2006). These layers of support typically include at least two tiers. Tier One is the general curriculum that organizes and structures children's daily learning opportunities within the classroom. Tier One in every preschool classroom should include at least one large-group storybook reading experience and, ideally, the opportunity for children to experience one or more small-group or one-on-one reading interactions with teachers, assistants, and volunteers. When the adult reader organizes these reading experiences strategically and intentionally to address specific inside-out and outside-in skills, we can expect the majority of children to benefit (e.g., Wasik & Bond, 2001; Whitehurst et al., 1994). Put another way, for many children, the Tier One layer of support ensures that they achieve adequate age-appropriate language and literacy skills, and enter kindergarten poised for success in beginning reading instruction.

Tier Two comprises supplemental experiences given to children who need something more than the general curriculum can offer to achieve age-appropriate language and literacy skills. Tier Two experiences are provided as an extra layer of support to children who do not respond to the learning experiences of Tier One at the same pace as other children in the classroom; that is, these children do not learn as quickly or as easily as others. Tier Two might, for instance, take the form of individual or small-group instruction for 20- or 30-minute sessions once or twice per week, in which teachers, assistants, or specialists use structured lesson plans to provide children with an extra "dose" of the same language and literacy objectives addressed in the general curriculum. Tier Two experiences constitute an important vehicle for closing the achievement gap at the earliest stage possible between children who learn readily within the classroom and those who do not; these experiences serve as a mechanism to close the gap between higher- and lower-achieving children, rather than allowing it to widen over time.

Importantly, shared storybook reading interactions can constitute an important element of supplemental Tier Two experiences. These reading interactions can replicate those of the Tier One, giving children extra opportunities to learn the inside-out and outside-in skills targeted within the Tier One reading experiences. Below we present an example of how one Early Reading First program, the Delaware Early Reading First (DERF) project, uses shared storybook reading as a research-based instructional strategy with its young children needing additional support, beyond that available to them through the general curriculum.

The Delaware Early Reading First Project's Tier Two Learning Support

The DERF project systematically layers a second tier of support upon 20% of the preschool children participating in its 12 classrooms using Tier Two structured, one-on-one book reading interactions between children and instructors.

How Are Children Selected?

At the start of the academic year, staff assess all project children using a norm-referenced measure of receptive vocabulary knowledge and a criterion-referenced measure of alphabet knowledge. Based on a composite score of these two measures, the children in each classroom are rank-ordered; the lowest performing 20% of the children are selected for Tier Two support. Additionally, monthly progress monitoring checks of language and literacy skill development track the children's learning and provide the data for Tier Two instructors to prepare narrative reports describing the children's performance for their teachers.

How Are Tier Two Sessions Structured?

Tier Two instructors deliver one-on-one, book-centered, 20- to 30-minute sessions to the Tier Two children 2 days each week. Initially, the plan was to provide the Tier Two support in the classroom, but this did not work, because other children wanted to join in to hear and talk about the story! Today the Tier Two support is provided in the hallway outside each classroom. Although it affords some benefits, this space presents other challenges. For example, these children at times are easily distracted, and adults and other children often move through this space.

Each Tier Two session involves the one-on-one reading of a single storybook. The storybook shared in each session is the same one the classroom teacher uses in large-group storybook reading sessions in a big book format, because this allows Tier Two children to use what they learn in their one-on-one sessions to participate more fully in the classroom group storybook reading sessions. In addition, this allows for strong support and reciprocity between the classroom and Tier Two teaching and learning.

So what might a session "sound like"? Each session includes a before, during, and after component. In the before component, the instructor focuses on helping the child understand that the title is the name of the book, and the author is the person who wrote the book; that pictures help us get a sense of what the book is about; and that based on the title and pictures, readers make predictions about the story's content. In addition, the instructor highlights an aspect of the print (e.g., the number of words in the title, the beginning sound of the words in the title, or the rhyming words in the title).

During reading, the instructor asks the child to show where she should begin reading and occasionally to point to the words as she reads. She invites the child to read the predictable sentences with her or to finish a sentence with a rhyming word. She uses a child-friendly definition to teach the meaning of unknown vocabulary and sometimes includes actions or manipulative materials. She asks questions and invites the child to ask questions to construct the meaning of the text and to connect the text to the child's life. She focuses on the sounds in the words, calling the child's attention to words that begin with the same sound, end with the same sound, rhyme, or begin with the same letter as the child's name.

After reading, the instructor revisits the prereading predictions and talks about the story's content with the child. She also focuses the child's attention on the print. For example, the instructor might ask the child to search for a particular letter or provide a word that rhymes with a key word from the story. Typically, the instructor also reviews the vocabulary that was introduced during the reading. Through it all, the instructor works to make the reading a pleasurable, playful, fun activity.

As shown by this description of book-centered Tier Two opportunities from the DERF project, educators can strategically and intentionally draw upon the book reading context to facilitate children's skills in particular areas. These learning opportunities within individual and small-group contexts with greater scaffolding from an adult are particularly important for children who learn relatively slowly compared to their peers, such as children with poor vocabulary skills (Gray, 2004). We now turn to a description of how educators can be intentional and strategic when reading to help young children develop specific inside-out and outside-in skills, whether using books within the general Tier One environment or, as occurs in the DERF program, as a Tier Two supplemental instruction technique.

Developing Inside-Out Skills through Interactive Reading

In this section, we describe how explicit attention to developing children's print knowledge and phonological awareness can be integrated into storybook reading interactions. Print knowledge refers to young children's emergent knowledge about the print or orthographic structure of written language, including the names of individual alphabet letters (alphabet knowledge) and the way in which print is organized and carries meaning in various texts (print concepts; see Justice & Ezell, 2004). Phonological awareness refers to young children's awareness of the phonological segments comprising spoken language. These segments include words, syllables, the intrasyllabic units of onset and rime, and phonemes (see Table 11.1). Both print knowledge—particularly alphabet knowledge—and phonological awareness represent important elements of emergent literacy development that pave the way for children's eventual "unlocking" of the alphabetic principle.

Print Knowledge

When educators share books with young children, they can make both meaning and print an explicit focus of the interaction. We later discuss strategies for heightening a meaning focus; here we focus on how educators can point to print, track print, comment on print, and ask questions about print to make it an object of salience within the adult–child reading interaction (Justice & Ezell, 2000, 2002). Although many adults (including teachers, parents, and speech–language pathologists [SLPs]) report that they make print an explicit element of their reading interactions with young children, most studies that have carefully examined the extent to which adults reference print when reading with preschoolers—either verbally or nonverbally—indicate that references to print to occur at very low rates, if they occur at all (Ezell & Justice, 2000; Phillips & McNaughton, 1990; van Kleeck, Gillam, Hamilton, & McGrath, 1997).

Nonetheless, including an explicit focus on print in reading interactions with children can significantly accelerate their print knowledge, and adults can readily do so using two approaches (Justice & Ezell, 2002):

TABLE 11.1. Phonological Segments: Dimensions of Phonological Awareness

Segment	Definition	Example of task(s)
Words	Awareness of words as units of spoken language	Child identifies that the spoken phrase "The black cat" has three words
Syllables	Awareness of syllables as units of spoken language	Child claps once for each of the three syllables in the word *butterfly*; child segments the syllable "ball" from the multisyllabic word *baseball*
Onsets	Awareness of the onset in a word; the onset is the initial consonant or consonant cluster (e.g., *spl*at; *sp*at; *s*at)	Child identifies /d/ as the first sound in the word *duck*; child segments the sound /b/ from the word *big*
Rimes	Awareness of the rime unit in a single-syllable word; the rime unit is the vowel and any consonants following the vowel (e.g., spl*at*; b*oo*; b*ought*)	Child produces two words that rhyme (e.g., *fly* and *buy*); child matches two words that share a rime unit from among three choices (*fly, map,* and *buy*)
Phonemes	Awareness of the individual speech sounds that make up spoken words	Child claps once for each sound in the word *cat*; child segments a word to identify each of the individual sounds in the word

- Selecting print-salient books for reading interactions
- Incorporating print references into reading interactions

"Print-salient" books are storybooks in which print is a notable design characteristic. Storybook illustrators produce "print-salient illustrations" by integrating print into illustrations with labels, environmental print, and visible speech and sounds (Smolkin, Conlon, & Yaden, 1988). Some illustrators make print salient through changes in the style, color, size, and orientation of print within the narrative text, whereas others feature print that forms patterns or three-dimensional objects (Smolkin et al., 1988). Books in which print is a salient feature (see Table 11.2) make print worth talking about, and adults can do this by incorporating print references into their book-sharing interactions. "Print references" comprise any verbal or nonverbal reference to print that adults make when they share books with children: They can simply track the print when reading (a nonverbal reference), point to print within the illustrations, or question (e.g., "Do you think you know what this word says? What is this letter?") or comment about print (e.g., "This word says 'Danger!' This letter is an *S*, like in your name").

When adults reference print, they typically are calling attention to one of four dimensions of print knowledge: (1) print concepts, (2) letters, (3) words, and (4) print-to-speech connections. The definitions of each of these dimensions, with examples of print references, are provided in Table 11.3. When educators read books with children, particularly those with print-salient features, it is relatively easy to embed attention to print within these interactions and heighten not only children's interest in print but also their understanding of how it works and what it does, as shown in this excerpt from a large-group reading session in a Head Start classroom:

TEACHER: Today we'll read one of my favorite books, *There's a Dragon at My School.* Here is where it says the title. (*Runs finger along the title.*)

CHILDREN: That's the title.

TEACHER: Yes, the title is the name of the book. This title has a lot of words in it. One, two, three, four, five, six words. And they are written with red letters. Does anyone see a letter they know?

CHILDREN: (*calling out*) S . . . T . . . S . . . A . . .

TEACHER: That's a lot of letters. I heard someone say S (*points to* S), and I heard *T* (*points to* T). You have sharp eyes today. Let's think about what this book might be about. It's called *There's a Dragon at My School.* I guess it's about a mouse in a house . . .

CHILDREN: (*calling out*) No! It's about a dragon.

As should be evident, this teacher has not only made print a salient characteristic of the book reading session with her pupils, but she has shown children that print is an object worthy of their interest. With her focus on print concepts, letters, and words, she is accelerating children's develop-

TABLE 11.2. Examples of Print-Salient Storybooks

Title	Author (year)
Chicka Chicka Boom Boom	Bill Martin, Jr. and John Archambault (1989)
Click, Clack, Moo: Cows That Type	Doreen Cronin (2000)
Growing Vegetable Soup	Lois Ehlert (1987)
My Little Brother	Debi Gliori (1992)
Silver Seeds	Paul Paolilli and Dan Brewer (2001)
The Crunching Munching Caterpillar	Sheridan Cain (2000)
The Gigantic Turnip	Aleksei Tolstoy and Niamh Sharkey (1998)
The Runaway Orange	Felicity Brooks (1999)
There's a Dragon at My School	Tyler and Hawthorn (1996)

TABLE 11.3. Dimensions of Print Knowledge Addressed by Print Referencing

Dimension	Definition	Print-referencing examples
Print concepts	Children's understanding of print and text features such as cover page elements (title, author, illustrator), print organization (left-to-right directionality), and book organization (left-to-right page turning)	• "Show me where the title is." • "This is the author's name; it says Lois Ehlert." • "I'm going to start reading right here, at the top of the page."
Letters	Children's understanding of letters as discrete units of written language that link up to make words	• "This letter is *S*." • "Do you know this letter?" • "This letter *G* is the first letter in your name!"
Words	Children's understanding of words as discrete units of written language that are composed of letters	• "This word and this word are exactly the same." • "These are two words: *Happy Birthday.*" • "This word *GO!* has two letters in it." • "Can you show me the space between two words?"
Print-to-speech connections	Children's understanding of the relationship between words and letters in print and in speech	• "What sound does this letter *B* make?" • "This word says *danger.*" • "Can you point to the words as I read?"

Note. Adapted from Justice and Ezell (2002, 2004).

ment of print knowledge beyond that which would normally occur in book reading sessions in which print is only an implicit focus (Justice & Ezell, 2000, 2002). As this excerpt also reveals, educators need not bombard children with questions about print to stimulate their curiosity and understanding; rather, they can embed references to print in much the same way that they do so for other topics more traditionally associated with book reading interactions, such as discussion of book characters or main events of the story.

Phonological Awareness

When educators share books with young children, they can embed conversations into their interactions that explicitly highlight the phonological aspects of spoken language and, in turn, children's development of phonological awareness. As noted previously, phonological awareness refers to children's sensitivity to the phonological segments of spoken language, including words, syllables, onsets and rimes, and phonemes (see Table 11.1). Phonological awareness has consistently been linked to children's later achievements in reading, particularly their word recognition (Storch & Whitehurst, 2002); consequently, educators who work with young children have been encouraged to promote children's phonological awareness as a preventive tactic for reducing later reading difficulties (Snow, Burns, & Griffin, 1998). Because the improvement of phonological awareness, for at least some children, requires relatively explicit and direct instruction, some educators might express concerns over its "fit" in early education. However, some of these concerns can be alleviated if educators would marry direct instruction in phonological awareness with the naturalistic scaffolds and contexts provided by storybooks that feature phonological patterns as a salient design characteristic. Books that feature compound words, rhyming patterns and verses, and alliteration provide a naturalistic context in which educators can embed explicit and direct instruction in the sound segments of spoken language. To capitalize on the storybook reading context in this way, educators must go about:

- Selecting phonologically salient books for reading interactions
- Incorporating sound references into reading interactions

Just as print-salient books are storybooks in which print is a notable design characteristic, phonologically salient storybooks make sound come alive. They do so with stories told

- With verse: "There's a dragon at my school, and he's broken every rule" (Tyler & Hawthorn, 1996)
- With rhyming phrases: "crunching munching" and "Mrs. Piggle-Wiggle" (Cain [2000] and MacDonald [1985], respectively)
- With alliterative patterns: "Tessa the teacher," "Gerda the goose," and "Tooth trouble" (Litchfield & Brooks [2006], Oram [2000], and Clarke & Johansson [2003], respectively)
- With plays on words: "Olive, the other reindeer" (Seibold & Walsh, 1997)
- With words at play: "Chicka chicka boom boom" and "Cat goes fiddle-i-fee" (Martin & Archambalt [1989], and Ziefert [2005], respectively)

But text selection is not enough when educators are considering the use of books as a tool for promoting children's phonological awareness. Just as critical, in fact, is for the teacher to pause during reading to prompt children's awareness of these phonological aspects of language and to make these features of text an explicit, rather than implicit, aspect of the reading session. Here, we provide a contrast between the two:

Implicit Attention to Phonological Features

"This book is called *Tooth Trouble*. It looks like the walrus has a toothache!"

Explicit Attention to Phonological Features

"This book is called *Tooth Trouble* (accentuating the /t/ sounds). That's interesting. Each word in the title starts with the sound /t/. Listen for it. I'll read the title again: *Tooth Trouble*. It looks like the walrus has a toothache!"

When adults reference the phonological features of language within reading sessions (i.e., when they make sound references), they call attention to one of four dimensions of phonological awareness: (1) words, (2) syllables, (3) onsets, and (4) rimes. Although educators can incorporate attention to phonemes within their interactions with young children, many preschool-age children are not sensitive enough to the phonological structure of language to recognize the individual phonemes that make up words and syllables. Thus, attending to words, syllables, onsets, and rimes makes the most sense developmentally. Importantly, educators should be aware that there is no reason to believe that attention to these concepts needs to be developmentally ordered, such that children's awareness of words needs to be developed before their awareness of syllables, or that awareness of syllables and words needs to precede awareness of rime units, and so forth. Although many early childhood curricula organize phonological awareness instruction to follow a developmental sequence, doing so does not appear to be necessary given that preschool-age children show sensitivities to all of these aspects of phonology, indicating that phonological awareness development does not follow a strict linear developmental continuum (Anthony, Lonigan, Driscoll, Phillips, & Burgess, 2003).

Educators who read phonologically salient storybooks with children find that it is relatively easy to embed attention to these sound features within these interactions, and that doing so invokes children's curiosity and enjoyment of the sounds and sound patterns of words. Importantly, rather than bombard children with explicit references to the phonological features of books, teachers can sensitively point out these features in ways that simply accentuate the reading experience for children. What seems particularly important is making children's exposure to phonological awareness learning experiences an explicit one. Research findings that involved parents reading to their preschool-age children with language impairment (Justice, Kaderavek, Bowles, & Grimm, 2005) indicated that when parents heightened the explicitness of children's experiences with rhyme and alliteration tasks embedded into storybook reading sessions, children showed accelerated phonological awareness development over a 10-week reading program.

Developing Outside-In Skills through Interactive Reading

Helping children to draw meaning from text is an important goal of reading instruction throughout most of the elementary school years (National Reading Panel, 2000). Skilled readers are able to think beyond literal levels and essentially read between the lines. However, it is not necessary that comprehension development be postponed until children are able to decode fluently (e.g., Pearson & Duke, 2002). Indeed, the abilities that underlie reading comprehension are important elements of language development during the preschool years, particularly vocabulary development and inferential language skills. Both aspects of development can be readily developed within high-quality language environments that provide children with many opportunities to hear "rare" words and to participate in conversations that require inferencing. The storybook reading context provides an excellent vehicle for the intentional development of vocabulary and inferential thinking through high-quality extratextual conversations between teachers and young children.

Vocabulary

When educators share books with young children, they can enhance children's vocabularies by providing an explicit focus on word meanings. In this section, we discuss strategies for supporting vocabulary development through repeated readings that highlight words children are unlikely to know. Through storybook reading, children are introduced to words that they may not encounter in everyday speech, which we call "rare words." Indeed, even a children's storybook has many more instances of rare words than a prime-time television sitcom (Cunningham & Stanovich, 2003). Giving young children repeated opportunities to hear rare words is an important goal of vocabulary instruction. Research shows that although children may be able to form a general representation of a word with just a single exposure, really knowing a word's meaning takes time (McGregor, Friedman, Reilly, & Newman, 2002).

Although much vocabulary is gained incidentally through multiple exposures to books (Elley, 1989; Penno et al., 2002), elaboration on word meanings by teachers may provide greater vocabulary growth than simply rereading texts and may be especially crucial for children with poor vocabularies (Justice, Meier, & Walpole, 2005; Penno et al., 2002). To capitalize on the storybook reading context in this way, educators must consider:

- Selecting appropriate words
- Elaborating on word meanings
- Engaging children in conversation

When selecting words to highlight during book sharing, it is important for educators to consider which words likely have the highest impact on vocabulary growth. Beck, McKeown, and Kucan (2002) describe how teachers select Tier Two words (not to be confused with Tier Two intervention) for elaboration during storybook readings and other classroom activities to build children's vocabulary knowledge. Tier Two words are relatively rare words that add precision to one's ability to express ideas. Children do not need elaboration for Tier One words such as *sad* or *like*, because these words are already firmly established in children's vocabularies. In addition, educators need not focus on Tier Three words, which include words that are specific to particular domains, such as *peninsula* or *xylophone*. Tier Two words are ideal because they include words that children are likely to encounter frequently, yet present some challenge, such as *furious, pleasant,* and *gigantic.* Teachers should carefully consider choosing words that children are unlikely to figure out from the context; contrary to popular belief, contexts often do not provide much assistance in figuring out word meanings. We recommend that educators choose at least three to five Tier Two or rare words per storybook.

After preselecting words prior to the reading, educators can then focus on how they will elaborate on the word meanings. Instead of using a dictionary, which often contains difficult-to-understand definitions of words, educators should prepare child-friendly definitions in language that young children can readily understand (Beck et al., 2002). In addition, educators can provide one-sentence explanations that help children situate the word meaning into the context of the book. Also, children can benefit from connecting word meanings to their everyday experience. In the following example, consider how the teacher elaborates on the word *impatient* from the storybook *Click, Clack, Moo: Cows That Type* (Cronin, 2000) after the line of text that indicates the cows were becoming impatient with the farmer:

> "*Impatient* means not being able to wait for something. The cows couldn't wait for Farmer Brown to make up his mind. Sometimes I

feel *impatient* when I have to stand in long lines at the grocery store. When do you feel *impatient?*"

The teacher chose the word *impatient* for elaboration, because she knew that children could grasp its underlying concept (i.e., not wanting to wait for things!), and because children would repeatedly encounter the word throughout school. Note how the teacher provides a child-friendly definition and situates the word in the context of the reading. Finally, she provides an opportunity for the children to engage actively with the word by supplying their own extensions of its meaning. To facilitate the management of this technique, educators can write their child-friendly definitions and explanations on sticky notes, placing each note on the page containing the word. During the storybook reading, educators are then ready to elaborate on the preselected word.

Spontaneous discussion and conversation during book reading also contribute to growth in children's vocabularies (e.g., Penno et al., 2002; Whitehurst et al., 1988). As in the previous example, an open-ended question (e.g., "When do you feel impatient?") can be a good way to encourage conversation. An open-ended question usually requires more than a one-word response from children and does not have just one correct answer. A closed-ended question (also called a test question), on the other hand, does not facilitate conversation and is often rhetorical (e.g., "What color is it? "What is his name?") In addition to asking questions, educators need to be attuned to children's interests and follow their lead, as they look for opportunities to build on children's understandings (Weitzman & Greenberg, 2002). If a child points to an illustration during a storybook reading session the educator can build on that opportunity by commenting on the picture, then waiting expectantly for the child to respond. When a child makes a comment about the book, the educator can *expand* the comment by recasting what the child said with correct grammar and syntax or by adding a new thought to the comment. Expanding on children's comments is a key way to facilitate children's growth in oral language (Fey, Long, & Finestack, 2003). Consider how the teacher expands on the child's comments in the following example and reinforces a story concept at the same time, after reading text concerning how the cows want some electric blankets in *Click, Clack, Moo* (Cronin, 2000):

CHILD: I like my mine.

TEACHER: [expanding] You like your blanket.

CHILD: (*Nods without speaking*)

TEACHER: [Follow-up question] What do you like about your blanket?

CHILD: It's warm.

TEACHER: [expanding] Your blanket keeps you warm and cozy at night. That's why the cows want blankets, too. They are asking the farmer to get them blankets.

It is important to note that the gains in vocabulary demonstrated by storybook interventions are modest (e.g., Sénéchal et al., 1995), and it is critical that educators provide a rich oral language environment beyond storybook reading interactions to boost children's vocabulary. We are not advocating storybook reading as the sole means for vocabulary acquisition; rather, educators can use the storybook context as one of many ways to enhance vocabulary development.

Inferential Language

When educators share books with young children, they can embed conversations into their interactions that stimulate children's higher-level thinking and understanding of abstract language, and provide opportunities for children to reason and to problem-solve using language as a tool. We refer to this as "inferential language," that is, language that children and adults use to represent cause and effect, to reason and to problem-solve, and to represent abstract events taking place beyond the here and now. Inferential language is related to reading comprehension in that strategic comprehension of text requires children to make conscious inferences about many elements of the book to understand its meaning, such as the mental states of characters, the nonliteral meaning of words and phrases, and different outcomes that may have occurred due to some particular event (van Kleeck, 2006). Comprehension is considered an essential component of reading instruction (National Reading Panel, 2000), and it is highly associated with a child's oral language competence (Storch & Whitehurst, 2002). Toward that end, researchers have stressed the importance of teaching explicit comprehension strategies, such as predicting and making inferences, to readers in the upper elementary grades. Children in the upper elementary school grades are required to use comprehension strategies independently as they read to learn new information. To help prevent later comprehension difficulties, educators can engage young children in inferential thinking and be proactive in helping them build language skills that are directly linked to later comprehension skills. Indeed, preschool children are able to interact with text beyond the literal level, and listening comprehension can be enhanced in young children before they begin formal reading instruction through the shared reading context.

Reading comprehension can be conceptualized as spanning a continuum progressing from literal (lower-level) to inferential (higher-level) language (van Kleeck et al., 2006). Literal language is used to discuss or understand ideas that are "right there" in the text. Adults who engage children in literal language activities may ask them to provide labels for objects, and may ask questions, such as "What color is this?" or "What is the girl doing?" Literal language is typically focused on the here and now, and on more perceptually focused events (e.g., size, color, shape).

Inferential language requires that we go beyond the text or the illustrations, to read between the lines—that is, to abstract or infer. Adults can positively impact children's abstract, higher-order thinking during book sharing by asking questions and promoting discussion that requires children to think beyond the literal level and to use or comprehend abstract language (van Kleeck et al., 1997, 2006). Importantly, there is a direct and positive relationship between young children's opportunities to practice their abstract language skills during book sharing interactions and their language abilities within the elementary grades (van Kleeck et al., 1997).

Educators can promote inferential language during shared book reading by using the following strategies:

- Creating and confirming predictions
- Posing stimulating questions to children

Creating and confirming predictions comprise an important problem-solving strategy readily employed by skilled readers. To develop this skill in young children, educators can engage children in creating hypotheses about what will happen in the story. In the example below, the teacher encourages inferential thinking:

"The title of this book is *Wemberly Worried* (Henkes, 2000). When I look at the cover of this book, I see a picture of a nervous-looking mouse. Hmm . . . I think her name is Wemberly, and she looks worried about something. She is holding her doll tightly. I predict that Wemberly is worried that she will lose her doll. Let's begin reading and see what happens."

In addition to "thinking aloud" about the book, educators can involve children in making predictions by asking, "What do you think will happen in the story?" As long as children's responses make sense, they have answered correctly. It is important to revisit and revise predictions during the storybook session, as the teacher here does:

"As we read the first few pages, we learn that Wemberly is worried about everything, little things and big things. Remember the prediction I made in the beginning of the story? I thought Wemberly would be worried about her doll. Hmm. . . . Is that true? Well, even though the author doesn't say that yet, it could be true, because Wemberly worries about everything. What do you think will happen next? Why?"

"Why" and "how" questions also tend to stimulate inferential thinking and use of inferential language. For example, a teacher might ask the following questions:

"Why do you think Wemberly is worried?"
"How do you think the three bears felt when they saw Goldilocks?"
"Why do you think Goldilocks went into the three bears' home?"

When educators ask questions like these, they are encouraging children to stretch their thinking. If children respond by saying "I don't know," a think-aloud could again be employed to help children develop higher-order thinking skills and model use of inferential language.

High-Quality Storybook Reading Sessions within Multitiered Programs

We discussed earlier in this chapter how strategic and intentional storybook reading interactions can serve children's needs within programs utilizing multitiered frameworks to layer the support that children receive. Within multitiered programs, all children receive Tier One (the general curriculum), whereas Tier Two supplemental instruction is provided to those children who require additional learning opportunities to close the emerging gap between high- and low-achieving children as the school year progresses, characteristic of the Matthew effect (Stanovich, 1986). Importantly, within multitiered programs at any grade level, the objectives of Tier One and Tier Two supports must be articulated to ensure that Tier Two extends children's Tier One experiences, thus providing children with multiple opportunities to achieve the critical objectives of the preschool curriculum.

We used the ERF project to illustrate how shared storybook reading experiences can be used to articulate goals and objectives between Tier One and Tier Two instruction. Specifically, Tier Two instruction (one-on-one or in small groups) that comprises storybook reading tutorials can be used strategically to support children who need additional learning opportunities in the preschool classroom. In a storybook reading tutorial, a teacher, assistant, specialist, or volunteer provides small-group or one-on-one supplemental instruction for children identified as requiring additional learning opportunities beyond those provided by Tier One, and this instruction is organized around a storybook reading event; that is, these Tier Two tutorials utilize storybook reading exchanges between adults and children to strategically foster children's skills in the four key areas discussed in this chapter: print knowledge, phonological awareness, vocabulary, and inferential language. We provide an example of a Tier Two framework adapted from that of the DERF project in Appendix 11.1. One of the benefits of such a set of procedures for organizing Tier Two instruction is that it not only capitalizes upon a research-based activity that has repeatedly been associated with improved language and literacy outcomes in children (e.g., Justice & Ezell, 2002; Penno et al., 2002; Whitehurst et al., 1988), but it is also inexpensive and relatively easy to implement. Novice educators can follow these procedures quite easily—and they appreciate knowing what is expected of them. The procedures also serve as a concrete tool to coach Tier Two instructors in the use of these research-based strategies in their storybook reading, and to monitor adults' use of these strategies. Of course, no single, one-on-one session includes all of the items on the procedures list.

Throughout this chapter, we have highlighted the importance of shared storybook reading that is both strategic and intentional. We have not only provided the reader with specific suggestions to enhance the quality of storybook reading sessions, but we have also described a larger framework for implementation that is practical and relatively easy to apply to the classroom setting. Shared storybook reading provides an ideal and naturalistic context for emphasizing both inside-out skills, such as print knowledge and phonological awareness, and outside-in skills, including vocabulary and inferential language. Developing these skills is essential to children's success as readers, both at the early stages of reading acquisition and during the later elementary school grades. Teachers can embed extratextual talk into the shared storybook reading session to create rich, interactive learning opportunities that stimulate children's thinking to extend beyond the words on the page.

References

Anthony, J. L., Lonigan, C. J., Driscoll, K., Phillips, B. M., & Burgess, S. R. (2003). Phonological sensitivity: A quasi-parallel progression of word structure units and cognitive operations. *Reading Research Quarterly, 38,* 470–487.

Beck, I. L., McKeown, M. G., & Kucan, L. (2002). *Bringing words to life: Robust vocabulary instruction.* New York: Guilford Press.

Brooks, F. (1999). *The runaway orange.* Tulsa, OK: Educational Development Corporation.

Cain, S. (2000). *The crunching munching caterpillar.* New York: Scholastic.

Chaney, C. (1994). Language development, metalinguistic awareness, and emergent literacy skills of 3-year-old children in relation to social class. *Applied Psycholinguistics, 15,* 371–394.

Clarke, J., & Johansson, C. (2003). *Tooth trouble.* New York: Scholastic.

Cronin, D. (2000). *Click, clack, moo: Cows that type.* New York: Scholastic.

Cunningham, A., & Stanovich, K. (2003). Reading can make you smarter. *Principal, 83,* 34–39.

Ehlert, L. (1987). *Growing vegetable soup.* New York: Scholastic.

Elley, W. B. (1989). Vocabulary acquisition from listening to stories. *Reading Research Quarterly, 24,* 174–187.

Ezell, H. K., & Justice, L. M. (2000). Increasing the print focus of adult–child shared book reading through observational learning. *American Journal of Speech–Language Pathology, 9,* 36–47.

Fey, M. E., Long, S. H., & Finestack, L. H. (2003). Ten principles of grammar facilitation for children with specific language impairments. *American Journal of Speech–Language Pathology, 12,* 3–15.

Fuchs, L. S. (2003). Assessing intervention responsiveness: Conceptual and technical issues. *Learning Disabilities Research and Practice, 18,* 172–186.

Gliori, D. (1992). *My little brother.* Cambridge, MA: Candlewick Press.

Gough, P. B., & Tunmer, W. E. (1986). Decoding, reading, and reading disability. *Reading and Special Education, 7,* 6–10.

Gray, S. (2004). Word learning by preschoolers with specific language impairment: Predictors and poor learners. *Journal of Speech, Language, and Hearing Research, 47,* 1117–1132.

Hammett, L. A., van Kleeck, A., & Huberty, C. (2003). Clusters of parent interaction behaviors during book sharing with preschool children. *Reading Research Quarterly, 38,* 442–468.

Hart, B., & Risley, T. R. (1995). *Meaningful differences in the everyday experience of young American children.* Baltimore: Brookes.

Henkes, K. (2000). *Wemberly worried.* New York: Scholastic.

Juel, C. (1988). Learning to read and write: A longitudinal study of 54 children from first through fourth grades. *Journal of Educational Psychology, 80,* 437–447.

Justice, L. M. (2006). Evidence-based practice, response to intervention, and the prevention of reading difficulties. *Language, Speech, and Hearing Services in Schools, 37,* 284–297.

Justice, L. M., & Ezell, H. K. (2000). Stimulating children's print and word awareness through home-based parent intervention. *American Journal of Speech–Language Pathology, 9,* 257–269.

Justice, L. M., & Ezell, H. K. (2001). Written language awareness in preschool children from low-income households: A descriptive analysis. *Communication Disorders Quarterly, 22,* 123–134.

Justice, L. M., & Ezell, H. K. (2002). Use of storybook reading to increase print awareness in at-risk children. *American Journal of Speech–Language Pathology, 11,* 17–29.

Justice, L. M., & Ezell, H. K. (2004). Print referencing: An emergent literacy enhancement strategy and its clinical applications. *Language, Speech, and Hearing Services in Schools, 35,* 185–193.

Justice, L. M., Kaderavek, J., Bowles, R., & Grimm, K. (2005). Language impairment, parent–child shared reading, and phonological awareness: A feasibility study. *Topics in Early Childhood Special Education, 25,* 143–156.

Justice, L. M., Meier, J., & Walpole, S. (2005). Learning new words from storybooks: An efficacy study with at-risk kindergarteners. *Language, Speech, and Hearing Services in Schools, 36,* 17–32.

Litchfield, J., & Brooks, F. (2006). *Tessa the teacher.* London, UK: Usborne.

MacDonald, B. (1985). *Mrs. Piggle-Wiggle.* New York: HarperTrophy.

Martin, B., Jr., & Archambalt, J. (1989). *Chicka chicka boom boom.* New York: Aladdin Paperbacks.

McGregor, K. K., Friedman, R. M., Reilly, R. M., & Newman, R. M. (2002). Semantic representation and naming in young children. *Journal of Speech, Language, and Hearing Research, 45,* 332–346.

National Reading Panel. (2000). *Report of the National Reading Panel: Teaching children to read.* Washington, DC: National Institute of Child Health and Human Development.

Neuman, S. B. (2006). The knowledge gap: Implications for early education. In D. K. Dickinson & S. B. Neuman (Eds.), *Handbook of early literacy research: Volume 2* (pp. 29–40). New York: Guilford Press.

Oram, H. (2000). *Gerda the goose.* Hauppauge, NY: Barron's Educational Series.

Paolilli, P., & Brewer, D. (2001). *Silver seeds.* New York: Puffin Books.

Pearson, P. D., & Duke, N. K. (2002). Comprehension instruction in the primary grades. In C. C. Block & M. Pressley (Eds.), *Comprehension instruction: Research-based best practices* (pp. 247–258). New York: Guilford Press.

Penno, J. F., Wilkinson, I. A. G., & Moore, D. W. (2002). Vocabulary acquisition from teacher explanation and repeated listening to stories: Do they overcome the Matthew effect? *Journal of Educational Psychology, 94,* 23–33.

Phillips, G., & McNaughton, S. (1990). The practice of storybook reading to preschool children in mainstream New Zealand families. *Reading Research Quarterly, 25,* 196–212.

Seibold, J. O., & Walsh, V. (1997). *Olive, the other reindeer.* San Francisco: Chronicle Books.

Sénéchal, M., Thomas, E., & Monker, J. (1995). Individual differences in 4-year-old children's acquisition of vocabulary during storybook reading. *Journal of Educational Psychology, 87,* 218–229.

Smolkin, L. B., Conlon, A., & Yaden, D. B. (1988). Print salient illustrations in children's picture books: The emergence of written language awareness. In J. E. Readence & R. S. Baldwin (Eds.), *Dialogues in literacy research: Thirty-seventh yearbook of the National Reading Conference* (pp. 59–68). Chicago: National Reading Conference.

Snow, C. E., Burns, M. S., & Griffin, P. (Eds.). (1998). *Preventing reading difficulties in young children.* Washington, DC: National Academy Press.

Stanovich, K. E. (1986). Matthew effects in reading: Some consequences of individual differences in the acquisition of literacy. *Reading Research Quarterly, 21,* 360–407.

Storch, S. A., & Whitehurst, G. J. (2002). Oral language and code-related precursors to reading: Evidence from a longitudinal structural model. *Developmental Psychology, 38,* 934–947.

Tolstoy, A., & Sharkey, N. (1998). *The gigantic turnip.* Cambridge, MA: Barefoot Books.

Tyler, J., & Hawthorn, P. (1996). *There's a dragon at my school.* Tulsa, OK: Educational Development Corporation.

van Kleeck, A. (2006). Fostering inferential language during book sharing with prereaders: A foundation for later text comprehension strategies. In A. van Kleeck (Ed.), *Sharing books and stories to promote language and literacy* (pp. 269–317). San Diego: Plural.

van Kleeck, A., Gillam, R. B., Hamilton, L., & McGrath, C. (1997). The relationship between middle-class parents' book-sharing discussion and their preschoolers' abstract language development. *Journal of Speech, Language, and Hearing Research, 40,* 1261–1271.

van Kleeck, A., Vander Woude, J., & Hammett, L. (2006). Fostering literal and inferential language skills in Head Start preschoolers with language impairment using scripted book-sharing discussions. *American Journal of Speech–Language Pathology, 15,* 85–95.

Wasik, B. A., & Bond, M. A. (2001). Beyond the pages of a book: Interactive book reading and language development in preschool classrooms. *Journal of Educational Psychology, 93,* 243–250.

Weitzman, E., & Greenberg, J. (2002). *Learning language and loving it: A guide to promoting children's social, language, and literacy development in early childhood settings* (2nd ed.). Toronto: Hanen Centre.

Whitehurst, G. J., Epstein, J. N., Angell, A. L., Payne, A. C., Crone, D. A., & Fischel, J. E. (1994). Outcomes of an emergent literacy intervention in Head Start. *Journal of Educational Psychology, 86,* 542–555.

Whitehurst, G. J., Falco, F. L., Lonigan, C. J., Fischel, J. E., DeBaryshe, B. D., Valdez-Menchaca, M. C., et al. (1988). Accelerating language development through picture book reading. *Developmental Psychology, 24,* 552–559.

Whitehurst, G. J., & Lonigan, C. J. (1998). Child development and emergent literacy. *Child Development, 69,* 848–872.

Ziefert, H. (2005). *Cat goes fiddle-i-fee.* New York: Sterling.

TEMPLATE FOR ORGANIZING
TIER TWO STORYBOOK READING SESSIONS

Adult reading cues	Focus	Date	Child's response
Before Reading			
Show front of the book • Tell: This is the cover. • Ask: What is this?	Print knowledge		
Read title, point to each word • Tell: This is the title. • Ask: What is this?	Print knowledge		
Read author's name • Tell: This is the person who wrote the book. Her/his name is . . . • Ask: What does an author do?	Print knowledge		
For titles containing alliteration, read title, emphasizing beginning sounds (e.g., *Tooth Trouble*)	Phonological awareness		
Picture walk • Tell: Let's look at all the pictures in the book . . . • Predict: What will this book be about?	Inferential language		
During Reading			
Read the left page • Ask: Where should I read next?	Print knowledge		
Point to each word in a line • Ask: Can you point to each word with me?	Print knowledge		
Read a line with return sweep • Ask: Where should I read next?	Print knowledge		
Read and emphasize • Beginning sounds • Rhyming words	Phonological awareness		
Choral reading (rhyming words) • Ask: Finish the sentence for me with a word that rhymes.	Phonological awareness		

(continued)

Adult reading cues	Focus	Date	Child's response
Content: Vocabulary elaboration • Provide child-friendly definition • Explain word in context or relate vocabulary word to child's experience	Vocabulary		
Content: Character thought • Ask: What might X be thinking? • Ask: Why did the character say X?	Inferential language		
Content: Predictions • Ask: What do you think will happen next? • Revisit and revise predictions.	Inferential language		
Content: Text-to-self connections • Relate story to child's experiences	Inferential language		
After Reading			
Letters (select one activity) • Ask child to name a letter • Ask child to identify as a capital or a lowercase latter • Demonstrate how to form letter • Ask child to form a letter • Find letter in a word	Print knowledge		
Phonological awareness (select one activity) • Tell: Two words that rhyme • Ask: What is a word that rhymes with X? • Tell: Two words begin the same sound • Ask: What is another word with the same beginning sound as X? • Clap and Tell: Words in sentence • Ask: Clap words in sentence.	Phonological awareness		
Choose one word to extend: • Revisit definition • Act out word (if applicable) • Discuss word meaning	Vocabulary		
Content: Predictions • Revisit predictions	Inferential language		
Content: Connection • Ask: What is your favorite part of the story? Why?	Inferential language		

CHAPTER 12

★★★★★★★★★

Differentiating Instruction in the Preschool Classroom

Bridging Emergent Literacy Instruction
and Developmentally Appropriate Practice

Terri Purcell
Catherine A. Rosemary

In response to the heightened press for literacy instruction in preschools, many early childhood teachers find themselves struggling with the question of how to infuse literacy into their daily routines and simultaneously recognize and appreciate the great variability in what children bring to the classroom. Put simply, how can preschool teachers differentiate instruction? The purpose of this chapter is to address this "how" question. Knowing how to differentiate instruction relies on a good understanding of what differentiation is and why it is important in early literacy teaching. Therefore, we begin the chapter with background on the underlying tension at the heart of this question, which is the commonly held belief that teaching literacy during the preschool years is developmentally inappropriate. This belief, however, is contrary to findings from a plethora of early literacy research that documents the important role of preschool teachers in teaching foundational reading and writing concepts through carefully planned group *and* individualized literacy experiences.

In the second section, we define "differentiated instruction" and describe some similarities between developmentally appropriate practice (DAP) and differentiated instruction. We present some principles of differentiated instruction and a framework that can be used to guide organization and early literacy instruction in the preschool classroom. We then explain why differentiated instruction in the teaching of early literacy concepts and skills is critically important. Finally, in the third section we present practical suggestions for implementing differentiated instruction in the classroom—recognizing that many teachers consider it to be "easier said than done" (Bodrova & Leong, 2006).

DAP and Early Literacy Research: What Is the Tension?

Both experts' claims and research reports substantiate the need for "differentiating instruction"—an approach in which teachers acknowledge children's unique needs and interests, and purposely act on this understanding, taking into account what children know and can do, to teach well what children need to learn. Over a decade ago, the position statement of the National Association for the Education of Young Children (NAEYC, 1996) called for teachers to meet individual children's needs: " . . . individual variation is not only to be expected but also valued and requires that decisions about curriculum and adult interactions with children be as individualized as possible" (p. 6). More recently, the joint position statement of the International Reading Association (IRA) and the NAEYC (1998) touted the need for teachers to understand that children differ in their developmental levels, and the National Institute of Child Health and Human Development (2000) provided evidence that effective teachers use various instructional approaches to accommodate children's differences.

Within the current educational context of mounting research that underscores the importance of literacy instruction in preschool programs, and the strong stance of IRA and NAEYC (1998) in support of early literacy teaching in preschools, however, some members of the early childhood community continue to question the appropriateness of literacy instruction in preschool (Bodrova & Leong, 2006) and its impact on the social–emotional well-being of children (Elkind & Whitehurst, 2001). Such views may be fueled by a concern about the inappropriateness of reading instruction observed in some preschool settings and the common misinterpretations of DAP. DAP, as advocated by NAEYC (1996), promotes a constructivist and interactive definition of "instruction" that comprises three major dimensions: age appropriateness, individual appropriateness, and social/cultural awareness. The definition states that the learning environment, teaching practices, and other program components should be planned and modified, based on what is expected of children at a particular age and on differences between children. Other concerns may be grounded in a "readiness view" of literacy development, which assumes that there is a specific time at which reading and writing instruction should begin (NAEYC, 1998).

More than a decade ago, Sue Bredekamp (1991), then Director of Professional Development of the National Association for the Education of Young Children, identified two misconceptions about DAP that have influenced the instructional practices in preschools then and now:

> *Misconception 1*: *Teachers should never use directed instruction with individual children or with small groups.* Instead, DAP implies a continuum of teaching practices ranging from teacher directive or didactic to low directive or child choice (Johnson & Johnson, 1992, p. 7). Through flexible grouping patterns (whole group, small group, partner and individual) children are provided a range of support and practice. In all of these experiences, however, teachers must refrain from activities that require children to sit for long periods of time.

> *Misconception 2*: *The curriculum is derived solely from student interests.* Instead, DAP suggests that teachers must understand the curriculum areas and child development related to the curriculum. More importantly, teachers must be able to use this information to plan instruction and provide for learning opportunities accordingly (Johnson & Johnson, 1992, p. 3).

Such misconceptions have resulted in confusion and tension for preschool teachers, who have been torn between supporting children's emotional growth through warm and supportive relations and directly teaching children information and skills (Pianta, 2006).

Another misconception held by many early childhood educators is that literacy instruction in preschool involves practices that should be reserved for school-age students. The instructional practices often cited are paper-and-pencil tasks, lots of seatwork, workbook work, and teacher lectures (NAEYC, 1998). These perceptions likely stem from their own schooling experiences, when transmissive teaching was widespread. Though these practices are still observed in many elementary classrooms, we also see a shift to constructivist teaching or learner-centered approaches in elementary classrooms.

Emergent literacy instruction that is developmentally appropriate for all learners engages children in meaningful learning activities (Morrow & Schickedanz, 2006; Whitehurst & Lonigan, 1998). It is sensitive to developmental differences among children (Walpole, Justice, & Invernizzi, 2004; Salinger, 2006), and adapts to children's changing needs. To teach effectively, teachers need to be knowledgeable about development, the content they are teaching, and assessments that can guide their planning. They need to be skillful observers, planners, and implementers. While directing the instruction toward achieving specific learning goals, effective teachers also provide ample opportunity for children to learn on their own and from each other in a language and print-rich environment. A blend of teacher-directed and learner-centered instruction ensures that children are taught with a clear academic focus and are provided numerous opportunities to practice and explore content and materials on their own (Landry, Swank, Smith, Assel, & Gunnewig, 2006). Importantly, studies have indicated that addressing literacy during the preschool years supports children's transition to more formal reading instruction in kindergarten (Bus & van IJzendoorn, 1999; National Institute of Child Health and Human Development, 2000) and "waiting" until kindergarten or first grade for reading instruction places many children at further risk for reading failure (Smith & Dixon, 1995).

Clearly, teaching early literacy concepts and skills need not be at odds with developmentally appropriate practice. Teaching sounds and words, how to listen to stories with purpose and anticipation, and how to write a name or a message can be done well through teacher-directed instruction that engages children in learning, addresses their needs, and provides ample opportunities for them to explore and practice on their own. Teachers who rely on these principles and practices are able to develop the literacy skills of children who differ in many qualities, development, interests, and learning approaches.

What Is Differentiated Instruction?

Differentiated instruction is a pedagogical approach to teaching that acknowledges and responds to student differences in readiness, interests, and learner profiles (Tomlinson, 2003). In this context, "readiness" refers to a child's developmental level, which can be determined through high-quality assessment data and careful observations. Attention to child "interests" means that teachers recognize the importance of motivation in learning. Teachers need a range of activities and materials that appeal to a variety of interests, so that children *want* to participate in the learning process. Finally, "student profiles," like learning styles, refer to children's modes of learning, which include visual, auditory, and kinesthetic pathways. Because children learn in different ways, teachers must broaden their teaching practices to include various teaching approaches to maximize effectiveness.

Differentiated instruction is a way of thinking about learning and teaching. With differentiated instruction, teachers understand that children are different and require different teaching materials, experiences, and support. Therefore, at the heart of differentiated instruction is the process of modifying and adjusting instruction to meet the needs of children with varying abilities, learning styles, and interests. Differentiated instruction resists the "one size fits all" approach to teaching and learning, and relies on established learning goals, child assessment, and observations to guide instruction. Teachers who incorporate differentiated instruction into their classrooms spend less time in whole-group activities, and more time working with children in small groups and individually, so that instruction is tailored to children's individual needs.

Though much has been written about differentiated instruction in recent years, the concept of differentiation is not a new idea. A review of the literature shows that researchers have long recognized the importance of considering the unique characteristics and interests of their children when planning instruction. Skilled teachers know the curriculum, use assessment data and direct observations to plan instruction, then carry out their plan with the targeted goal of assisting children's learning. They know what the children know, know what to teach, and know how to assist children's learning. They are working in what is often referred to as Vygotsky's (1978) zone of proximal development (ZPD). The ZPD refers to an optimal instructional level at which children learn skills and competencies that are just beyond their level of mastery. Application of this principle is based on the belief that when children are not challenged enough, they do not perform at their highest level of ability, because the brain is understimulated (unmotivated; see Tomlinson, 2003). Conversely, working within children's ZPD also prevents overchallenging the brain, which can lead to frustration and negatively affect motivation. Brain-based research shows that when the brain is overchallenged, it is not engaged, and it releases fewer neurochemicals (Kapusnick & Hauslein, 2001). Thus, differentiated instruction is based on the premise that children learn best when instruction is geared specifically to their level of development— within their reach, with some support from the teacher, or a more knowledgeable or skilled peer.

Tomlinson's (2001) perspective on differentiation is particularly well accepted because of her attention to student differences in readiness levels, interests, and learning profiles when planning instruction—recognizing that each of these characteristics impacts learning. Tomlinson established a set of principles to illustrate her ideas for effective differentiation within the classroom. She proposed that effective differentiation (1) is proactive rather than reactive; (2) employs flexible grouping patterns; (3) varies materials used by different children; (4) varies in instructional pacing; (5) is knowledge-centered (teachers must be knowledgeable about instructional practices and how children develop to support them at each stage); and (6) is learner centered (builds on each child's prior knowledge and experiences). Together these principles present a comprehensive arrangement of characteristics, instructional practices, and underlying knowledge that teachers must have to implement differentiated instruction successfully in their class. Table 12.1 illustrates these six principles and provides examples of how teachers may apply them in their classrooms.

Obviously, DAP and differentiated instruction share many important characteristics related to learning and teaching. First, both practices are based on the premise that children learn well in different ways; therefore, they require different approaches, materials, and pacing to be successful. Second, both practices encourage learning opportunities that promote student interaction with and without the teacher—including small-group guided instruction, as well as independent practice and child choice time. Finally, both DAP and differentiated instruction encourage teachers to rely upon assessment data and child observations in planning instruction that reflects the changing needs and interests of the children. In addition, continuous observation and assessment allow teachers to monitor each

TABLE 12.1. Tomlinson's (2001) Principles of Differentiated Instruction Applied to Practice

Tomlinson's principles of differentiated instruction	Applied to practice
Instruction is proactive, rather than reactive.	Teachers plan instruction based on assessment data to identify needs and interests of the children.
Instruction employs flexible grouping patterns.	Teachers organize children to work in a variety of formats, such as groups of three to five children with a teacher, partner groups, and/or independently. These varied grouping patterns allow teachers to better plan for the specific needs of their children and to monitor student progress throughout the year.
Instruction varies in materials.	Teachers use a variety of instructional materials that relate to student interests and developmental levels.
Instruction varies in instructional pacing.	Teaching is fast-paced for children who are reviewing a specific concept or skill and is slow paced for children who are developing an awareness of the concept or skill.
Instruction is knowledge-centered.	Teachers use their knowledge to teach what children need to learn. They know how children develop, the concepts and skills that need to be taught, appropriate instructional strategies, and the strengths and needs of their children.
Instruction is learner-centered.	Teachers place children's learning at the center of planning, teaching, and assessing instructional effectiveness.

child's progression toward identified goals. It is clear that effective literacy practices complement DAP by promoting learning experiences that value and respond to children's differences in ways that capture their attention and promotes continued success and development.

What Do Teachers Need to Know to Implement Differentiated Instruction?

Teachers who successfully meet specific literacy objectives with culturally and developmentally diverse learners have an understanding of how children learn and develop, and of the instructional strategies that promote learning. The following section presents three knowledge bases that influence the effectiveness of literacy instruction for preschool children:

1. Knowledge of literacy goals and the developmental progression of important literacy foundations.
2. Knowledge of assessments and how to use them as teaching tools.
3. Knowledge of how to modify instruction for all learners.

Knowledge of Literacy Goals and Understanding the Developmental Progression of Important Literacy Skills

Tomlinson (2003) asserts that effective differentiation is "knowledge centered." Before teachers can plan and differentiate instruction, they must have a clear understanding of the important concepts that need to be taught. Familiarity with the literacy goals and objectives appropriate for preschool-age learners helps teachers maintain a focus on the skills that need to be addressed—with the understanding that children differ in their knowledge and in developmental progression of each of these skills. When teachers are knowledgeable about the literacy expectations established by state and local administrators, they begin to analyze activities more critically in terms of "what" skills are being taught, thus selecting more meaningful and purposeful experiences for children. When teachers have a solid grasp of the content they are teaching, they are more likely to demonstrate precise and purposeful teaching to support children's learning. For example, teachers who understand the critical importance of phonological awareness in reading development are likely to spend more time sharing nursery rhymes with their children and engaging children in sound play activities than teachers who may view these kind of activities solely as fun and do not recognize their teaching value.

In addition to understanding the appropriate literacy goals for preschool-age children, effective teachers have a clear understanding of how specific skills develop over time. Building on and extending student knowledge relies on the teacher's understanding of the direction and developmental progression of the skills (Hollins, 1993). These teachers know the next rung in children's progress in literacy learning, and they plan instruction that scaffolds or supports children's learning. For example, research in the area of phonological awareness has shown that children often detect larger units of sound before they are able to perceive smaller units of sound (Lonigan, Burgess, Anthony, & Barker, 1998). This general knowledge has great implications for the sequence of phonological awareness instruction and expectations that teachers set for children. Relying upon this research, most teachers introduce children to rhymes and syllables before they introduce individual phonemes.

Knowledge of Assessments and How to Use Them as Teaching Tools

Preschool teachers can find out what children know about early literacy concepts and what skills they possess by observing children as they engage in literacy activities. Informal observations may occur in day-to-day teaching, and the collaborative and individual activities of the classroom. For example, singing the alphabet song gives children a natural, rhythmic way to learn the letter names. It can be done orally, with or without reference to an alphabet chart. If an alphabet chart is used, the teacher begins by modeling how to point to each letter when singing the letter names. He or she then turns over the pointer to individual children to practice on their own. During tracking, the teacher observes an individual child's facility with matching the names of the letters to their corresponding symbols when the letters are named in sequence. This practice builds the child's familiarity with the names of letters and their distinct symbols.

It is important to know what concepts and skills children have already learned, so teachers can introduce new concepts in ways that make meaningful connections between children's prior knowledge and new concepts (Hollins, 1993). Teachers' informal observations are an important part of assessing children' performance, but these are not the only types of assessments that should be used to guide planning and instruction (Moon, 2005). Instructional decisions should also be based on assessments that yield valid and reliable data. "Reliability" refers to how consistent the observations are over time and across observers. For example, Michelle, a preschool teacher, uses an alphabetic recognition assessment with a set of standardized procedures. She carries out those procedures the same way each time she uses the assessment, so the observations she makes are likely to be consistent. If another teacher were to conduct the same assessment with the same children, following the same procedures and using the same assessment materials, that teacher would likely obtain the same results. Assessments yield reliable data when teachers use the same tools and follow the administration procedures consistently. "Validity" means that the assessment measures what it is intended to measure. For example, a teacher who wants to assess listening comprehension reads a story rather than a list of words to a child. As the child listens, the teacher asks some questions about the text and documents the child's responses. In this way, the teacher is measuring listening comprehension directly, and the assessment results can be interpreted as valid. The use of assessments that lead directly to observations of reading and writing behaviors are essential. Teachers need to administer these assessments using standardized procedures (i.e., to ensure reliability), which include tasks that allow teachers to observe directly what children know and can do (i.e., to ensure validity).

Beyond selection of quality instruments, knowing what capabilities to look for is the most critical component to assessment. Teachers who have a broad understanding of the literacy concepts and skills that children need to acquire at a particular point in time are better able to examine these important literacy constructs through observations and interactions with children. For example, research has shown that oral language abilities (receptive and expressive), phonological awareness, and print/alphabet knowledge predict a child's success in learning to read; consequently, preschool teachers should periodically check student development in each of these fundamental areas, with the understanding that some children require more frequent checks than do others.

For example, teachers need to set a regular time to observe what children are learning about the alphabet. The plan may involve setting aside 5 minutes each day during a particular week, several times throughout the year. Documentation of alphabet knowledge should capture several aspects of the assessment, such as observations at various times and in various situations in which children encounter print. Using a checklist of upper- and lowercase letters, a teacher dates the observation and records a "U" if the child identified the uppercase form of a letter, or an "L" if the child identified the lowercase form. By knowing who knows which letters, the teacher can gear instruction to the letters that children have not yet learned. A teacher may also gauge the effectiveness of her own teaching by noting individual children's progress and reselecting the kinds of activities she provided earlier. Patterns of slow or of rapid progress suggest that the teacher needs to make adjustments in the instruction.

Continuous monitoring of child progress (progress monitoring) is vital to effective teaching, because it informs teachers of the specific needs of their children, ensures that instruction is within children's optimal learning level, or ZPD, and that children are progressing toward the learning goal. This connection makes "assessment" a fundamental component of differentiated instruction as teachers continuously alter instruction and vary the grouping patterns to meet children's changing needs.

Knowledge of How to Modify Instruction, Materials, and Grouping Patterns for All Learners

Differentiated instruction is based on the premise that instructional approaches should be varied and adapted for individual, diverse children in classrooms (Hall, 2002). Despite the increase in teacher awareness of children's differences, studies indicate that teachers continue to support traditional practices such as extended whole-group instruction, whereby all children receive the same instruction at the same time. Even special educators have reported using whole-group practice with children in resource rooms, because they felt that doing so was "right," and that it kept children from being stigmatized (Schumm, Moody, & Vaughn, 2000). Others have suggested that the problems in differentiating instruction lies in the teacher's difficulty in modifying the curriculum for children who need more or less support (Tomlinson et al., 2003). Modifying instruction in this manner requires teachers to be "knowledgeable decision makers," which is a challenge, because many teachers have grown accustomed to teaching "to the middle" (average children) or following strictly the scope and sequence presented in curricula materials. As decision makers, however, knowledgeable and skilled teachers make choices about curriculum content and the sequence of instruction based on children's needs. More importantly, they are willing to plan multiple levels of instruction, so that all of their children achieve success every day.

Modifying instruction starts with a high-quality curriculum and instruction that addresses key concepts, ideas, and skills (Tomlinson et al., 2003), and promotes active learning, incorporates real-life experiences, and connects to a child's interests. With a learning-powered lesson as a foundation, teachers can maximize instruction for all children by adjusting, or *tiering*, instruction so that there is additional support for less capable children and extension activities for more advanced children.

In a tiered activity, the teacher takes one curricular concept and introduces it to the entire class. The teacher varies the complexity of the task by adjusting one or more elements of the lesson: the content—what children are learning; the process—the activities in which children are engaged; the product—the projects that require children to apply and extend what they have learned; and the learning environment—the way the classroom supports student learning and practice (Tomlinson, 2003). Tiered activities allow all children to work at their comfort level and pace. By tiering the instruction, the teacher is differentiating the task so that all children learn a common concept at a comfortable level and pace. Table 12.2 illustrates how teachers may tier instruction in phonological awareness.

TABLE 12.2. Tiered Activity

Skills	Level 1—highest level of teacher support	Level 2—moderate teacher support	Level 3—least amount of teacher support
Phonological awareness: listening for and producing rhyming words	Children listen for and identify the rhyming words in a familiar rhyme as the teacher reads: "Hickory, Dickory **Dock**. The mouse ran up the **clock** [emphasizing boldfaced words]." Teacher explains that *dock* and *clock* sound alike because they are rhyming words. Teacher and children say the rhyming words together.	Children fill in the missing rhyming word in a familiar rhyme: "Hickory, Dickory, Dock. The mouse ran up the _____." Teacher asks children to fill in the rhyming words. They continue this activity with other nursery rhymes.	Children identify and match pairs of words presented on picture cards on the basis of rhyme.
Notice that the concept being taught—rhyming—is the same across all three activities. The environment/ materials are also the same for the first two tasks. The tasks differ in *process* and *product*.	In this activity, the teacher introduces the concept of rhyming to the children. The children are expected to listen and attend to the rhyming words. The focus here is on the *process*.	In this activity, the process is more challenging because the children are expected to use their understanding of rhyming words and familiarity with the nursery rhyme to *produce* or fill in the missing word.	This is the most challenging of the three phonological awareness activities. Children are familiar with rhymes and are expected to pair picture cards based on rhyming words.

Differentiated Instruction Involves Modifying the Materials and Activities in the Environment

To provide rich learning experiences for a broad range of children, teachers must have a wide range of materials to accommodate each child's unique readiness, interests, and learning style. The activities presented in the environment are very important to differentiated instruction, because they support children's development by allowing them to practice. Bodrova and Leong (2006) assert that differentiation is never accomplished if the teacher is perceived as the only source of assistance. Instead, teachers can rely on the environment to support higher levels of functioning by providing children with materials and activities that reinforce what they have learned in small-group instruction. When children practice with new content on their own, they are moving closer to independence, thus expanding their ZPD (Bodrova & Leong, 2006). When selecting materials to appeal to children's interests, teachers must be willing to integrate culturally responsive resources and materials for these children (Ladson-Billings, 1990). With this in mind, it is imperative that teachers frequently monitor the learning centers and rotate activities to reflect children's changing needs, interests, and leaner profiles.

We know that choice is a powerful motivator (Ginsberg, 2005). When children are allowed to choose the activities and texts that interest them, they spend more time trying to learn or understand the materials. Therefore, learning centers must be well-stocked with books and materials that appeal to their interests and encourage creativity in all children. Open-ended activities provide opportunities that allow children to mold activities to their interests and values (Turner & Paris, 1995). For instance, asking children to draw a picture or to create an object in response to a story or a discussed theme/concept gives them tremendous freedom to interpret the story in their own way.

Table 12.3 illustrates how children of varying abilities may use a writing center. Notice that whereas some children may want to produce their own stories, others choose to use the classroom environment in creating a story. These differences demonstrate how children require different materials and environmental support as they explore various centers. For instance, some children spontaneously begin to write when given a paper and pencil, whereas others require additional support from the alphabet chart, environmental print, or pictures available in the center. Still, children may differ in the utensils and materials that they choose to use. Some children prefer to write on chalkboards or dry-erase boards, whereas others may select to write on chart paper or use sandpaper letters to create words. It is important to understand that in all of these writing

TABLE 12.3. Ways That Different Children Use the Writing Center Activities

Student A: older and/or more advanced student	Student B: average student	Student C: younger and/or less capable student
Student often uses a pencil and paper to create a story. Writing demonstrates partial phonetic spelling (I LK CTZ for *I like cats*). Student sometimes elects to type stories on the computer.	Student enjoys writing words that are displayed in the classroom. Student chooses to write on dry-erase boards, chart paper, and chalkboards.	Student writing is characterized by scribbles and pictures. Student prefers to use crayons, markers, and colorful pencils to write and draw.

activities, despite differences in the level of understanding or materials used, children are furthering their knowledge of print and how words work.

Differentiated Instruction Involves Modifying the Ways We Support Children

One of the most distinguishing characteristics of differentiated instruction is that children work in a variety of grouping patterns, or "flexible grouping," which is a classroom organizational strategy that allows teachers to address a wide range of ability levels within a single classroom (Castle, Deniz, & Tortora, 2005). Teachers plan activities and choose materials that specifically address the needs and interests of the individual child, not the entire group. For instance, in the course of a school day, children may work in whole groups, small groups, dyads or partner groups, one-on-one with the teacher, and independently. Flexible groupings support "scaffolded instruction," which is supportive instruction that moves children to a level of independence, because children receive varying levels of support ranging from one-to-one or guided, small-group practice with the teacher to working with a partner or independently.

Flexible groupings are sometimes confused with ability groupings for an obvious reason: Children in both types of groupings may work with others of similar abilities. However, in ability groups, children are often stigmatized, because they remain in the same group throughout the school day and the school year. However, in flexible groups, children move in and out of a variety of grouping arrangements based on their changing needs, interests, and learning preferences. Table 12.4 describes the various ways that teachers may group children for instruction.

As should be evident, preschool teachers and children have many opportunities to work in a variety of grouping arrangements throughout the school day. In addition to helping teachers address the specific needs of children, these grouping arrangements build a positive classroom environment in which children work both cooperatively with their classmates and independently.

Avoiding Common Pitfalls

Like anything new, implementing differentiated instruction takes time and requires careful planning by the preschool teacher. In this section, we discuss how preschool teachers can make differentiated instruction work in their classrooms by avoiding a few common pitfalls. It is important to understand that there is no "right" way to differentiate instruction

TABLE 12.4. Flexible Grouping for Instruction

Types of groupings	Primary uses	Preschool activities
Whole-class grouping	Community building, planning, introducing new concepts or skills, reading–writing–thinking strategies	Morning circle calendar Shared reading
Teacher-led groups	Common need, guided practice, and task-focused help	Small-group lessons in which teacher addresses specific needs of children (e.g., name-writing practice, letter recognition, phonological awareness activity)
Student-led small groups	Supported practice, shared tasks, collaborative responses, common interest, sharing reading and writing	
Partners (dyads)	Supported practice, mentoring, tutoring, shared tasks	Student partner reading, games, or center exploration
Individual	One-on-one instruction, individual assessment, independent practice, individual response	Center exploration or independent practice

Note. Data from Chapman (1995).

(Tomlinson, 2003). Instead, we present four guiding principles that may ease the transition into differentiated instruction and increase the effectiveness of this practice:

1. Continually monitor student progress and regroup children.
2. Create a supportive environment that engages all learners.
3. Plan and start slowly.
4. Plan for student transitions.

Continually Monitor Progress and Regroup Children

Before teachers can create a strong literacy program for all learners, they must understand the range of skills and capabilities that is represented in their classroom. Therefore, the use of assessment data is a vital component of this practice, because it helps to maintain an instructional focus on the needs of all children. Because children's needs and abilities change over time and in response to instruction, teachers need to assess children before, during, and after the instructional episode, and at various points throughout the school year. Assessments should help to answer critical questions regarding children's needs and optimal learning:

1. What do my children know?
2. What do my children need to know?
3. How do my children vary in their knowledge of important literacy concepts?

Answering these three questions related to language and literacy skills informs teachers of the instructional focus that is necessary for each child, as well as which materials will support the learner. In addition, continuous progress monitoring guides teachers in updating literacy centers, reorganizing flexible groups, and expanding materials and activities to accommodate children at various stages of development.

It is important that teachers select a method of keeping track of the assessment data that they collect on each child (McGee & Richgels, 2003). A simple way to organize assessment data is to create a separate assessment folder, or a notebook with tabs, for each child. Within each folder or tab, teachers should store assessment information that informs them of the child's development in important literacy concepts (along with benchmarks). Referring to this information often ensures that teachers are designing instruction that targets children's needs. Teachers may want to schedule particular assessments early in the year, again at midpoint, and at the end of the year (McGee & Richgels, 2003). However, natural observations of children and "quick checks" of literacy skills should occur weekly. For example, some preschool teachers plan weekly observations of four to five children by using anecdotal records. In these observations, for example, teachers may closely examine a child's name writing or his or her interaction with print, book reading, and language development.

Create a Supportive Environment that Engages All Learners

In addition to planning for more targeted instruction, teachers must arrange the environment in a way that invites children to engage in learning activities without the teacher. Because the environment serves as a source of support for children's learning, differentiated instruction can only occur in well-organized classrooms where children are encouraged to work collaboratively and independently. In such classrooms, materials are easily accessible to children, and literacy centers are stocked with activities and materials that appeal to a range of student interests and developmental needs. In this capacity, the classroom environment has the potential to scaffold student learning, because children are able to explore and practice skills that are within their comfort zone or ZPD.

Appealing to children's interests and preferred learning styles is important to consider when organizing the environment, because high-interest activities heighten the learning experience and motivate children to continue making the effort. Therefore, teachers should select materials that are appropriate for children's age and developmental levels, interests, and learning profiles.

Plan and Start Slowly

Effective differentiated instruction requires multilevel planning, including *whole-group instruction* (to introduce new concepts and skills), *small-group instruction* (to provide more targeted instruction), and *centers* (to allow for independent practice). Planning for and managing these diverse learning experiences takes time and practice for both teachers and children. We suggest starting slowly by examining elements of differentiated instruction that are already in place. For most preschool teachers, this may include use of centers that permit independent practice. Here, teachers can set the stage for individualized instruction. Teachers are able to monitor children's learning in various centers and make necessary adjustments that promote increased levels of success and/or interests.

Nonetheless, teachers must model and direct children in the use of learning centers. Through continuous teacher modeling, children learn to select appropriate materials that are within their comfort range. Children also develop important skills, such as working cooperatively and independently in activities designed to serve as practice of skills and concepts they have already been taught. When children are engaged in learning centers, teachers are better able to work with smaller groups of children in more targeted instruction.

Plan for Transitions

Clear transition practices are also important in reducing the feeling of "chaos" in the classroom. To avoid noisy and unorganized transitions, teachers and children must consistently practice how to walk and move from one area of the classroom to the next. Preschool children need clear directions in how to clean up their center areas, to transition to a new learning center (e.g., walking with their hands by their sides), and to respond to classroom signals from the teacher (e.g., lights turned off—time to be quiet; clapping—look for the teacher); bell ringing—move to small groups. For example, Mrs. Ford, a Head Start teacher, uses animal noises from a portable piano to signal when children are to clean up their areas and move to the kidney-shaped table for small-group instruction. In her classroom, the sound of a *lion* signals Group 1; the sound of an *elephant* signals Group 2, and the sound of *birds* signals Group 3.

As teachers and children become more confident in this process of transitioning in and out of centers, teachers are able to expand differentiated instruction to include teacher-led, small-group instruction and one-to-one instruction for high-risk children.

Pulling It All Together: Differentiated Instruction in One Classroom

Figure 12.1 illustrates how one Head Start teacher meets the needs of all children during language and literacy instruction. In the course of 2 hours, children work in whole groups, partner groups, and small groups with the teacher and independently. Children also engage in activities that address important literacy concepts daily.

Conclusions

Children enter preschool with an array of knowledge about language and print. Through their literacy experiences in the home, including rich conversations, storybook readings, and opportunities to observe adults engaged in literacy activities, children become aware of the print around them and the many ways that people use language. Preschool teachers have a special opportunity to further children's awareness of language and print through a well-designed literacy program that is both engaging and developmentally appropriate. Creating an instructional program that meets children *where they are* requires that teachers embrace differentiated instruction—a way of teaching that recognizes children learn well in different ways, and benefit from instruction that accommodates their differences (Sternberg & Zhang, 2005). Such teachers strive to create equity in learning by planning instruction that responds to student differences related to readiness, interests, and learning profiles.

Teaching emergent literacy in this manner is supportive of developmentally appropriate practice, because children are encouraged to work at their level of comfort and pacing. Teachers plan opportunities to guide students' development with instruction that is designed specifically to move children just beyond this comfort zone. For example, in one group of children, a teacher may assist students in writing their names, whereas in another group, children may be learning to distinguish letters from

Time and activity	Language and literacy skills addressed	Grouping pattern	Materials	Procedure
9:00–9:15 Morning movement and song	Phonological awareness	Whole group, teacher led	Poetry chart Finger-play chart	Teacher and students recite a familiar nursery rhyme or poem while acting it out.
9:15–9:30 Shared-Book reading and conversation (questioning)	Oral language, print awareness, vocabulary, concept knowledge	Whole group, teacher led	Selected book	Teacher shares book with children (prereading, during reading, after reading activity).
9:30–10:30 Centers and independent practice	Alphabet knowledge, print awareness, concept development, oral language, and collaboration	Independent center exploration, child-centered	Center activities that correspond to a wide range of student needs and interests	Children move to several centers throughout the classroom.
9:30–10:00 Small-group instruction	Targeted language and literacy skills based on student assessments	Small group, guided instruction	Small-group materials that support instructional focus	Teacher works with several small groups of children to address specific literacy needs.
10:30–11:00 Recall and sharing	Print awareness and concept of word	Small group	Chart paper and markers	Language Experience Approach (LEA)— students recall activities they enjoyed as teacher writes them down

FIGURE 12.1. Sample daily language and literacy block.

numbers. In such an environment, children are curious and active learners, consistently engaged in activities and learning experiences in which they can feel successful. Acknowledging that each child is a unique individual, and planning instruction that embraces these differences, is not only a characteristic of effective and responsible teaching, but it also demonstrates a sense of caring and compassion that is always an important element in teaching young children.

References

Adams, C. (1990). *Beginning to read*. Cambridge, MA: MIT Press.

Bodrova, E., & Leong, D. (2006). Vygotskian perspectives on teaching and learning early literacy. In D. Dickinson & S. Neuman (Eds.), *Handbook of early literacy research* (pp. 243–268). New York: Guilford Press.

Bredekamp, S. (1991). Redeveloping early childhood education: A response to Kessler. *Early Childhood Research Quarterly, 6*, 199–209.

Bus, A. G., & van IJzendoorn, M. H. (1999). Phonological awareness and early reading: A meta-analysis of experimental training studies. *Journal of Educational Psychology, 91*(3), 403–414.

Castle, S., Deniz, C., & Tortora, M. (2005). Flexible grouping and student learning in a high-needs school. *Education and Urban Society, 37*(2), 139–150.

Chapman, M. L. (1995). Designing literacy learning experiences in a multiage classroom. *Language Arts, 72*(6), 416–428.

Elkind, D., & Whitehurst, G. J. (2001). Young Einsteins. Much too early: Much too late. *Education Matters, 1*, 8–21.

Ginsberg, M. (2005). Cultural diversity, motivation, and differentiation. *Theory into Practice, 44*(3), 218–225.

Hall, T. (2002). *Differentiated instruction*. Wakefield, MA: National Center on Accessing the General Curriculum. Retrieved February 2, 2007, from *www.cast.org/publications/ncac/ncac_diffinstruc.html*.

Hollins, E. R. (1993). Assessing teacher competence for diverse populations. *Theory into Practice, 32*(2), 93–99.

Johnson, J., & Johnson, K. (1992). Clarifying the developmental perspective in response to Carta, Schwartyz, Atwater, and McConnell. *Topics in Early Childhood Special Education, 12*(4).

Kapusnick, R. A., & Hauslein, C. M. (2001). The "silver cup" of differentiated instruction. *Kappa Delta Pi Record, 37*(4), 156–159.

Ladson-Billings, G. (1990). Blurring the borders: Voices of African liberatory pedagogy in the United States and Canada. *Journal of Education, 172*(2), 72–88.

Landry, S. H., Swank, P., Smith, K., Assel, M., & Gunnewig, S. (2006). Enhancing early literacy skills for preschool children: Bringing a professional development model to scale. *Journal of Learning Disabilities, 39*(4), 306–324.

Lonigan, C. J., Burgess, S. R., Anthony, J. L., & Barker, T. A. (1998). Development of phonological sensitivity in 2- to 5-year-old children. *Journal of Educational Psychology, 90*(2), 294–311.

McGee, L., & Richgels, D. (2003). *Designing early literacy programs: Strategies for at-risk preschool and kindergarten children.* New York: Guilford Press.

Moon, T. (2005). The role of assessment in differentiation. *Theory into Practice, 44*(3), 226–233.

Morrow, L., & Schickedanz, J. (2006). The relationship between sociodramatic play and literacy development. In D. K. Dickenson & S. Neuman (Eds.), *Handbook of early literacy research* (pp. 269–280). New York: Guilford Press.

National Association for the Education of Young Children. (1996, July). *Developmentally appropriate practice in early childhood programs serving children from birth through age 8.* Retrieved February 2, 2007, from *www. naeyc.org/about/ positions/pdf/psdap98.pdf.*

National Association for the Education of Young Children. (1998, May). *Learning to read and write: Developmentally appropriate practices for young children.* Retrieved February 2, 2007, from *www.naeyc.org/about/positions/pdf/psread98. pdf.*

National Institute of Child Health and Human Development. (2000). *Report of the National Reading Panel: Teaching children to read: An evidence-based assessment of the scientific research literature on reading and its implications for reading instruction* (NIH Pub. No. 00-4769). Washington, DC: U.S. Government Printing Office.

Pianta, R. (2006). Teacher–child relationships and early literacy. In D. K. Dickenson & S. Neuman (Eds.), *Handbook of early literacy research* (pp. 149–162). New York: Guilford Press.

Salinger, T. (2006). Policy decisions in early literacy assessments. In D. K. Dickenson & S. Neuman (Eds.), *Handbook of early literacy research* (pp. 427–444). New York: Guilford Press.

Schumm, J. S., Moody, S. W., & Vaughn, S. (2000). Grouping for reading instruction: Does one size fit all? *Journal of Learning Disabilities, 33*(5), 477–488.

Smith, S. S., & Dixon, R. (1995). Literacy concepts of low- and middle-class four-year-olds entering preschool. *Journal of Educational Research, 88*(4), 243–253.

Sternberg, R., & Zhang, L. (2005). Styles of thinking as a basis of differentiated instruction. *Theory into Practice, 44*(3), 245–253.

Tomlinson, C. (2001). *How to differentiate instruction in mixed-ability classrooms* (2nd ed.). Alexandria, VA: Association for Supervision and Curriculum Development.

Tomlinson, C. A. (2003). *Differentiated of instruction in the elementary grades* (ERIC Digest). Retrieved February 2, 2007, from *www.ericdigests.org/2001-2/elementary.html.*

Tomlinson, C. A., Brighton, C., Herberg, H., Callahan, C., Moon, T., Brimijoin, K., et al. (2003). Differentiated instruction in response to student readiness, interest, and learning profile in academically diverse classrooms: A review of the literature. *Journal for the Education of the Gifted, 27*(2/3), 119–145.

Turner, J., & Paris, S. (1995). How literacy tasks influence children's motivation for literacy. *Reading Teacher, 48*(8), 662–673.

Vygotsky, L. (1978). *Mind in society: The development of higher psychological processes.* Cambridge, MA: Harvard University Press.

Walpole, S., Justice, L., & Invernizzi, M. (2004). Closing the gap between research and practice: Case study of school-wide literacy reform. *Reading and Writing Research Quarterly, 20,* 261–283.

Whitehurst, G. J., & Lonigan, C. J. (1998). Child development and emergent literacy. *Child Development, 69*(3), 848–872.

CHAPTER 13

★★★★★★★★★

Language and Literacy Practices for English Language Learners in the Preschool Setting

M. Adelaida Restrepo
Virginia Dubasik

English language learners (ELLs) have an increasing presence in preschool programs within the United States (National Center for Education Statistics [NCES], 2004). Over 9 million children attending U.S. schools speak a language other than English at home, a 162% increase in the last 15 years. Currently, 1 child in 5 in the U.S. is born to an immigrant family. The educational community faces several challenges in providing educational services to these pupils, because children of immigrants are more likely to live in poverty and, if they have difficulty speaking English, are also more likely to score below their English peers in reading and math (NCES, 2006). These factors put preschool ELLs at risk for academic difficulties, which in turn places them at risk of not completing high school and college, thus significantly impacting their future work, education, and income potential.

For the purposes of this chapter, the term "English language learner" refers to children in the United States who are learning English as a second language, and who are being raised in homes in which languages other than English are spoken. The process of acquiring a second language after age 3 years is called "sequential bilingualism," and these children are considered to be second language learners (Genesee, Paradis, & Crago, 2004). Although the age of 3 years is used in this definition as a cutoff, and includes the assumption that these youngsters have developed their native language by this time, it is often the case that the process of acquiring their native language is not complete at this age; that is, young ELLs are still in the process of acquiring grammatical forms, building complexity in their sentences and stories, and learning new vocabulary as they expand the breadth and depth of their knowledge of that vocabulary. Because of this, ELL preschoolers who attend English-only programs may experience inhibited native language growth, especially if native language stimulation in the home is not rich (Tabors, 1997).

This is an important point given that in the U.S., where English is considered the majority language and is the dominant language used in many publicly funded preschool programs, the home language of ELLs is considered the minority language. Raising children in environments where their native language is a minority language that is not valued can negatively affect their cultural identity and overall academic progress (Hamers & Blanc, 2000). However, many parents of young ELLs enroll their children in preschool programs with the expectation that their children will learn English, and that this will help to prepare them for kindergarten and later schooling. Therefore, preschool programs should ensure that ELLs in their programs are prepared to succeed academically and to learn English as a second language for this purpose.

In this chapter we discuss how to optimize English language acquisition, and native language and literacy development, for ELLs attending preschool programs in the United States. We address topics such as how to emphasize the relationship between oral language skills and literacy development, how preschool staff can help ELLs develop English language skills, and how school personnel can connect with ELL families given the important role they have in children's language and literacy development. In addition, we address best practices for situations in which teachers do not speak the child's language.

The Need for Quality Preschools for ELLs

Across the United States, ELLs underperform in reading and math at all grade levels. ELLs entering kindergarten are often behind their language-majority peers in the skills necessary for reading. Unfortunately, this gap in achievement remains throughout their school years. The 2005 National Assessment of Educational Progress (NAEP) results indicated that 73% of fourth-grade ELLs and 71% of eighth-grade ELLs scored below basic levels in reading ability. Although these statistics are discouraging, research indicates that ELLs can achieve literacy skills appropriate for their grade level if they receive effective literacy instruction. Their gains are not instantaneous, but with time they can succeed (Waits, Campbell, Gau, Jacobs, & Hess, 2006). Even more encouraging is the finding that preschool programs have a direct impact on children's academic skills, and can close the gap with appropriate quality education (Garcia & Gonzalez, 2006). Given the potential for ELLs to become bilingual and biliterate adults—thus, making strong contributions to a society that increasingly recognizes the importance of bilingualism—education should support this potential rather than minimize its importance and value.

Given the growing numbers of ELLs in the United States, preschool programs need to be ready to address the needs of these pupils, especially those of youngsters at risk of academic failure due to the limited educational achievement of their primary caregivers and the far-reaching impact of poverty. Latinos, who make up the largest group of ELLs in the United States, tend to live in lower economic conditions and have higher unemployment rates than their European American peers (Garcia & Gonzalez, 2006). ELL preschoolers who live in poverty are more likely than their advantaged peers to know fewer words and to have poorer language and phonological awareness skills (Hart & Risley, 1992, 1995; Raz & Bryant, 1990; Smith et al., 1997; Washington & Craig, 1999). In addition, these children tend to experience more reading problems than their middle-class peers later in their lives (Alwin & Thornton, 1984; Teale, 1986; White, 1982). Quality preschool programs that focus on ELLs' specific needs and whose aim is to enhance their language and preliteracy skills can prevent their academic failure.

In the remainder of this chapter, we utilize a three-pronged approach to suggest how educators might optimize ELL preschoolers' learning in preschool programs:

1. Building and supporting ELLs' native language development, so that they exhibit strong communication skills at home and build on their native language, which in turn predicts English skills.
2. Using English as a second language (ESL) strategies to facilitate children's learning of English.
3. Connecting homes and schools to ensure that parents of ELLs understand the goals and expectations of preschool programs, to help children feel connected to home and school, and to help school staff to understand, value, and respect the home culture.

Developing Native Language and Literacy

Supporting ELL children's native language development in preschool programs serves many functions: It supports the foundation of good English acquisition, facilitates literacy development and academic achievement, and it helps to reinforce cultural identity and healthy social–emotional development (Gutierrez-Clellen, 1999; Kohnert, Yim, Nett, Kan, & Duran, 2005). Here, we describe specific elements necessary for a quality preschool program for ELLs, in which one of the main goals is to build strong native language skills. This foundation serves as the basis for children's long-term literacy development and supports the transfer of native language and literacy skills to English.

According to the Simple View of Reading (Gough & Tunmer, 1986), oral language is critical for both reading comprehension and the development of phonemic awareness and letter knowledge, all of which are necessary to improve children's later skills in reading. Language skills in the preschool years, such as phonemic awareness, syntactic abilities, and vocabulary knowledge, have been found to predict later reading skills (Campos, 1995; Craig, Connor, & Washington, 2003; Naslund, 1990; Scarborough, 1990, 1991, 2001). Furthermore, children with reading difficulties may exhibit problems in phonological awareness (Bryant et al., 2000; Lonigan, Burgess, & Anthony, 2000), letter knowledge (Bond & Dykstra, 1967; Stevenson & Newman, 1986), and vocabulary (Share, Jorm et al., 1984) during the preschool years. The same skills that have been found to predict reading success in English speakers predict success in ELLs' reading in English (August & Shanahan, 2006). Moreover, research indicates that native language skills may facilitate or transfer to literacy development in English, and that early native language skills predict later English literacy skills acquisition (Branum-Martin et al., 2006; Cisero & Royer, 1995; Durgunoglu, 2002; Durgunoglu, Nagy, & Hancin-Bhatt, 1993).

Why Should Preschool Practitioners Be Concerned with Children's Native Language If They Live in an English-Majority Context?

The goal of an excellent preschool program for ELLs should be to support the continued development of children's native/home language, because it facilitates a variety of positive outcomes. First, it ensures that families develop effective communication skills necessary for the transmission of culture, the children's social–emotional development, and strong parent–child relations. Second, strong native language knowledge has been found to transfer to the second language, and may help children to build English knowledge (Kohnert & Derr, 2004; Kohnert et al., 2005) and increase their academic achievement (Campos, 1995; Saville-Troike, 1984). Third, preschool children who attend programs in their second language are at risk of loss or stagnation in their native language (Leseman, 2000). Therefore, building on the native language prevents native language loss, which impacts communication and ethnic identity (Anderson, 2004).

Strong native language skills predict second language skills within and across a variety of language and literacy skills (Branum-Martin et al., 2006; Cisero & Royer, 1995; Dickinson, McCabe, Clark-Chiarelli, & Wolf, 2004; Durgunoglu, 2002; Durgunoglu et al., 1993; Wang, Park, & Lee, 2006). Vocabulary, phonemic awareness, rapid naming and phonological memory in the native language predict children's second language word-level reading (Lesaux & Geva, 2006). For example, Proctor, August, Carlo, and Snow (2006) found that native language vocabulary in second-grade ELLs was a strong predictor of these students' fourth-grade English reading comprehension. This suggests that native Spanish vocabulary knowledge is important for English comprehension. In addition, there is some evidence that alphabet knowledge in the native language transfers to English, and that this is facilitated by the similarity in the languages' alphabetic principles (August, Calderon, & Carlo, 2002; Bialystok, McBride-Chang, & Luk, 2005; Wang et al., 2006). Letter names in one language can transfer to the second language when alphabetic instruction occurs in the native language and the alphabets are similar, as they are in Spanish and English (Rolla San Francisco, Carlo, August, & Snow, 2006). If alphabetic instruction is provided solely in English, however, there is a negative relationship between letter knowledge in the native language and letter knowledge in English. Typically, the more letters the children know in English, the fewer letters they can identify in their native language. These results suggest that children need to receive alphabetic instruction in both of their languages. Therefore, it is important for preschool programs to provide for ELLs instruction in the native language, along with second language instruction. This provides for these children the best chance for school success in later years.

Research indicates that those children who have strong native language skills do better academically than those who do not (e.g., Campos, 1995; Saville-Troike, 1984). For example, Campos (1995) found that Spanish-speaking children who attended a preschool program that focused on building their Spanish oral language skills performed significantly better on fifth-grade standardized assessments than their peers who attended English-only preschool programs. In addition, they exhibited lower retention rates and higher grades.

How Do We Encourage Bilingual Language and Literacy Development?

The goal of developing children's competence in two languages requires that the children receive sufficient instruction in both languages

(Genesee et al., 2004). Children who have limited native language communication in the home, and are exposed to English only at school, are at risk of not developing their language skills fully, or at least of not developing strong native language skills (Kan & Kohnert, 2005; Wong Fillmore, 1991). Similarly, if the children do not receive sufficient English input, then they are at risk for not developing the English proficiency necessary to succeed in schools where English is the majority language and the language of instruction.

Bilingual Programs

Ideally, preschool programs should instruct children in the most frequently used languages of the classroom, one of which is English. These programs, termed "dual-language programs," are used in regular schools and serve children who speak the majority language and are learning the minority language (Genesee et al., 2004). This model lends itself well to preschool if adequately trained staff are available. These programs not only support ELLs but they also promote bilingualism in all children, regardless of their language background.

Many traditional preschool programs do provide instruction in two languages, but often these programs are for mostly language-minority children (Rodriguez, Diaz, Duran, & Espinosa, 1995). This kind of model is often seen in Head Start programs in places where there are large communities of language-minority children (Snow & Tabors, 1993; Tabors, 1997; Tabors, Paez, & Lopez, 2003). Having bilingual staff in the classroom is necessary for bilingual and dual-language programs, but it is not sufficient. Kan and Kohnert (2005), for example, found that Hmong children attending a bilingual Head Start program with bilingual Hmong–English staff did not develop their native language vocabulary while they were in the program. They did, however, develop their English vocabulary skills. The investigators concluded that most of the instruction actually occurred in English, although the staff communicated with the children in their native language for other purposes, such as classroom management. These results suggest that the language of instruction should be used systematically and purposefully, and that it should not be limited to English; that is, bilingual staff should plan specifically which lessons are to be taught in each language. If the language of instruction varies, the default language becomes what is easy and accessible to the teacher, which in the United States tends to be English, though instruction is in some cases provided in only the teacher's native language. In these cases, the children's English language development suffers.

Rodriguez and colleagues (1995), in contrast to Kan and Kohnert (2005), found that ELLs made gains in both languages in a dual-language program in a variety of language skills areas, including vocabulary, verb complexity, and receptive language. What was critical in such programs, however, was the use of planned and purposeful native language instruction; that is, the goal of the program was to ensure that the children made gains in both English and Spanish, so activities were planned accordingly.

Add-On Programs

Another available model—a "limited add-on program"—ensures that language-minority children receive some native language intervention, although it may not be as intensive as in dual-language or bilingual programs. This model works when availability of bilingual staff is limited due to the paucity of professionals who speak the minority language in a given community. Restrepo and colleagues (2007) developed an add-on Spanish literacy and oral language program for ELLs who spoke Spanish as their native language and attended English-only preschools. In this model, ELLs received 30 minutes of Spanish a day in small groups (no more than five children per group). Daily instruction was provided in two or three of the following skills: phonemic awareness, letter knowledge, vocabulary, and book reading. In this limited add-on program, ELLs with native language instruction made significant native language gains in sentence length and complexity, in addition to learning valuable English language skills. The ELLs in the control classrooms made no gains in Spanish.

Programs to Facilitate Home Language Use

If bilingual programs and/or add-on programs are not available, the goal of a preschool program should still be to encourage, value, and promote home language use. Programs can facilitate home language use by having readily available home lending libraries of books in the children's native language and by emphasizing, through parent education, the importance of building oral language in the children's native languages (Campos, 1995; Tabors, 1997). In addition, the preschool curriculum should place a strong emphasis on cultural diversity, using materials, such as books and songs, that represent children from a variety of cultures. Furthermore, engaging the parents and community volunteers to teach about the language and culture is critical. Parents and volunteers should be encouraged to read in their native language at home and in the classroom, and to participate in activities that are relevant and appropriate for the children; these activities encourage the use of the native language and demonstrate respect for and value of linguistic and cultural diversity.

What Language and Literacy Areas Should Teachers Encourage in the Native Language?

Vocabulary

Vocabulary is one area that is crucial to ELLs and directly affects later reading comprehension. ELL children from low-income homes, where the exposure to literacy and strong language skills is limited, may be at particular risk for limited vocabulary development; indeed, these children are at risk for demonstrating limited vocabulary in both their native language *and* their second language. This can impact reading comprehension and academic achievement in English in the years beyond preschool (August, Carlo, Dressler, & Snow, 2005; Carlo et al., 2004; Proctor et al., 2006; Rolla San Francisco et al., 2006).

Preschool programs should specifically target vocabulary in a direct, systematic, and focused manner. This suggests the use of implicit and explicit approaches to vocabulary building. Implicit approaches involve storybook reading and repeated book reading, whereas explicit approaches include dialogic reading (Elley, 1989; Justice, Weber, Ezell, & Bakeman, 2002), use of weekly, specific, target vocabulary words connected to the classroom theme, and selection of vocabulary that is neither prototypical nor high frequency (Schwanenflugel et al., 2004). High-frequency vocabulary does not need explicit teaching, because it is learned by children in their natural environments. Attention to the reinforcement of vocabulary through themes and units that are shared with the children's families through book reading, projects, and newsletters in each child's native language encourage family involvement and help parents to assume a coteaching role with the teacher.

An important question that warrants consideration is whether vocabulary transfers between languages. The answer to this question is inconclusive; however, we know that children learn a new concept faster in their native language (Kiernan & Swisher, 1990; Perozzi, 1985; Perozzi & Chavez-Sanchez, 1992). In addition, being exposed to vocabulary in two languages allows children to gain depth and greater conceptual development, while acquiring more basic English skills.

Phonemic Awareness, Letter Knowledge, and Print Awareness

Recent research confirms that development of phonemic awareness, letter knowledge, and print awareness should be a central curricular foci for all preschool children (National Early Literacy Panel, 2006). Evidence that these skills do, in fact, transfer from native language to second language and, for some skills, from second language to first language, creates a strong reason to address each of these skills in the children's native language.

Preschool programs for ELLs can address these preliteracy skills through classroom activities, centers, dialogic reading, and dramatic play. If the languages are similar in alphabet and orthography, as are English and Spanish, the same letter sounds can be addressed for the most part in the two languages. For example, children's study of the letter name and sound /m/, and identification of words that start with /m/, would work in both languages. ELLs can learn to distinguish differences in pronunciation or sounds. Teaching these skills in the two languages does not confuse children or delay reading (August & Shanahan, 2006).

Environmental Print

An active bilingual classroom includes both dual-language instruction and environmental print in the languages spoken in children's homes; therefore, signs for classroom items, areas, and centers should be at eye level and in the different languages evident in the classroom. If the teacher does not speak the minority language, parents can assist in creating the labels for the preschool classroom, so that the children can use them as a reference. Bilingual staff and parent volunteers should actively use the classroom print environment to encourage children's print awareness. In addition, print from the children's languages (e.g., menus, storefront names, and post office items) should be embedded into the children's play activities. Print should also include commercially available materials (e.g., information books, magazines, and storybooks). All of these elements create a bilingual environment and a bilingual context that demonstrates to children the various uses and function of print in their native languages.

What Techniques Help ELLs Develop English Language Skills?

Children who enter preschool as monolingual speakers of a language other than English go through a series of stages in English acquisition. Many children attempt to communicate with other children and their teachers in their native language, then find that their attempts are ineffective and unsuccessful. Once they realize this, children often exhibit what is called a "silent period" (Tabors, 1997); they observe but do not actively participate in language interactions. This period can be both frustrating and quite difficult for some children. Many become sad or angry, and tell their parents that they dislike school.

Importantly, this period of language learning can be eased by establishing routines that ELLs can easily follow, with predictable language that the children can learn to use. At this stage, peer modeling is invaluable. A child in the silent period can be paired with a child who speaks the same language for peer support and play. The teacher should attempt to make sure that the child feels welcome by facilitating peer interaction and initiating communication. Once fear subsides, the child may feel comfortable and begin slowly to increase his or her active participation in classrooms routines. Routines with predictable language in small-groups settings are particularly helpful to the child at this point. For example, circle time routines in which the children share how they are feeling or choose the activity of day can be done with the support of visual aids. The child can point to the visual aid, while the teacher models the full response; this may decrease feelings of anxiety as it helps the child learn the language of the routine. During these times, the ELL child should not be forced to participate. The following dialogue illustrates the language of this support system in operation:

TEACHER: How are you, Luis? (*Points to each of three visual choices: happy face, sad face, and sick face.*)

CHILD: (*Points to happy face.*)

TEACHER: Luis feels happy today.

When children begin using more of the English language, they use telegraphic speech, or formulaic language (Tabors, 1997), chunks or phrases that they have learned. At this stage, they continue to need many visual aids, hands-on experiences, and predictable language in routines, although they can now participate more independently in these activities. At this level, the teacher's role is to ensure that the language is predictable, that children understand the general idea of the activity, and that they have time to respond and to formulate their ideas. Placing ELLs in small groups with children who are fluent in English is helpful, because it provides appropriate peer models for the ELL children. In addition, selection of books to be shared with the children needs careful consideration. Appropriate books for children at this level include pattern books, short stories, and books with clear pictures. At this stage, bilingual books are especially effective in teaching vocabulary and stories in both languages. Teachers might have children take these books home for family use and enjoyment.

With more time, the ELL children then enter a more productive stage of language development, using more and longer sentences that are still characterized by grammatical errors, such as incorrect word order and omission of morphemes, and limited vocabulary (Tabors, 1997). Children in this stage increasingly use sentences to communicate their needs and to participate verbally in activities. Modeling or recasting their incorrect productions without explicit correction helps them to benefit from all the language around them. At the same time, however, the children should be engaged in meaningful activities with the class, such as reading books and hands-on activities. The following dialogue illustrates interaction with a child in this stage of second language learning:

> TEACHER: Luis, what is going to happen to Goldilocks when the bears come home?
>
> CHILD: Bears be mad.
>
> TEACHER: The bears are going to be mad. Why do you think the bears are going to be mad?
>
> CHILD: Because chair broken, soup gone.
>
> TEACHER: That is right; she broke the chair and drank all the soup.
>
> CHILD: She broke the chair and drank soup.

Even in this stage, children still need a lot of repetition and hands-on experiences with target vocabulary. Teachers should plan activities in which the children experience the target vocabulary, and they should provide props that help ELL children learn the words/concepts in multiple ways. For example, using the story *Goldilocks and the Three Bears*, the children may be taught words such as *medium, rest, hard,* and *soft*. Participating in activities such as categorizing and describing objects with those attributes helps ELLs develop more complex vocabulary. At the same time, children at this stage comprehend the story in general, but not necessarily the details. Therefore, the teacher should monitor children's basic story comprehension.

As these children become more fluent in English and have fewer grammatical errors and better vocabulary, they are still in the process of learning the second language. Teachers should not assume that they can do everything a monolingual child can do. At this level, vocabulary should continue to be a strong focus of the preschool program, with higher-level vocabulary incorporated into daily lessons; that is, the preschool program should provide a language-rich environment in which ELLs understand the language of the classroom, have opportunities to use it, and engage in learning about both the language and the world (Tabors, 1997). In addition, the children at this point need many more experiences with abstract language to help them develop comprehension, with story retelling, and with scaffolded conversations (van Kleeck, Gillman, Hamilton, & McGrath, 1997). These are skills that majority-language children are able to use, but ELL children have not been afforded the opportunity to practice them, because they have spent their time learning the basics of the language. The teacher's role, then, is to ensure that the children have

TABLE 13.1. ELL Stages and Appropriate Activities

Silent period	Early English acquisition	Productive English	Fluent English skills
		Characteristics	
Child does not interact with others; observes others silently, and may be sad or angry.	Child uses formulaic or telegraphic speech.	Child speaks in complete sentences but language is still ungrammatical and limited in vocabulary.	Child is able to use language fluently, although minor grammar and word errors are still apparent.
		Activities	
Small groups/peer guides; short bilingual books connected to the daily theme; hands-on activities; opportunities to participate in simple routines with modeling; use gestures and visual aids; use routines and repetition	Small-group activities/peer models; short bilingual books connected to the daily theme; opportunities to participate using formulaic speech or telegraphic speech with modeling; high use of gestures, visual aids, and multisensory hands-on activities; use routines and repetition	Small groups; provide time to respond; choose bilingual books connected to the daily them; hands-on activities and multisensory techniques; expect short phrases and sentences; check for comprehension; start using scaffolded conversations and higher vocabulary levels	Build abstract language; select books that have good stories, information texts, and wordless books connected to the classroom theme; small-group interactions with science and art using target high-level vocabulary; practice story retelling; have scaffolded conversations

plenty of language, math, science, and literacy opportunities from which to learn. The focus is to teach beyond English skills and to prepare students to be successful in kindergarten and elementary school. Table 13.1 provides a summary of the ESL stages and activities appropriate for each level.

Connecting Homes and Schools

Making the connection between home and school is a critical element in facilitating ELLs' school success. In many federal programs, it is obligatory that all communication be provided to parents in the native language of the home. If resources are available, this is an excellent way to ensure that families are kept current on school happenings and are simultaneously informed about the school's expectations. When there is no consistent communication with the home, the child's parents may assume that things are going well, and they may be unaware of what their child is expected to know. In addition, communication with the home empowers the families to help their children. However, in many cultures it is not traditional or appropriate to involve the families in schoolwork. Therefore, if preschool staff expect to include children's families in their education, then they must be willing to educate them on the importance of reinforcing the lessons taught at school and to communicate clearly their expectations for parent involvement. For many parents, staying out of the teacher's way is a form of respect and involvement (Rodriguez & Olswang, 2003). For some families, what may be perceived as lack of involvement in school is actually respect for the school professional.

Encouraging Families to Come to School

One of the most important ways of fostering connections between homes and schools is to encourage families to come to school. If economics and circumstance allow, families often appreciate coming to school. Having caregivers and other family members come to children's schools can serve several functions (adapted from Civil & Quintos, 2006):

- *To be informed*: They like to learn about and see what the child is doing.
- *To learn*: They might learn English with their child.
- *To teach*: They might learn how to teach the child.
- *To volunteer*: They can help the school.
- *To be a leader*: They can help others by being a liaison to other parents, who may not be as confident in their language and cultural skills.

To accomplish this successfully, school personnel should be easily accessible to the parent or other family members and actively encourage family participation; that is, they must ensure that the parents can communicate with someone who ensures that they feel valued and appreciated. This time should not be used to discuss their children's problems, if any exist. Prior to their entering the classroom, the teacher should provide parents with a quick overview of the activities, the theme of the week, and the concepts the children are working on that week. Familiarizing them with what is happening in the classroom helps to contextualize parents' experience. They can participate in specific activities or help where they are needed. They can read to the ELLs in their native language and teach other children another language. They can assist by placing environmental print around the classroom or by bringing songs from their own culture to share—that is, if they are comfortable and have the skills to do so. Many successful family literacy programs integrate parent and child learning. These opportunities are golden, because they allow preschool staff to work in collaboration with the parents rather than as separate units.

Other programs have designated parent and children together (PACT) time. These programs are well structured and involve fun activities for parents to do with their child in the classroom. Again, it is important to make sure that the activity is easily accessible to the parent—that they understand it. Parents of ELLs are often very hesitant to ask questions or to interfere in the schooling process. The staff must therefore be proactive in their interactions to ensure that the parents of ELLs are comfortable and successful in the classroom.

An additional important technique for involving families is to ask parents to share their skills (recipes, songs, artifacts, etc.) with the school; this technique shows that the school values the children's languages and cultures, and that parents can be active members of the preschool community. Making them part of the curriculum is simple, and the children take great pride in having their culture acknowledged, valued, and showcased in the classroom.

Bringing School to the Home to Connect Two Worlds

A second way to connect home and school is by sharing materials (e.g., books, activities, songs) with families. The teacher may need to teach parents to use these materials, such as how to share a particular book with their children, by providing a handout that describes specific techniques. During parent orientation, the teacher might suggest that the parents save the activities in a binder, so they can check what target words, letter names and sounds, numbers, and themes the children are studying or should know. Teachers should encourage parents to conduct all home activities in the native language. Use of the native language builds children's communication skills and knowledge of both languages, prevents language loss, and builds strong bicultural identities.

Some programs use book bags (with bilingual books), backpacks, or material exchanges that parents or children can borrow for home use. Other programs use a special toy that the child takes home. The toy is returned with an accompanying journal describing what happened to the toy during its journey within a child's home. If the family writes in Spanish, school staff should encourage the parent to write the story of the toy's adventures in Spanish. The teacher should read the journal entry to the class in Spanish, translating as needed.

Summary and Conclusions

Optimizing language and literacy learning should be the direction taken by quality preschool programs for ELLs. Supporting native language instruction and providing opportunities to learn a second language not only promote future academic success but also enhance overall communication between parents and children. With the numerous resources available, educators can create programs with the best interests of the child and family in mind. The possibilities are endless. By providing ELLs with a positive school experience that is conducive to language and literacy development, in addition to supporting the learning that occurs in the context of their homes, parents and educators can work as a team rather than separate entities.

School staff must facilitate language and literacy development in preschool and carefully consider the methods used to teach this unique group, while continuing to hold high expectations of these children. The goal of an excellent preschool program for ELLs should be to support and encourage continued development of the children's native/home language and growth in the second language, English.

References

Alwin, D. F., & Thornton, A. (1984). Family origins and the schooling process: Early versus late influence of parental characteristics. *American Sociological Review, 49,* 784–802.

Anderson, R. T. (2004). First language loss in Spanish-speaking children: Patterns of loss and implications for clinical practice. In B. Goldstein (Ed.), *Bilingual language development and disorders in Spanish-English speakers* (pp. 187–212). Baltimore: Brookes.

August, D., Calderon, M., & Carlo, M. (2002). *The transfer of skills from Spanish to English: A study of young learners.* Washington, DC: Center for Applied Linguistics.

August, D., Carlo, M., Dressler, C., & Snow, C. (2005). The critical role of vocabulary development for English language learners. *Learning Disabilities Research and Practice, 20,* 50–57.

August, D., & Shanahan, T. (2006). *Developing literacy in second language learners: A report of the National Literacy Panel on Language Minority Children And Youth.* Mahwah, NJ: Erlbaum.

Bialystok, E., McBride-Chang, C., & Luk, G. (2005). Bilingualism, language proficiency, and learning to read in two writing systems. *Journal of Educational Psychology, 97,* 580–590.

Bond, G., & Dykstra, R. (1967). The cooperative research program in first-grade reading instruction. *Reading Research Quarterly, 2,* 5–142.

Branum-Martin, L., Mehta, P. D., Fletcher, J. M., Carlson, C. D., Ortiz, A., Carlo, M., et al. (2006). Bilingual phonological awareness: Multilevel construct validation among Spanish-speaking kindergarteners in transitional bilingual education classrooms. *Journal of Educational Psychology, 98,* 170–181.

Bryant, D. P., Bryant, B. R., & Hammill, D. D. (2000). Characteristic behaviors of students with LD who have teacher-identified math weaknesses. *Journal of Learning Disabilities, 33,* 168–177, 199.

Campos, J. (1995). The Carpinteria Preschool Program: A long-term effects study. In E. Garcia & B. McLaughlin (Eds.), *Meeting the challenge of linguistic and cultural diversity in early childhood education* (pp. 34–48). New York: Teachers College Press.

Carlo, M., August, D., McLaughlin, B., Snow, C., Dressler, C., Lippman, D., et al. (2004). Closing the gap: Addressing the vocabulary needs of English language learners in bilingual mainstream classrooms. *Reading Research Quarterly, 39,* 188–215.

Cisero, C. A., & Royer, J. M. (1995). The development and cross-language transfer of phonological awareness. *Contemporary Educational Psychology, 20,* 275–303.

Civil, M., & Quintos, B. (2006). Engaging families in children's mathematical learning: Classroom visits with Latina mothers. *New Horizons for Learning Online Journal, XII*(1). Available at *www.newhorizons.org/spneeds/ell/Civil%20quintos.htm.*

Craig, H. K., Connor, C. M., & Washington, J. A. (2003). Early positive predictors of later reading comprehension for African American students: A preliminary investigation. *Language, Speech, and Hearing Services in Schools, 34,* 31–43.

Dickinson, D., McCabe, A., Clark-Chiarelli, N., & Wolf, A. (2004). Cross-language transfer of phonological awareness in low-income Spanish and English bilingual preschool children. *Applied Psycholinguistics, 25,* 323–347.

Durgunoglu, A. Y. (2002). Cross-linguistic transfer in literacy development and implications for language learners. *Annals of Dyslexia, 52,* 189–204.

Durgunoglu, A. Y., Nagy, W. E., & Hancin-Bhatt, B. J. (1993). Cross-language transfer of phonological awareness. *Journal of Educational Psychology, 85,* 453–465.

Elley, W. B. (1989). Vocabulary acquisition from listening to stories. *Reading Research Quarterly, 24,* 174–187.

Garcia, E. E., & Gonzalez, D. M. (2006). *Pre-K and Latinos: The foundation for America's future* (Rep. No. Research Series). Pre-K Now.

Genesee, F., Paradis, J., & Crago, M. (2004). *Dual language development and disorders: A handbook on bilingualism and second language learning.* Baltimore: Brookes.

Gough, P. B., & Tunmer, W. E. (1986). Decoding, reading and reading disability. *Remedial and Special Education, 7,* 6–10.

Gutierrez-Clellen, V. F. (1999). Language choice in intervention with bilingual children. *American Journal of Speech–Language Pathology, 8,* 291–302.

Hamers, J. S., & Blanc, M. H. A. (2000). *Bilinguality and bilingualism* (2nd ed.). Cambridge, UK: Cambridge University Press.

Hart, B., & Risley, T. R. (1992). American parenting of language learning children: Persisting differences in family–child interactions observed in natural home environments. *Developmental Psychology, 28*(6), 1096–1105.

Hart, B., & Risley, T. R. (1995). *Meaningful differences in the everyday experience of young American children*. Baltimore: Brookes.

Justice, L. M., Weber, S. E., Ezell, H. K., & Bakeman, R. (2002). A sequential analysis of children's responsiveness to parental print references during shared book-reading interactions. *American Journal of Speech–Language Pathology, 11*, 30–40.

Kan, P. F., & Kohnert, K. (2005). Preschoolers learning Hmong and English: Lexical–semantic skills in L1 and L2. *Journal of Speech, Language and Hearing Research, 48*, 1–12.

Kiernan, B., & Swisher, L. (1990). The initial learning of novel English words: Two single-subject experiments with minority language children. *Journal of Speech and Hearing Research, 33,* 707–716.

Kohnert, K., & Derr, A. (2004). Language intervention with bilingual children. In B. Goldstein (Ed.), *Bilingual language development and disorders in Spanish–English speakers* (pp. 315–343). Baltimore: Brookes.

Kohnert, K., Yim, D., Nett, K., Kan, P. F., & Duran, L. (2005). Intervention with linguistically diverse preschool children: A focus on developing home language(s). *Language Speech, and Hearing Services in Schools, 36,* 251–263.

Lesaux, N., & Geva, E. (2006). Synthesis: Development of literacy in language-minority students. In D. August & T. Shanahan (Eds.), *Developing literacy in second-language learners. Report of the National Literacy Panel on Language-Minority Children and Youth* (pp. 53–74). Mahwah, NJ: Erlbaum.

Leseman, P. (2000). Bilingual vocabulary development of Turkish preschoolers in the Netherlands. *Journal of Multilingual and Multicultural Development, 21,* 93–112.

Lonigan, C. J., Burgess, S. R., & Anthony, J. L. (2000). Development of emergent literacy and early reading skills in preschool children: Evidence from a latent-variable longitudinal study. *Developmental Psychology, 36,* 596–613.

Naslund, J. C. (1990). The interrelationships among preschool predictors of reading acquisition for German children. *Reading and writing: An interdisciplinary Journal, 2,* 327–360.

National Early Literacy Panel. (2006, March). *Findings from the National Early Literacy Panel: Providing a focus for early language and literacy development*. Presented at the National Conference of the National Center for Family Literacy, Louisville, KY.

Perozzi, J. A. (1985). A pilot study of language facilitation for bilingual language handicapped children: Theoretical and intervention implications. *Journal of Speech and Hearing Disorders, 50,* 403–406.

Perozzi, J. A., & Chavez-Sanchez, M. L. (1992). The effect of instruction in L1 on receptive acquisition of L2 for bilingual children with language delay. *Language, Speech, and Hearing Services in Schools, 23,* 348–352.

Proctor, C. P., August, D., Carlo, M. S., & Snow, C. (2006). The intriguing role of Spanish language vocabulary knowledge in predicting English reading comprehension. *Journal of Educational Psychology, 98,* 159–169.

Raz, I. S., & Bryant, P. (1990). Social background, phonological awareness and children's reading. *British Journal of Developmental Psychology, 8,* 209–225.

Restrepo, M. A., Castilla, A. P., Arboleda, A., Schwanenflugel, P., Neuhart Prittchett, S., & Hamilton, C. (2007). *Sentence length, complexity and grammaticality growth in Spanish-speaking children attending English-only and bilingual preschool programs.* Manuscript under review.

Rodriguez, B. L., & Olswang, L. B. (2003). Mexican-American and Anglo-American mothers' beliefs and values about child rearing, education, and language. *American Journal of Speech Language Pathology, 12,* 452–462.

Rodriguez, J. L., Diaz, R. M., Duran, D., & Espinosa, L. (1995). The impact of bilingual preschool education on the language development of Spanish-speaking children. *Early Childhood Research Quarterly, 10,* 475–490.

Rolla San Francisco, A., Carlo, M., August, D., & Snow, C. (2006). The role of language of instruction and vocabulary on The English phonological awareness of Spanish–English bilingual children. *Applied Psycholinguistic, 27,* 229–246.

Saville-Troike, M. (1984). What really matters in second language learning for academic achievement. *TESOL Quarterly, 17,* 199–219.

Scarborough, H. S. (1990). Very early language deficits in dyslexic children. *Child Development, 61,* 1728–1743.

Scarborough, H. S. (1991). Early syntactic development of dyslexic children. *Annals of Dyslexia, 41,* 207–219.

Scarborough, H. S. (2001). Connecting early language and literacy to later reading (dis)abilities: Evidence, theory, and practice. In S. Neuman & D. Dickinson (Eds.), *Handbook for research in early literacy* (pp. 97–110). New York: Guilford Press.

Schwanenflugel, P., Hamilton, C. E., Bradley, B., Ruston, H., Neuharth-Pritchett, S., & Restrepo, M. A. (2005). Classroom practices for vocabulary enhancement in prekindergarten: Lessons from Paved for Success. In H. E. Hiebert & M. Kamil (Eds.), *Bringing scientific research to practice: Vocabulary* (pp. 155–177). Hillsdale, NJ: Erlbaum.

Share, D. L., Jorm, A. F., MacLean, R., & Matthews, R. (1984). Sources of individual differences in reading acquisition. *Journal of Educational Psychology, 76,* 1309–1324.

Smith, M. W. (2001). Children's experience in preschool. In D. K. Dickinson & P. O. Tabors (Eds.), *Beginning literacy with language* (pp. 149–174). Baltimore: Brookes.

Smith, J., Brooks-Gunn, J., & Klebanov, P. (1997). Consequences of living in poverty for young children's cognitive and verbal ability and early school achievement. In G. Duncan & J. Brooks-Gunn (Eds.), *Consequences of growing up poor* (pp. 132–189). New York: Russell Sage Foundation.

Snow, C., & Tabors, P. O. (1993). Language skills that relate to literacy development. In D. Spodek & O. Saraco (Eds.), *Yearbook of early childhood education* (Vol. 4, pp. 1–20). New York: Teachers College Press.

Stevenson, H. W., & Newman, R. S. (1986). Long-term prediction of achievement in mathematics and reading. *Child Development, 57,* 646–659.

Tabors, P. O. (1997). *One child, two languages.* Baltimore: Brookes.

Tabors, P. O., Paez, M. M., & Lopez, L. M. (2003). Dual language abilities of bilingual four-year-olds: Initial findings from the early childhood study of language and literacy development of Spanish-speaking children. *NABE Journal of Research and Practice, 1,* 70–91.

Teale, W. H. (1986). Home background and young children's literacy development. In W. H. Teale & E. Sulzby (Eds.), *Emergent literacy: Writing and reading.* Norwood, NJ: Ablex.

van Kleeck, A., Gillman, R. B., Hamilton, L., & McGrath, C. (1997). The relationship between middle-class parents' book-sharing discussion and their preschoolers' abstract language development. *Journal of Speech, Language, and Hearing Research, 40,* 1261–1271.

Waits, M. J., Campbell, H. E., Gau, R., Jacobs, E., & Hess, R. K. (2006). *Why some schools with Latino children beat the odds and others don't.* Tempe, AZ: Morrison Institute for Public Policy and Center for the Future of Arizona.

Wang, M., Park, Y., & Lee, K. R. (2006). Korean–English biliteracy acquisition: Cross-language phonological and orthographic transfer. *Journal of Educational Psychology, 98,* 148–158.

Washington, J. A., & Craig, H. K. (1999). Performance of at-risk, African American preschoolers on the Peabody Picture Vocabulary Test–III. *Language, Speech, and Hearing Services in Schools, 30,* 75–82.

White, K. (1982). The relation between socioeconomic status and academic achievement. *Psychological Bulletin, 91,* 461–481.

Wong Fillmore, L. (1991). When learning a second language means losing the first. *Early Childhood Research Quarterly, 6,* 323–347.

PART IV

★ ★ ★ ★ ★ ★ ★ ★ ★ ★ ★

MAKING DATA-BASED DECISIONS

Chapters 14 through 17 of this book consider the important topic of data, specifically, how educators and administrators can use data to achieve excellence in classroom instruction. In this era of educational accountability, the use of data has achieved a prominent position within the area of preschool education. Policymakers and administrators who are invested in elevating the quality of preschool programs are interested in data on teachers (e.g., credentials, experiences, beliefs, practices), classrooms (e.g., teacher–child ratio, furnishings, instructional climate), children (e.g., presence of disability, indicators of school readiness, ethnicity), and families (e.g., household income, parental educational attainment, school involvement). Within this volume, we are most interested in data concerning the quality of language and literacy instruction and how these data might be used to promote children's preschool achievement in language and literacy. No doubt preschool administrators and teachers who are vested in making data-based decisions will find the four chapters in this section particularly informative.

Kathy Roskos and Carol Vukelich (Chapter 14) describe their use of a tool designed specifically to evaluate the fundamental characteristics of packaged early literacy programs. They illustrate how use of a structured review tool, the Early Literacy Program Review Tool, can help program personnel make more objective, data-based decisions when selecting new programs for use in their classrooms. Khara L. Pence (Chapter 15) provides a comprehensive description of program evaluation techniques, and describes the types of questions evaluators might ask, as well as the types of outcomes one can expect from a quality evaluation.

Chapters 16 and 17 describe data-based decision making as it applies to children's skills and how pupil assessment can be used sensibly and sensitively within preschool programs vested in achievement excellence. Many preschool programs today use tools not only to screen children when they enter and exit programs but also to monitor progress within the curriculum. Using such tools correctly, outcomes include provision of important guidance in ensuring children's growth within the high-quality learning environments and making sure that every moment counts. Christopher Schatschneider, Yaacov Petscher, and Kellee M. Williams (Chapter 16) discuss fundamental characteristics of quality screening tools, and provide explicit guidance to preschool administrators and teachers on not only how to understand the vocabulary of screening tools (e.g., sensitivity, specificity) but also how to study the quality of individual tools themselves. Readers will find that this chapter provides an important resource in their search for the best tools to use for conducting screening of children. Tanis Bryan, Cevriye Ergul, and Karen Burstein (Chapter 17) discuss progress-monitoring tools and how these can be used effectively in preschool programs to monitor children's progress within the general curriculum, as well as in supplemental tiers. Of particular use to readers is the step-by-step guidance provided by the authors on how programs might develop their own curriculum-based measures that map onto their own learning goals and techniques.

While reading these chapters, generate responses to the following five questions, and be prepared to share your responses in guided discussions with others:

1. What is important to consider when choosing a language and early literacy program (often called a curriculum) for preschoolers?

2. How might preschool teachers use curriculum-based measurement to monitor and increase children's learning of language and early literacy skills?

3. How can direct and indirect measures be used to evaluate a preschool language and early literacy program?

4. If you were the mother of a child screened for potential reading difficulties, which rating—false positive or false negative—would be of greatest concern to you? Why?

5. How might program evaluation, curriculum-based measurement, the Early Literacy Program Review Tool, and screening tools col-

lectively be used to address the effectiveness of preschool programs?

After you have completed your reading, complete one or more of the
following four activities to expand your knowledge further:

1. Examine a preschool language and early reading program. How
   does it address the three essential dimensions of an early literacy
   program? Is any dimension missing?
2. Go to *ggg.umn.edu* to learn more about the Individual Growth
   and Development Indicators (IGDI) preschool assessment tool.
   Readers who work with preschool children might wish to down-
   load and use the IGDI to assess a child's language and literacy
   development.
3. Look on the U.S. Department of Education's website (*www.*
   ed.gov/programs/earlyreading) to locate the nearest Early Reading
   First project. Contact the project to arrange to interview the project's evaluator to learn about the assessment tools the project is
   using, the types of data he or she is using to make judgments
   about the project, and the questions he or she is asking (and
   answering).
4. Study a screening tools manual. What information does the
   author or publisher provide about the quality and specificity of
   measurement of the assessment tool's diagnostic efficiency? How
   does this tool "measure up" when you consider the qualities of
   screening tools described by Schatschneider and colleagues in
   Chapter 16?

CHAPTER 14

★★★★★★★★★

Quality Counts

Design and Use
of an Early Literacy Program Review Tool

Kathleen A. Roskos
Carol Vukelich

A growing recognition of the significance of early literacy skills for future reading achievement has led to an explosion of early literacy materials in the early childhood classroom. The preschool is fast becoming a place for a variety of early encounters with print, from alphabet letter games to e-books to full-blown early reading programs. But unlike the wealth of guidance for choosing quality educational toys and playthings for young children, early years educators have little to go on when making decisions about the quality of early literacy programs and resources. How to select CD-ROM storybooks for young children is a good example. Studies show that despite publishers' claims about the instructional value of this software, many such storybooks in fact contribute little to children's emerging understandings of literacy (DeJong & Bus, 2003; Korat & Shamir, 2004): Amusing, yes, but value-added as early literacy skill-builders? Probably not.

The lack of measuring sticks for gauging the quality of early literacy instructional materials is a serious problem for several practical reasons. Early educators depend on these curricular resources as tools for early literacy instruction. They use them as sources of information to build their own professional knowledge about literacy. And they must make decisions about purchasing early literacy programs best suited to their child populations—a major responsibility in early education, where funding resources are often meager. With the new starting line for early reading instruction at the preschool level, it is clear that quality counts in the curricular resources developed for this purpose.

In this chapter we describe the design and development of the Early Literacy Program Review Tool (ELPRT), a tool for evaluating the quality of packaged early literacy programs. We define an early literacy program from a resource perspective as a set of materials for early literacy instruction. Packaged programs serve the overall early childhood program by providing realia (books, kits, puppets, activity pages) and a description of activities and procedures to be followed in the use of the materials with the children.

The chapter begins with a brief overview of the design of the ELPRT. We describe the curricular framework and early literacy research base that serve as the tool's conceptual bases. All tools (even hammers) are the result of design work, which lays out the ideas that give shape and meaning to the tool. Next we describe the development of the ELPRT in a research setting where we "tested" it with several packaged early literacy programs. We highlight key findings from this research work, which occurred over a 2-year period. From here we move to the application of the ELPRT in a field setting and what we are learning about its usability in comprehensive early childhood programs. This is promising information that we hope will improve the ELPRT as a viable tool in helping early childhood educators make decisions about early literacy program materials for their classrooms. The chapter closes with a brief summary of the past, present, and future of the ELPRT, and its potential contribution to the early literacy education field.

Design of the ELPRT

You may have heard the statement: Form follows function. This is a guiding principle of design, which basically asserts that the structure of an object (e.g. a chair) should be suited to its purpose (e.g., sitting). The same principle applies in designing tools for evaluation purposes; form should align with function.

Adhering to this principle we designed the ELPRT to perform as a tool that examines three essential dimensions of an early literacy program as an instructional resource. The first dimension is the structural organization of the program. Early childhood experts (Bredekamp, Knuth, Kunesh, & Schulman, 1992; Strickland, 1989), backed by the strong support of early childhood professional organizations (National Association for the Education of Young Children and National Association of Early Childhood Specialists in State Departments of Education [NAEYC and NAECS/SDE], 2004), have consistently argued that rather than a loose collection of activities, a sound educational program for young children should reflect four basic curricular elements that cohere (i.e., provide structure to) the program. These elements are (1) instructional goals, (2) instructional content, (3) learning activities, and (4) assessments. The arrangement of these elements helps to define the *why, what, and how* of a program (i.e., the overarching purpose of the program); the knowledge, skills, and attitudes children will learn; and different ways to help them learn (Bowman, Donovan, & Burns, 2001). Curriculum experts recommend that programs include a clear conceptual framework (Frede, 1998; Wiggins & McTighe, 1998) that describes the research foundations and alignment to early learning expectations. In addition, quality programs should provide teachers with clear guidance and lesson plans that sequence activities to support children's accomplishments (Siraj-Blatchford, 1998).

A second critical dimension of a program is the instructional content it contains to guide the teacher to teach. Within the early literacy field, there is a growing consensus as to the early literacy concepts and skills that are the building blocks of learning to read (see Dickinson & Neuman, 2006; Neuman & Dickinson, 2001; Snow, Burns, & Griffin, 1998). To become skilled readers, children need a rich language and conceptual knowledge base, a broad and deep vocabulary, and verbal reasoning abilities to understand messages that are conveyed through print (Hirsch-Pasek, 2004; Neuman, 2001; Scarborough, 2001). Children also must develop code-related skills. These include the understanding that spoken words comprise smaller elements of speech (phonological awareness); the idea that letters represent these sounds (the alphabetic principle); the many systematic correspondences between sounds and spellings; and a repertoire of highly familiar words that can be easily and automatically recognized (Lonigan, Burgess, & Anthony, 2000; McCardle, Scarborough, & Catts, 2001; McGee, 2004). To attain a high level of skill, young children need opportunities to develop these strands, not in isolation, but interactively (Neuman, Copple, & Bredekamp, 2000).

Research syntheses point to early literacy content in five major learning categories (Rathvon, 2004):

- Phonological awareness, defined as *sensitivity to sounds in words and the ability to manipulate them; conscious awareness of the sound structure of speech as opposed to its meaning* (Whitehurst & Lonigan, 2001).
- Alphabet letter knowledge, defined as *ability to name, write, and identify the sound of alphabet letters* (McBride-Chang, 1999).
- Print knowledge, defined as *conceptual knowledge of the purposes and*

conventions of print: concept of word; print awareness; knowledge of reading terms, rules, and procedures (Mason, 1984).

- Vocabulary, defined as the words an individual knows and can use; words used in speaking (expressive vocabulary) and/or recognized in listening (receptive vocabulary) (Beck, McKeown, & Kucan, 2004; Bloom, 2000).
- Oral language comprehension, defined as *ability to listen and speak with understanding* (Snow, 1983).

Each of these learning categories in turn includes important concepts and skills that are essential to it. It is this domain-specific content that young learners must acquire to make progress as readers and writers. For example, knowledge of letter names and their corresponding sounds must be acquired as building blocks for learning the alphabetic principle (Ehri, 1979). Category-specific knowledge and skills constitute the essentials of learning in that category—the nutrients, as it were, for growth. An early literacy program, therefore, contains the instructional content that helps children learn essential ideas and skills.

The third dimension of a program is its organization of learning activities. How will children be introduced to concepts and skills? How will they be taught? Three grouping arrangements are commonly used in early childhood educational programs as contexts for learning: whole-group, small-group, and/or indoor play areas, often referred to as "centers." Research supports the organization of multiple activity settings (Estrada, Sayavong, & Guardino, 1998) and small-group instruction (Foorman & Torgesen, 2001) as keys to instructional effectiveness. Programs that support different grouping arrangements offer opportunities for the teacher to draw and build on children's existing ideas; to promote learning concepts along with skills; and to differentiate instruction to help all children learn more deliberately (Bransford, Brown, & Cocking, 2000; Tharp, Estrada, Dalton, & Yamauchi, 2000).

To summarize, the three critical dimensions of early childhood programs are structure, content, and setting. Consequently, we intentionally designed the ELPRT to reflect these three critical dimensions of early literacy programs cited in the professional knowledge base as quality factors in program materials. To represent these dimensions, the tool is organized into two parts.

Part I surveys a program's materials for evidence of five structural features that describe the why, what, and how of the program. These features are summarized in Table 14.1.

Feature A—elements of curriculum—requires a broad look at the instructional materials to identify the program goals (the *why*), a scope and sequence (the *what*), and a set of activities, including an informal assess-

TABLE 14.1. Structural Features of an Early Literacy Program

A. Includes *elements* of curriculum.
  - Goals/expectations
  - Content
  - Learning activities
  - Assessments (informal)

B. Identifies a *conceptual framework*.
  - Philosophy or theory of action
  - Research-base
  - Alignment with national/state standards

C. Provides a *teacher's guide*.

D. Provides *lesson plans*.
  - Adequate time (20–30 minutes teacher-led; 45–60 minutes play/centers).
  - Developmentally appropriate materials
  - Developmentally appropriate procedures

E. Describes *integration* into the early childhood program.
  - Diverse grouping arrangements.
  - Program planning (e.g., themes).
  - Integrating into total program day.

ments (the *how*). Often this information is found in the front matter of a program guide or in the program description.

Feature B—conceptual framework—guides the program reviewer to look for evidence of a guiding theory or philosophy for the program, a description of the program's research base, and whether the program developers provide information about how the program content aligns with early literacy learning expectations or standards.

Feature C—teacher guide—is a concrete form of evidence that shows the user how to use the instructional resource. Most early literacy programs provide some kind of teacher guide or directions for use.

Feature D—lesson plans—are another concrete form of evidence that provide guidance about how the instructional materials should be used in the classroom. Lesson plans typically outline amount of time for instruction, materials needed, instructional procedures, and follow-through activities. Some programs offer highly detailed plans (even scripts), whereas others outline general planning steps.

Feature E—integration of instruction—is identifiable in program guidance about how to plan (units, weeks, days), how to group children (whole, small, play), and how to incorporate the specific program materials into the broader early childhood program. Program materials may describe how to integrate instruction in the form of theme planners, suggested time schedules, and routine activities for whole groups, small groups and play centers.

The benchmark for exhibiting adequate structural quality is set at 80% of the features present in the early literacy program, or four out of the five features. This level is derived from consensus in the field on the benefits of a planned curriculum in a preschool program (Bowman et al., 2001) and the research base on learning (Bransford et al., 2000).

Part II of the ELPRT examines evidence of a program's instructional content and the primary settings used for instruction. For this purpose, the content knowledge of the early literacy domain is organized into five learning categories identified by early literacy research. These categories are phonological awareness (PA), alphabet letter knowledge (AK), print knowledge (PK), vocabulary (VOC), and language comprehension (LC).

For each learning category, the instructional components needed to help children learn essential concepts and skills are identified. The instructional components describe the *guidance* the program should provide users to support instruction. The tool is used to locate evidence of guidance statements for each instructional component by category in the program materials (primarily the teacher guide). The instructional components for each of the five learning categories are listed in Table 14.2.

In addition to locating evidence of guidance for the instructional component, the tool design allows for indicating the setting(s) where instruction may occur. When program reviewers find evidence that a program *guides instruction in phonological awareness*, for example, they can also record evidence of the setting where instruction is guided to occur, namely, *whole group, small group, play*, or some combination thereof. Figure 14.1 illustrates how the tool is used to document evidence of instructional content and setting.

The tool also attempts to document evidence of a sequence of instruction in guidance for an instructional component. An "instructional sequence" is a related string of ideas or skills carried over from one activity to another, from one setting to another, and/or from one lesson to another. As a case in point, guidance for the instructional component *that provides suggestions for engaging children in writing for a variety of purposes* (PK-13) in the print knowledge learning category could be offered for whole-group activities, followed up in a small-group activity, then suggested for play center activities. For example, children may read about and record facts about fish in whole group, label different kinds of fish in small group, and create a play aquarium in a dramatic play center. The tool allows reviewers to record evidence of instructional sequences in program samples. Instructional sequences are important, because they afford multiple exposures to new ideas, facts and skills, and opportunities for children to practice using them. From a program-design perspective, in-

TABLE 14.2. Instructional Components in the Five Essentials of Early Literacy

Learning category	Instructional component
Phonological awareness	• PA-1. Guides instruction in phonological awareness • PA-2. Integrates PA activities into learning activities • PA-3. Links PA activities to learning alphabet letters (e.g., name writing) • PA-4. Provides informal assessment of PA • PA-5. Provides additional instruction for special needs
Alphabet letter knowledge	• AK-6. Guides instruction in letter-naming activities • AK-7. Guides instruction in letter–sound activities • AK-8. Integrates alphabet letter practice in other learning activities • AK-9. Supports informal assessment of children's letter knowledge • AK-10. Provides additional instruction for children needing more support
Print knowledge	• PK-11. Guides instruction in book and print concepts • PK-12. Integrates theme-related print into learning environment • PK-13. Provides suggestions for engaging children in writing for a variety of purposes • PK-14. Supports children learning environmental signs (e.g., STOP) and simple sight words (e.g., mother)
Vocabulary	• VOC-15. Guides instruction in vocabulary • VOC-16. Integrates opportunities for children to use target vocabulary in learning activities • VOC-17. Provides vocabulary instruction in different genres (narrative, informational, poetry) • VOC-18. Provides suggestions to support children's use of new words in activities • VOC-19. Provides suggestions and techniques for additional vocabulary instruction for special needs
Language comprehension	• LC-20. Guides instruction in language comprehension during book reading • LC-21. Provides questions or topic suggestions to stimulate conversation and discussion • LC-22. Provides examples for engaging children in conversations in different settings • LC-23. Provides suggestions that prompt/cue children's use of language (speaking and listening) in activities • LC-24. Provides suggestions and techniques for additional instruction for children needing more support • LC-25. Supports informal assessment of children's language abilities (e.g., listening comprehension, word-use fluency, sentence completion, story retelling)

	Instructional Component	Evidence		
		Whole Group	Small Group	Play/ Center
Phonological Awareness	**PA-1.** Guides instruction in phonological awareness.	Insert page numbers from teacher guide		
	PA-2. Integrates phonological awareness activities into other learning activities.			
	PA-3. Links phonological awareness activities to learning alphabet letters (e.g., name writing) *Emphasis is **on listening** to increase sound awareness.*			
	PA-4. Provides for informal assessment of phonological awareness by the teacher.			
	PA-5. Provides suggestions and techniques for additional instruction for children needing more support.			
	Total Number of References (*tally those cited*)			
	Combined Total for Skill Area			

FIGURE 14.1. Example of locating evidence of an instructional component by setting.

structional sequences are indicators of program coherence—a difficult quality to observe in instructional materials.

How Well Does It Work?: ELPRT in the Research Setting

As in all design work, a tool can be created, but the critical bottom line is: *How well does it work?* To probe this question, we conducted a 2-year study to examine how well the tool performed as an evidence-finder of quality factors in early literacy program materials (Roskos, Vukelich, & Neuman, 2005). Prime quality factors, as discussed previously in this chapter, focus on evidence of structural features in the instructional resource and inclusion of research-based instructional components that guide the user. Our research brief, which follows, describes how we tested the tool, what it produced, and modifications that we made to improve it.

Testing the ELPRT

The initial phase of our study comprised gathering samples of early literacy program materials that might serve as good candidates for testing the tool design. This is not as straightforward as it might seem. Early literacy programs come in different stripes, from "off the shelf" commercial programs to embedded programs in comprehensive curricular models to home-grown sets of literacy activities. Our starting point was a pool of 15 early literacy programs identified by the U.S. Department of Education (2002) as commercially available. From this list, we selected seven early literacy programs to serve as optimal resources for testing the tool design. We based our selections of these programs on three criteria: (1) The program was developed primarily as an early literacy program; (2) it met the 80% criterion of structural features; and (3) it was produced by a reputable publisher in early childhood curricular materials.

Our primary source material for testing the ELPRT was the program teacher's guide, because this document supplies the most direct program information and instructional guidance to the user. The tool was applied to the program description provided in each guide and a 25% sample of the lessons from each program. For programs arranged hierarchically, samples were drawn from the beginning, middle, and end of the program. For all others, the samples were drawn from lessons in a unit theme. An item of evidence comprised a statement, or set of related statements, that indicated the presence of a structural feature or an instructional component. Here's an example of a set of statements constituting an item of evidence for an instructional component [AK-7] from a teacher's guide:

> **Letter/Sound Matching.** Display *Big Alphabet Card Ff* and point to the fish. Tell children that *F* stands for the /f/ sound—the sound you hear at the beginning of fish. Ask them to watch as you say /f/, emphasizing the sound so that they can watch your mouth. Invite them to say: /f/, *fish* with you several times. Repeat with *Picture Word Cards* 15 (firefighter), 17 (fork), and 18 (fox). (Scholastic, 2000, p. 16)

A three-member research team obtained an interrater reliability score of .90 on a three lesson sample using the procedures outlined in Figure 14.2.

Evaluating the Evidence

Our main research interest was in determining how well the tool performed in locating evidence of design qualities that characterize a program as an instructional resource. Results from the sample test of the tool on seven programs showed the tool's functionality in revealing a program's structural features and profiling its patterns of instructional guid-

Part I—Structural Features

- Step 1: Locate the program guide, description, scope, and sequence (if available) and general program information in the program materials.

- Step 2: Read the program materials to locate evidence of goals, a content-focus (e.g., learning the alphabet), kinds of learning activities (e.g., games), and informal assessments (e.g., observe children's responses). Mark YES if all the basic elements are present. Record the page number(s) of the evidence found in the program materials in the text box.

- Step 3: Read the program description for evidence of a conceptual framework, indicated by statements of a philosophy, the program's research base, *and/or* alignment to national or state standards. Mark YES if evidence is present. Record the page number(s) of the evidence found in the program materials in the text box.

- Step 4: Locate evidence of a teacher's guide in the program material. Mark YES if there is a teacher guide. Record the name of the document or an abbreviation thereof.

- Step 5: Locate evidence of lesson plans as shown by a description of learning activities *and/or* procedures. Mark YES if the evidence is present. Record page numbers of *examples*. (Briefly describe four or five examples.)

- Step 6: Locate evidence of integration in the program materials as shown by use of (a) different grouping arrangements (individual, small group, whole group); (b) program planning (e.g., around units or themes); *and/or* (c) guidance in the teacher's guide for integrating learning across the program day. Mark YES if there is evidence. Record page numbers of *examples* in the text box. (Briefly describe four or five examples.)

- Step 7: Calculate the total percentage of curriculum features found in the program. A benchmark criterion of 80% is recommended for moving to Part II of the program review.

Part II—Instructional Components and Settings

- Step 1: Identify the program sample for coding. Prepare the sample for coding by highlighting the major sections of the material (e.g., a lesson plan).

- Step 2: Search for evidence of each instructional component in each learning category. **Evidence consists of a statement or set of statements that describe guidance for an instructional component.** Each statement item is tallied as a piece of evidence. Mark the page number of the evidence in the setting column (whole group, small group, play/center) where it occurs.

- Step 3: Calculate the number of instructional components present by setting and in total.

- Step 4: Determine the total number of instructional components present; calculate percentages by learning category.

- Step 5: Tally the number of instructional components in each category cited in the program sample; graph the frequency for each component.

- Step 6: Determine the frequency of components by setting; calculate the percentages for each setting.

FIGURE 14.2. Procedures for Program Review

ance in relation to the early literacy knowledge base. We learned, for example, that programs tended to be stronger in some structural features than others, such as Feature A (elements of curriculum) being stronger than Feature E (integration of instruction). This kind of information is helpful, because it provides insight about what may be needed to ensure effective use of a program as an instructional resource in the overall early childhood educational program.

The tool also made clearer how programs differ in their instructional emphases of essential early literacy skills. Programs showed considerable variation in the degree to which specific instructional components in each learning category were addressed. Guidance in LC, for example, ranged from 16% of components present in one program to 50% of components present in another; that for PK ranged from as low as 6% of components present in one program to 23% in another; that for AK, again a low of 6% of components present in one program to 32% in another; and PA had as few as 8% of components present in one program and 28% present in another. Guidance related to VOC showed the least variation between programs, with most programs including about 15% of the instructional components.

Figure 14.3 shows the distribution of instructional components for each program in the seven-program sample. Program 1, for example, offers proportionally more instruction in oral LC than in PA, resembling the mean profile of all programs. Program 7, on the other hand, concen-

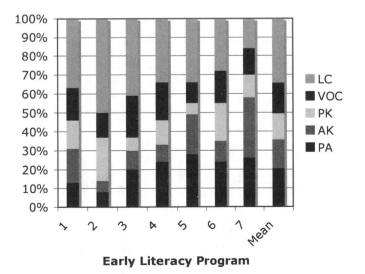

Early Literacy Program

FIGURE 14.3. Percent of instructional components by program sample.

trates instruction on AK and PA, offering more activities for developing these skill areas.

Evidence of such program profiles is useful, because it shows how different programs offer different "menus" of early literacy instruction. This kind of information is indeed needed to make decisions about what instructional resource, or combination of resources, might best meet the specific needs of a specific group of children in a specific educational setting.

The tool also probed the instructional guidance of programs more deeply, measuring most and least referenced instructional components per learning category. These results, summarized in Figure 14.4, indicate the frequency of components in the program sample.

Frequently referenced components, such as PA-1, *guides instruction in phonological awareness*, and LC-23, *prompts/cues children's use of language in activities*, for example, support basic skills instruction fundamental to the domain. Children need to be taught to listen for sounds, recognize letters, use new words, and join in reading and writing activities, and these components direct teachers toward these goals. Least-referenced components, such as PA-5, *provides additional instruction for special needs*; VOC-17, *contextualizes vocabulary in high quality children's literature*; and LC-22, *provides examples for engaging children in conversations*, on the other hand, suggest less support regarding instructional flexibility, differentiating instruction, and assessment activities that help teachers pinpoint needs and implement more strategic instructional interactions. Recognizing that

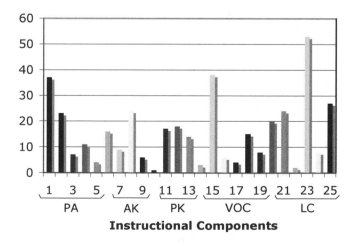

FIGURE 14.4. Frequency of instructional components in the program sample. PA, phonological awareness; AK, alphabet knowledge; PK, print knowledge; VOC, vocabulary; LC, language comprehension.

programs emphasize some instructional components over others, and what these components are, provides much-needed information about the professional development that may be necessary for effective program implementation, and for knowing where to fill in the instructional gaps.

In addition to profiling patterns of instructional components in programs, the tool mapped the settings for implementing instructional components provided in the guidance. Across the seven-program sample, the preferred setting for instruction was whole group followed by play centers in all early literacy learning categories. Thus, the tool documents a preference for whole-group instruction, which itself may reinforce this instructional practice. In this respect, our screening results using this tool sound a warning. Given the complexities of developing early literacy skills in young children (e.g., listening for letter sounds), instruction needs to occur in situations where adults can provide contingent responses that build individual understandings and skills (Rogoff, 1990; Wood, Bruner, & Ross, 1976). Whole-group instruction alone cannot possibly fill this need, nor can play center talk. Multiple configurations for learning that afford many opportunities to learn early literacy skills offer more optimal conditions for early literacy learning. Early childhood educators and program developers need to be alert to this information, and endeavor to better design and use program materials to support instruction in multiple settings in early literacy practice.

Finally, although the tool is capable of tracking instructional sequences within and across a lesson sample, this function of the tool was not tested in the research setting.

Modifying the Tool

The test of the tool over the 2-year period demonstrated not only its functional strengths but also several of its weaknesses. Although we had developed a procedure for selecting a program sample, and for identifying data statements and marking page numbers within the sample, the procedure lacked the specificity to ensure proper entry of abbreviated evidence of each instructional component (e.g., citing each instance of instructional guidance related to a component). More detail, therefore, added in the directions for data entry, directed reviewers to carefully record the page number of each piece of evidence cited for each component. Several guidance statements for *guides instruction in phonological awareness* (PA-1), for example, may be found in one lesson, and the page number of each should be cited.

Transferring data from the recording forms for each learning category + setting to the summary tables and the graphs proved cumbersome and inefficient, thus lengthening the time needed to complete a full review and increasing the chances for error. To streamline data entry and the accuracy of resulting computations, the ELPRT was converted to an EXCEL software application. This allowed easy entry of each page number documenting evidence of each instructional component in each learning category + setting and the follow-up, automatic conversion of raw frequency data into tables and graphic displays. Additionally, learning categories and settings were color-coded to highlight visually patterns of instructional components and to map grouping arrangements. The interactive software improved the accuracy and efficiency of data entry, and supported the interpretation of results.

We also found directions in how to use the ELPRT to be vague, serving more as brief guides for our research team. Sets of directions for data entry, analysis, and interpretation were expanded to include more explicit coding guidance on how to use the tables and graphs, and sample program profiles to aid interpretation.

Questions also emerged around the intended users of the tool: state office directors, program directors, or classroom teachers? In addition, what processes and procedures need to be in place to use the tool effectively in a decision-making context? How would users be oriented to the tool? Who would be responsible for data entry? How would results be treated and disseminated? Who would have access to the results? How might results be used to inform decision making and professional development? Finding answers to these questions clearly went beyond the scope of our study, which we undertook to test the viability of ELPRT, and led us to examine the tool in the practical world of early childhood programs. In the next section, we describe efforts to apply ELPRT in the field, and what we are learning from these applications.

How Well Does It Work?: ELPRT in the Field

From our "laboratory" test of the tool, we could see that it had promise for helping early childhood educators make decisions about early literacy programs based on evidence of some key quality indicators. Using a program review tool in a research context, however, is one thing, and under the practical conditions of an early childhood program, quite another. After two rounds of presentation of the ELPRT at national conferences (Roskos, Vukelich, & Neuman, 2005; Roskos, 2006), we approached a few of our colleagues in the field (and several approached us) to ask whether they might try out the tool in their settings. We made specific arrangements with program directors in two different locales (Michigan and Ohio) to apply the tool in a way that made sense in their programs.

At the Michigan site, which offers comprehensive early childhood services in a large area, the program director was in the process of selecting early literacy program materials for early childhood classrooms in 28 school districts. She viewed the ELPRT as a means of guiding and informing this critical decision-making process. She invited her staff to join her in learning to use ELPRT for purposes of evaluating several early literacy programs under consideration for adoption. Nine teachers accepted her invitation. Following the training on the ELPRT by one of the researchers, the program director held a one-day ELPRT training session for her volunteer teachers.

What did this training look like? How did it go? After orienting her teacher team to the ELPRT, the program director worked collaboratively with the group to examine a program sample. They located statements of evidence, made data entries using the software, examined the results displayed in the tables and graphs, and discussed what they meant. She reported that, in the course of using the tool, the group engaged in lots of discussion about what constituted evidence, how to tag statements of evidence, definition of terms (e.g., target vocabulary), clarity and organization of the instructional guidance, and issues of developmental appropriateness related to early literacy instruction. Training on the tool, in short, evolved into a spirited exchange on early literacy teaching and learning, and how the program sample supported this effort. To follow up, the director provided teacher trios with different sets of program materials for review and the ELPRT CD-ROM. Each trio spent about 2 weeks conferring and completing its reviews. Reconvening the group, the program director guided a discussion of the results and worked with the team to rank-order the early literacy programs for adoption.

At the Ohio site, a campus-based preschool program in a small city setting, the program director and staff had recently adopted a new early childhood curriculum that featured embedded early literacy instruction. The program director hoped the ELPRT might provide additional information about the early literacy instructional content of the selected curriculum. She oriented her teaching staff to the tool. Together the group selected a 25% sample from the beginning, middle, and end of the early childhood curriculum. Using a portion of their regular staff meeting time, they searched for evidence of each instructional component and entered the data into the EXCEL spreadsheet. They kept track of the unfolding patterns in the program's guidance through the tables and graphs. They also paid close attention to any instructional sequences found in the sample as evidence of program coherence. The meeting time, although brief, allowed them the opportunity to discuss the strengths and gaps in the instructional guidance for each skills learning category, and to consider ways to improve the curricular resource. In this respect, the director reported, use of the ELPRT facilitated a kind of "on the spot" professional development and planning that informed their overall curriculum implementation.

These are two abbreviated examples of the ELPRT put to the test in the everyday professional work of early educators. We find them instructive on several counts. We observe, for example, the leadership role of program directors, who actively engaged their staff in the critical work of program review. In both instances, the directors set aside time to orient staff, to provide training and support, and to allow for thorough discussion of results and what they mean for practice.

We note how the ELPRT, a means for program review, also served as a catalyst for professional development in early literacy development and learning. Both directors reported how learning to use the ELPRT created a rich professional development context for those involved, generating spirited discussion and opportunity to clarify concepts, issues, and principles of early literacy instruction.

Use of the tool helped participants to become more informed consumers and users of program materials. Teachers commented on how well (or poorly) program directions were organized, on what early literacy content was emphasized, and on qualities of instructional guidance. According to program directors, several teachers expressed concerns that program guidance offered neither sufficiently detailed directions nor research-based information about early literacy development that might expand a teacher's understanding. Interpreting the ELPRT results led to considerable discussion about how to adapt program materials to address particular student needs, to target specific learning goals, and to align with the overall early childhood program.

We are more sensitive now than before to the need for a better, fuller set of directions in how to use the ELPRT. We also see more clearly the importance of describing the *who–when–how* of effective application of the tool to meet the specific goals and needs of an early childhood program. We more deeply appreciate the need for sufficient time and support to use the ELPRT in meaningful ways that result in teachers' effective use of available program materials.

ELPRT: Past, Present, Future

Developing young children's early literacy understandings and skills is a serious matter, as critical to their life chances as other areas of physical, emotional, and social growth, for when children do not thrive and grow as future literate persons, they realize less of their human potential as adults (Heckman, 2002). The foundations of literacy are laid in careful, thoughtful, enriching early literacy instruction that prepares children for the phonological, alphabetic, semantic, and syntactic demands of learning to read, along with an abiding eagerness to undergo the task. Well-built program materials—strong in design and content—contribute to children's early literacy development and learning by laying out a set of activities that guide them from nascent literacy understandings to beginning literacy skills. Claims, therefore, that early literacy programs are strong, research-based curricula cannot be taken at face value or left to individual judgment. Critical reviews of early reading programs are necessary to assess the extent to which prepared early literacy programs address instructional priorities. ELPRT provides a helpful tool for educators to engage in critical reviews and thoughtful analyses. Efforts to use the tool in research and field settings proved productive in that we gained useful information about what early literacy programs can offer, but we are also discovering what early literacy programs need if we are to ensure that all young children receive the best early literacy education.

References

Beck, I. L., McKeown, M. G., & Kucan, L. (2004). *Bringing words to life: robust vocabulary instruction.* New York: Guilford Press.

Bloom, P. (2000). *How children learn the meanings of words.* Cambridge, MA: MIT Press.

Bowman, B. T., Donovan, M. S., & Burns, M. S. (2001). *Eager to learn: Educating our preschoolers.* Washington, DC: National Research Council.

Bransford, J., Brown, A., & Cocking, R. R. (2000). *How people learn: Brain, mind, experience, and school.* Washington, DC: National Academy Press.

Bredekamp, S., Knuth, R. A., Kunesh, L. G., & Schulman, D. D. (1992). *What does research say about early childhood education?* Oak Brook, IL: North Central Regional Educational Laboratory.

De Jong, M. T., & Bus, A. G. (2003). How well suited are electronic books for supporting literacy? *Journal of Early Childhood Literacy, 3*(2), 147–164.

Dickinson, D., & Neuman, S. B. (Eds.). (2006). *Handbook of early literacy research* (Vol. 2). New York: Guilford Press.

Ehri, L. C. (1979). Linguistic insight: Threshold of reading acquisition. In T. G. Waller & G. F. MacKinnon (Eds.), *Reading research: Advances in theory and practice* (Vol. 1, pp. 63–111). New York: Academic Press.

Estrada, P., Sayavong, P., & Guardino, G. M. (1998). *Patterns of language arts instructional activity in first and fourth grades: pedagogy, simultaneity/diversification of activity, diversification of persons, and student performance* (Technical Report No. 2, Project 5.8). Santa Cruz: University of California, Center for Research on Education, Diversity and Excellence (CREDE) and the Office of Educational Research and Improvement.

Foorman, B. R., & Torgesen, J. (2001). Critical elements of classroom and small group instruction promote reading success in all children. *Learning Disabilities Research and Practice, 16*(4), 203–212.

Frede, E. C. (1998). Preschool program quality in programs for children in poverty. In W. S. Barnett & S. S. Boocock (Eds.), *Early care and education for children in poverty: Promises, programs and long-term outcomes* (pp. 77–98). Buffalo: State University of New York Press.

Heckman, J. (2002). Human capital: Investing in parents to facilitate positive outcomes in young children: Opening session remarks. In *The first eight years: Pathways to the future* (Summary of Conference Proceeding, pp. 6–15). Washington, DC: Head Start Bureau, Mailman School of Health and the Society for Research in Child Development.

Hirsch-Pasek, K. (2004). *Pathways to reading: The role of oral language in the transition to reading.* NICHD Early Child Care Research Network. Rockville, MD: National Institute of Child Health and Human Development.

Korat, O., & Shamir, A. (2004). Do Hebrew electronic books differ from Dutch electronic books?: A replication of a Dutch content analysis. *Journal of Computer Assisted Learning, 20*(4), 257–268.

Lonigan, C. J., Burgess, S. R., & Anthony, J. L. (2000). Development of emergent literacy and early reading skills in preschool children: Evidence from latent variable longitudinal study. *Developmental Psychology, 36,* 596–613.

Mason, J. M. (1984). Early reading from a developmental perspective. In P. D. Pearson, R. Barr, M. L. Kamil, & P. Mosenthal (Eds.), *Handbook of reading research* (Vol. 1, pp. 505–543). New York: Longman.

McBride-Chang, C. (1999). The ABCs of the ABCs: The development of letter–name and letter–sound knowledge. *Merrill–Palmer Quarterly, 45,* 285–308.

McCardle, P., Scarborough, H., & Catts, H. (2001). Predicting, explaining and preventing children's reading difficulties. *Learning Disabilities Research and Practice, 16*(4), 230–239.

McGee, L. (2004, December). *The role of wisdom in evidence-based preschool literacy curriculum.* Keynote Address at the National Research Conference, San Antonio. TX.

National Association for the Education of Young Children and National Association of Early Childhood Specialists in State Departments of Education (NAEYC and NAECS/SDE). (2004). *Early childhood curriculum, child assessment and program evaluation: Building an accountable and effective system for children birth through age eight.* Retrieved July, 2004, from *naeyc.org/resources/position_statements/.*

Neuman, S. B. (2001). The role of knowledge in early literacy. *Reading Research Quarterly, 36,* 468–475.

Neuman, S. B., Copple, C., & Bredekamp, S. (2000). *Learning to read and write: developmentally appropriate practice.* Washington, DC: National Association for the Education of Young Children.

Neuman. S. B., & Dickinson, D. (2001). *The handbook of early literacy research* (Vol. 1). New York: Guilford Press.

Rathvon, N. (2004). *Early reading assessment: A practitioner's handbook.* New York: Guilford Press.

Rogoff, B. (1990). *Apprenticeship in thinking: Cognitive development in social contexts.* Oxford, UK: Oxford University Press.

Roskos, K. (2006). *An early literacy program review tool: The ELPRT.* Paper presented at the NAEYC Leadership Conference, San Antonio, TX.

Roskos, K., Vukelich, C., & Neuman, S. B. (2005, June). *Are early literacy programs research-based?: A critical review of the evidence.* Presented at the 15th National Institute for Early Childhood Professional Development, Miami, FL.

Siraj-Blatchford, I. (Ed.). (1998). *A curriculum development handbook for early child-hood educators.* Staffordshire, UK: Trentham Books.

Scarborough, H. (2001). Connecting early language and literacy to later reading (dis)abilities: Evidence, theory, and practice. In S. B. Neuman & D. Dickinson (Eds.), *Handbook of early literacy research* (Vol. 1, pp. 97–110). New York: Guilford Press.

Scholastic, Inc. (2000). *Building language for literacy teacher guide.* New York: Author.

Snow, C. E. (1983). Literacy and language: Relationships during the preschool years. *Harvard Educational Review, 53,* 165–189.

Snow, C., Burns, S., & Griffin, P. (1998). *Preventing reading difficulties in young children.* Washington, DC: National Academy Press.

Strickland, D. (1989). A model for change: Framework for an emergent literacy curriculum. In D. S. Strickland & L. M. Morrow (Eds.), *Emerging literacy: Young children learn to read and write* (pp. 135–146). Newark, DE: International Reading Association.

Tharp, R. G., Estrada, P., Dalton, S. S., & Yamauchi, L. A. (2000). *Teaching transformed: Achieving excellence, fairness, inclusion, and harmony.* Boulder, CO: Westview Press.

U.S. Department of Education, Office of Elementary and Secondary Education. (2002). *Early Literacy Programs.* Washington, DC: Author.

Whitehurst, G. R., & Lonigan, C. J. (2001). Emergent literacy: Development from prereaders to readers. In S. B. Neuman & D. K. Dickinson (Eds.), *Handbook of early literacy research* (Vol. 1, pp. 11–29). New York: Guilford Press.

Wiggins, G., & McTighe, J. (1998). *Understanding by design.* Alexandria, VA: Association for Supervision and Curriculum Development.

Wood, D., Bruner, J. S., & Ross, G. (1976). The role of tutoring in problem solving. *Journal of Child Psychology and Psychiatry, 17,* 89–100.

CHAPTER 15

★★★★★★★★★

Indicators and Goals
of High-Quality Program Evaluation
for the Preschool Classroom

Khara L. Pence

Program evaluation is an integral part of the process of creating early childhood education programs that exhibit excellence in language and prereading instruction. *Program evaluation* refers to "systematic inquiry designed to provide information to decision makers and/or groups interested in a particular program, policy or other intervention" (Gredler, 1996, p. 15). When applied to preschool programs, it can provide information about teacher credentials, teaching effectiveness, classroom climate, room organization, child outcomes, and many other important program characteristics. To be effective, program evaluation activities should be planned and executed with the same degree of care as all other elements of a program,[1] such as selecting curricula and organizing professional development activities for center staff.

This chapter provides a two-part overview of the indicators and goals of high-quality program evaluation. The first part describes *what* evalua-

---

[1] In this chapter, "program" refers to the overarching project concerned with implementing an educational innovation or intervention; it encompasses the approach to promoting children's learning and development, the curriculum adopted, and all project stakeholders (e.g., children, educators, parents). The term "curriculum" describes the aggregate of lessons and activities that a program adopts. The term "center" describes a program's affiliation, in most cases, the physical location where a program is housed.

tions of early childhood programs should examine (e.g., aspects of the classroom environment; teacher knowledge and qualifications; teacher instruction and planning; and children's language, cognitive, and pre-literacy skills). The second part of this chapter describes *how* evaluation of early childhood programs should occur. Procedures related to the types of questions evaluators should ask, the kinds of data they should collect, and the types of measures they should use are discussed.

What Evaluations of Early Childhood Programs Should Examine

Before undertaking a program evaluation for an early childhood program, the evaluation team and program staff (e.g., administrators, teachers, paraprofessionals) should develop a series of questions to organize the program evaluation. Examples of such questions are presented in Table 15.1 and organize this section of the chapter.

To What Degree Are a Preschool Program's Objectives, Activities, and Materials (i.e., Curriculum) Consistent with One Another?

"Systematicity" describes the degree to which a program's objectives, activities, and materials are consistent with one another. Systematicity is important for the success of a program, because having objectives, activities, and materials that are consistent with one another increases the likelihood that teachers and staff will know what to do, how to do it, and why. Promising preschool centers of excellence should begin by establishing program objectives with clear goals for children's language and literacy learning and development (i.e., oral language, phonological awareness, print awareness, and alphabet knowledge), and these goals should be reflected in a center's selected language and literacy curriculum. Simply

---

TABLE 15.1. Questions to Organize Program Evaluation

- To what degree are a preschool program's objectives, activities, and materials (i.e., curriculum) consistent with one another?

- Is the program appropriate for the participating schools or centers, staff, children, and their families? Are participating educators able to implement the program?

- To what extent do the classroom environments and instruction demonstrate scientific and research-based practices in cognition, language, and early reading?

- Have the classroom environment, the teachers' knowledge and qualifications, the teachers' planning and instruction, and the children's language, cognitive, and preliteracy skills improved?

---

adopting an early childhood curriculum, even one that is well-known, does not guarantee that a program will be systematic; not all early childhood curricula include clear goals for language and literacy learning and development, and of those that do, not all stipulate how activities and materials are related to the goals. Thus, one of the evaluator's roles is to determine the systematicity of the program by examining how the curriculum is integrated into the overall preschool program, how the preschool program's educators implement the curriculum, and how the children experience different aspects of the curriculum.

What does program systematicity look like in an early childhood center and how can it be evaluated? The following vignette illustrates how an early childhood center might demonstrate a high degree of systematicity.

The Bright Futures Early Learning Center has adopted the fictitious Model Early Childhood Curriculum (MECC), which claims to be grounded in scientifically based reading research (SBRR) to support children's oral language, phonological awareness, print awareness, and alphabet knowledge development. Prior to the beginning of the academic year, the center administrators provided the teachers with a 2-day professional development workshop that introduced them to the MECC. A large portion of the workshop time was devoted to allowing the teachers to discuss the curriculum's scope and sequence, and how it is structured to support children's developing competencies in oral language, phonological awareness, print awareness, and alphabet knowledge. The professional development staff facilitated teachers' discussions of how they would use weekly lesson plans and daily schedules, and how they would incorporate the MECC materials throughout the entire day in explicit and intentional ways. Teachers also learned about how to introduce new concepts using teacher-directed strategies (during whole-group instruction), with the goal of moving toward small-group instruction and practice, and, eventually, individual instruction and practice.

When the Bright Futures teachers returned to their classrooms, they established classroom centers (e.g., block area, dramatic play area, art area), incorporated books, writing materials, and language and literacy props (e.g., phones, clipboards) in all centers, and modeled proper use of the materials for children. Teachers also implemented the weekly lesson plans and daily schedules that they had discussed during the professional development workshop, and they promoted children's language and literacy development throughout the entire day in intentional ways (e.g., by reading storybooks and discussing new vocabulary to minimize downtime between multiple school bus arrivals). The teachers introduced new concepts in whole-class and large-group settings (e.g., by introducing specific alphabet letters), and reinforced these concepts by practicing with children in small-group and one-on-one settings (e.g., by having children practice writing letters). Eventually, children were able to work independently on the concepts they had learned (e.g., by writing letters on notepads as they took orders for food in the dramatic play area). Follow-up professional development sessions were scheduled once per month, so that teachers and administrators could share ideas and support one another in their use of the curriculum.

The Bright Futures Early Learning Center demonstrates a high degree of program systematicity due to the consistency among its program objectives, professional development activities, instructional practices, and materials. Table 15.2 provides several indicators of program systematicity that evaluators might examine.

One important task for evaluators of early childhood programs is to determine how systematic a program is, with the goal of making recommendations for improvement. Important components for evaluators to consider include the curriculum adopted by the program; the amount and type of professional development provided to the staff; the extent to which teachers implement the curriculum and integrate program activi-

TABLE 15.2. Indicators of Program Systematicity

Indicator	Example
Program objectives are consistent with professional development activities, instructional practices, and materials.	The curriculum provides a specific scope and sequence to support children's oral language development, phonological awareness, print awareness, and alphabet knowledge.
Professional development activities are consistent with program objectives, instructional activities, and materials.	Professional development balances information on the curricular scope and sequence with exploration and practice with curricular materials and instructional activities.
Classroom instructional practices are consistent with program objectives, professional development activities, and materials.	Instructional practices are integrated throughout the entire day in intentional and explicit ways. Teachers introduce new concepts (e.g., using whole-group instruction and practice), and move toward small-group instruction and practice, and eventually individual instruction and practice, just as they learned to do in their professional development sessions.
Materials are consistent with program objectives, professional development activities, and classroom instructional activities.	Teachers integrate books, writing materials, and language and literacy props in all centers and model use of the materials for children.

ties throughout the day; and the extent to which learning objectives, activities, and materials are aligned. The second part of this chapter provides information concerning *how* evaluators might measure the systematicity of early childhood education programs.

Is the Program Appropriate for the Participating Schools or Centers, Staff, Children, and Their Families? Are Participating Educators Able to Implement the Program?

"Applicability" describes the suitability of a program to the participants, whereas "feasibility" describes the extent to which a program can be carried out. When examining the applicability and feasibility of a program, the evaluator should consider factors such as the length of the instructional day (e.g., half day, full day) and the length of the week (e.g., 4 days per week, 5 days per week) to determine whether the program is suitable for the amount of instructional time available.

With respect to the staff, the evaluator should consider whether the program is suitable and possible given the educational backgrounds of the administrators, educators, literacy coaches, and other paraprofessionals. For example, do the teachers have the recommended levels of training and educational background to implement a particular curriculum? Do project staff have appropriate credentials to implement all components of their program (e.g., family literacy component)?

When considering the suitability of the program for the children, the evaluator should determine whether the program addresses the diverse learning needs of children in the program (e.g., children learning English as a second language, children with speech and language delays). Consideration of the ages of the children attending the program is also important. For example, 3-year-olds are very different developmentally from 5-year-olds who are preparing to transition into kindergarten, and likely require different kinds of activities to support their language and early literacy development.

Finally, the program evaluator should consider the extent to which the program is applicable to the children's families. For instance, if there is a high degree of illiteracy in the community, does the program make provisions for family literacy? If the community speaks a language, or languages, other than English, are materials available in those languages for parents, and are there staff members who are bilingual in English and the predominant language of the community? The vignette that follows illustrates how the early childhood center described previously demonstrates a high level of applicability and feasibility.

The Bright Futures Early Learning Center is located on a Native American reservation in the rural Midwest and operates 5 days per week in 7-hour sessions. Most of the children and families participating in center activities are very low-income. Bright Futures serves children ranging in age from 3 to 5 years, who attend one of two kinds of classrooms: One type of classroom includes children who plan to attend kindergarten the following year, and the other includes children who do not plan to attend kindergarten the following year (i.e., children who are age 3 or who recently turned 4). Within each classroom, teachers and staff provide individualized instruction to all children by building sufficient time for one-on-one practice into each day's schedule. All educators have at least a bachelor's degree, and at least one person in each classroom (e.g., teacher, assistant) is bilingual in English and in the local Native American language. A family literacy coordinator makes regular home visits with parents to discuss strategies for incorporating literacy in the home. The family literacy coordinator also arranges social events at the local library and community hall, and assists parents in pursuing their general equivalency degree (GED), if necessary. Bright Futures Early Learning Center also has hired a literacy coach who specializes in educating children who are learning English as a second language to rotate between the center's classrooms.

The Bright Futures Early Learning Center demonstrates applicability to all program participants (including children, educators and staff, and parents), and is feasible given the number of hours the program operates, and staff members' amount and kinds of educational experience. Table 15.3 provides several indicators of program applicability and feasibility that evaluators might examine.

"Applicability" concerns the suitability of the early childhood program to all stakeholders, each of whom brings different educational backgrounds, experiences, knowledge, and developmental capabilities to the program. "Feasibility" describes the extent to which implementing the project is possible. Thus, the role of the evaluator is to consider the extent to which the program is suited to all stakeholders, and to make recommendations on how the program might make adjustments in its allocation of resources, staff, and services to best achieve the overall goals of the program. The second part of this chapter includes information concerning *how* evaluators might measure a program's applicability and feasibility.

To What Extent Do the Classroom Environments and Instruction Demonstrate Scientific and Research-Based Practices in Cognition, Language, and Early Reading?

Evaluators of early childhood education programs also have the important role of determining the extent to which classroom environments and instruction demonstrate scientific and research-based practices in cognition, language, and early reading, also known as the "scientific and theo-

TABLE 15.3. Indicators of Program Applicability and Feasibility

Indicator	Example
Program is suitable for the amount of instructional time available and is possible to implement given the amount of time.	The program is a full day in duration (7 hours long) and operates 5 days per week.
Program is suitable to the educational backgrounds of the program staff and is possible for the program staff to implement.	Educators, staff, and paraprofessionals have relevant degrees and training appropriate to the program. For example, educators hold at least a Bachelor's degree, and at least one person in each classroom is bilingual in English and the language of the local community.
Program is suitable to the diverse needs of the children and is possible to implement.	The program addresses children's diverse learning needs by enrolling children in classrooms according to their age and developmental level. The program builds time into each day for one-on-one instruction with teachers and staff.
Program is suitable to meet the needs of families and is possible to implement.	The program includes a family literacy component and makes the family a partner in fostering children's language and literacy development by sponsoring educational opportunities and social events for families. Families who do not have transportation are able to benefit from the home visits, as well as the local educational and social opportunities.

retical groundedness" of the program. Programs that are scientifically and theoretically grounded are those driven by the current best available evidence and theory concerning how children develop and learn, and how children's outcomes relate to program quality, specific activities, and caregiver characteristics. The following vignette illustrates a high degree of scientific and theoretical groundedness in the Bright Futures Early Learning Center.

> The Bright Futures Early Learning Center has partnered with a local university to select an early childhood program that is scientifically and theoretically well-grounded. The university team undertook a comprehensive review of the recent early childhood literature to find such a program. First, the university team used the guidelines proposed by the U.S. Department of Education, Institute of Education Sciences, National Center for Education Evaluation and Regional Assistance (2003) to learn how to evaluate whether an intervention is backed by strong evidence of effectiveness. After identifying three such programs, the university team searched the literature for peer-

reviewed journal articles that described studies of each of the three early childhood programs in greater detail. They were particularly interested to learn how children's outcomes related to the quality of implementation, to specific activities that were a part of the program (e.g., how activities surrounding print concepts contributed to children's print awareness), and to characteristics of the educators (e.g., whether outcomes were stronger for children who had closer relationships with their teachers). The university team selected the single early childhood curriculum that was backed by several such peer-reviewed journal articles, the MECC.

Throughout the school year, teachers and staff at Bright Futures made it their priority to implement components of the MECC (including oral language, phonological awareness, print awareness, and alphabet knowledge activities) with an awareness of how children were developing in each area. The center's literacy coach helped the teachers conduct progress-monitoring assessments throughout the year and helped them to make adjustments to their instruction using the results of the progress monitoring assessments (i.e., data-based decisions). Staff members also met twice monthly with the university team, as part of a journal club, to discuss articles pertinent to early childhood language and literacy development. The university team encouraged the staff members to consider not only the quality of the instructional environment they were creating for the children but also the social and emotional environment, using current scientific and theoretical evidence on the subject.

The Bright Futures Early Learning Center exhibits strong scientific and theoretical groundedness. See Table 15.4 for indicators of scientific and theoretical groundedness that evaluators might examine.

When a program is not theoretically or scientifically grounded, evaluators may need to recommend that new activities, materials, or even a new early childhood curriculum be implemented. Evaluators might additionally make recommendations for professional development that emphasize the linkages among the program's instructional activities, classroom social and instructional processes, and children's outcomes, so that program staff can make intentional efforts to continue to improve in these areas in theoretically and scientifically driven ways (e.g., by making data-based decisions about instruction). For more information about *how* evaluators might measure a program's scientific and theoretical groundedness, see the second part of this chapter ("How Evaluations of Early Childhood Programs Should Be Conducted").

Have the Classroom Environment; the Teachers' Knowledge and Qualifications; The Teachers' Planning and Instruction; and the Children's Language, Cognitive, and Preliteracy Skills Improved?

TABLE 15.4. Indicators of Program Scientific and Theoretical Groundedness

Indicator	Example
Curricular materials and activities are scientifically and theoretically grounded.	The curriculum is backed by evidence of effectiveness. Published studies in peer-reviewed journals (especially studies using random assignment of participants) indicate that the curriculum promotes children's language and early literacy development.
Instructional decisions are driven by data.	The literacy coach and teachers conduct progress-monitoring assessments over the course of the academic year and use the results of these assessments to inform instructional decisions.
Intentional efforts are made to support children's social and emotional competencies in conjunction with their academic competencies in the areas of language and early literacy.	The university team collaborates with the center staff to discuss scientific and theoretically motivated research concerning children's academic, social, and emotional development.

An evaluation of an early childhood education program would not be complete without examining the program's contributions to improvement in the identified areas. Although improvement in children's outcomes is the program's desired end, improvement in the areas of classroom environment and educators' knowledge, qualifications, and instructional practices are an important means to that end, and should be evaluated as well. The vignette that follows illustrates a high level of demonstrated improvement in several important areas.

> The Bright Futures Early Learning Center made dramatic changes in its classroom language and literacy environment by the end of the year, as measured by two observational instruments. For example, the center improved the literacy richness of the classroom environment by purchasing and displaying a variety of new materials (e.g., books, puppets, writing center materials, large dry-erase boards). Additionally, Bright Futures offered monthly professional development sessions designed to build teachers' understanding of language and early literacy development. Portions of each professional development session were focused on how to document and preserve evidence of children's learning and development in ways that did not take away from instructional time (e.g., children had to "sign in" at centers each day, and these sign-in sheets were saved as documentation of their emerging writing abilities). Teachers from the center also learned in their professional development sessions how to con-

duct progress-monitoring assessments at the beginning, middle, and end of the academic year, not only to inform instructional decisions but also to provide a more formal measure of children's developing language and early literacy competencies to accompany the informal documentation procedures. By the end of the year, children demonstrated marked improvement in their phonological awareness, print awareness, alphabet knowledge, and oral language, as evidenced by an increase in their scores on standardized assessments from fall to spring. (See Table 15.5 for indicators of demonstrated improvement that evaluators might examine.)

The evaluator's role, therefore, is to determine what improvements are evident both in environmental and instructional aspects of a program, and in children's language and literacy outcomes. Once he or she has determined what improvements have been made, the evaluator can recommend how the program might move to the next level of improvement. For example, if improvements are demonstrated in only structural aspects of the program, the evaluator can recommend professional development tailored toward improving instructional processes and making data-based decisions. The next part of this chapter provides detailed information on *how* an evaluator might measure a program's demonstrated improvement.

TABLE 15.5. Indicators of Demonstrated Improvement

Indicator	Example
The program demonstrates improvement in the classroom environment.	Classrooms include a variety of literacy centers, materials, and props, including books, puppets, a writing center, and a library center, to name a few.
The program demonstrates improvement in teacher knowledge and qualifications.	Program staff participate in intensive and sustained professional development opportunities and make progress toward completing higher education degrees.
The program demonstrates improvement in planning and instruction.	Program staff plan and execute progress-monitoring assessments to inform instructional decisions and document children's developing competencies. They also document children's developing competencies in informal ways (e.g., by collecting writing samples).
The program demonstrates improvement in children's outcomes.	Children demonstrate marked improvement from fall to spring on standardized measures of phonological awareness, print awareness, alphabet knowledge, and oral language.

How Evaluations of Early Childhood Programs Should Be Conducted

So far, this chapter has discussed aspects of an early childhood education program that should be evaluated, including the program's systematicity, applicability and feasibility, and theoretical and scientific groundedness. Also discussed was the need to determine the extent to which the program contributes to improvements in the language and literacy richness of the environment, teachers' instructional planning and practices, and children's language and literacy outcomes. The remainder of this chapter addresses *how* evaluators should conduct a high-quality evaluation with attention to these areas. Specifically, this section examines the types of questions evaluators should ask and the kinds of data they should collect and use.

Types of Questions Evaluators Should Ask

A variety of governmental agencies (e.g., U.S. Department of Education, U.S. Department of Health and Human Services, U.S. Environmental Protection Agency, U.S. Government Accountability Office) commonly incorporate specific types of questions as part of their program evaluations that might serve as models for evaluations of early childhood programs. This chapter introduces three types of questions that evaluators of early childhood programs might ask: impact questions, normative questions, and descriptive questions.

Impact Questions

Impact questions are concerned with the following: (1) determining a program's outcomes; (2) determining whether a program has been implemented as intended, and how the implementation has contributed to the outcomes; (3) providing evidence to funding agencies about program resources that have been allocated wisely; and (4) informing decisions about replicating or extending a program (Owen & Rogers, 1999). Evaluators of potential early childhood centers of excellence are specifically interested in posing impact questions about whether a program has made a demonstrable impact on any, or all, of the following areas: (1) classroom quality (e.g., language and literacy richness, physical arrangement); (2) teacher qualifications and training (e.g., experience, background, efficacy, sense of community); (3) teacher instruction (curriculum choices, instructional strategies); or (4) child and family outcomes (e.g., transition to kindergarten, family literacy beliefs and practices).

To pose a question about the impact of a program, it is preferable to compare classrooms, teachers, and children who were part of an intervention (adoption of the MECC with the surrounding support of literacy coaches, professional development for the teachers, etc.) to a comparison group that did not participate in the intervention. Impact questions can be posed in the context of a true experimental design or a quasi-experimental design. True experimental designs are those in which participants are randomly assigned to a group that receives the program under evaluation (treatment or intervention group) or to a group that does not receive the program under evaluation (comparison or control group). Quasi-experimental designs are those in which random assignment to treatment and comparison conditions is not possible. With quasi-experimental designs, every effort should be made to ensure that the intervention, rather than preexisting differences between the treatment and comparison groups, is responsible for any observed program impact. Following are two examples of how an evaluator might ask an impact question. The first example takes place within the context of a true experimental design in the Bright Futures Early Learning Center, and the second takes place within the context of a quasi-experimental design in the Discovery Daycare Center.

IMPACT QUESTION, EXAMPLE 1

Through random assignment, three classrooms in the Bright Futures Early Learning Center participated in an early childhood education innovation, whereas three additional classrooms in the center maintained their prevailing early childhood education program. The evaluator posed the following impact question concerning the print richness of the classroom environments: How do Bright Futures Childcare Center's treatment classrooms compare in print richness to their comparison classrooms at the end of the academic year? Figure 15.1 illustrates the impact of the program on Bright Futures Early Learning Center's classroom print richness. By examining the mean scores of the treatment and the comparison groups on a print richness measure, we see that the treatment group outperformed the comparison group. Because the sample size was small ($n = 6$) and the data were not normally distributed, the evaluator presented the data in a graphic form and discussed their implications according to the impact question posed—an appropriate choice.

IMPACT QUESTION, EXAMPLE 2

The three classrooms in the Discovery Daycare Center were not randomly assigned to treatment and comparison groups. Instead, three preschool teachers from classrooms in a nearby center, who were not participating in a new educational innovation, volunteered to complete the same surveys as the treatment teachers at the beginning and the end of the year.

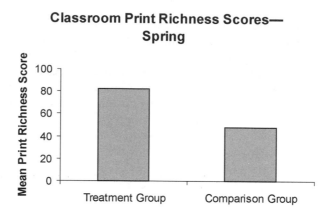

FIGURE 15.1. Impact of program on Bright Futures Early Learning Center's classroom print richness.

One such survey measured teachers' perceived instructional self-efficacy. "Instructional self-efficacy" describes a teacher's feelings about being able to instruct competently. The program evaluator asked the following impact question concerning instructional self-efficacy: To what extent did the early childhood innovation impact teachers' feelings of instructional self-efficacy? Figure 15.2 depicts results of the instructional self-efficacy survey for treatment and comparison teachers in the fall and spring of the academic year. Notice that treatment and comparison teachers reported similar degrees of instructional self-efficacy in the fall and that by the spring, the treatment teachers, but not the comparison teachers, reported greater levels of self-efficacy.

Normative Questions

Another type of question that evaluators might ask is normative. "Normative questions" provide information about a child relative to an identified comparison group and are answered with the aid of "norm-referenced assessments," or assessments that are capable of spreading out individuals' scores, so that performance differences can be clearly identified, and provide "performance norms," or the typical performance of a population (Gredler, 1996). When used in the context of a program evaluation, normative questions provide information concerning the range of performance within a group of individuals, and also differences between individuals who are part of a program and those who participated in the norming sample. For example, to evaluate the performance of Smart Stars Early Learning Center's 109 children on a measure of receptive

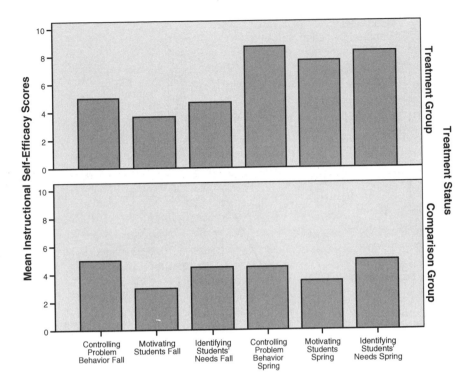

FIGURE 15.2. Impact of program on Discovery Daycare Center's instructional self-efficacy.

vocabulary in the spring of the academic year, the evaluator might ask the following: How do children in Smart Stars Early Learning Center perform on a measure of receptive vocabulary at the end of the academic year in comparison to the normative sample? How much do children in the Smart Stars Early Learning Center differ from one another compared to children in the norming sample? The evaluator used a measure of receptive vocabulary in which the norming sample had a mean score of 100 and a standard deviation of 15. As illustrated in Figure 15.3, students in the Smart Stars Early Learning Center had a mean score of 98, and thus performed similarly, when considered as a group, with the children in the norming sample. The data in Figure 15.3 also illustrate that children in the Smart Stars Early Learning Center demonstrated a similar level of variability, or the same spread in scores, to that of the norming sample (both samples had a standard deviation of 15).

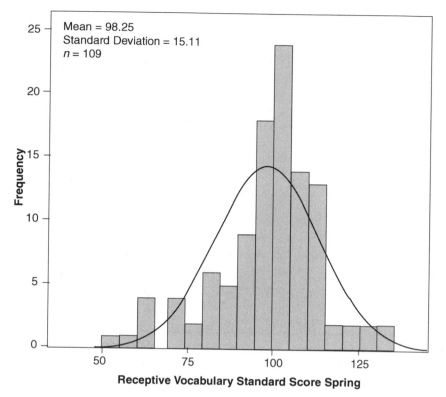

FIGURE 15.3. Scores for Smart Stars Early Learning Center's receptive vocabulary measure.

Descriptive Questions

The final type of question evaluators might ask about a program is descriptive, designed to elicit answers that *describe* an aspect of an early childhood education program. Descriptive questions are particularly useful with small samples (where inferential statistics are inappropriate) and with nonexperimental research designs (when a comparison group is not available). Answers to descriptive questions can provide a general picture of program performance for stakeholders. For example, if Bright Futures Early Learning Center implemented an early childhood education innovation designed to improve classroom quality in the areas of emotional support, behavioral management, and instructional support, the evaluator might ask the following: What does the quality of Bright Futures Early Learning Center's classrooms look like at the end of the academic year? As shown in Figure 15.4, this center scored in the middle to middle-to-high range on all three of the classroom quality indicators measured by

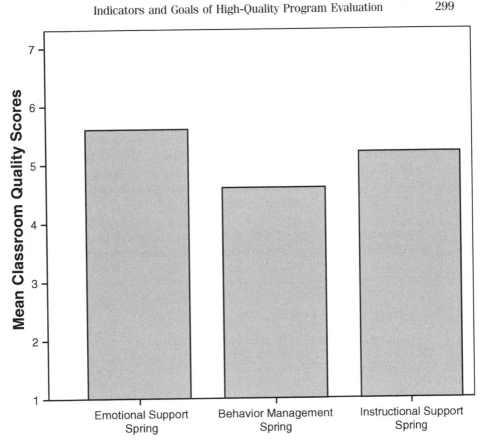

FIGURE 15.4. Scores for Bright Futures Early Learning Center's descriptive measure of classroom quality.

the evaluator using the Classroom Assessment Scoring System: Preschool Version (Pianta, La Paro, & Hamre, 2006). Using this descriptive information, the evaluator might also recommend that the center direct additional effort toward improving behavior management strategies, because the center scored relatively lower in the area of behavior management than in the areas of emotional support and instructional support.

Kinds of Data Evaluators Should Collect and Types of Measures They Should Use

When asking impact questions, normative questions, and descriptive questions as part of a program evaluation, evaluators also must consider what kinds of data to collect and the types of measures to use. In this section of the chapter I discuss two distinct types of data, formative and summative, and also describes how evaluators may use direct and indirect measures to evaluate a program.

Formative Data

Formative data are used to discover problems and successes in intermediate stages of program implementation, to inform ongoing activities, and to guide decision making over time (Scriven, 1967). The focus of formative data collection is on processes and mechanisms of change. Consider the following two examples of formative evaluations provided to the Discovery Daycare Center midway through the academic year.

Formative Evaluation of Classroom Environment for Discovery Daycare Center. Discovery Daycare Center's classroom environments are strong and have been substantially improved already this year. School district personnel are exploring space issues, particularly for storing classroom materials, and are developing a resource library for family literacy.

Formative Evaluation of Curriculum Implementation for Discovery Daycare Center. The teachers and assistants have expressed that the complexities of implementing a new curriculum are challenging, but they are on their way to feeling more comfortable with the curriculum. They have agreed on the importance of collaborating with other preschool programs, particularly those within the same county. The curriculum specialist is implementing an observational protocol to monitor classroom climate to assist the teachers in achieving excellence in curriculum and instruction.

Formative evaluations such as those presented in the preceding examples do not rely on a specific set of procedures. They may take the form of interviews, focus groups, record reviews, or observations, all with the goal of identifying both ways that a program is operating according to plan and ways that it departs from the original plan. Royse, Thyer, Padgett, and Logan (2006) recommend the following types of data in a formative or process evaluation: student demographic information, staff demographic information (degrees, amount of experience), program activities (meetings, professional development provided, measures of implementation fidelity), meeting minutes, correspondence and internal memos, and financial data (program costs and expenditures). Notice that many of these types of data are *qualitative* rather than *quantitative* in nature (they utilize narrative to a greater degree than numbers). Scriven (1967) further recommended that, if possible, persons conducting the formative evaluation of a program be distanced from those conducting the summative evaluation (discussed in the next section) to preserve the objective nature of the evaluation.

Summative Data

In contrast to formative data, summative data focus on the end point and final outcome, or the *product*, of a program. Summative components of program evaluations provide an empirically based appraisal of the results or final outcomes of a program (Royse et al., 2006). Although summative data may determine whether meaningful changes have occurred within a given program, more complex research designs are required to determine whether a program is *responsible* for observed improvements (Royse et al., 2006), such as a true experimental design. For this reason, evaluators should conduct summative evaluations only to the extent to which their program design permits. For example, on the one hand, a program evaluator using a nonexperimental design would not be able to make adequate causal claims about a program (i.e., to determine that the program is responsible for observed improvements). On the other hand, a program evaluator using a true experimental design that employs random assignment to the treatment may have an adequate basis on which to make causal claims about a program's effectiveness.

Direct Measures

Direct measures are those instruments that go straight to the source for answers. The most important types of direct measures for evaluating potential preschool centers of excellence include measures of early language and literacy abilities administered directly to children. Direct measures address children's competencies in specific areas targeted by the program, namely, oral language, phonological awareness, print awareness, and alphabet knowledge. Evaluators might use two types of direct measures: *progress-monitoring assessments* and *outcome assessments.*

"Progress-monitoring assessments" should be conducted a minimum of three times over the academic year to chart a child's growth and make data-based decisions for instruction. Because they are used to inform and support instructional decisions, progress-monitoring instruments are generally conducted internally by program staff or teachers, and the results may be provided to evaluators as a means to chart children's growth and progress. Progress-monitoring instruments do not need to be lengthy or intensive, but it is important that they be administered repeatedly, with the objective of monitoring a child's progress in a specific area.

"Outcome assessments" need to be conducted at the end of the academic year or the end of a program. Like progress-monitoring instruments, outcome assessments also measure children's competencies in oral language, phonological awareness, print awareness, and alphabet knowledge. However, outcome assessments may be lengthier and more intensive than progress-monitoring assessments, and they may measure students' competencies generally rather than in a way that is specific to the curriculum or instructional activities implemented. For example, an outcome measure of oral language might measure children's receptive and expressive vocabulary competencies, whereas a progress-monitoring assessment of oral language might measure vocabulary specific to a curricular unit just completed. For thorough descriptions of direct assessments appropriate for progress monitoring, and measuring language and literacy outcomes, see Pence (2007) and Rathvon (2004).

Indirect Measures

Indirect measures are obtained through a secondary source. As an example, surveys may be administered to teachers or parents to gather information about children's language and literacy competencies. Surveys might also be administered to teachers or parents to gain a better understanding of children's social and behavioral competencies, and how these competencies might have changed over the course of the preschool year. Other indirect measures include attendance records to assess the dosage or amount of intervention a child has received and a teacher's lesson plans to determine the extent to which the intervention was implemented with fidelity. Pence (2007) and Rathvon (2004) also provide thorough descriptions of indirect measures that evaluators might use.

When deciding on the kinds of data and types of measures to use, evaluators should use a variety of measures to achieve convergence and to paint the most complete picture possible regarding the degree to which a program is systematic, applicable and feasible, and scientifically and theoretically grounded; and the extent to which it demonstrates improvements in classroom environment, in teacher knowledge and qualifications, in teacher instruction and planning, and in children's language, cognitive, and preliteracy skills.

Regardless of which measures evaluators select, measures should demonstrate reliability and validity. Reliability describes the consistency and dependability of a measure over time and across examiners. Validity describes the extent to which an instrument measures the construct it purports to measure. Both of these issues are extremely important in program evaluations, because conclusions and recommendations provided by an evaluator are only as accurate as the data used to support them.

Conclusions

In summary, high-quality program evaluations of promising preschool centers of excellence should be implemented with the same level of integrity and importance as the design and implementation phases of a program. Evaluators should be objective and fair in their examination of a program's systematicity, applicability and feasibility, scientific and theoretical groundedness; and the extent to which the program demonstrates improvement in classroom environment, in teacher knowledge and qualifications, in teacher instruction and planning, and in children's language and literacy outcomes. Evaluators have a range of methods for evaluating these components. High-quality program evaluations should consider the types of questions to ask, the kinds of data to collect, and the types of measures to use.

References

Gredler, M. E. (1996). *Program evaluation.* Englewood Cliffs, NJ: Prentice-Hall.

Owen, J. M., & Rogers, P. J. (1999). *Program evaluation forms and approaches.* London: Sage.

Pence, K. L. (Ed.). (2007). *Assessment in emergent literacy.* San Diego, CA: Plural.

Pianta, R. C., La Paro, K., & Hamre, B. (2006). *Classroom Assessment Scoring System: Preschool Version.* Charlottesville: Center for Advanced Study of Teaching and Learning, University of Virginia.

Rathvon, N. (2004). *Early reading assessment: A practitioner's handbook.* New York: Guilford Press.

Royse, D., Thyer, B. A., Padgett, D. K., & Logan, T. (2006). *Program evaluation: An introduction, fourth edition.* Belmont, CA: Thomson Higher Education.

Scriven, M. (1967). The methodology of evaluation. In R. Tyler, R. Gagne, & M. Scriven (Eds.), *AERA Monograph Series on Curriculum Evaluation: Perspectives of curriculum evaluation.* Chicago: Rand McNally.

U.S. Department of Education Institute of Education Sciences, National Center for Education Evaluation and Regional Assistance. (2003). *Identifying and implementing educational practices supported by rigorous evidence: A user friendly guide.* Available from *www.ed.gov/rschstat/research/pubs/rigorousevid/index.html.*

CHAPTER 16

★★★★★★★★★

How to Evaluate a Screening Process

The Vocabulary of Screening and What Educators Need to Know

Christopher Schatschneider
Yaacov Petscher
Kellee M. Williams

One of the most critical issues facing researchers today is to devise appropriate methods of identifying students who are likely to require special education services. With the passing of the No Child Left Behind Act of 2001, researchers and practitioners alike have recognized the pressing need for accurate identification methods. Concern about how to identify those students who are at risk for various types of difficulties (i.e., learning disabilities, reading comprehension problems) has emerged as an issue for administrators and education researchers alike, and the use of screening tools within early childhood programs makes this an important concern for early educators in the 21st century.

Recent research has reported that students with poorer reading skills have difficulty in closing achievement gaps (Vadasy, Sanders, & Peyton, 2006), and high-risk students often come from demographically challenged neighborhoods and schools. Longitudinal analyses have found that third-grade students failing at least one subject and reading below grade level are unlikely to complete high school (Slavin, Karweit, & Wasik, 1992), and students referred for special education services are typically identified based upon reading failure. Although early success does not equate with future success, it is important that early, appropriate screening properly identify students who are in preliminary stages of failure for particular outcomes.

Accurate identification is necessary to remediate the difficulties a student is encountering, yet given the variety of methodological approaches available to researchers, nonoptimal techniques have often been attempted. Methods to identify students who appear to be at risk for difficulties have included simple bivariate correlations, interrater reliability, low achievement cut points (i.e., percentile rank), and achievement–IQ discrepancies. However, one of the most useful processes to evaluate the accuracy of student identification and the prevalence of a problem in a population is through the examination of classification decisions from screening outcomes.

Diagnostic and screening processes used extensively in the fields of medicine and clinical psychology have only relatively recently been adopted by educational researchers. Use of screening processes to identify children needing extra support with preschool literacy programs is an important design feature of the Early Reading First program authorized by the U.S. Department of Education. Much has been gained in applying classification decisions to the identification of individuals with psychological disorders and determination of whether a person may have a life-threatening illness, or whether a student might gain from additional, immediate intensive interventions. As these examples show, the results of such screenings may have considerable impacts on the individuals who are being assessed for difficulties. Therefore, the quality and specificity of measurement in diagnostic efficiency are key in determining the validity of the screening assessment's results.

Although screening can be an important tool for use in preschool programs today, particularly for identifying children who require additional instructional services, there has been a communication gap between educational researchers who are developing screening procedures and those who need or want to implement a system by which students are identified as potentially needing further services. Researchers have generated a large amount of information regarding the development and evaluation of screening instruments, and this has spurred a "vocabulary of screening" that may be foreign to those schools or districts that may want to develop a screening system. Our goal in this chapter is to introduce people to this vocabulary and to provide recommendations for evaluating and implementing a screening process.

The Vocabulary of Screening

The early identification of children who may be at risk for developing a learning problem has been identified as an important step in the prevention and early remediation of academic problems. "Screening" in this context is defined as a process by which students are identified as being either at risk (i.e., not achieving some predefined educational outcome) or not at risk according to a given measure. Already in the explanation we have introduced a level of ambiguity that needs to be discussed. First is the concept of risk (or being at risk). The concept of risk can be viewed in many ways, but for the purposes of this presentation, let's view risk as a "percent chance" number that exists between 0 and 1, with 0 meaning that there is no chance at all that a particular student will develop a problem, and 1 being no chance that the student will *not* develop a problem. It should be obvious that almost all children lie somewhere between 0 and 1 on the risk continuum, and being identified as "at risk" is relatively arbitrary. When one is employing some kind of process to identify children who are "at risk," this is typically a yes–no decision based upon some kind of "cut point" along a continuum of risk. For example, two students from different districts may have the same chance of developing a particular learning problem, but whereas one may be identified as being at risk for that problem, the other may not, depending on the placement of the cut-point used in each district that divides at-risk and not-at-risk students.

Second, we also need to define the condition for which a student is at risk. Typically this is some future measure of student achievement, of which a similarly arbitrary cut-point must be defined. Oftentimes this future measure of achievement is a state's high-stakes assessment. Most statewide, high-stakes assessments also measure achievement along a continuum and provide some kinds of standard score that describes the performance of the students. Presumably, to make decisions about students and schools, a cut point is chosen that determines whether a student has passed or failed the statewide assessment.

Many other terms that are used when discussing the utility of screening for problems can be derived from a 2 × 2 classification table (see Table 16.1). A 2 × 2 classification table typically shows the number of students that have been placed into one of four categories: students identified by the screening process as being at risk for some outcome who actually do develop the problem (cell a), students identified by the screening process as being at risk for some outcome who do not develop the problem (cell b), students not identified by the screening process as being at risk for some outcome who do develop the problem (cell c), and students *not* identified by the screening process as being at risk for some outcome who do not develop the problem (cell d). Cells a and d are correct classifications, and cells b and c are incorrect classifications.

TABLE 16.1. A 2 x 2 Classification Table

		Outcome	
		Problem	No problem
Screen	Risk	a	b
	No risk	c	d

To make this clearer, let's borrow a classification table from the technical report of the development of the Texas Primary Reading Inventory (TPRI; Texas Education Agency, 1998) on whose development team Christopher Schatschneider served. The five TPRI screening instruments (one for kindergartners, two for first graders, and two for second graders) were designed to identify children who may need more detailed assessments to determine their risk status for developing a reading problem. To develop the screening portion of the TPRI, we used a preexisting longitudinal sample of 945 students from kindergarten through second grade. When developing this screen, we had a number of decisions to make. Among other decisions about what assessments to include in our screen, we also had to define the "at risk for what" question and to identify particular cut points on the screen that would classify students into at-risk categories.

For the kindergarten screen for the TPRI, we chose two prereading skills that have been shown to be predictive of future reading performance—letter name knowledge and phonological awareness (Schatschneider, Fletcher, Francis, & Foorman, 2004). From our longitudinal sample, we were able to select a group of kindergarten children who were assessed in December and followed until the end of first grade, at which point they were assessed on a measure of reading ability (the Woodcock–Johnson–Revised Basic Skills Cluster). We then made an arbitrary decision to operationalize the "at risk for what" question. The goal of the Texas Education Agency (TEA) at the time was to have every third grader reading at grade level. On this basis, we then defined "at risk" at the end of first grade as any student performing half a grade level below grade level on the Woodcock–Johnson–Revised Basic Skills Cluster. After that decision, we developed cut points on the screening measure that would meet certain properties (which we describe shortly). Now, having created two decision rule cut points, we were able to construct a 2 × 2 table (see Table 16.2).

From this relatively simple table, a cornucopia of (sometimes) confusing information can be used to evaluate the performance of the screening tool. Our goal here is to introduce and define several terms that may be provided along with the screening tool, and that educators and researchers can use to evaluate the effectiveness of the tool. An understanding of

TABLE 16.2. 2 x 2 Classification Table from Kindergarten TPRI

		Outcome		
		Problem	No problem	
Screen	Risk	87	121	208
	No risk	9	204	213
		96	325	421

these indices is critical in evaluating the potential effectiveness of any screening tool.

True Positive

A "true positive" is defined as a student who was identified as being at risk, subsequently developed the problem. In Table 16.2, 87 students were identified as true positives.

True Negative

A "true negative" is defined as a student who was not identified as being at risk, and did not develop the problem. In Table 16.2, 204 students were identified as true negatives.

False Positive

A "false positive" is defined as a student who was identified as being at risk, but did not subsequently develop the problem. From Table 16.2, 121 students were identified as false positives.

False Negative

A "false negative" is defined as a student who was not identified as being at risk, but did develop the problem. In Table 16.2, nine students were identified as false negatives.

Overall Classification Accuracy

Both true positives and true negatives are considered correct classification decisions. Adding those numbers together and dividing by the total number of students yields the overall classification accuracy of the screening process. In the TPRI example, the overall classification accuracy is $(204 + 87)/421 = 69\%$.

Base-Rate of the Problem

The "base-rate occurrence" of the problem, which plays an important role in determining the effectiveness of any screening process, is simply defined as the percentage of students who end up having a problem. In this example, the base rate of occurrence is $96/421 = 23\%$.

Using these simple categories to characterize students, we can also define more terms that describe the performance of the screening process. These indicators are often provided with the screening instrument or process and can be used to estimate how well this process might work in any school or district setting.

Sensitivity

"Sensitivity" is a proportion that essentially can be defined in the following way: Out of all the children who will eventually develop a problem, what percentage were identified by the screening process? In our example, the sensitivity of this screen is .91, which is calculated by dividing 87 (the number of students correctly identified as at risk for developing a problem) by 96 (the total number of students who develop a problem). It can also be defined as the number of true positives divided by the sum of true positives and false negatives; from Table 16.1, the equation is $a/(a + c)$.

False-Positive Rate

The "false-positive rate" is defined as the number of students who are incorrectly identified by the screen as being at risk, divided by the total number of students who do not end up developing a problem. In the previous example, the false-positive rate is .37 and was determined by dividing the number of false positives (121) by the number of students who do not develop a problem (325). From Table 16.1, we compute the false-positive rate as $b/(b + d)$. It can also be defined as the number of false positives divided by the sum of false positives and true negatives, or $1 -$ specificity, which we discuss next.

Specificity

"Specificity" which is also a proportion, is defined as the percentage of children not identified as being at risk by the screen, who do not develop the problem in the future divided by all children who do not develop the problem. In our example, the specificity of this screen is .63, which is calculated by dividing 204 (the number of students correctly identified as not being at risk to develop a problem) by 325 (the total number of students who develop a problem). It can also be defined as the number of true negatives divided by the sum of true negatives and false positives, or, from Table 16.1, $d/(b + d)$.

False-Negative Rate

The "false-negative rate" is defined as the number of students who are incorrectly identified by the screen as not being at risk, divided by the total number of students who end up developing a problem. In the previous example, the false-negative rate was determined by dividing the number of false negatives (9) by the number of students who develop a problem (96). The false-negative rate for this example is $9/96 = .09$. From Table 16.1, it would be computed as $c/(a + c)$. It can also be defined as the number of false negatives divided by the sum of false negatives and true positives, or $1 -$ sensitivity.

Sensitivity, specificity, false-positive, and false-negative rates are typically thought of as properties of the screening instrument (Streiner, 2003). This means that when this information is reported along with the instrument, these numbers are expected to remain the same from sample to sample, and not change depending upon the base rate of the problem at a particular school or district. They may vary somewhat due to a number of other factors (e.g., the representativeness of the sample in which these values were obtained and how a school or district matches this sample), but the expectation is that these values will hold. This is not true for the next two indices we discuss, even though these numbers are critical for understanding how well (or poorly) an established screening instrument will perform at any particular school or district.

Positive Predictive Power

Sometimes called positive predictive value, positive predictive power (PPP) is the proportion of students who end up developing a problem out of all of the students identified by the screen as being at risk. In this example, the PPP of this screen for this sample is defined as the number of students correctly identified as being at risk for a reading problem (87), divided by the number of students identified by the screen as being at risk (208), or .42, or, from Table 16.1, $a/(a + b)$. This means that, for this sample, only 42% of the children identified as being at risk for a reading problem will actually develop a reading problem.

Negative Predictive Power

Sometimes called negative predictive value, negative predictive power (NPP) is the proportion of students who end up not developing a problem, divided by the number of students identified by the screen as not being at risk. From Table 16.1, NPP would be computed by $d/(c + d)$. In our TPRI example, the NPP of this screen is defined as the number of students correctly identified as not being at risk for a reading problem (204), divided by the number of students identified by the screen as not being at risk (213), or .96. This means that of the students identified in kindergarten as not being at risk, 96% did not develop reading problems by the end of first grade.

PPP and NPP are typically not considered properties of the screen; rather, they are sensitive to the context in which the screen is used (Meehl & Rosen, 1955; Streiner, 2003). More specifically, PPP and NPP are highly related to the base rate of occurrence of the problem for which the screen is being implemented. When the problem being screened for occurs at a low rate, PPP will also be lower, and NPP will be higher (all else being equal). The reverse is also true. When there is a high rate of occurrence of a problem, PPP will be higher and NPP will be lower.

Oftentimes PPP and NPP are not provided by the creators of a screen (Kessel & Zimmerman, 1993). In many ways this makes sense, because PPP and NPP vary considerably according to the local base rate of occurrence. Fortunately, if the reported sensitivity and specificity of the test are available, and the base rate of the problem is known (or can be estimated) in the sample in which the screen is to be employed, PPP and NPP can be computed with the following formulas (Streiner, 2003).

$$PPP = \frac{(Base\ rate)(Sensitivity)}{(Base\ rate)(Sensitivity) + [(1 - Base\ rate)(1 - Specificity)]}$$

$$NPP = \frac{(1 - Base\ rate)(Specificity)}{(1 - Base\ rate)(Sensitivity) + [(Base\ rate)(1 - Sensitivity)]}$$

These formulas reveal something very interesting. It is possible for a screen that has both high sensitivity and specificity actually to have a relatively poor PPP, if the base-rate of occurrence is low. Let's take a hypothetical example in which both the sensitivity and specificity are relatively high (.90). Using the formula for PPP, and assuming a base-rate of occurrence of .5 (50%), the PPP will also be .9. This means that in this context, 90% of the students identified by the screen are truly at risk for developing a problem. However, if the base-rate of occurrence is only .1 (10%), then the PPP drops to .5. In this context, only half of the students identified by the screen are at risk for developing a problem—same screen, two different contexts, two different results.

Relative Risk

A relative risk (RR) is a ratio of two probabilities. It estimates the probability of developing a problem if a certain risk factor is present versus that of developing a problem when the risk factor is absent. To compute the RR, or risk ratio, as it is often called, we first need to compute the probability of developing a problem for those identified as being at risk, which we have already defined as the PPP of the screen. This is defined in Table 16.1 as $a/(a + b)$, or .42 from our example. We then divide that by the probability of a student who was not identified by the screen developing a problem: $c/(c + d)$, or in our example, $9/(9 + 204)=.04$. Dividing .42 by .04 yields a relative risk ratio of 10.5 (which we can round off to 11); this means that students identified by the screen develop a problem 11 times more often than students not identified by the screen. An RR greater than 1 depict a positive relationship between being identified by the screen and developing the problem, which means there is an increase in the risk of developing the problem if the risk factor is present. An RR equal to 1 means that no relationship exists between the risk factor and the problem. An RR less than 1, which is rare in the context of screening, means that the situation in which students identified by the screen do develop a problem occurs at a lower rate than that in which children not identified by the screen.

Odds Ratio

An odds ratio (OR), like the RR ratio, describes the relationship between two numbers. Whereas the RR is the ratio of two probabilities, the OR is the ratio of two odds: the odds of the group with the risk factor developing the problem, divided by the odds of the group without the risk factor developing the problem. Odds are, oddly enough, the ratio of two probabilities—the probability of something occurring over the probability of something not occurring. In the context of our screening example, we could compute the odds of students identified by the screen developing a problem by taking the probability of developing a problem given a positive screen identification (previously computed as .42) and divide it by the probability of not developing the problem given an at-risk designation on the screen (calculated as 1 – .42, or .58). Dividing .42 by .58 yields .72. Odds less than 1 imply that the likelihood of a student not developing a problem (given that he or she was identified by the screen) is greater than the likelihood of developing a problem. This may seem surprising, but it is supported by the data in the 2×2 table, indicating that only 42% of the children identified by the screen as being at risk actually go on to develop a reading problem. The odds we just computed, however, are only half of the OR.

We can compare these odds to the odds of developing a problem given that a student has actually passed the screen. This we obtained by computing the probability of a student developing a problem given that he or she was not identified by the screen as being at risk [in our example, $9/(9 + 204) = .042$] divided by the probability of not developing a problem given that a student has passed the screen ($1 - .042$, or .958). Dividing .042 by .958 gives the odds of developing a problem given that the student has passed the screen of .044. Now that we have the two odds, we can create an OR by dividing .72 by .044; this gives us an OR of 16.4. We simplify this calculation immensely by realizing that the OR can also be computed directly from the 2×2 table as ad/bc. As with the RR, an OR greater than 1 shows a positive relationship between the risk factor and problem, or that the event is more likely to occur in the group with the risk factor present. An OR of 1 shows no difference between risk groups in terms of the likelihood of the event occurring, and an OR less than 1 shows a reduced likelihood of the event or problem occurring if the risk factor is present. The ratio obtained from our TPRI example can be interpreted by saying that students who were identified as being at-risk from the screening process have 16 times the odds of developing the problem than those not identified by the screen.

Some Guidelines for Educators

As shown in the previous section, we have generated an enormous amount of information from a simple 2×2 classification table. We now turn to answering an important question: Upon what should educators and administrators focus when deciding how a particular screening instrument or process will work in their own school or district? Here are some guidelines.

1. Define the "at risk for what" question for your school or district. To establish a screening process, some problem must be identified and made explicit. Is the school passing the statewide assessment? Is it scoring above a certain cut point on a standardized achievement test? Or on some other benchmark? No screening process can succeed until a clearly defined end point has been selected.

2. Establish a goal for the screening process. Do you want a screening process to identify students who simply may need more follow-up assessments to determine whether they are at risk? Do you want to use the screen to assess at-risk status directly? Do you plan on assessing all of the students? Answering these questions will help you select the screening process that best fits the needs of the school and/or district. For example, if a school district or school personnel want to use a screening device to

identify children who may need follow-up assessments or further monitoring, it may be wise to set up the initial screen in such a way that the NPP is high. Using this strategy, their goal would be to remove students with a very low chance of developing a problem from further monitoring or assessments. This type of screening process would probably be fairly quickly and easily administered. The downside is that many students identified by the screen are probably not at risk.

Additionally, even if a school or district does not plan to assess everyone (perhaps only teacher-nominated children would be assessed), it is still the case that all students participate in the screening process, with teacher nomination as the first level of the screen. If this approach is employed, it is advisable to investigate how well the teachers perform in classifying children.

3. If you select an established screen, investigate how it was developed. Unless the established screening process was developed with the same "at risk for what" criterion and on a sample similar to the students where the screen has yet to be implemented, different results may occur when it is used locally. Investigate the criterion used in the development of the screen. See whether there is any information about how well that criterion correlates with what is being implemented locally. Additionally, you need to know how the cut points (pass–fail rule) were selected in the established screen. For example, the cut points on the TPRI screen were developed to identify students who did not need further assessments to assess risk. This means that although passing the screen is very informative, being identified by the screen is less so. Using the screen by itself to assess risk status probably leads to a great number of children than necessary being identified as being at risk. Knowing the purpose of the existing screen and how it was developed helps to minimize poor screening performance.

4. Determine the base rate of occurrence of the problem to be detected. Once the problem is made explicit, knowledge about its prevalence aids the development of a process for screening. Base rates have a large impact upon how a screening process functions in a local context, because the base rate greatly affects the positive and negative predictive power of the screen, which tell you how well the screen functions in the context of educational setting.

5. Pay attention to PPP and NPP. In most cases, they provide the best information as to how the screening process will work in a particular educational context. PPP and NPP combine information from sensitivity and specificity, respectively, along with base-rate information, to provide users of the screen with information they most likely need to know. Specifically, the PPP is the expected percentage of students who will develop a problem given that they have been identified by the screen, and the NPP is the expected percentage of students who will not develop a problem given

that they have passed the screen. If the base rate of the problem is low in your setting (perhaps under 15%), you will most likely end up identifying many students who really are not at risk for a problem. If this is the case, it may be advantageous to develop a "gated" screening approach (Meehl & Rosen, 1955) whereby students go through a multitiered, or gated, process in which students safely identified on the first pass as not being at risk are removed from the process. Those that remain go through a second screening. This has the beneficial effect of "raising the base rate" for students going through the second screen and increasing the expected PPP and NPP.

6. Pay attention to base-rates and overall classification accuracy. If 85–90% of students in a school or district develop a problem, it makes little sense to screen. Most screens do not exceed 85–95% classification accuracy. It is probably in the best interests of a school or a district with this kind of problem simply to assume that everyone is at risk, and to use its resources in other areas. Additionally, if the sample on which the screen was established has high overall classification accuracy, it doesn't necessarily mean that the screen is doing a good job. If the base rate in that sample is either very low or very high, it's possible that the high classification rate is due to the overwhelming presence of true positives or true negatives. Attention should be paid to the estimated PPP and NPP in the context in which the screen is delivered.

7. Collect local data on how the screening process is performing. Assuming that a particular screening process works the same way in all places is a bit naive. It is good practice to collect data on the students where the screening process is taking place. With the examples we provided earlier, educators can compute their own local indices of screening performance and make adjustments accordingly.

Concluding Thoughts

Nationally, there is an increased awareness of the need for early identification of students who are at risk for developing academic difficulties. For a number of years, educational researchers have been investigating ways to identify children who may be at risk for future difficulties, and have borrowed vocabulary developed from medicine and statistics to describe how these screens perform. However, a gap may exist in use and understanding of this terminology between these researchers and persons in the field who may have to implement a screening procedure. We hope that this chapter aids those in the field as they evaluate existing screening instruments and procedures, and provides useful focal areas for estimating how a particular screening process will work in a local context.

References

Kessel, J. B., & Zimmerman, M. (1993). Reporting errors in studies of the diagnostic performance of self-administered questionnaires: Extent of the problem, recommendations for standardized presentation of results, and implications for the peer review process. *Psychological Assessment, 5*, 395–399.

Meehl, P. E., & Rosen, A. (1955). Antecedent probability and the efficiency of psychometric signs, patterns, and cutting scores. *Psychological Bulletin, 52*, 194–216.

Schatschneider, C., Fletcher, J. M., Francis, D. J., Carlson, C., & Foorman, B. R. (2004). Kindergarten prediction of reading skills: A longitudinal comparative analysis. *Journal of Educational Psychology, 96*, 265–282.

Slavin, R. E., Karweit, N. L., & Wasik, B. A. (1992). Preventing early school failure: What works? *Educational Leadership, 50*, 10–18.

Streiner, D. L. (2003). Diagnosing tests: Using and misusing diagnostic and screening tests. *Journal of Personality Assessment, 81*, 209–219.

Texas Education Agency. (1998). *Texas Primary Reading Inventory technical report.* Retrieved February 20, 2007, from *www.tpri.org/researcher_information/19971998teachnicalmanual.pdf.*

Vadasy, P. F., Sanders, E. A., & Peyton, J. A. (2006). Code-oriented instruction for kindergarten students at risk for reading difficulties: A randomized field trial with paraeducator implementers. *Journal of Educational Psychology, 98*, 508–528.

CHAPTER 17

★★★★★★★★★

Curriculum-Based Measurement of Preschoolers' Early Literacy Skills

Tanis Bryan
Cevriye Ergul
Karen Burstein

The primary goal of preschool centers of excellence is to ensure that young children have the prerequisite language and literacy skills necessary for school success. To achieve this goal, centers of excellence must use a developmentally appropriate curriculum that includes direct, systematic instruction in oral language, phonemic awareness, alphabet letter naming, and print awareness, taught through activities such as interactive storybook reading, print-rich classroom environments, writing activities, and dramatic play (Burns, Griffin, & Snow, 1999; Lonigan & Whitehurst, 1998; National Early Literacy Panel, 2004). Teachers within such centers need reliable and valid measures to monitor students' acquisition of the key language and literacy skills. An integral part of teaching is monitoring children's learning gains and modifying instruction when children fail to make adequate progress.

Our purpose in this chapter is to describe how preschool teachers can use curriculum-based measurement (CBM) to monitor children's learning of the early literacy skills taught in preschool classrooms and to modify instruction when the information gathered indicates that a modification is needed. This chapter summarizes the types of assessments that are typically used with young children, and the origins and applications of CBM, followed by descriptions of two CBMs developed for preschool education: (1) the Preschool Individual Growth and Development Indicators (IGDIs) (Early Childhood Research Institute on Measuring Growth and Development, 1998), a packaged computer-based CBM; and (2) a teacher-constructed CBM developed specifically to monitor English language learners' acquisition of literacy skills taught in the Early Reading First Project, Academic Centers of Excellence (ACE³). Thus, preschool educators are presented with a description of how they might adopt a packaged program or construct their own CBMs tailored to their curricula.

Commonly Used Assessment Approaches in Preschool Programs

Standardized Tests

The most frequently used tests in preschool programs are commercially available, norm-referenced, standardized tests. Standardized tests serve several important purposes, including state and national school and district comparisons, program evaluation, and determination of eligibility for special education services. Few investigations have examined preschool teachers' use of these tests. Much of the available research is outdated (prior to 1987) and often consists of state or regional organizations' summaries that were not conducted systematically, and that failed to describe procedures or verify that preschool teachers were sampled (Pretti-Frontczak, Kowalski, & Brown, 2002). One statewide survey indicates that preschool teachers reported using 21 different commercially available assessment instruments; 35% reported using at least one norm-based, standardized test, and many listed an average of nearly three different assessments (Pretti-Frontczak et al., 2002). This is consistent with state regulations and recommended practice to use multiple norm-based and standardized tests for screening and determining eligibility for special education services.

However, teachers perceive the results of norm-referenced standardized tests as inadequate for making instructional decisions (Thurlow & Ysseldyke, 1982). Available tests typically lack content validity; they do not measure children's learning linked directly with the classroom curricula (Fuchs, Fuchs, & Maxwell, 1988). They also tend to be insensitive to short-term academic gains, and may fail to identify gains when pupils have made actual improvements (Marston, 1989). Additionally, these tests generally are time-consuming, expensive, and can only be administered at a single point in time or on a pre- to posttest basis; the latter characteristic makes these tests inadequate and unreliable for tracking progress and making instructional decisions (Fuchs, Fuchs, & Hamlett, 1989a, 1989b; Marston & Magnusson, 1988; McCurdy & Shapiro, 1992). Thus, although assessment is an important component of education, the tests that typically are used have limited utility at best for guiding teachers' instructional decision making.

Critical Skills Mastery Approaches

Another form of assessment commonly used in early childhood settings is based on critical skills mastery approaches, which assume that certain skills emerge before others, and that there is a hierarchical developmental sequence that must be identified for an assessment to be constructed. Subskills within a developmental sequence become short-term instructional objectives. Early childhood special education has a long-standing and strong tradition of applying critical skills mastery approaches to screen children, to identify children who may need evaluation or early intervention, and to conduct program planning and curricular evaluations (Bricker & Waddell, 1996; Fewell, 2000; McLean, Bailey, & Wolery, 1996; Meisels, Liaw, Dorfman, & Nelson, 1995).

These tools are common components of early childhood programs, as indicated by a recent survey indicating that preschool teachers used 21 instruments based on critical skills mastery approaches, many linked to commercial curricula being used in the classroom (Pretti-Frontczak et al., 2002). Although these measures often exhibit direct linkages to classroom curricula, they have been criticized because they provide little or no information for making comparative evaluations of individual children or for characterizing children's rate of growth over time or progress toward long-term, desired outcomes (McConnell, 2000). Thus this approach also appears to have limited utility for preschool classrooms.

Curriculum-Based Measurement

Curriculum-based measurement, or CBM, is a third type of assessment tool that is increasingly being used in preschool classrooms. For the most part, however, CBM has been used as an assessment tool in elementary and secondary programs. CBM was first used at the University of Minnesota in the mid-1970s, when the original Individual with Disabilities Education Act (IDEA) was passed. At that time, Stanley Deno and colleagues began to develop a measurement system to assist special educators in tracking student growth in basic skills (Deno, 1985; Fuchs, Deno, & Mirkin, 1984; Marston, Mirkin, & Deno, 1984). The original intent was that teachers use technically sound but simple data in a meaningful fashion to document student growth and to determine the necessity for modifying instructional programs (Stecker, Fuchs, & Fuchs, 2005).

CBM is based on the direct assessment of child performance on a standard task, with a common growth metric of performance that can be collected across an extended period of time (Deno, 1985, 1992; Fuchs & Deno, 1991). CBM is meant to be a reliable, valid, and efficient procedure for obtaining child performance data to evaluate intervention programs. The two most salient features are (1) the assessment of proficiency on global outcomes toward which the entire curriculum is directed, and (2) reliance on a standardized, prescriptive measurement methodology that produces critical indicators of performance (Fuchs & Deno, 1991). CBMs are evaluated in terms of the extent to which they (1) measure important outcomes for children; (2) can be used efficiently and economically; (3) are standardized and replicable; (4) rely on generalized or "authentic" child behaviors; (5) are technically adequate; and (6) are sensitive to growth and change over time and to effects of intervention. CBM has been used primarily to monitor students' reading and, to a lesser extent, spelling, written expression, and mathematics computation skills.

CBMs are developed by identifying a behavior of interest, with a focus specifically on behaviors that are tied to the curriculum. A set of standard stimulus materials related to the behavior are then developed, and performance is measured through repeated observations. Developers have been concerned with demonstrating that CBMs meet the psychometric criteria established for standardized tests, which includes showing that CBM data are predictive of standardized test performance (Deno, Mirkin, & Chiang, 1982; Fuchs & Fuchs, 2002). A particularly critical issue concerning use of CBMs has been to identify the conditions under which teachers' use of CBMs has a positive effect on student achievement. Research has demonstrated that students show higher growth rates when teachers use CBM frequently, compare slopes of progress against a goal line, make instructional modifications when slopes are less steep than the goal line, and meet with teacher trainers or consultants on a regular basis to decide on CBM data-utilization procedures (Fuchs et al., 1984; Fuchs, Fuchs, Hamlett, & Ferguson, 1992; Jones & Krouse, 1988). CBM alone has not been found to have a positive effect on student achievement. For CBM to have a positive impact on student achievement, teachers must use the CBM information in their instructional decision making.

Computer applications are a relatively recent advance in CBM progress-monitoring assessment. Teachers using computer-based CBM were found to develop more specific goals, to cite more objectives and frequent data sources for evaluating student progress, and to modify instructional programs more frequently than teachers in a noncomputer CBM condition (Fuchs, Fuchs, & Stecker, 1989). Computer-based CBM appears to have great promise for helping teachers use student performance data.

In this next section, we turn to the use of CBM in preschool education, a newly emerging area that has been stimulated by the emphasis in

No Child Left Behind on using evidence-based curricula and explicit in-struction in early literacy skills in preschool classrooms.

Early Childhood Assessment

The Impact of Early Reading First

Aside from screening and evaluating children to determine their eligibil-ity for special education services, assessment in early childhood education has been controversial regarding its appropriateness (McConnell, 2000). The controversy has reflected lack of agreement about developmental goals for early childhood education and ambiguity about curriculum. Without consensus, it has been difficult to establish standards against which to evaluate children. The recent implementation of Early Reading First (ERF), however, has promoted the use of scientifically based reading research (SBRR) in preschool programs to teach early literacy skills. ERF, a component of the 2001 No Child Left Behind Act, is the first national initiative to establish that SBRR should set the standard for early child-hood education. Since 2001, the U.S. Department of Education has invested more than $400 million in ERF projects nationwide in preschools that serve children from communities where families tend to have low socioeconomic and education status. The introduction of SBRR into early childhood education is based on a large body of research on early brain development, language development, and acquisition of reading skills conducted over the past 50 years (e.g., Liberman, Shankweiler, & Liberman, 1989; Shonkoff & Phillips, 2000; Torgesen, 1999). This re-search consistently has shown that early childhood is a critical period for language and preliteracy development, that young children's development of language and literacy skills predict their facility in learning to read, and that early education should teach early literacy skills to prevent the later development of reading problems (Dickinson, McCabe, Anastasopoulos, Peisner-Feinberg, & Poe, 2003; National Reading Panel, 2000). The ERF stipulation that SBRR be implemented in preschool classrooms as a crite-rion for funding established the specific behaviors of interest as language and preliteracy skills.

The introduction of SBRR into early childhood education made it possible to develop CBM to assess young children's acquisition of early lit-eracy skills. With identification of the specific behaviors of interest, a set of standard materials could be developed to assess the specific behaviors of interest, and performance could be measured through repeated ob-servations. Within early childhood programs, the critical skills to be addressed through SBRR are oral language, phonological awareness, and alphabet letter naming. Oral language refers to children's ability to com-prehend spoken language and to express themselves verbally. These abilities share a strong relationship with later academic success involving oral and written language (Liberman et al., 1989). Young children need to acquire about three new word meanings per day and to have a vocabulary of approximately 2,500–5,000 words by kindergarten and first grade, and 6,200 root words by second grade for grade-level reading comprehension (Biemiller & Slonim, 2001). Children adding less than one word per day generally fall below grade level by third grade in reading comprehension (Hart & Risley, 2003) and seldom manage to erase the deficit (Juel, Griffith, & Gough, 1986).

Phonological awareness refers to awareness of and ability to manipulate the phonological components in words (Kaminski & Good, 1996). Phonological awareness includes the ability to segment a word into its component phonemes and to pronounce the word that is left, after the initial phoneme of a word is removed. Many research studies have shown that phonological awareness is a strong predictor of the speed with which children acquire reading skills in the early grades (Adams, 1990; Torgesen, 1998).

Alphabet letter naming refers to the child's ability to identify the letters of the alphabet. This skill appears to have a causal impact on the development of phonemic awareness (Wagner, Torgesen, & Rashotte, 1994) as prereaders use letter names to access letter sounds and make connections between graphemes and word pronunciations. Integrating instruction in alphabet knowledge and phonemic awareness and starting early have a strong impact, because the two skills are among the best predictors of first-grade reading achievement (National Reading Panel, 2000) and have a strong influence on reading and spelling in sixth grade (Badian, 1995).

CBM in Early Childhood Education

Over the last 10 years, researchers have begun to use CBM to assess young children's acquisition of early literacy skills, including those discussed earlier in this chapter (Good & Kaminski, 2003; Kaminski & Good, 1996; McConnell, Priest, Davis, & McEvoy, 2002) and at length by James F. Christie (Chapter 2, in this book). Researchers at the Universities of Kansas, Minnesota, and Oregon collaborated as part of the Early Childhood Research Institute on Measuring Growth and Development (ECRI-MGD) to produce general outcome measures for infants and toddlers, preschoolers, and kindergarten students (Phaneuf & Silberglitt, 2003). From 1996 to 2001, three teams of researchers worked together to develop a set of general outcome measures of child growth and development for use with children from ages birth to 8 years. They produced a list of desired developmental outcomes for all children, ages birth to 8 years (Priest et al., 2002), as well as sets of measures for infants and toddlers (Greenwood,

Luze, & Carta, 2002), preschool-age children (McConnell et al., 2002), and elementary children (Good, Gruba, & Kaminski, 2002).

At the preschool level the IGDIs (Early Childhood Research Institute on Measuring Growth and Development, 1998) were designed to be quick, efficient, and repeatable progress-monitoring measures used to assess children ages 30–66 months. Preschool IGDIs are used to identify children needing early intervention and to monitor the effects of an intervention. Like CBM for older children, preschool IGDIs (1) demonstrate criterion or construct validity and treatment validity (sensitivity to the effects of interventions); (2) provide an index of the rate of development over time through frequent and repeated assessment, and by using common measurement procedures; and (3) are socially valid in that they help teachers and parents make decisions in a particular developmental domain. Three measures of the IGDIs were developed to assess children's early literacy skills: Picture Naming, Alliteration, and Rhyming. All three tools are available at no cost via the Internet (*ggg.umn.edu*).

"Picture naming" provides a measure of expressive language, particularly children's fluency in producing single vocabulary words in response to pictured stimuli. In this task, children are asked to name as many pictures as they can in 1 minute, following a demonstration of the task by the examiner. Pictures used in this task are drawings or photos of objects that are commonly found in a child's environment.

"Rhyming" is a measure of phonological awareness. A child is shown a card with the target word illustrated at the top and three other illustrations in a row at the bottom of the card. One of the illustrations has the same ending sound as the target word. Following two sample items and practice, the teacher shows each card, sounds out the words, and asks the child to point to one of the three pictures that rhymes with the target picture. The score is based on the number of items the child identifies correctly in 2 minutes.

"Alliteration" also is a measure of phonological awareness. Similar to rhyming, the teacher shows the child a card with the target word illustrated at the top and three other illustrations in a row at the bottom of the card. One of the illustrations has the same initial sound as the target word. Following demonstration and practice, the teacher shows each card and sounds out all words, then asks the child to point to one of the three pictures at the bottom with the same initial sound as the target picture. The child's score is the number of items identified correctly in 2 minutes.

To use IGDIs, a teacher must register on the IGDI website. Once registered, the teacher can enter the assessment data, generate score recording forms, and obtain graphical reports of performance for an individual child. The teacher can then create a report for an individual child that includes a table and graph of IGDI scores, a trend line, and an aim line.

The trend and aim lines offer a visual comparison between the child's actual rate of progress (trend line) and the desired rate of progress (aim line). The trend line allows comparison of the child's progress at different points over time and indicates whether the child is progressing at the desired rate (the aim line) or failing to make progress.

The aim line is based on a study group of English-speaking preschool children without identified disabilities. This aim line may be of limited use for monitoring the progress of English language learners (ELLs), and children from diverse socioeconomic and ethnic communities. Teachers are advised to create an aim line based on a suitable comparison group from the local classroom, school, or district. This aim line can then be used over time to determine whether individual children are following the group trend, catching up, or failing to make progress.

An evaluation of IGDIs revealed that the time needed for administration and scoring is minimal, that IGDIs provide valuable information for measuring the effects of an intervention and monitoring children's progress over time, and that teachers' instruction is influenced by the results (Phaneuf & Silberglitt, 2003).

CBM in the Academic Centers of Excellence

Here, we discuss a set of CBMs developed and tailored specifically to the curriculum being taught in the Academic Centers of Excellence (ACE[3]), a federally funded ERF program. ACE[3] involved 23 preschool classrooms serving 425 children in two Head Start and two local education agencies located in southwest Arizona on the U.S.–Mexico border, an agrarian, Spanish-speaking community. The goal of the CBM development was to provide teachers a rapid (2-minute) way to frequently (weekly) monitor monolingual Spanish preschoolers' acquisition of the English language and early literacy skills being taught in the Doors to Discovery curriculum (Wright Group/McGraw-Hill, 2002). No CBMs were available at that time to meet these specific needs. In the next sections, we describe the ACE[3] curriculum, how the team custom-made CBMs to monitor children's progress within this curriculum, how they used the graphed results to make instructional decisions, and the impact of CBM on children's learning outcomes.

ACE[3] Curriculum

The Doors to Discovery curriculum was adopted in ACE[3] because it has a fairly even distribution of research-based instructional components for developing essential early literacy skills. The Doors curriculum is organized into a series of 1-month "explorations" that focus on books on topics appealing to young children, such as *Vroom! Vroom!* (transportation) (Wright Group/McGraw-Hill, 2002); *Backyard Detectives* (nature) (Wright Group/McGraw-Hill, 2002); and *Tabby Tiger's Diner* (food and restaurants) (Wright Group/McGraw-Hill, 2002). The Doors curriculum includes three interrelated instructional blocks: (1) large-group time (shared reading of big books) (2) discovery centers (children self-select activities in a variety of learning centers), and (3) small-group time (teachers conduct activities with small groups of students). English was the primary language of instruction for the curriculum, although teachers used Spanish when children required explanations, clarification, expansions, and discipline. Because the developmental origins of children's ability to learn a second language and to acquire prereading skills occur in the preschool period (Lonigan, Burgess, & Anthony, 2000; McCardle, Scarborough, & Catts, 2001), the ACE[3] project personnel assumed that a focus on English language and early literacy in preschool might provide a special advantage for ELLs. The focus on English also reflected the recommendations of Proctor, Carlo, August, and Snow (2005), who suggested that ELLs from low socioeconomic status (SES) families should provide taught in English, because their families were likely to have limited literacy skills in their primary language.

Uses of CBM in ACE[3]

CBM was developed to allow ACE[3] teachers to monitor ELLs' acquisition of instructional targets in vocabulary, phonemic awareness, and alphabet knowledge. CBMs in the ACE[3] were used in three ways: (1) to examine individual ELLs' responses to each unit in the instructional program to provide ongoing feedback to teachers on children's acquisition of discrete skills in vocabulary, phonemic awareness, and alphabet letter naming; (2) to test whether children administered CBM made greater progress than children who did not participate in CBM; and (3) to compare the learning trajectories across time of children who were typical learners, children at risk for learning disabilities, and children with disabilities.

Implementation of CBM in ACE[3]

Each teacher selected four children to participate in weekly CBM: (1) a child identified as having disabilities, (2) a child at risk for disabilities, (3) a child with typical achievement, and (4) a child with high achievement. The scores of typically achieving children functioned as an aim line and also were used to assess how well ELLs with disabilities and those at risk were performing relative to ELLs who represented typical development in the local context.

The CBM test stimuli were drawn from the curriculum, standardized across participating classrooms, and administered by teachers weekly across the school year. Two hundred eighteen words were selected for a CBM vocabulary pool. Project staff and mentors used the pool to select six to eight words from each Doors to Discovery exploration. Teachers used the CBM weekly to monitor children's acquisition of the vocabulary (expressive and receptive), phonemic awareness (alliteration), and letter identification taught the preceding week.

On the Receptive Vocabulary subtest, children were shown a poster or page from the Doors exploration and the teacher instructed the child to "Show me _____." On the Expressive Vocabulary and Letter Identification subtests, the children were shown a poster or book page and asked to name the object or letter to which the teacher pointed. The Receptive and Expressive Vocabulary subtests had three to four items weekly throughout the year. The Letter Identification subtest included one to two target letters each week in the first semester, but included all letters cumulatively in the second semester. On the Alliteration subtest, children were shown a card with the target word illustrated at the top and three other illustrations in a row at the bottom of the card (see Figure 17.1). One of the illustrations had the same initial sound as the target word. Following two sample items, the teacher displayed the card and sounded out the words, then asked the child to point to one of the three pictures at the bottom with the same initial sound as the target picture. The Alliteration subtest had two items each week in the first semester and four in the second semester. The initial sounds matched the letters targeted that particular week. The selected words were familiar to preschoolers.

A score sheet prepared for each child included administration and scoring instructions (e.g., which Doors poster to use), as well as space for comments and descriptions of the types of errors (e.g., OK with initial sounds but unable to pronounce the rest of the word, mispronunciation of the whole word, certain types of mispronunciations of words or letters) or any other condition (e.g., off-task behavior, sick, weather too hot) (see Figure 17.2). The comments helped teachers to reflect on possible reasons for the children's errors, and to communicate to staff what they should consider when evaluating results. Teachers administered the CBMs at the same time each week, allowed equal wait time for each child, and followed standard administration procedures.

At the end of each Doors monthly exploration, each child's weekly performance was displayed on a graph (see Figure 17.3). The horizontal axis indicated the week of the unit, and the vertical axis presented the percentage of correct responses on each CBM subtest. Teachers and mentors reviewed the graphs, and compared the performances of children with special needs and those at risk, typically achieving, and high achieving.

FIGURE 17.1. A sample Alliteration card.

ACE³ CBM SCORE SHEET—UNIT [VROOM! VROOM!]/WEEK 1

Child's Name _____ School _____

Date of Test _____ Examiner _____

Purpose: Track how well the child is learning the vocabulary words and letters you are teaching using Doors.

Directions: Read the script in the box below. Enter the scores on the left side column.

Letter Identification Letter Card (card with all letters) Dd _____ Ll _____ Mm _____ Jj _____ F1 _____ Pp _____ Hh _____ Tt _____ # correct _____	**LETTER IDENFICATION:** Present the letter card to the child and say, **"We are going to look at this card with all these letters. Tell me the name of the letter I point to."** SCORE: **1** Point = correct answer or self-correction within approximately 3 seconds. **0** Points = incorrect answer. **NA (No Answer)** = Asked twice and no answer at the end of 3 seconds.
Show Me *Our Big Book of Driving*: Pages 2–3. Van _____ Bicycle _____ Motorcycle _____ Fire truck _____ # correct _____	**SHOW ME (Identification):** Open the lap book version of *Our Big Book of Driving* to pages 2–3. Place the book in front of the child and say, **"We are going to look at these pictures. Point to the picture that I tell you."** **"Show me the _____."** SCORE: **1** Point = correct answer or self-correction within approximately 3 seconds. **0** Points = incorrect answer. **NA (No Answer)** = Asked twice and no answer at the end of 3 seconds.
Tell Me Picture Word Cards: Pull the word cards for the followng items: Taxi _____ Bus _____ Tire _____ Stop sign _____ # correct _____ Comments: _____ _____	**TELL ME (Production):** Place the word cards in front of the child and say, **"We are going to look at these pictures. Tell me the name of the picture I point to."** Point to each picture and say, **"Tell me the name of this?"** SCORE: **1** Point = correct answer or self-correction within approximately 3 seconds. **0** Points = incorrect answer. **NA (No Answer)** = Asked twice and no answer at the end of 3 seconds.

FIGURE 17.2. A sample score sheet (page 1).

ACE[3] SCORE SHEET (ALLITERATION)
VROOM! VROOM! WEEK 1

Alliteration
Picture cards:

Teacher	Tricycle
T-shirt ________	**Truck** ________
Toy	Toilet
Toaster ________	**Toes** ________

\# correct ________

Comments: ____________________
____
____
____

ALLITERATION (Identification of initial sounds):

Use alliteration picture cards.

1. Sample item 1
Say, **"Here is a picture of bread. It starts with the 'b' sound.** Repeat the word and say, **"Now look at these pictures. Which one starts with 'b'?** Name each bottom picture. If the child does not get the correct answer, say the top picture's name and correct answer, emphasizing initial sounds.

2. Sample item 2
Repeat the instructions of sample item 1 using the picture names in this sample.

3. Test items 1, 2, 3, and 4
Say, **"Here is a picture of a (picture name). Now, which one of these pictures starts with the same sound?"** Name the top picture and then point to each picture in the bottom and say out loud.

SCORE:

1 Point = correct answer or self-correction within approximately 3 seconds.

0 Points = incorrect answer.

NA (**N**o **A**nswer) = Asked twice and no answer at the end of 3 seconds.

FIGURE 17.2. A sample score sheet (page 2).

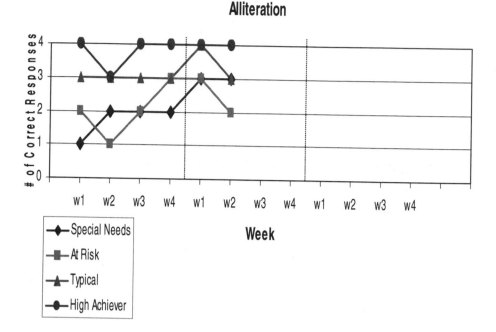

FIGURE 17.3. A sample graph of comparative performances of children with special needs, at risk, typical, and high-achievement.

The performance line for the typically achieving child in the graph was considered as the aim line for children with disabilities and children at risk.

Teachers then used the Decision Tree (see Figure 17.4) to determine whether the graphs indicated that instructional changes should be made for individual children or the group. The Decision Tree included three rules.

- Decision Rule 1: If the child's performance is not consistently above or below the aim line (i.e., more than three consecutive data points), make no instructional changes (see Figure 17.5).
- Decision Rule 2: If a child's performance shows three consecutive data points below the aim line, the teacher explored child-related and instruction-related reasons that performance failed to meet expectations (see Figure 17.6). For instance, had the child been ill or absent, had attention or behavior problems, or were there upsetting events in the home? Were the CBM items too difficult, inadequately taught (not adequately explained, infrequently presented), or was the child not given sufficient opportunities to practice (e.g., called on to answer questions)? Sugges-

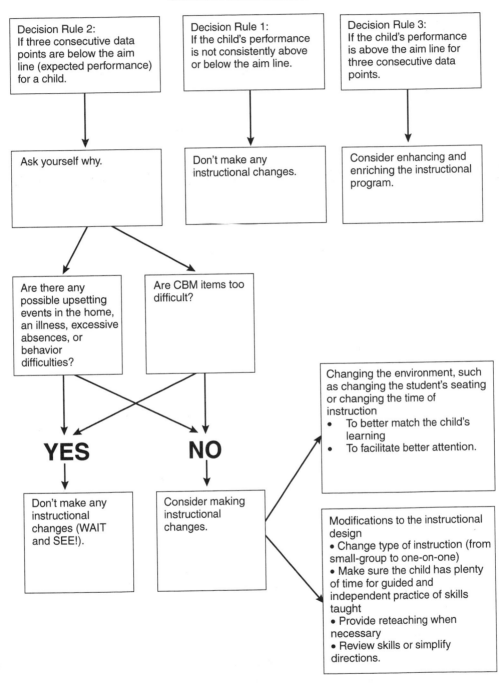

FIGURE 17.4. CBM Decision Tree.

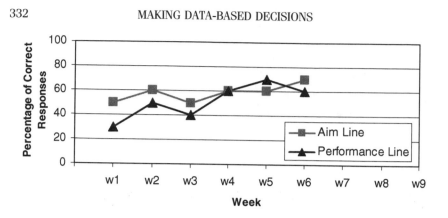

FIGURE 17.5. A sample graph for Decision Rule 1.

tions for instructional changes included: change the classroom environment (e.g., seating, time of instruction or testing), and/or modify instruction (use more structured activities during small-group time or one-on-one instruction, reteach and recycle, simplify directions, increase number of times the child actively responds).

• Decision Rule 3: If the child's performance was above the aim line for three consecutive data points, consider enhancing and enriching the instructional program (see Figure 17.7), and continue to monitor.

Teachers were encouraged to explain CBMs to parents by sharing the words and letters that were the focus in each exploration and in the child's graph. A written note might include an explanation of the child's progress on the graph, noting positive changes. Parents also were provided a list of suggested activities to support classroom learning at home and in the community.

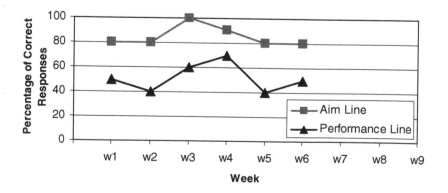

FIGURE 17.6. A sample graph for Decision Rule 2.

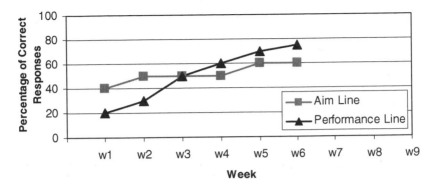

FIGURE 17.7. A sample graph for Decision Rule 3.

Outcomes of CBM in ACE[3]

CBM participants made greater gains in phonological awareness, receptive and expressive language, and alphabet knowledge compared to nonparticipants. Although higher-achieving children outperformed typical children, who in turn outperformed children at risk and those with disabilities, the ELLs with disabilities and those at risk showed more significant gains in acquiring literacy skills. These results lend support to Proctor et al.'s (2005) recommendation that children from non-English-speaking low SES families be taught in English.

The ACE[3] teachers evaluated CBM very positively, because it was fast (2 minutes per child weekly), inexpensive, easy to administer, and provided useful information related to daily instruction. CBM allowed these teachers to measure their students' growth in performance continuously, to determine whether their students were learning at the expected rate, and to evaluate instructional strategies when students failed to demonstrate expected growth.

A number of reasons might account for the benefits of CBM. First, children became acclimated to test taking; thus, they learned the routine and began to anticipate the contents of the next test. For instance, teachers reported that children would ask whether the words in a story were going to be on the assessment. Teachers described children as comfortable with CBMs and looking forward to the testing. Children not in the CBM group asked when they would have a chance to show the teacher what they had learned. CBM provided children with individual attention and praise from teachers. Second, teachers reported that CBMs alerted them to individual children's needs for additional instruction and rehearsal, and that they used the Decision Tree to guide them in making instructional adaptations. Having information about children's performance over short periods of time was clearly very useful to teachers for planning and evaluating instructional adaptations.

Do-It-Yourself

We strongly recommend that preschool teachers use CBM to (1) assess children's acquisition of early literacy skills, and (2) evaluate the data to make decisions about instruction. Teachers can take advantage of the IGDIs computerized program or use the ACE[3] example as a model to tailor their own CBMs to ensure that children are learning the skills being taught in their curriculum. Although developing CBMs takes effort and time, the anticipated payoff is great. Teachers have been using quizzes and tests to assess children's learning since the beginning of education. Developing CBMs should be construed as one additional step in good lesson planning. Bear in mind that the ACE[3] CBM worked as an intervention. Children who were administered ACE[3] CBM outperformed children not administered CBM in every literacy area that was assessed. It is recommended that preschool teachers within a school or district work as a team, and arrange schedules to accommodate shared planning time. Teachers can then collaborate on developing CBMs, interpret the results of individual and group performance on CBMs, and brainstorm ideas for activities and materials that respond to the data.

Steps to Develop Preschool CBM

1. Create a vocabulary pool and alphabet list grouped by units and weeks. Select words, sounds, and alphabet letters to be targeted each week. Use the same number of items for each CBM.
2. Select four children from each classroom to participate in weekly CBMs (teachers may want to form 4 groups of children and rotate the groups, so that all children are tested monthly):

- One child who has been identified as having disabilities: Children in this group have individualized education plans (IEPs) and receive special education services.
- One child who is at risk for disabilities: Children in this group score below the 25th percentile on any screening measure used by the school.
- One child with typical achievement: Children in this group score in the 26th to 75th percentiles on screening measures. Use the scores of typically achieving children as an aim line to determine how well at-risk children and those with disabilities are performing.
- One child with high achievement: Children in this group score above the 75th percentile on screening measures. The high-achieving child is included to determine potential expectations for children in this school context.

3. Determine where and when CBM testing will take place.

4. Identify four items each week from the vocabulary pool and an alphabet list for each CBM section: Letter Identification, Receptive Vocabulary, Expressive Vocabulary, and Alliteration.

5. Prepare for each child a score sheet (see Figures 17.1 and 17.2 for examples) weekly that includes the four CBM sections with administration and scoring instructions (e.g., which materials to use).

6. Be sure to emphasize each week's targeted vocabulary, letters, and sounds during large- and small-group time, and in discovery center activities.

7. Administer the CBM to all four students following the described standard administration procedures (e.g., at the same time each week, allowing equal wait time for each child, and using same type of prompts).

8. Develop a graph for each CBM section. The horizontal axis indicates the week of the unit, and the vertical axis presents the number or percentage of correct responses on that CBM subtest.

9. Display each child's weekly performance on the graph. Review the graphs, examine trends, and compare the performance of children with special needs, and at-risk, typical achieving, and high achieving children. Use the typical achieving child's scores in the graph as the aim line for children with special needs and those at risk.

10. Go to the CBM Decision Tree (Figures 17.5, 17.6, and 17.7) and apply the rules to the findings.

References

Adams, M. J. (1990). *Beginning to read: Thinking and learning about print.* Cambridge, MA: MIT Press.

Badian, N. A. (1995). Predicting reading ability over the long term: The changing roles of letter-naming, phonological awareness and orthographic processing. *Annals of Dyslexia, 45,* 3–25.

Biemiller, A., & Slonim, N. (2001). Estimating root word vocabulary growth in normative and advantaged populations: Evidence for a common sequence of vocabulary acquisition. *Journal of Educational Psychology, 93,* 498–520.

Bricker, D., & Waddell, M. (1996). *AEPS measurement for three to six years* (Vol. 3). Baltimore: Brookes.

Burns, S., Griffin, P., & Snow, C. (1999). *Starting out right: A guide to promoting children's reading success: Specific recommendations from America's leading researchers on how to help children become successful reading.* Washington, DC: National Academy Press. (ERIC Document Reproduction Service No. ED 439781)

Deno, S. L. (1985). Curriculum-based measurement. *Teaching Exceptional Children, 20,* 41–47.

Deno, S. L. (1992). The nature and development of curriculum-based measurement. *Preventing School Failure, 36*(2), 5–10.

Deno, S. L., Fuchs, L., Marston, D., & Shin, J. (2001). Using curriculum-based measurement to establish growth standards for students with learning disabilities. *School Psychology Review, 30,* 507–524.

Deno, S. L., Mirkin, P., & Chiang, B. (1982). Identifying valid measures of reading. *Exceptional Children, 49,* 36–45.

Dickinson, D. K., McCabe, A., Anastasopoulos, L., Peisner-Feinberg, E. S., & Poe, M. D. (2003). The comprehensive language approach to early literacy: The interrelationships among vocabulary, phonological sensitivity, and print knowledge among preschool-aged children. *Journal of Educational Psychology, 95,* 465–481.

Early Childhood Research Institute on Measuring Growth and Development. (1998). *Theoretical foundations of the Early Childhood Research Institute on Measuring Growth and Development: An early childhood problem-solving model* (Tech. Rep. No. 6). Minneapolis: Center for Early Education and Development, University of Minnesota.

Espin, C. A., Shin, J., & Busch, T. W. (2005). Curriculum-based measurement in the content areas: Vocabulary matching as an indicator of progress in social studies learning. *Journal of Learning Disabilities, 38,* 352–363.

Fewell, R. R. (2000). Assessment of young children with special needs: Foundations for tomorrow. *Topics in Early Childhood Special Education, 20,* 38–42.

Fuchs, D., & Fuchs, L. S. (2002). Curriculum-based measurement: Describing competence, enhancing outcomes, evaluating treatment effects, and identifying treatment nonresponders. *Peabody Journal of Education, 77*(2), 64–84.

Fuchs, L. S., & Deno, S. L. (1991). Paradigmatic distinctions between instructionally relevant measurement models. *Exceptional Children, 57,* 488–500.

Fuchs, L. S., Deno, S. L., & Mirkin, P. K. (1984). The effects of frequent curriculum-based measurement and evaluation on pedagogy, student achievement, and student awareness of learning. *American Educational Research Journal, 21,* 449–460.

Fuchs, L. S., Fuchs, D., & Hamlett, C. L. (1989a). Effects of alternative goal structures within curriculum-based measurement. *Exceptional Children, 55,* 429–438.

Fuchs, L. S., Fuchs, D., & Hamlett, C. L. (1989b). Effects of instrumental use of curriculum-based measurement to enhance instructional programs. *Remedial and Special Education, 10*(2), 43–52.

Fuchs, L. S., Fuchs, D., Hamlett, C. L., & Ferguson, C. (1992). Effects of expert system consultation within curriculum-based measurement using a reading maze task. *Exceptional Children, 58,* 436–450.

Fuchs, L. S., Fuchs, D., Hamlett, C. L., & Stecker, P. M. (1990). The role of skills analysis in curriculum-based measurement in math. *School Psychology Review, 19,* 6–22.

Fuchs, L. S., Fuchs, D., & Maxwell, L. (1988). The validity of informal reading comprehension measures. *Remedial and Special Education, 9*(2), 20–28.

Fuchs, L. S., Fuchs, D., & Stecker, P. M. (1989). Effects of curriculum-based measurement on teacher instructional planning. *Journal of Learning Disabilities, 22,* 51–59.

Good, R. H., Gruba, J., & Kaminski, R. A. (2002). Best practices in using dynamic indicators of basic early literacy skills (DIBELS) in an outcomes-driven model. In A. Thomas & J. Grimes (Eds.), *Best practices in school psychology* (4th ed., Vol. 1, pp. 699–720). Washington DC: National Association of School Psychologists.

Good, R. H., & Kaminski, R. A. (2003). *Dynamic indicators of early basic literacy skills.* Longmont, CO: Sopris West.

Greenwood, C. R., Luze, G. J., & Carta, J. J. (2002). Best practices in assessment and intervention results with infants and toddlers. In A. Thomas & J. Grimes (Eds.), *Best practices in school psychology* (4th ed., Vol. 2, pp. 1219–1230). Washington, DC: National Association of School Psychologists.

Hart, B., & Risley, T. (2003). The early catastrophe. *American Educator, 27*(4), 6–9.

Jones, E. D., & Krouse, J. P. (1988). The effectiveness of data-based instruction by student teachers in classrooms for pupils with mild learning handicaps. *Teacher Education and Special Education, 11,* 9–19.

Juel, C., Griffith, P. L., & Gough, P. B. (1986). Acquisition of literacy: A longitudinal study of children in first and second grade. *Journal of Educational Psychology, 78,* 243–255.

Kaminski, R. A., & Good, R. H. (1996). Toward a technology for assessing basic early literacy skills. *School Psychology Review, 25,* 215–227.

Liberman, I. Y., Shankweiler, D., & Liberman, A. M. (1989). The alphabetic principle and learning to read. In D. Shankweiler & I. Y. Liberman (Eds.), *Phonology and reading disability: Solving the reading puzzle* (pp. 1–33). Ann Arbor: University of Michigan Press.

Lonigan, C. J., Burgess, S. R., & Anthony, J. L. (2000). Development of emergent literacy and early reading skills in preschool children: Evidence from a latent-variable longitudinal study. *Developmental Psychology, 36,* 596–613.

Lonigan, C. J., & Whitehurst, G. J. (1998). *Getting ready to read: Emergent literacy and family literacy.* Unpublished manuscript. (ERIC Document Reproduction Service No. ED 450418)

Marston, D., & Magnusson, D. (1988). Curriculum-based assessment: District-level implementation. In J. Graden, J. Zins, & M. Curtis (Eds.), *Alternative educational delivery systems: Enhancing instructional options for all students* (pp. 137–172). Washington, DC: National Association of School Psychologists.

Marston, D., Mirkin, P., & Deno, S. (1984). Curriculum-based measurement: An alternative to traditional screening, referral, and identification. *Journal of Special Education, 18,* 109–117.

McCardle, P., Scarborough, H. S., & Catts, H. W. (2001). Predicting, explaining, and preventing children's reading difficulties. *Learning Disabilities Research and Practice, 16,* 230–239.

McConnell, S. R. (2000). Assessment in early intervention and early childhood special education: Building on the past to project into our future. *Topics in Early Childhood Special Education, 19,* 43–48.

McConnell, S. R., Priest, J. S., Davis, S. D., & McEvoy, M. A. (2002). Best practices in measuring growth and development for preschool children. In A. Thomas & J. Grimes (Eds.), *Best practices in school psychology* (4th ed., Vol. 2, pp. 1231–1246). Washington, DC: National Association of School Psychologists.

McCurdy, B. L., & Shapiro, E. S. (1992). A comparison of teacher monitoring, peer monitoring, and self-monitoring with curriculum-based measurement in reading among students with learning disabilities. *Journal of Special Education, 26,* 162–180.

McLean, M., Bailey, D., & Wolery, M. (1996). *Assessing infants and preschoolers with special needs*. Englewood Cliffs, NJ: Prentice-Hall.

Meisels, S. J., Liaw, F. R., Dorfman, A., & Nelson, R. N. (1995). The Work Sampling System: Reliability and validity of a performance assessment for young children. *Early Childhood Research Quarterly, 10,* 277–296.

National Early Literacy Panel. (2004). *Report on the synthesis of early reading predictors*. Louisville, KY: Author.

National Reading Panel. (2000). *Teaching children to read: An evidence-based assessment of the scientific research literature on reading and its implications for reading instruction* (National Institute of Health Publication No. 00-4769). Washington, DC: National Institute of Child Health and Human Development.

Phaneuf, R. L., & Silberglitt, B. (2003). Tracking preschoolers' language and preliteracy development using a general outcome measurement system. *Topics in Early Childhood Special Education, 23,* 114–123.

Pretti-Frontczak, K., Kowalski, K., & Brown, R. D. (2002). Preschool teachers' use of assessments and curricula: A statewide examination. *Exceptional Children, 69,* 109–123.

Priest, J. S., McConnell, S. R., Walker, D., Carta, J. J., Kaminski, R. A., McEvoy, M. A., et al. (2002). General growth outcomes for children between birth and age eight: Where do you want young children to go today and tomorrow? *Journal of Early Intervention, 24,* 163–180.

Proctor, C. P., Carlo, M., August, D., & Snow, C. (2005). Native Spanish-speaking children reading in English: Toward a model of comprehension. *Journal of Educational Psychology, 97,* 246–256.

Shonkoff, J. P., & Phillips, D. A. (Eds.). (2000). *From neurons to neighborhoods: The science and ecology of human development*. Washington, DC: National Academy Press.

Stecker, P. M., Fuchs, L. S., & Fuchs, D. (2005). Using curriculum-based measurement to improve student achievement: Review of research. *Psychology in the Schools, 42,* 795–819.

Thurlow, M. L., & Ysseldyke, J. E. (1982). Instructional planning: Information collected by school psychologists vs. information considered useful by teachers. *Journal of School Psychology, 20,* 3–10.

Torgesen, J. K. (1998, Spring/Summer). Catch them before they fall. *American Educator,* pp. 1–8.

Torgesen, J. K. (1999). Phonologically based reading disabilities: Toward a coherent theory of one kind of learning disability. In R. J. Sternberg & L. Spear-Swerling (Eds.), *Perspectives on learning disabilities* (pp. 231–262). Boulder, CO: Westview Press.

Wagner, R. K., Torgesen, J. K., & Rashotte, C. A. (1994). Development of reading-related phonological processing abilities: New evidence of bidirectional causality from a latent variable longitudinal study. *Developmental Psychology, 30,* 73–87.

Wright Group/McGraw-Hill. (2002). *Doors to Discovery*. Bothell, WA: Author.

Index